TOTALITARIAN and AUTHORITARIAN REGIMES

TOTALITARIAN and AUTHORITARIAN REGIMES

Juan J. Linz

LYNNE
RIENNER
PUBLISHERS

BOULDER
LONDON

Published in the United States of America in 2000 by
Lynne Rienner Publishers, Inc.
1800 30th Street, Boulder, Colorado 80301
www.rienner.com

and in the United Kingdom by
Lynne Rienner Publishers, Inc.
3 Henrietta Street, Covent Garden, London WC2E 8LU

Chapters 1–6 of this book were published originally in the
Handbook of Political Science, Volume 3, *Macropolitical Theory*,
edited by Fred I. Greenstein and Nelson W. Polsby. Reading, Mass.:
Addison-Wesley, 1975.

Library of Congress Cataloging-in-Publication Data
Linz, Juan J. (Juan José), 1926–
    Totalitarian and authoritarian regimes / Juan J. Linz.
    Includes bibliographical references and index.
    ISBN 978-1-55587-866-5 (hc. : alk. paper)
    ISBN 978-1-55587-890-0 (pbk. : alk. paper)
    1. Totalitarianism. 2. Authoritarianism. I. Title.

JC480.L59   2000
321.9—dc21   00-028259

British Cataloguing in Publication Data
A Cataloguing in Publication record for this book
is available from the British Library.

Printed and bound in the United States of America

∞   The paper used in this publication meets the requirements
     of the American National Standard for Permanence of
     Paper for Printed Library Materials Z39.48-1992.

10   9   8   7   6   5   4   3

CONTENTS

ACKNOWLEDGMENTS

I want to thank Fred I. Greenstein and Nelson W. Polsby, who asked me to write a *Handbook* contribution that, thanks to their tolerance, became a book; and Larry Diamond and Lynne Rienner, who did excellent editing. It has been a pleasure to work with Lynne. Houchang E. Chehabi also made excellent suggestions.

I want to acknowledge, as well, Rocío de Terán's critical reading and editing and Winnie Travers's constant retyping of the manuscript.

— *Juan J. Linz*

FURTHER REFLECTIONS
ON TOTALITARIAN AND
AUTHORITARIAN REGIMES

Facing the prospect of the publication of a study written twenty-five years ago, inevitably I feel ambivalent.[1] So much has happened both intellectually and on the political scene that there is the temptation to rewrite, extend, and add to the original text. At the same time, I feel that the original work has value just as it was written in 1973–1974. Within the limitations of space imposed then by the editors of the *Handbook of Political Science,* the work is in some way the centerpiece of a trilogy including *Crisis, Breakdown and Reequilibration* (Linz, 1978)* and *Problems of Democratic Transition and Consolidation: Southern Europe, South America, and Post-Communist Europe* (Linz and Stepan, 1996). The three cover the period between 1914 and 1989, which François Furet (1999), Ernst Nolte (1987), and Eric Hobsbawm (1994) have analyzed as the shortened twentieth century and the age of totalitarianism.

The 1978 book and my work on fascism (Linz, 1976, 1980) could be seen as part of the present book insofar as they contribute to our understanding of why and how democracies broke down and nondemocratic regimes became established, as well as why some democracies survived. The work on democratic transitions could well be the last chapter, since it deals with the crisis of the regimes studied in the present book, their breakdown, and the transition to stable or fledgling

---

*All citations in this chapter refer to the notes and bibliography (pages 38–48) following the chapter. In subsequent chapters, citations refer to the notes and bibliography at the end of the book.

1

democracies. Although my writings on fascism were not related to the German debate on the theory of fascism as an alternative to the study of authoritarianism (Kraushaar, 1997), I hope they contribute to our understanding of one of the great antidemocratic movements of this century. I underline the focus on fascist movements, since I share, to a large extent, De Felice's (1975) distinction between fascism as a movement and as a regime.

Many scholarly efforts to substitute fascism for totalitarianism as a category for describing or understanding the Nazi regime were based largely on Marxist, more or less sophisticated theories of fascism. Simultaneously, new empirical comparative research on fascist movements—their successes and failures, their leaders, members, and social bases—was in progress from a non-Marxist or strictly historical perspective (Lacqueur, 1976; Larsen, Hagtvet, and Myklebust, 1980; Griffin, 1991; and the monumental work by Stanley Payne, 1995, that also includes the fascist regimes until their demise). My own writings on fascism were part of the latter effort.

The relatively short section on sultanistic regimes in the original *Handbook* essay has been expanded by Houchang Chehabi and myself (1998) in a long introduction to a collection of essays dealing in detail with that type of regime. Sultanism is a regime type that should be seen as clearly distinct from authoritarian regimes in their various manifestations, a point that escaped some readers of my original work. Mark Thompson (1995) has written an excellent monograph on the Marcos regime in the Philippines from this perspective.

When I wrote on totalitarianism in the early 1970s, the intellectual community was questioning the concept and ready to abandon it for good and bad reasons. Among the latter was the largely hopeless debate about the association of the concept with the polemics generated by the Cold War, ignoring its intellectual origins before World War II. Another mistaken reason was that the concept did not allow us to differentiate Soviet and Nazi totalitarianism. I never doubted the need for such differentiation, and I hope that I contributed to an appreciation of it in the *Handbook* essay. But I also felt strongly that a simple dichotomy between democratic regimes and nondemocratic rule obscured the distinctiveness of the totalitarian phenomenon.[2] More recently, Sartori (1993) has argued against a simple dichotomy of democratic and nondemocratic regimes.

A legitimate reason for questioning the concept of totalitarianism, one that I tried to take into account, was that by the 1970s and thereafter it did not adequately capture the political reality of Soviet-type regimes. I paid attention to this fact by reviewing the growing literature on changes in communist countries, particularly the Soviet Union. But I did not formulate as clearly as I would later the distinctive characteristics of what I call "post-totalitarian political systems." In part this was the result of my sheer exhaustion after undertaking the comparative analysis of all types of nondemocratic regimes; but it also was due to the nature of a contribution to a handbook intended to reflect the state of the art. (A few scholars tried to apply my analysis of authoritarian regimes to late communist systems, an approach that could contribute some insights, but one that I found misleading.)

With the liberalization in Eastern Europe, scholars and activists there discovered the Western literature on totalitarianism (Rupnik, 1984). There was a strange resurgence of the totalitarianism approach being applied to systems that at one time were clearly totalitarian but that, in my view, were now better analyzed as post-totalitarian (Linz and Stepan, 1996; Thompson, 1998). Although in the West some scholars wanted to ditch the concept of totalitarianism as politically tainted by the Cold War—these scholars emphasized the positive aspects of communism compared to the totally negative view of fascism and particularly Nazism—paradoxically, but understandably, opposition forces in Eastern Europe (with the significant exception of several authors writing on Poland [Djilas, 1993; Staniskis,1986]) were discovering the fruitfulness of the totalitarianism perspective. In fact, many opponents of authoritarian regimes, for example in Spain, felt that to characterize the regimes as authoritarian—instead of totalitarian—would serve to legitimize them.

Since my thinking about the distinction between totalitarian and authoritarian regimes was initially a reflection of my knowledge of the politics of Franco's Spain—particularly from the late 1940s to the early 1960s—a number of critics in Spain have stressed the totalitarian character or tendencies in early phases of the Franco regime (Ramírez, 1978). Some did not ever surrender the totalitarian label for the regime, perhaps because they felt that it gave greater moral legitimacy to their opposition. Ironically, this position is the reverse of that held by those who would question the category totalitarian as a result of the Cold War. I never would deny the totalitarian ambitions of the Spanish Falange and the totalitarian tendencies of the Franco regime during the hegemony of the Axis powers in Europe. I would, however, stress the legacy of limited pluralism in the origin of the regime, which Franco subordinated to his personal power and designs. This personalization frustrated the creation of a true and modern totalitarian regime. Javier Tusell's (1988) excellent study of Franco during the Civil War tells us much about the origins of Franco's power and his regime, which made genuine totalitarianism unlikely, except in the event of an Axis victory in World War I (and perhaps the displacement of Franco).[3] I also refer the reader to Stanley Payne's (1987, 1999) excellent history of the Falange during the Franco years, which shows the complex relation between the Caudillo and the party, and to my own work on the transformation of the single party (Linz, 1970). In addition, studies of the elites of the regime have described in detail its limited pluralism (Miguel Jerez, 1982; Amando de Miguel, 1975; Viver Pi-Sunyer, 1978).

As I developed in my essays in Daalder (1997) and Söllner et al. (1997), my commitment to the concept of totalitarianism is based on an intellectual need to distinguish a particular historical form of regime and society from other nondemocratic polities. It is not based as much on the distinction between democracy and totalitarianism, which I considered from the start to be obvious, nor on Hannah Arendt's emphasis on terror, but focuses instead on a regime form for completely organizing political life and society.

The historian François Furet (1999) reiterated the need to retain totalitarianism as a distinctive type when he wrote:

> Stalinized Bolshevism and National Socialism constitute the two examples of twentieth-century totalitarian regimes. Not only were they comparable, but they form a political category of their own, which has become established since Hannah Arendt. I am well aware that this notion is not universally accepted, but I have yet to discover a concept more useful in defining the atomized regimes of societies made up of individuals systematically deprived of their political ties and subjected to the "total" power of an ideological party and its leader. Since we are discussing an ideal type, there is no reason why these regimes must be identical or even comparable in every way; nor need the characteristic in question be equally prominent throughout the history of such regimes. Hitler's Germany and Stalin's Russia were two different universes. Nazi Germany was less totalitarian in 1937 than it was in 1942, whereas Stalinist terror was more virulent before and after the war than during the war. But this does not preclude the possibility that both regimes, and they alone, set in motion the destruction of the civil order by the absolute submission of individuals to the ideology and the terror of the party-state. It was only in these two cases that the mythology of the unity of the people in and by the party-state, under the leadership of an infallible Guide, killed

millions and presided over a disaster so complete that it destroyed the history of two nations, the Germans and the Russians, making their continuity all but inconceivable. . . .

From a "totalitarian" perspective, the relation between the two regimes refutes the apparent simplicity of their comparison along ideological lines. Nazi Germany belonged to the family of Fascist regimes; and Stalin's Russia to the Bolshevik tradition. Hitler imitated Mussolini; Stalin followed Lenin. Such a classification is supported by the history of ideas, or of intentions, for it distinguishes two revolutionary ambitions—one founded on the particular, the nation or the race, the other on the universal, if we accept that the emancipation of the proletariat prefigures that of all humanity. This classic point-by-point comparison of the two ideologies does not rule out the possibility that either one of them constituted a closed system, based on an immanent interpretation of human history and offering something like salvation to all those suffering the ravages of bourgeois egoism. (pp. 181–181)

I never would question the need for systematic comparison and the highlighting of the specific differences (as well as similarities) between the Soviet- and Nazi-type regimes within the genus totalitarianism. Nor do I dispute the need for a nuanced comparative analysis of communist totalitarian systems, particularly between the Soviet Union and China and also between those two giants and other systems like Cuba, North Korea, Cambodia, and the East European countries. I have insisted that Poland was, for many years before 1989, closer to the authoritarian regime type than the totalitarian or the standard post-totalitarian. The limits on terror in Cuba influenced my thinking toward the view that totalitarianism did not necessarily require terror on the scale of the Soviet Union, and the same would be true for the DDR (East Germany).

Totalitarianism and Post-totalitarianism

In the case of the Soviet Union and to a lesser extent other East European communist regimes, scholarly questioning of a simplified model of totalitarianism, together with the realities of the post-totalitarian regimes, led to the emergence of more sociological- and economics-based analyses to replace the political approach. The emphasis of modernization theory, in particular, was on industrialization, occupational and educational development, welfare state policies, and a presumed social contract between rulers and the people. At a later stage, attention turned to the failures of the modernization model of economic and social change: first, stability was attributed to the success of modernization; later, crisis and a breakdown to stagnation and the loss of dynamism and the capacity for innovation (Müller, 1997). In these perspectives, political and institutional structures, which in my view were and continued to be central, lost salience.

I would never argue that the more sociological and economic analyses were not legitimate (and to a greater or lesser extent, empirically valid); but I do argue that they did not provide the key to understanding political stability or crisis in these regimes. Totalitarianism was stable—not only due to coercion, though that was an important factor—during periods of both economic hardship and growing economic success, and post-totalitarianism survived for a long time during the increasingly serious signs of crisis. That crisis, particularly in Eastern Europe, became more acute after Khrushchev's 1956 "secret" speech denouncing Stalin; and changes in those communist regimes ultimately were conditioned by a change in the Soviet leadership. That leadership, after considerable delay, initiated a political response that aimed at reform. But, somewhat as de Tocqueville wrote about the *ancien régime,* when reform finally was seriously considered, the crisis became even more acute. The unintended consequences of Gorbachev's actions did not lead to the survival of a reformed system, but to the break-up and breakdown of the the Soviet Union (Brown, 1996). The regime collapse, while perhaps accelerated by social and economic changes, ultimately was triggered by the political decisions of the political leadership—a leadership that long ago had lost faith in the totalitarian utopia and its ideologically defined goals, lost the capacity to mobilize the masses, and lost the will to use violence when challenged on the periphery of the system (Friedheim, 1993). The loss of capacity to use force fits into a Paretian type of analysis, and the loss of ideological faith at different levels can be analyzed in terms of Weberian concepts of legitimacy.

In my work with Alfred Stepan (1996) on the transition from post-totalitarianism to democracy (which did not include the failed democratizations), we limited ourselves to distinguishing post-totalitarian regimes from both authoritarian regimes and the previous totalitarian regime. We did not enter into a detailed analysis of the change from totalitarianism to post-totalitarianism, although we did point to different paths and degrees of change in the different European communist countries. Certainly much of the sociological literature on social changes in those countries, the structure of the economy (as analyzed, for example, by Zaslavskaya's [1984] Novosibirsk School), and the politico-administrative structures (like the work of Jerry Hough [1977]) would be relevant in this context. A systematic comparative study of society, economy, and politics in the post-totalitarian phase in different countries deserves top priority. The study of the legacy of the earlier totalitarianism on that phase and the continuing legacies from totalitarianism and post-totalitarianism in the new and the failed democracies would be challenging.

The lesson to be learned from the study of the politics of post-totalitarianism is, to quote Klaus Müller (1997) in his work on neototalitarianism theory, "the stress it lays on domination and its specific irrationalities, variables which were indeed neglected by mainstream sociology and, after the Soviet breakdown, are ignored by liberalist optimism of neoclassic reform programs."

Was Fascist Italy Totalitarian?

I have been hesitant to characterize the Italian fascist regime as totalitarian, even though the term was invented by opponents of the regime to characterize it and assumed later by the fascists themselves (Petersen, 1996). I wrote of "arrested totalitarianism" to indicate not only the clearly totalitarian intention and conception of the fascists, but also the limitations that Italian society and certain institutions—the monarchy, the army, the church—imposed on its ambitions. Unlike Hannah Arendt, I did not reach that position on the basis of the limited terror, the smaller number of victims (particularly deaths after the takeover of power, until the later years of the war), since I had not included terror as a defining element of totalitarianism. However, more recent work by Italian scholars on the ideological commitment, the workings of the regime, the weakness of the institutions putting any limit on the party hegemony, and the personal power and sacralization of Mussolini could convince one of the more totalitarian character of the regime. Mussolini's statement quoted on pages 166–167 of this book was perhaps more an excuse for his failure than a description of the circumstances under which his regime developed for many years.

As Emilio Gentile (1986) summarizes the position of the great scholar de Felice:

> Fascism was never completely totalitarian; firstly, because it did not adopt mass terror and the concentration camp system; secondly, because it did not impose the supremacy of the party on the State, but brought about, instead, the "depoliticization" of the PNF (Partito Nazional Fascista) and its subordination to the State and to the *duce;*

finally, because it never aimed "at a complete transition from the State based on right to the police State." In short, the fascist political system should be defined as an "imperfect totalitarianism." (pp. 200–201)

Gentile, however, writes:

> There has been a fascist conception of totalitarianism, and this cannot be overlooked. Once one attributes a "totalitarian tendency" to fascism, which distinguishes it from traditional authoritarian regimes, one then has to study how this tendency originated, how it was formed in reality, and how it operated to modify reality, conditioning the lives of millions of men and women in the process. The failure of fascist totalitarianism is not a proof of its non-existence. The gap between myth and achievement is not an argument against the importance of myths in the politics of fascism and in its conception and mode of organization of the masses. (p. 201)

He concludes:

> Consequently, an exact classification within one or other category is not possible. If authoritarian fascism characterized the construction phase of the "regime," it was totalitarian fascism, developing in fascism's second decade in power, which provided the dynamism and the goal of "transforming the State." (p. 203)

Placing Other Nondemocratic Regimes

I never intended the *Handbook* essay to be an exhaustive comparative analysis of all nondemocratic regimes, partly due to the lack of prior monographic research and, in a few cases, difficulty in finding an adequate conceptualization (for example, in the complex and fluid case of Mexico). In the meantime, it has become easier to incorporate Japan and Cuba in the discussion.

Japan

Japan, between the failure or breakdown of party democracy (Scalapino, 1953) and the postwar democratization under Allied supervision, had not been included in the comparative study of nondemocratic regimes. Much of the debate among scholars hinged on its characterization as a fascist regime—military fascist, emperor fascist—from more or less Marxist perspectives. That approach fails since there was no fascist movement, no fascist civilians taking power, and the reception of only some parts of fascist ideology. The commitment to the imperial legitimacy, including even the formal Meiji constitution among other factors, limited the possible rise of true fascism. However, as Kasza (1995, 1999) has pointed out, the global fascist *Zeitgeist,* while not producing a fascist movement and party state in Japan, had considerable impact on some of the policies of the military-bureaucratic-intellectual elites who assumed power between 1937 and 1945 and on some efforts at social mobilization. Kasza, describing this authoritarian, *Kakushin* (i.e., renovationist) right, has noted its similarities with authoritarian mobilizational policies on the right (and the left) in other countries. Indeed, he argues for the characterization of certain authoritarian military-bureaucratic regimes as *Kakushin* regimes. His review of the literature on Japanese politics in the 1930s once more shows the need to keep totalitarian and authoritarian regimes distinct, as well as the importance of the fascist *Zeitgeist* (and models) without overextending the term "fascist" to characterize a wide range of nondemocratic and noncommunist regimes.

Cuba

Although the *Handbook* essay was written when the Castro regime had consolidated its power, it did not include a reference to Cuba except in a long footnote. I likely found the topic too close and too polemical at the time. Most of the early studies of the revolution focused on its utopian elements, its social achievements, and the hopes associated with breaking free of dependency on the United States and pursuing independent economic development and even industrialization. Later the focus was on the hostility to U.S. imperialism. Even when some analysts had already noted the frustration of hopes for democracy, the positive social changes and popular support and mobilization were seen to compensate. The massive outmigration (12 percent of the population, mostly to the United States and Spain) limited the scale of repression, although a recent summary shows the extent of state terror and the similarity to the Soviet model in the patterns of repression, including the harsh punishment of former revolutionaries turned dissidents (Fontaine, 1997). Almost no scholarly effort was made to place the system in a comparative perspective. The hostility to the concept of totalitarianism precluded its use, although in my view the basic elements were there. I see the indisputable charismatic appeal of Castro and his links with the Latin American tradition of *caudillismo* as no obstacle to characterizing the institutionalization of the regime and its policies as totalitarian. The question is to what extent the charisma and the nationalist appeal are still the basis of what we might characterize as a post-totalitarian regime.

Castro's political survival after the fall of the communist regimes that had supported him has raised questions of whether, when, and how a transition to democracy will take place in Cuba. The many papers on the subject focus on the creation of capitalist enclaves, particularly in tourism, the greater tolerance of private economic activity, the dollarization of part of the economy, occasional tolerance of some dissidence, the new *modus vivendi* with the Catholic Church after years of conflict, and some speculations about the attitude of the armed forces. The analyses and speculations turn on the nature of the post-totalitarian character of the regime and the potential for transition (Mujal-León and Saavedra, 1977; Krämer 1993, 1995; Centeno and Font, 1996).

Cuba presents us therefore with an almost complete cycle, from the revolutionary overthrow and abdication of a sultanistic dictator, to a provisional government that some hoped would lead to democracy, to the consolidation of a dictatorship that in the 1970s could fit perfectly into the totalitarian type, to a process of transition to post-totalitarianism by decay, societal conquest, and partial and reluctant liberalization (Perez-Stable, 1999). Some of the best conceptual analyses deal with this last phase, characterized as charismatic or *caudillo* post-totalitarianism. While the earlier phases—the takeover by Castro, the failure of the provisional government, and particularly the totalitarian phase—were not placed in a comparative perspective, the opposite is happening with the post-totalitarian phase.

Traditional Authority as Distinct from Modern Authoritarian Regimes

Also in the category of "other nondemocratic regimes" are some of the traditional monarchies. These include Saudi Arabia; some like Kuwait with oligarchic democratic institutions; Morocco and Jordan, now perhaps starting processes of democratization; Nepal until the democratic transition in 1990–1991; and Bhutan. Without analyzing the politics of these countries, I want to note that the basis of legitimacy of the nondemocratic rule is traditional (at least for parts of the population and the elites), and that therefore these regimes should not be confused with modern authoritarian regimes.

There are those who call Latin American authoritarian regimes or sultanistic regimes "traditional"; some even do so in the cases of Franco's Spain and Salazar's Portugal. This interpretation is fundamentally flawed, however, since the basis of legitimacy in the regimes is not traditional dynastic legitimacy.

Excursus on the
Scholarly Literature of Recent Decades

In the twenty-five years since publication of the *Handbook of Political Science,* much has been learned about some of the nondemocratic regimes around the world. It would be foolish to attempt to summarize those developments here, since there are other works that accomplish that task. For example, Volume 2 of the *Traité de science politique,* edited by Madeleine Grawitz and Jean Leca (1985), includes excellent essays by L. Ferry and E. Pisier-Kouchner, P. Ansert, K. D. Bracher, H. Carrère d'Encausse, and J. L. Domenach on different totalitarianisms and by G. Hermet on authoritarianism. The recent essay by Archie Brown (1999) is an excellent source of work done in the United Kingdom. It is impossible to refer in this limited space to the flood of books and articles on Nazi rule that have appeared; the anthology edited by Karl Dietrich Bracher, Manfred Funke, and Hans-Adolf Jacobsen (1983) offers an interesting selection and a selected systematic bibliography. More recently, Eckhard Jesse (1996) has compiled an outstanding reader that includes writings on totalitarianism from different perspectives.

With the exceptions I have already noted and a few others, the work in the last twenty-five years has been mostly excellent historical monographs and descriptive country studies. With the opening of the Soviet archives, we can expect additional work along these lines. Such work would allow us to understand better the different phases of Soviet totalitarianism from its inception after the revolution to the Stalinist period, the real meaning of Khrushchev's reforms (which can be seen either as a process of liberalization or as an attempt to revitalize totalitarianism without terror), the years of detotalitarianization (by default more than by intent) under Brezhnev (Bialer, 1980), and the active reforms by Gorbachev that led to the breakdown of the Soviet Union and to democratization.

While Italian archives have been open for decades, political scientists have not added much to our systematic knowledge of the nature and transformation of Italian fascist rule, from a theoretical perspective, that would allow us to understand better why totalitarianism was ultimately arrested in Italy. We do have, however, the monumental historical work of Renzo de Felice and the interesting writing of another historian, Emilio Gentile, mainly on the ideological origins of the regime. The Franco regime also has been the subject of excellent historical research that illuminates some of the origins of its limited pluralism, as well as excellent studies of the regime's elite. For Portugal, the work of Antonio Costa Pinto places Salazar's regime in the broader context of authoritarian European politics and the rise of fascism, focusing on Portugal's small fascist party and its fate under authoritarian rule. Manuel de Lucena (1976) has written an excellent study of Portuguese corporatism. There is still much scholarly work to be done by historians and social scientists on the nondemocratic regimes in Latin America, beyond the recent focus on transitions to democracy.

There have been some valuable newer studies of authoritarian nonfascist and even antifascist regimes: Ben-Ami (1983) on the Primo de Rivera dictatorship in Spain; Kluge (1984) on Austria; Lucena (1976), Wiarda (1977), Schmitter (1979), and Costa-Pinto (1995) on Portugal; Özbudun (1995) on Turkey; Paxton (1972) on Vichy France; Stepan on Brazil (1973) and Peru (1978); Wynot (1974) on Poland; Lieven (1973) on the Baltic states; Jowitt (1978) on Romania; Liddle (1996) on Indonesia; Winckler on China (1999). The most important contribution to the debate on the new authoritarianism in Latin America, largely generated by O'Donnell's thesis of bureaucratic authoritarianism, is the book edited by David Collier (1970), with contributions by, among others, Albert Hirschman and Fernando Henrique Cardozo. The breakdown of military regimes in South America and Greece has led to new thinking about the military in authoritarian regimes. Alfred Stepan (1988) formulated the distinction between regimes in which the "hierarchial" military assumed power through its top leadership and those where a "nonhierarchical" military (i.e., officers of lower rank) assumed power, displacing their superiors, as happened in Greece. This distinction became very important in the analysis of the role of the military in the transition to democracy and particularly the problems of democratic consolidation (Linz and Stepan, 1996).

The various transitions—to democracy, to an uncertain future of nonconsolidated democracy, or to failed democratization processes—together with the end of hopes for the democratization of some authoritarian regimes in the third world have created conditions for an objective, intellectual analysis of regimes in comparative politics. For example, the three volumes of *Democracy in Developing Countries* on Africa (1988), Asia (1989) and Latin America (1999), edited by Larry Diamond et al., cover developments in countries that have experienced both authoritarian and democratic rule, by country experts.

Some Thoughts on the Origins of Totalitarianism

The reader of my work—and that of most of the contributors to the volumes that Alfred Stepan and I edited on the breakdown of democracy—would realize that we should not overestimate the capacity of antidemocratic leaders and the success of antidemocratic mass movements, but instead take into account the failures of democratic governments and leaders, their inability to confront their opponents in defense of liberal democracy, and, for some, their semiloyalty to democracy.[4] From that perspective, the taking of power by Mussolini (Lyttelton, 1987) and Hitler was not inevitable, nor were the October Revolution and Lenin's rise to power. Totalitarianism was not the inevitable outcome of the European crisis created by World War I and even less the outcome of the Great Depression. It was one of the possible fruits of modernity; but democracy was another. The victory of communism in Russia and the communist threats in Europe met with different responses, some democratic and some authoritarian, and not—*pace* Nolte (1987)—an inevitable struggle between fascism and communism.

A healthy corrective to any overdetermined view of the history of the twentieth century is the reading of Henry A. Turner's (1989) counterfactual history based on the assumption that Hitler died in a car accident in the summer of 1930. This thoughtful exercise makes excellent reading, providing us with much food for thought. Had that death occurred in 1930, it would have prevented me from writing many of the pages of this book. Still remaining, however, would be the question of the development of totalitarianism in the Soviet Union and other communist countries. And it would not have assured an earlier consolidation of democracy in many European and Latin American countries and in Japan.

The Shortened Century of Totalitarianism

The history of the origins of the political disasters of the "short century" should start with 1914, World War I and its aftermath. As Hobsbawm

(1994), François Furet (1999), Ernst Nolte (1987), and Karl Bracher (1984) emphasize, the old bourgeois order was shattered by the guns of August. Without the war there would not have been the split of socialism between Bolsheviks and Social Democrats, nor the rise of Italian interventionist nationalism, Mussolini and fascism, the German radical left, and the Nazi success in destroying Weimar democracy. Certainly, the intellectual roots of the ideological response to the war and its aftermath were there, as Bracher, Mosse, Gentile (1975), Sternhell (1978), and Furet among others stress. The war generated among respectable intellectuals, as Mommsen (1997–1998) has shown, a nationalist-chauvinist, militarist reaction that may be difficult to understand today. With the mass slaughter, its revolutionary aftermath, the new nationalisms, and the displacement of millions from their homes, the war desensitized people to the violence and horrors to come, a point eloquently made by Hobsbawm.

That legacy became articulated and institutionalized in the great antidemocratic movements and the regimes studied in this book. In the common matrix of the war and its aftermath, the intellectual seeds of revolutionary Marxism, irrationalist philosophy, social Darwinism, and racism would bear new and poisoned fruit. (A more complete discussion would include an analysis of those origins, but the works cited should allow the reader to fill that gap.) The generational composition of the founders and top elites of fascist and communist parties all over the world, and certainly of the German Nazi and communist parties, reflects the centrality of the experience of World War I, in contrast to the older elites of the Christian Democrats and even more the socialist parties (Linz, 1978, pp. 43–47, especially Table 1).

Reading Furet and a number of other works of intellectual and cultural history gives us considerable insight into why totalitarianism seduced so many outstanding minds—though not always for long. There is no fully equivalent work on the attraction of fascism, although there is a useful review by Hamilton (1971) and the writings on Heidegger, Carl Schmitt, and Gottfried Benn and on the fascist graduates of the Ecole Normale Supérieure (Rubinstein, 1990). Would those regimes have had the same success without that appeal to intellectuals? Possibly yes, considering their appeal to common men, the desire for security, and above all the fear that their terrorism created. We should not forget their ability to mobilize participation through the single party and the administered mass organizations, nor the gratification derived from, or dependent on, on that participation. Within the scope of my early work it was not possible to convey sufficiently the importance of that "democratic" participatory dimension.

Nolte (1987) has rightly stressed the importance of the fear of revolution in Europe in generating reactionary sentiments. That fear was stimulated by the unsuccessful but bloody revolutionary attempts and the widespread revolutionary rhetoric in the socialist movement, by the efforts of communist emissaries to kindle revolution, by the conflicts in the new nations bordering on the Soviet Union, and by the militias and army officers involved in repressing revolution, many of whom turned against even the democratic governments that were successfully stopping revolution.

Anticommunist, antirevolutionary sentiments were an essential component of the antidemocratic wave in Europe (not always led by the fascists). Fascism and Nazism were the beneficiaries of that response to communism, but anticommunism, in my view, was not the only, and in many cases not the most important, ideological basis and appeal of fascism. Nazism was not just anticommunism. Hitler's racism may have been reinforced and legitimized by an emphasis on the Jewish leadership of some of the revolutionary movements of the time, but it had prewar and deeper intellectual and cultural roots. Fascism was a more complex phenomenon and movement than anticommunism. As any reader of the work of Gentile (1975) knows, Italian fascism's antiliberal, antibourgeois, even anticlerical elements, as well as its overall style, are not the reaction to communism or the result of "learning" from the Soviet experience, as Nolte argues in his scholarly but one-sided analysis.

While anti-Semitism and the Holocaust occupy a central and unique place in the analysis of Nazi ideology, it should be considered as part of a broader racist ideology: "a full blown system of thought, an ideology like Conservatism, Liberalism" (Mosse, 1985, p. ix). That racism was reflected in the mass murder of gypsies and in the sterilization of the German children of black soldiers (World War I). Such social-Darwinist eugenic thinking was part of a larger body of scientific thought, which had a broad appeal beyond Germany and counted many followers in the democratic left. (We tend to forget the scientific and pseudoscientific pedigree of racist thinking, of Gobineau, Vacher de Laponge, Houston Stewart Chamberlain, and the eugenic movement.) Even when Nazism, as other fascist movements, was fundamentally nationalist (and therefore "particularistic" rather than "universalistic," to use Furet's terminology), its racism was in a sense "universalistic," ready to sacrifice the nation and those citizens not identifying with the racist-biological myths, and attempting to mobilize racists beyond its borders. The racist-eugenic utopia was something quite different from nationalism (Mosse, 1983).

Liberal democrats, however, should not ignore the contribution of the "civil war" atmosphere in the crisis of democracy that made possible the fascist and particularly the Nazi appeal: there was an atmosphere generated by the rhetoric of the class struggle, the futile violence of German communist party (KPD) activists, the growth of the communist parties, and the ambiguity toward liberal democracy of some sectors of the socialist movement. Anticommunism could lead, and did lead in a number of countries, to authoritarian regimes and to repression, but not to a totalitarian system with its revolutionary efforts at social transformation. Also, a number of democracies, some incorporating the socialist parties into the government, were able to oppose both fascism and communism. The totalitarian ambitions of fascists, the totalitarian dimension of Italian fascism, cannot be understood as a reflection of anticommunism. The radical and fully totalitarian rule of Hitler adds Nazism's distinctive anti-Semitism and even more broadly conceived racism to fascist ideological elements and the Italian model. Indeed, Nazi racism went beyond the characteristic nationalism of fascist movements. (In this context, it is significant that "neofascist" groups and skinheads today do not connect that much with the fascist legacy, but instead use Nazi symbolism in their violence against foreigners).

The Totalitarian Temptation

Writing from the perspective of the year 2000, looking back at the forms politics has taken in the twentieth century, what strikes me most, besides the horrors and the inhumanity, is the enthusiasm, the hopes, the commitment, and the idealism generated by communism and fascism, including Nazism. The same has to some extent been true for anticommunism and antifascism. In contrast, the much weaker appeal of democracy in the first half of the twentieth century—in spite of its successes—and the measured hopes—and even disillusionment (*desencanto,* or *Entzauberung*)—associated with it in the last quarter are striking. The appeal of totalitarianism contrasts with the generally passive acceptance of authoritarian regimes and the apathy, opportunism, and cynicism in the response to sultanistic rule. The capacity for deception and temptation by totalitarianism is only equaled by its tragic legacy. Only work focusing more than my own does on the ideological dimension of totalitarianism, as seen sometimes in films, newsreels, and literature, can capture the basis for the political institutions discussed.

National Cultures and Authoritarianism

An issue that I did not deal with sufficiently in the *Handbook* is the inclination of some scholars to explain totalitarianism as the result of unique historical legacies. During World War II this was a popular interpretation of Nazism by politicians, historians, and psychologists focusing on Germany's historical uniqueness, the Prussian legacy, Lutheran political thought and ethics, a particular kind of national character, etc. Richard Hamilton (1995) has articulated well some of the difficulties with cultural arguments about the success of Nazism. I never sympathized with such interpretations, and the development of German democracy after the war only confirmed my skepticism. There were similar approaches in attempting to explain Leninism and Stalinism (Arnason, 1993). More recently, the historian Richard Pipes (1984, 1990) has argued that an exploration of Soviet totalitarianism "must be sought not in socialism but in the political culture which draws on socialist ideas to justify totalitarian practices," as summarized by Klaus Müller (1997, p. 32). Daniel Goldhagen's (1996) work on the roots of Hitler's holocaust in German anti-Semitism, which created a great deal of controversy (Schoeps 1996), is in the same tradition.

The emphasis on the Russian cultural matrix leads to a paradoxical effort to stress a discontinuity between Leninism and Stalinism. The argument is that many of Stalin's policies reflected a break with the leftist ideological heritage and led to a rightist-nationalist regime that reconstructed traditional authoritarian patterns and implemented repressive ethnic policies. With that line of thinking, the concept of totalitarianism can encompass both Nazism and Stalinism. The latter can even be interpreted as a variant of fascism; and in that way, the original Marxist-Leninist ideology can be saved from responsibility for totalitarianism. A new falsification of history, by ignoring the Leninist roots of totalitarianism, would serve to cover the failure of the communist utopia revealed with the fall of the Berlin Wall in 1989.

Samuel Huntington's *Clash of Civilizations* (1996) may encourage a revival of such cultural explanations of nondemocratic rule. However, considering the example of Confucianism, the democratic politics of contemporary Taiwan and South Korea make such a culturalist perspective questionable (Stepan, 2000). Obviously, I do not totally dismiss such approaches—as long as they are not given a dominant place, and cultures and religions are not considered homogeneous and unchangeable. But a cast-iron political culture interpretation in my view is untenable. Perhaps I am allergic to such interpretations because they recall many writings on the incompatibility of Catholicism and democracy and the inherent propensity for authoritarianism in the Spanish culture, ignoring a wealth of other social, economic, and political factors.

Mass Society and Totalitarianism

I have kept my distance from the mass-society perspective in explaining totalitarianism, which probably is my main reason for not agreeing with Hannah Arendt's analysis. This reluctance is based on the facts about the rise of Nazism in German society stressed by Rainer Lepsius (1993) and Sheridan Allen (1984), among others, but also on the theoretical-empirical critique of the concept by Theodor Geiger (1954) and Salvador Giner (1976) and, going farther back, Simmel's analysis of the individualizing consequences of modernity. Many, if not most, of the people who joined the Nazi movement were not lone individuals, but did so as members of "civil society" groups taken over by Nazi activists or went to Nazi rallies with friends.

The successes of totalitarian movements were not the result of alienation generated by a "mass society," of the loneliness of individuals in modern industrial or capitalist societies. In fact, in some cases those successes were facilitated by the integration of individuals into close groups that rejected the larger more complex and open society. Some of those groups, like the Italian veterans (the *Arditi)* and the German *Freikorps,* had been formed on the basis of close emotional relations developed during World War I and the violent postwar years. The "mass society" approach to some extent reflects the search for an alternative to the "class society" and class conflict view of disappointed Marxists.

However, the mass-society perspective does help us to understand the success of totalitarian rule once consolidated. The destruction of civil society—which could not function without the freedoms guaranteed by the liberal state based on the rule of law (the *Rechtsstaat)*—the penetration of society by mass organizations controlled by a single party, and the fears generated by repression and terror certainly isolated individuals and facilitated mass manipulation and mobilization. Even such primary groups as the family and circles of friends were threatened. The diary (1918–1921) of a young French intellectual, Pierre Pascal, who joined the Bolsheviks in 1917, reveals how a contemporary, engaged observer perceived the impact of totalitarianism on society:

> A unique and heady spectacle: the demolition of a society. This is the very realization of the fourth psalm of the Sunday vespers, and the Magnificat: the powerful cast from their throne and the poor man lifted from his hovel. The masters of the house are confined to one room, and each of the other rooms houses a family. There are no more rich people: only poor and poorer. Knowledge no longer confers either privilege or respect. The former worker promoted to director gives orders to the engineers. Salaries, high and low, are getting closer to each other. The right to property is reduced to the rags on one's back. Judges are no longer obliged to apply the law if their sense of proletarian equity contradicts it. Marriage is merely registration with the civil authorities, and notice of divorce can be served by postcard. Children are instructed to keep an eye on their parents. Sentiments of generosity have been chased out by the adversity of the times: the family sits around counting mouthfuls of bread or grams of sugar. Sweetness is now reputed to be a vice. Pity has been killed by the omnipresence of death. Friendship subsists only as camaraderie. (quoted in Furet, 1999, pp. 102–103)

The difficulties in re-creating civil society even in new post-totalitarian democracies show the lasting impact of a "flattened social landscape" (Marc Howard, 1999).

Totalitarianism and "Democracy"

The relation between democracy, as I have defined it, and totalitarianism remained underdeveloped in the *Handbook,* but today it deserves further thought. My earlier position was determined by the fact that totalitarian rule had not ever been established by free choice in a competitive electoral setting, contrary to the misinterpretation (if not outright lie) that Hitler came to power as the result of a free election. However, I have not thought enough about the possibility of the democratic decision of a majority to do away with the freedoms that are the essence of democratic government—a possibility that we should not dismiss lightly. As de Tocqueville cautioned, democracy as a supreme value, without giving equal or greater value to freedom, can be risky. Certainly, the probability is that a functioning democratic system will not lead to an unfree, nondemocratic political system, but we can not exclude that frightful possibility. In our enthusiasm for the victory of democracy, as Daniel Bell warned me, we should not forget that freedom is as important as (if not more important than) democracy—that is, government by those elected by the people. The liberal freedoms certainly are important as an instrumental requirement for democratic political processes, but above all they are valuable in themselves. We should not forget that both fascism (especially Nazism) and communism were profoundly antiliberal, but claimed to be "democratic" in a way that authoritarian regimes did not.

The Centrality of Ideology

The reading of François Furet's *The Passing of an Illusion: The Idea of Communism in the Twentieth Century,* with its focus on ideology (and in passing, fascism) and the ideological manipulation of antifascism and later, anti-anticommunism, is perhaps the best complement to the political-science analysis in this book. Nolte in a sense does the same with how anticommunist sentiments were used by fascism. Both extremist ideologies sought to obscure the realities of their respective totalitarian systems, gaining support from those who should have been their enemies—liberal democrats, social democrats, Christians, nationalists, and above all bourgeois and (although it might sound strange to those weaned on the Marxist theories of fascism) capitalists—and who were seen by both ideologies as enemies to be destroyed. This deliberately created confusion led many to see the shortened twentieth century as one of conflict between communism and fascism—as Nolte does with great knowledge but also simplification—ignoring the roots of fascist thought before the October Revolution and of Nazism in a tradition of racist thinking, social Darwinism, pseudo-biological science, and anti-Semitism.

The differing ideologies are, of course, one of the main distinctions between communism and fascism. What are striking, however, are the similarities in communism's and fascism's commitment to ideas, their use of ideas to derive policies (sometimes very concrete measures, even in realms otherwise remote from politics such as art, music, scientific debates), their fanatic effort to implement those policies, the murderous consequences, and the extent to which large numbers of cadres, party members, and citizens believed in them.

No one will question that the ideologically grounded and argued debates among the contenders for Lenin's mantle up to the purges in the 1930s were part of a gigantic and ultimately murderous power struggle. But it would be a mistake to ignore the seriousness of the debates, the intellectual articulation of the positions. That Stalin finally became the despot he was and the only source of ideological formulations could be seen as the deterioration of the ideological pillar of totalitarianism and the strengthening of another (i.e., the concentrated monopoly of power in the leader and his trusted lieutenants, who control the apparatus of the one-party state and its organizations).

It is the centrality of ideological belief that made so devastating to the system Khrushchev's 1956 revelations, the loss of faith in the communist utopia and its replacement with an emphasis by the leadership on "really existing socialism," and the realization by common people of the "living lie." This in spite of the ritual reiteration and recitation of ideology and the remaining loyalty of some cadres, activists, and fewer and fewer intellectuals. The crisis of totalitarianism and the drift into post-totalitarianism is largely, but not only, a crisis of the ideological way of thinking. However, the "wooden language" of the regime had become a mentality for the apparatchiks and even citizens, which survives today in the new democracies.

I want to emphasize that ideology shaped the behavior and actions of social groups and individuals operating from widely varying motives. As Kershaw (1991, p. 74) put it, these actors "shaped the progressive dynamic of Nazi rule by interpreting Hitler's *presumed* wishes without any need for close central direction. At the same time, it allowed the functional importance of Hitler's ideology to be seen less as concrete aims to be implemented than as interpreted, utopian 'directives for action' integrating different forms of social motivation and gradually coming into focus as realizable objectives without the necessity of close steerage from the dictator himself." This was probably even more true for Stalin, as Bialer (1980) noted when writing about "preemptive obedience." In any case, the ideology, intentions, and actions of the dictator, while far from unimportant, are insufficient to explain the processes in totalitarian systems. They are admittedly more important than I recognized in the *Handbook*—where I did not make reference to the growing biographical literature on political leaders—but certainly much less important than is claimed by those who want to put all the weight on the leaders' personalities.

The real conflict was between freedom and liberal democracy on one side and the two revolutionary totalitarianisms on the other, as Raymond Aron and K. D. Bracher, among many others, emphasized. The underlying perspective of my own work is part of that tradition, except that I also include the noncommunist and nonfascist authoritarian and sultanistic threats to freedom as part of the political and social history of the twentieth century.

One of the shortcomings of the *Handbook* essay is that I did not, because of space limitations, consider how nondemocratic political regimes affected other spheres of society: religion, intellectual life, the arts (Antonova and Merkert, 1995; Council of Europe, n.d.), the bureaucracy, and the military, as well as the daily lives of ordinary citizens. My lack of reference to "economic" society was more deliberate, since it would have required a different expertise and probably another book.

Political Religion, Religion, and Regimes

If—the constant if—I had been writing a book rather than a contribution to a *Handbook,* I would have devoted considerable attention to the relation between political regimes and religion. I have done so in several subsequent essays, mainly on the *"nacional-catolicismo"* in the context of the Spanish authoritarian regime (Linz, 1992a, 1993, 1997a).

While the literature to which I referred in the *Handbook* made use of the concept of "political religion" or at least noted the pseudo-religious element in totalitarian politics, I did not incorporate that concept in my analysis. However, two volumes edited by Hans Maier and Michael Schäfer (1997a) have reviewed classical writings on totalitarianism, emphasizing this dimension and applying the approach to concrete phenomena. My own contribution to those volumes (Linz, 1997) explores the whole range of relations between political regimes and religion, covering aspects neglected or underdeveloped in the *Handbook.*

Though I share some of the reservations expressed about the concept of political religion, I probably would agree with several themes linked to the debate on the subject to which Hans Maier (1996) has made an important contribution. One is the fundamental hostility of totalitarian regimes to existing organized religion: the effort to destroy it—as in the

Soviet case—or at least to limit, control, or manipulate religious institutions. This is compatible with pragmatic, cynical, or vague invocations of defending religion, like the "positive Christianity" of the Nazi program or Hitler's invocation of *Vorsehung* (providence). I also would agree that the success of totalitarian movements was greater in secularized societies, and that religious ties resulted in some capacity to resist. And I would accept that, despite the secularization of the fascist regimes, some of their leaders and especially some ideologists used a language and symbolism derived from religious traditions, making them profane.

It is worth notice that a contemporary observer like Thomas Mann perceived the common element of sacralization. Mann wrote in his diary (October 1, 1933):

> The honor guard of the Storm Troops posted like statues in front of the Feldherrnhalle is a direct and unabashed imitation of the guard the Russians keep in front of Lenin's tomb. It is the "ideological" arch-enemy they are imitating—as they do in their films—without reflecting, perhaps without even being aware of what they are doing. The similarity, in the *style of our time,* is far stronger than any rational differences in "ideology." (quoted by Furet, 1999, p. 526)

Even in Italy, as Emilio Gentile (1996) and the more ethnographic study by Mabel Berezin (1997) show, this process went far. Totalitarian regimes tried to fill the emotional vacuum created by secularization with political rituals and liturgies derived from or inspired by religion. What is more difficult to ascertain is to what extent leaders, party organization members, and ordinary citizens succumbed to those pseudoreligious efforts to give meaning to their lives, and the extent to which participation in those rituals evoked feelings comparable to those of religious rituals. I am quite skeptical on the first point, except for the ideologists themselves and some leaders; but I would consider the second quite relevant in understanding the hold of totalitarian movements and regimes on some of their supporters.

Fascism and Totalitarianism

I subscribe to the idea of a generic fascism as a type of political movement, ideology, and style, of which Nazism was a distinct (and even somewhat aberrant) variant. This does not, however, lead me to equate the Nazi and the Italian fascist regimes as a single type of totalitarianism. Some scholars reject any encompassing conception of fascism, though they many emphasize the commonalities among fascist regimes. Others reject the usefulness of any analysis that does not consider each case as unique. Still others conflate ideology, movements, and regimes under the category "fascism" (generally extending it to a wide range of rightist-conservative-capitalist antidemocratic parties and regimes). In this regard, the Italian political theorist of the democratic left, Norberto Bobbio, has formulated it well: "I agree with De Felice; fascism is a historical phenomenon; we can compare it with Nazism in spite of all the differences we know, but we can not attribute the characterization of 'fascism' to whatever authoritarian regime. There are dictatorships of a military nature, which insofar as they are autocratic regimes are also oppposed to democratic regimes, but they are not fascist" (1996, p. 29). Paradoxically, those who overextend the term "fascism" come to a position not too different from Ernst Nolte's in *Der europäische Bürgerkrieg* [The European Civil War], which treats the conflict between communism and fascism as the key to European history.[5] This position, in contrast to the perspective maintained by Bracher (1976) and myself, forgets that the great conflict in this century was between those two ideological movements and modern liberal democracy based on the rule of law. The recognition of that conflict has been the source of analyses by Aron and Bracher, among many others. In the present book, another intellectual source of the emphasis on the distinctiveness of totalitarianism was my need to describe and understand the whole range of nondemocratic and antiliberal regimes and the differences among them.

The reader of this book and of my essays on fascism will understand that I find myself more in agreement with François Furet in his *The Passing of an Illusion* than I am with Nolte. The two Western totalitarianisms had their own distinct origins and ideological bases, and it would be a mistake to interpret fascism as a reaction to communism, thereby ignoring its fundamental antiliberalism (as well as other "anti" positions) and its distinctive appeal. In fact, there were fascists in various countries who perceived an affinity with the communist revolution in Russia in their common hatred of liberal, parliamentary, bourgeois-plutocratic, and victorious democracies; for some, Stalinism was a kindred Russian national revolution.

Human Rights, State Terror, and Mass Murder

A major breakthrough in recent years has been the greater focus on human rights, on totalitarianism's terrible legacy of inhuman repression and on the new forms of authoritarian repression, state terror, and violence. However, the rich scholarly literature and solid official reports make little reference to any typology of regimes (Courtois et al., 1998). I have to confess that in an essay trying to link the typology of regimes and the terrible manifestations of inhumanity by states in the twentieth century I was, in many respects, inconclusive (Linz, 1992b). Totalitarianism certainly explains some of the worst violations of human rights, but totalitarian tendencies and regimes have not always led to the same type of state terror and repression—and certainly other nondemocratic regimes have contributed their share to the terrible legacies of the last century. The systematic analysis of the most obvious data on the mass murders, deaths, and jail sentences, the concentration camps, Gulags, and political prisoners, should be complemented with a comparison of the mechanisms of political and social control: the size of police forces; the recruitment, number, and activities of paid and "unofficial" informers; the presence of party activists that might be informers and the way they exercised pressures; the "political tests" for employment, travel, and educational opportunities. Even among communist countries there seem to have been significant differences. The mechanisms of control probably differentiated totalitarian regimes as much as the more obvious horrors of repression.

Although politics and ideological justifications are at the core of the explanation of the horrors of the twentieth century, microresearch on victims and their persecutors in various countries has shown the use by individuals of the machinery of repression for their personal goals, vendettas, and settling of private accounts. The paradox of the "privatization" of violence has been highlighted by Jan Gross (1988) and documented in many studies (e.g., Kalyvas). However, it is the absence of a liberal democratic *Rechtsstaat* that made this possible.

In this context, I want to mention Alexandra Barahona de Brito's *Human Rights and Democratization in Latin America* (1997) and her important observation on the South American military regimes:

> Finally, the level of "totalitarian" penetration in these regimes was not uniformly distributed. At one level, these regimes were typically authoritarian given their rhetorical adherence to democratic legalistic values, given their more porous quality, given the presence of limited pluralism, and their daily political and diplomatic confrontation with the values and rhetoric of the opposition and of the international community. It was only sections of the military institution which developed the totalitarian logic more fully in their implementation of repression. One saw a repressive ideological dynamic or "pockets"

within the military which operated according to a totalitarian logic. The "closer" to the repressive apparatus and the "further" from the limited pluralism at the regime level, the more the totalitarian elements of the ideology dominated and the more the totalitarian repressive dynamic took hold.

These coexisting tendencies occasioned paradoxical results. On the one hand, the totalitarian dynamic led the Armed Forces, so attached to legal conventions, to violate their own laws; on the other, it led them to attempt to pass constitutions which aimed at "protecting democracy." Thus, although the Uruguayan military tortured almost one-third of their population, they forced President Bordaberry to resign for his desire to destroy the traditional parties by abolishing them. In Chile, one could be abducted by an illegal and official nonexistent Comando Conjunto, but one's criminal abductors took the trouble to fill out forms with the relevant information.

The more the totalitarian ideology penetrated the Armed Forces, the worse the repression. Thus, the differences in repressive methods were partly shaped by the intensity and extension of the penetration of the totalitarian ideology within the Armed Forces. This is particularly clear when one compares Uruguay and Chile with Argentina. It is widely accepted that the penetration of this ideology in Argentina was the greatest of the three countries. Here, the total institutionalization of repression within the structures of the Armed Forces, together with the intensity of this ideological outlook, made repression the worst in the Southern Cone, as the military became more of a totalitarian institution or organization than it did in any other case.

This again shows how actual regimes combine elements in "mixed forms" that would fit more into one or another of the ideal types developed in the *Handbook* essay. In this case, regimes that in their dominant characteristics would be considered "authoritarian" had a totalitarian conception of repression. The same would be true of the strong sultanistic tendencies in Ceauşescu's Romania and in North Korea, which we would otherwise define as totalitarian, and of the sultanistic component in Suharto's rule in Indonesia.

Opposition and Resistance

One gap—among many—in my work is the neglect of the unsuccessful, but not nonexistent, dangerous and heroic resistance against totalitarianism. Over the years, an extensive scholarly historical literature on the resistance—*Widerstand*—against Hitler's rule has been published. Some interesting conceptual distinctions have been made between passive withdrawal, the assertion of autonomy by institutions and individuals, activities planning for a different future, and conspiratorial activities toward the overthrow of the regime (Hoffmann, 1979; Schmädeke and Steinbach, 1985). There also is an extensive literature on dissidents, particularly intellectuals and artists, in post-totalitarian regimes. In an essay on "Opposition In and Under an Authoritarian Regime: The Case of Spain" (Linz, 1973), I analyzed the different types of semi-opposition, alegal (tolerated) opposition, and illegal (persecuted) opposition in authoritarian regimes. Richard Löwenthal (1983) distinguishes among political opposition, societal refusal, and ideological dissent. Broszat (1987) has developed an interesting contrast between *Widerstand* and *Resistenz.*

The need for Soviet military intervention in Budapest in 1956 and Prague in 1978 to support and reequilibrate totalitarian rule after the death of Stalin is evidence of the limits or failure of totalitarian control (Ekiert 1996). The different forms of dissidence, opposition, and resistance deserve more attention. The demobilization of opposition and reequilibration of those regimes, however, represent the start of post-totalitarianism.

A question that might have been pursued further and explored more systematically in the *Handbook* essay is at what point, when, how, and by whom the establishment of totalitarian rule could have been prevented, arrested, or overthrown. Such a counterfactual analysis could help us to understand better the conditions and circumstances that made totalitarian control of society possible.

Totalitarianism and Daily Life

Since publication of the *Handbook,* a new perspective has led to much solid empirical research by historians, particularly on Nazi Germany, focused on a wide range of aspects of the daily lives of individuals. Working conditions, local community life, the letters of soldiers from the front, etc., are increasingly documented by what is called *Alltagsgeschichte* (Peukert, 1984, 1987). That literature in part has been used against the totalitarianism approach, arguing for the limits of Hitler's power and highlighting peoples' ways of evading the politicization of everyday life, but arguing also for individuals' spontaneous and unthinking assent to and participation in the policies of the regime against "racially inferior" people, Jews, and foreign workers.

In my view, these important contributions do not call into question the distinctive characteristic of a totalitarian regime (in contrast to other types of nondemocratic rule), nor the shaping of society, behavior patterns, and values by the system. They only question a simplistic view of totalitarianism that extrapolates from an ideal type a society totally penetrated and shaped by those in power. The essay by Henry A. Turner (1999), based on the diary of Victor Klemperer (1995), shows well how ordinary citizens expressed their discomfort with the regime—specifically its persecution of Jews—in little ways, as well as the fear surrounding those actions. It also puts a limit to the view that coercion and state terror (always latently present) were always overt and omnipresent. Certainly, people in their everyday lives—unless they were part of a targeted group (or an object of the hostility, for whatever reason, of those with access to power)—did not think of how their society was being ruled, just as people in a democratic free society do not see their daily lives shaped by the values of a free society. In a nondemocratic and particularly in a stable totalitarian society, many ordinary people are not necessarily aware of their lack of freedom; for them, that is the way life is. However, simultaneously and for a wide range of reasons (including personal benefits), many people are actively committed to building and sustaining such a society. After the fall of the system, they will claim (and even believe) they were just "ordinary" people ruled by an indeterminate and remote "them."

The Intellectual and Political History
of the Totalitarianism Debates

I believe that some of the most important contributions in the last few years to our understanding of totalitarianism have come from writings on the intellectual history of the concept and from the debates that work has generated. A book could and should be written on the intellectual and ideological history of these writings and debates. The works edited by Alfons Söllner (1997) and Hans Maier (1997) provide many of the needed elements. Moreover, we have the surveys by Wipperman (1997) and Gleason (1995). Gleason's book, while its title (*Totalitarianism*) suggests an updating of work on totalitarian regimes, really responds to its subtitle, *The Inner History of the Cold War*—that is, to the use of, and the political polemics surrounding, the term. The collection of essays edited by Evelyne Pisier-Kouchner (1983) provides us with a review of the analyses of Trotsky, Kautsky, Althusser, Castoriades, and Besançon, among others.

But a truly comprehensive book would have to discuss not only works by social scientists, but also literary writing ranging from Koestler's *Darkness at Noon,* Silone's *School for Dictators,* and Orwell's *1984* to Solzhenitsyin's *The Gulag Archipelago.* There is also an extremely rich body of autobiographical writings, mainly by former communists, that includes efforts at intellectual conceptualization and analysis. There are a few works—significantly few—by former fascists or fascist dissidents. The ideological, pseudo-scholarly efforts of intellectuals who identified with totalitarian regimes (and their contortions to hold their places in and under such regimes)—Carl Schmitt, Rudolf Huber, and the numerous Italian fascist jurists come to mind—would deserve to be included. François Furet, in *The Passing of an Illusion,* offers many insights into the delusions of such intellectuals. The pages (116–124) he devotes to Gyorgy Lukács convey well that overriding ideological commitment of a brilliant thinker: Lukács "never missed a chance to align himself with what was going on in the Bolshevik party," and he was so captive of the *idea* of the Soviet Union that it annulled his knowledge of its history.

An interesting chapter in the study of totalitarianism—one without any parallel in the case of authoritarian regimes—is the fascination with communism (including Stalinism and Stalin as a leader) (Marcou, 1982) and fascism, and even Nazism, of so many distinguished intellectuals, writers, and artists living in free societies. That response provides us with many insights into the nature of totalitarianism and its appeal.

Last, but not least, there are foreign "political pilgrims" (Hollander 1981) impressed by the positive aspects of such regimes. The *Handbook* essay makes little or no reference to them.

The outside responses to the Soviet and the Nazi totalitarianisms were shaped by those regimes' respective use of antifascism and anticommunism to cover up their distinctive characteristics, and at one point or another to gain the sympathy or tolerance of liberal democrats who otherwise would have been hostile to them. At the time of the Cold War, "anti-anticommunism" served the same purpose. Each of those "ideological" myths had a kernel of truth, but obscured the true nature of the two totalitarianisms. Since my student days in Spain, I have been familiar with Koestler, Monnerot, Merleau-Ponty, and Carl Schmitt. That intellectual baggage shaped my thinking, although it might not be reflected in the footnotes limited to the more scholarly literature.

Types of Regime and the Transition to Democracy

I have found the clear distinctions among modern forms of politics—democracy, totalitarianism, post-totalitarianism (as a distinctive type of nondemocratic rule), authoritarian regimes in all their varieties, and sultanistic regimes or regimes with strong sultanistic tendencies—to be extremely fruitful in understanding the patterns of transition to democracy as well as, or even more, some of the problems of democratic consolidation. In this regard, I refer the reader to my collaboration with Alfred Stepan on *Problems of Democratic Transition and Consolidation.*[6]

The type of regime that we (Linz and Stepan, 1996) briefly delineate and use in our analysis of European postcommunist transitions to democracy is explicitly linked to the analysis of totalitarianism in the present book. It shares the general approach of focusing on the political—the structure and use of power—rather than the social, economic, or even cultural factors, though the latter three of course should not be neglected. It does not explain the change in and from totalitarianism in terms of the emergence of new social strata like managerial elites and technicians, or the spread of education, or social mobility, or the functional requirements for economic efficiency. Those changes certainly took place, but they did not directly change the political system. In my view, it was the cadre's loss of ideological commitment, which set in after de-Stalinization, that was decisive. The decay, the ossification and ritualization of an ideology that could not serve as a mobilizing utopia, in the end meant that the cadres, particularly at the middle and lower levels, did not feel legitimized to use the intact and large coercive apparatus in a crisis situation. Negotiation with demonstrators and meetings (some public) of regime leaders and the oppositon were the consequence. The nomenklatura—hierarchical, bureaucratized, aging, sometimes corrupt, recruited to the end using political criteria—was in general unable to formulate innovative responses to the problems confronting the society. However, in the end, one of its members, Gorbachev, would start *perestroika* and *glasnost* to reform and shake up the system, abandon the outer empire, and allow electoral mobilization in nationalist peripheries, with the consequences we all know. It was clear that there was no plan to return to totalitarianism; but neither was there the intention to make a transition to Western-type democracy (Di Palma, 1995). It was a new dynamic setting and conflicts within the elite that accelerated the process of breakdown and transition to democracy or pseudodemocratic politics.

My and Stepan's thinking on post-totalitarianism should not be understood as a theory of neototalitarianism. We incorporated into our analysis not so much the social and economic changes before and after Gorbachev as the political changes that contributed to the breakdown of the Soviet-type regimes, particularly the political crisis in the relation of the rulers with the society and within the ruling elite. An analysis of the post-totalitarian phase—in its variations over time and across countries—is in our view particularly useful to understanding the difficulties post-totalitarian new democracies confront in the transition phase and especially during consolidation. It is unfortunate that we could not devote even more attention to the distinctive characteristics of post-totalitarianism. We believe that the development of societies—economies, intellectual life, religion, civil society—in new democracies with a post-totalitarian past, in contrast to those with an authoritarian past, proves the relevance of totalitarianism as a distinctive form of domination. It also should caution against cultural-civilizational interpretations of Russian history and of the history of some Eastern European countries.

In Eastern Europe, the different types of post-totalitarian regimes, as we analyze in some detail in *Problems of Democratic Transition and Consolidation,* underwent processes of liberalization (initiated by members of the elite) or confronted a more or less significant and mobilized civil society that had submitted before to the lies of the regime, whether passively or coerced. The regime elite in some cases tried to save as much as it could by substituting one leader for another, by negotiation, and ultimately by giving up power peacefully, having lost faith in its right to rule and its capacity to mobilize the party and its organizations.

The course of totalitarianism had gone full circle from the initial ideological-utopian impulse to the loss of ideological legitimacy. In the absence of free democratic electoral legitimation, what basis was there left on which to demand obedience? (The case of East Germany was even more dramatic: if it was not to be a socialist state, why should it exist at all?) Everything that had made totalitarianism so powerful and frightening had decayed, eroded, disintegrated; but its legacy has been a flattened society, which finds it difficult to articulate itself in the framework of democratic political institutions and a market economy.

The Primacy of Politics

In the nineteenth century there was an uneasy equilibrium between the primacy of economic and political change. The bourgeoisie was making an economic revolution—industrial, agrarian, and service—and demanding political change. At the same time, as Schumpeter noted, that revolution was in a sense protected by the political legitimacy of the preindustrial political structures. The constitutional monarchies were a result of the compromise between the ascendant bourgeoisie and the traditional structures.

The shortened twentieth century (1914–1989) was dominated by *politique d'abord*—to use the term coined by Charles Maurras—of Bolshevism, fascism, and Nazism with the terrible and destructive consequences we know, and even democracy and its Keynesian policies after World War II. It was a time in which everything became politicized and all hopes were centered on political action.

Now, at the turn of the century, the indisputable success of the capitalist market economy—under whatever regime—has opened the door to a neoliberal economic view of politics that ignores the importance of institutions and political legitimacy.

The primacy of politics led to power as an end in itself, its maximization in the society and among nations, military expenditure rather than consumption. The absolute primacy of the economy, property, and market can lead to private consumption, but the neglect of collective goods. There is a need for a balance between politics and economy, made possible (but not assured) by democracy.

From the "Age of Totalitarianism" to the "Age of Democracy"?

As we move away in time from the concrete institutional, social experience of totalitarianism—and as the concept is being less questioned—attention turns to a more philosophical perspective. What does it all mean? How much did it define a historical period, between World War I and 1989? What does it tell us about human nature, modernity, and our values? These are great and difficult questions.

It is logical that, after 1989 and the end of the Soviet Union, a broader—although still European—approach would become central in the intellectual debate. This is an approach that goes far beyond the "political science" perspective found in the *Handbook* essay, but it is highly relevant to it. From different perspectives and implicit value judgments, the works of Bracher, Furet, Nolte, and Hobsbawm are relevant to the debate on totalitarianism, the usefulness of the concept, and the differences as well as the similarities of totalitarian systems.

Were I to write a much longer essay, I would enter into those debates and highlight my agreements (considerable with Furet) and disagreements (more with Nolte and less so with Hobsbawm). In view of the horrors of Auschwitz and also the Gulag, the questions first raised by Hannah Arendt appear as more central than ever in a comparative study of regimes. The monstrosity of inhuman rule, in a historical-moral perspective, was the central fact of the twentieth century. Unfortunately, the ultimate crisis of the totalitarian ideologies, movements, and regimes may not be the end of that tragic story.

In the *Handbook* essay I certainly was wrong in my pessimism about the possibility of peaceful, orderly, even formally constitutional transition from nondemocratic regimes to democracy. At the time I was writing, in 1974, there had been only the Turkish transition after World War II and the Colombian power-sharing agreement (*concordancia*), and no one could foresee the pattern of transition initiated in 1976 in Spain that would be followed by so many countries in later years.

The twentieth century was the age of totalitarianism, true; but it also was the age of democracy, the consolidation and expansion of political—and to some extent, social—democracy. It was the age of decolonization and the end of colonial imperialism, the age of the emergence of new independent states, some democratic, most nondemocratic. The century will be remembered for the inhumanity of man toward fellow human beings, but also for the universal declaration and assertion of human rights. (The first characteristic sadly does not seem to be a monopoly of totalitarianism.) No better evidence for the gigantic historical change in the last twenty-five years can be found than the fact that in mid-1974, according to Larry Diamond (1999), there were only 39 democracies in the world—that is, only 27 percent of the existing independent states—and by the beginning of 1998 the number of electoral democracies (in which governmental offices are filled through competitive multiparty elections that place incumbents at real risk of defeat) had increased to 117, or 61 percent of the by then larger number of independent states.

However, our joy at the progress of the last quarter-century must be tempered by the fact that of these 117 formal democracies, only 81 (69.2 percent) could be characterized by Diamond, using the Freedom House ratings, as "free." In a significant number of countries, for example 93 in 1993, the freedom scores were declining (compared to improving scores in 18 countries). If I were to write a book on comparative democracies, it would have to include a section on failed transitions to democracy, defective or pseudodemocracies, which I would rather characterize as "electoral authoritarian" regimes—mostly ethnocratic, often plebiscitarian—where a democratic façade covers authoritarian rule, often with sultanistic components.

When I was writing in 1974, there were many "democracies" with adjectives such as "organic," "people's," "tutelary," "basic"—and it was the nondemocratic regimes, their ideologists and partisans, who were using those terms to describe themselves; many of those regimes are analyzed in this book. In the middle 1970s and through the 1980s, a clear consensus seemed to emerge about which governments deserved to be called democratic. In the 1990s, confusion again set in—but this time caused by the very scholars committed to democracy, a result of their desire to see democracy progress and their hopes for democratic developments below the state level. New adjectival democracies are labeled "pseudo," "semi," "illiberal (electoral)," or "delegative"—but these terms are in fact being used to describe nondemocratic regimes (or in a few cases, low-quality democratic governments) (Merkel, 1999; Collier and Levitsky, 1997; Collier and Adcock, 1999). The fact that these nondemocratic regimes do not fit into the basic types of nondemocratic polities leads to such conceptualizations; I myself surely have fallen into this trap. Thus, I would urge the search for conceptual clarity. We might positively value some aspects, by no means all, of these new regimes, but we should be clear that they are not democracies (even using minimum standards). To avoid confusion, I propose the addition of adjectives to "authoritarianism" rather than to "democracy": for example, electoral authoritarianism, multiparty authoritarianism, center authoritarianism with subnational democracy. These are only suggestions, and I have yet to work out more precise concepts and to define the dimensions needed to clarify this growing number of regimes.

A somewhat different question is the quality of political democracy. We see governments resulting from free and fair elections and attempting to rule according to a constitution, committed to the rule of law, and respecting human rights. We might not have doubts about the democratic convictions of their leaders, but they may govern with a state apparatus that does not respond to their demands. We see countries where those who hold power at the local level behave as if immune to the laws of the state (in several federal states); countries where the police and the military in charge of maintaining law and order are unresponsive to liberal values (and where their reorganization and retraining cannot be achieved easily); countries where terrorists and in-surgents contribute systematically to a spiral of violence and counter-violence (even though their demands could instead be expressed peace-fully and there are democratic institutions in place to respond to them), preventing citizens from exercising their democratic rights. The quality of democracy depends on the quality of the state—bureaucracy, judi-ciary, police, military—and of all major social forces and actors, some-thing that a democratic government cannot assure in the short run. In addition, democratic institutions and civil rights cannot always lure disloyal and violent oppositions into the arena of peaceful democratic politics.

Any analysis of the quality of democracy in "third wave" democ-racies (Huntington, 1994) has to take into account that totalitarian sys-tems did not create only political institutions (and in the communist systems, a command socialist economy), but also shaped the entire so-cial life and culture. It is that legacy—difficult to define, conceptualize, or describe—that cannot be ignored. The former Soviet Union is dif-ferent in this respect from Eastern Europe and even the Baltic re-publics, since at least one or two generations of Soviet citizens were socialized in that totalitarian and post-totalitarian society. Fortunately, Nazi totalitarianism, lasting less than a generation, could not have the same impact.

The Future of Nondemocratic and Illiberal Rule

A question that the reader might pose, and to which I am very hesitant to reply decisively, is: "What is the future of nondemocratic politics at the turn of the millennium?" I can not avoid stressing that we should not be overly optimistic. There have been a significant number of failed transitions to democracy. There is still a lot of uncertainty about the de-velopment of Cuba and some of the postcommunist Southeast Asian countries, as well as North Korea, where totalitarianism seems to com-bine with sultanistic elements. The strong sultanistic components of Suharto's authoritarian regime leave a difficult legacy for the transition to democracy in Indonesia. And although China is undergoing some significant processes of liberalization, in my view it is still a post-totalitarian communist regime; contrary to the hopes of many of my colleagues, the emergence of capitalism does not yet assure a transition to democracy.

What probably has changed is that, with one exception, there are no nondemocratic regimes that appeal to intellectuals as there were for those born in the first part of the twentieth century. The one exception is Islamic fundamentalism, which found a first state-institutional embodiment in the Islamic Republic of Iran.

It is difficult to fit the Iranian regime into the existing typology, as it combines the ideological bent of totalitarianism with the limited pluralism of authoritarianism and holds regular elections in which candidates advocate differing policies and incumbents are often defeated (Chehabi, 1998). In the early 1980s, Iran's Islamic regime held great attraction for Muslim activists worldwide: it seemed to combine popular participation with a commitment to cultural authenticity, the rule of the *shari'a,* and opposition to Western imperialism. But the inability of the regime to deliver on its promises of a better life for its citizens has led to widespread disenchantment within the country, while the inconclusive ending of the war against Iraq and the growing Shi'ite sectarianism in Iran's foreign policy have dampened enthusiasm for the Iranian model elsewhere in the Muslim world (Roy, 1994).

The failure of the Iranian model of nondemocratic rule to maintain its appeal among Muslims does not mean that other forms of Islamic nondemocratic rule cannot attract adherents. Afghanistan's Taliban, for example, seems to exert an ideological influence that can be detected in such places as the Caucasus. Moreover, the end of ideology, or better, the crisis of ideology, has not, outside of Western Europe, meant the end of the ideological appeal of nationalism, which has led to new forms of ethnocracy, sometimes dressed in democratic form. It is difficult to say whether new forms of nondemocratic rule have emerged, except perhaps for plebiscitarian, pseudodemocratic, ethnocratic authoritarianism with significant sultanistic strains, particularly in the periphery of the former Soviet Union. We cannot exclude the authoritarian tendencies in some Latin American presidential democracies with strong populist traditions, such as Peru under Fujimori and Venezuela under Chavez. In other parts of the world, the real question is the consolidation and stability of the state under whatever political regime, preventing what could be called *chaocracy*—the rule of chaos, the mob, mercenaries, militias—without a central authority with the monopoly of violence.

Class and ideological conflict were the main causes of authoritarianism and totalitarianism in the past. The crisis of ideology—the defeat of fascism and the disintegration of communist rule in the Soviet Union and Eastern Europe—and the economic revolution in many parts of the world have reduced those bases of authoritarian responses. However, the salience of nationalism is likely to create, in many multinational states, conflicts leading to authoritarian rule and repression, as is the case when dominant nation-builders try to integrate ethnic and cultural minorities into a nation-state (ethnocratic polities) and when different minorities claim the right of national self-determination and secession. Overpopulation and inequalities in development produce massive migrations that threaten the sense of national identity and economic interests, leading to discrimination and the repression of outsiders. I therefore see in nationalism in its different manifestations one of the main sources of authoritarianism in the future. What is not clear is what institutional forms these authoritarian responses will take.

In a paradoxical way, political and cultural nationalism is a not unlikely response to economic globalization, to the expansion of a worldwide market economy and certain cultural patterns of the consumer society associated with it. While that economic transformation may be necessary, even inevitable, and probably to a large extent (although not for everybody) beneficial, I am not so optimistic about its positive effects in the political realm. Will economic globalization assure the expansion and consolidation of liberal political democracy? I sometimes feel that we might fall into the trap of a "white Marxism"—a belief that a free-enterprise, liberal economic infrastructure assures the development of a liberal political democracy.

The use of violence—power "out of the barrel of the gun"—in the twentieth century created a political order based on an existential and deadly friend-foe distinction. At the turn of the century, that distinction is still there, in a sense privatized in the hands of independent entrepreneurs of violence who mix personal ambitions, greed, ethnic hatred, and religious fanaticism. Typically, these mobilizers of violence are unable to create political order in a larger political realm, but they are able to resist any effort to subdue them. The result is chaocracy, enclaves of unlimited power without legitimating (true or false) myths. The situations in Liberia, Somalia, Sierra Leone, and Rwanda, the rule of the Tamil Tigers in northern Sri Lanka, to some extent the Taliban in Afghanistan, the guerrillas in Colombia, the KLA in Kosovo (barely checked by NATO and the UN) all approach this model. We are not dealing with states, regimes, political systems, but with something new that certainly has little to do with the types of politics analyzed in this volume.

My present intellectual interests are focused on the comparative study of political democracies in all their varieties, particularly their institutional forms: presidential and parliamentary, unitary and federal, and specifically the relationship of federalism, democracy, and nation. I hope, perhaps believe, that the totalitarian illusion—temptation—will not be repeated. But who is to tell whether—after the failures of real democracies, the existence of many "bad" democracies, the unsolvable problems in many societies—in a few decades the dream of a homogeneous, egalitarian, conflictless (by eliminating the sources of conflict) polity will be resurrected. The power of the idea of the nation in the context of a world that is globalized economically, and to some extent culturally and politically, could serve as the basis for a new mobilizing effort by a demagogic leadership—a leadership propelled by resentment and cloaked in a response to the injustice in the world.

As I read the *Handbook* essay today, I confess that I probably erred in being pessimistic about the possibility of nonviolent transitions to (liberal) democracy and about the spread of democracy around the globe. I would not like to underestimate again the potential for change toward freedom and democracy. However, the title of *Democracy's Victory and Crisis* (Hadenius, 1997) reflects my own feelings. The growing literature on "defective democracies" (Merkel, 1999) (almost all of them nondemocratic regimes with an electoral façade), delegative democracy, the disillusionment with democracy, and a renewed debate about the quality of democracy (which tends to disregard the enormous gains in freedom and human dignity thanks to even far from perfect democracies) should make us wonder about the "victory" of democracy. Fortunately for all of us, there is (with the exception noted above) for now no alternative form for organizing political life that is attractive to intellectuals, students, young people—no alternative that is firing their imaginations. Perhaps we have learned the insight of Hölderlin (1970, p. 607, my translation):

> You accord the state far too much power. It must not demand what it cannot extort. But what love gives, and spirit, cannot be extorted. Let the state leave that alone, or we will take its laws and whip them to the pillory! By Heaven! he knows not what his sin is who would make the state a school of morals. The state has always been made a hell by man's wanting to make it his heaven.

Notes

1. The reader should keep in mind that the chapters that follow were written at the request of the editors of the *Handbook of Political Science,* Fred

Greenstein and Nelson Polsby. The material therefore is centered on the political dimension of regimes and hence makes only limited reference to such issues as social structure, economic development, economic institutions—capitalist or socialist—and religious traditions. I initially was given only a few pages in the *Handbook,* but I bargained constantly to expand the essay. My argument was that in the other contributions to the six volumes there was almost no reference—and even less, an extended discussion—of any aspects of nondemocratic regimes. The chapters on executives and legislatures, on parties, etc., were focused exclusively on liberal democracies—at a time when the majority of the world's population was living under nondemocratic rule.

2. I have written an essay (in Söllner, 1997) on how I came to formulate the distinction between totalitarianism and authoritarianism. I note there how the term *totalitarianism* was used in the 1930s in Spain (applied to both communism and fascism by a leftist bourgeois politician) and how Francesc Cambó, a Catalanist politician, formulated a distinction in his wartime diary (published many years later) between totalitarian and authoritarian regimes.

3. Manuel Azaña, the leader of the bourgeois left and president of the Republic, wrote in 1937 (in the middle of the Civil War):

> When one speaks of fascism in Spain, my opinion was this: There are or may be as many fascists as one may wish. But a fascist regime, there will be none. If the movement of force against the Republic were victorious, we would fall into a military and ecclesiastical dictatorship of the traditional type. For many "watchwords" translated and many labels they might use. Swords, chasubles, military parades and homages to the Virgen del Pilar. On that side the country does not produce anything else.

Azaña was right, although fascism contributed to the distinctive and, in a way, the modern character of the authoritarian regime. The regime was a failed and largely defeated totalitarian attempt.

4. There has been an extensive literature on the conditions for and the breakdown of democracies, which I cannot review within the scope of this piece. Dirk Berg-Schlosser and Gisèle De Meur (1994) offer an original systematic comparison of different theories, including my own work. A major contribution is Dietrich Rueschemeyer, Evelyne Huber Stephens, and John D. Stephens, *Capitalist Development and Democracy* (1992).

5. Incidentally, the conflict between fascists (and other authoritarians) and communists (and other revolutionary groups), particularly their militias, could be considered part of a civil war, but not so the extermination of entire social or ethnic groups. A civil war is a violent conflict between two or more groups that are part of the same social or political body. The total exclusion of groups of people as "insects" or a "disease," and their physical destruction, goes beyond civil war. Civil war implies groups fighting, with one perhaps winning, but not a conflict with a defenseless group that has no chance to offer resistance.

6. There is the ever growing literature on the transitions from nondemocratic regimes to democracy (or sometimes failed transitions), including O'Donnell, Schmitter, and Whitehead (1986), Di Palma (1990), Przeworski (1991), Higley and Gunther (1992), Huntington (1994), von Beyme (1994),

Offe (1994, 1997), Shain and Linz (1995), Linz and Stepan (1996), Bratton and van de Walle (1997), Diamond (1999), Merkel and Puhle (1999), and Merkel (1999).

Bibliography

Allen, William Sheridan (1984). *The Nazi Seizure of Power: The Experience of a Single German Town 1922–1945.* New York: Franklin Watts.

Antonowa, Irina, and Jörn Merkert, eds. (1995). *Berlin-Moskau, 1900–1950.* Munich: Prestel.

Azaña, Manuel (1968). *Obras Completas,* Vol. 4, *Memorias Políticas y de Guerra.* Mexico: Oasis. P. 813.

Barahona de Brito, Alexandra (1997). *Human Rights and Democratization in Latin America.* Oxford: Oxford University Press.

Bebler, Anton, and Jim Seroka, eds. (1990). *Contemporary Political Systems: Classifications and Typologies.* Boulder: Lynne Rienner.

Ben-Ami, Shlomo (1983). *Fascism from Above: The Dictatorship of Primo de Rivera in Spain 1923–1930.* Oxford: Clarendon Press.

Berezin, Mabel (1977). *Making the Fascist Self: The Political Culture of Inter-war Italy.* Ithaca: Cornell University Press.

Berg-Schlosser, Dirk, and Gisèle De Meur (1994). "Conditions of Democracy in Inter-War Europe: A Boolean Test of Major Hypotheses." *Comparative Politics* 26, 3: 253–279.

Beyme, Klaus v. (1944). *Systemwechsel in Osteuropa.* Frankfurt: Suhrkamp.

Bialer, Seweryn (1980). *Stalin's Successors: Leadership, Stability and Change in the Soviet Union.* Cambridge: Cambridge University Press.

Bobbio, Norberto, Renzo De Felice, and Gian Enrico Rusconi (1996). *Italiani Amici Nemici.* Milan: Donzelli.

Bracher, Karl Dietrich (1976). *Zeitgeschichtliche Kontroversen, Um Faschismus, Totalitarismus, Demokratie.* München: Piper.

——— (1984). *The Age of Ideologies: A History of Political Thought in the Twentieth Century.* Translated by Weald Osters. New York: St. Martin's Press.

——— (1992). *Wendezeiten der Geschichte: Historisch-politische Essays 1987– 1992.* Stuttgart: Deutsche Verlags-Anstalt.

Bracher, Karl Dietrich, Manfred Funke, and Hans-Adolf Jacobsen, eds. (1983). *Nationalsozialistische Diktatur 1933–1945: Eine Bilanz.* Düsseldorf: Droste.

Bratton, Michael, and Nicolas van de Walle (1977). *Democratic Experiments in Africa: Regime Transitions in Comparative Perspective.* New York: Cambridge University Press.

Broszat, Martin (1987). "Die Begriffsfrage: Widerstand und Resistenz." In Martin Broszat and Elke Fröhlich, *Alltag und Widerstand: Bayern im Nationalsozialismus.* Munich: Oldenbourg.

Brown, Archie (1996). *The Gorbachev Factor.* Oxford: Oxford University Press.

——— (1999). "The Study of Totalitarianism and Authoritarianism." In Jack Hayward, Brian Barry, and Archie Brown (eds.), *The British Study of Politics in the Twentieth Century.* Oxford: British Academy and Oxford University Press.

Browning, Christopher R. (1991). *Ordinary Men: Reserve Police Battalion 101 and the Final Solution in Poland.* New York: Harper Collins.

Buchstein, Hubertus (1997). "Totalitarismustheorie und empirische Politikforschung: Die Wandlung der Totalitarismuskonzeption in der frühen Berliner Polktikwissenschaft." In Alfons Söllner et. al. (eds.), *Totalitarismus,* pp. 239–267.

Centeno, Miguel Angel, and Mauricio Font, eds. (1996). *Toward a New Cuba: Legacies of a Revolution.* Boulder: Lynne Rienner.

Chehabi, Houchang (1991). "Religion and Politics in Iran: How Theocratic Is the Islamic Republic?" *Daedalus* 120, Summer.

——— (1995). "The Provisional Government and Transition from Monarchy to Islamic Republic in Iran." In Yossi Shain and Juan J. Linz (eds.), *Between States,* pp. 127–143, 278–281.

——— (1998). "Das politsche System der Islamischen Republik Iran." In Renate Schmidt (ed.), *Naher Osten, Politik und Gesellschaft.* Berlin: Berliner Debatte. Pp. 180–199.

Chehabi, Houchang, and Juan J. Linz, eds. (1998). *Sultanistic Regimes.* Baltimore: Johns Hopkins University Press.

Collier, David, ed. (1979). *The New Authoritarianism in Latin America.* Princeton: Princeton University Press.

Collier, David, and Robert Adcock (1999). "Democracy and Dichotomies: A Pragmatic Approach to Choices about Concepts." *Annual Review of Political Science* 2: 537–565.

Collier, David, and Steven Levitsky (1997). "Democracy with Adjectives: Conceptual Innovation in Comparative Research." *World Politics* 30, 4 (July): 477–493.

Costa Pinto, Antonio (1995). *Salazar's Dictatorship and European Fascism.* Boulder: Social Science Monographs.

Council of Europe, compiled and selected by Dawn Ades, Tim Benton, David Elliot, and Ian Boyd Whyte (1995). *Art and Power: Europe under the Dictators 1930–1945.* London: Hayward Gallery, National Touring Exhibitions and Arts Council. Distributed by Cornerhouse Publications, Manchester.

Courtois, Stéphane, Nicolas Werth, Jean Louis Panné, Andrzej Paczkowski, Karel Bartosek, and Jean-Louis Margolin (1997). *Le livre noir du communisme: Crimes, terreur, répression.* Paris: Robert Laffont. (Also published in English: *The Black Book of Communism: Crimes, Terror, Repression.* Cambridge, Mass.: Harvard University Press, 1999.)

Daalder, Hans, ed. (1997). *Comparative European Politics: The Story of a Profession.* London: Pinter.

De Felice, Renzo (1966). *Mussolini il fascista* (2 vols.). Torino: Einaudi.

——— (1974). *Mussolini il Duce,* vol. 1, *Gli Anni del Consenso, 1929–1936.* Torino: Einaudi.

——— (1975). *Intervista sul Fascismo a cura di Michael A. Ledeen.* Rome: Laterza.

—— (1981). *Mussolini il Duce,* vol. 2, *Lo Stato totalitario, 1936–1940.* Torino: Einaudi.

—— (1990). *Mussolini l'alleato* (2 vols.). Torino: Einaudi.

——, ed. (1991). *Bibliografia orientativa del fascismo.* Rome: Bonacci.

de Lucena, Manuel (1976). *A evolução do sistema corporativo portugués.* Lisbon: Perspectivas e Realidades.

de Miguel, Amando (1975). *Sociología del Franquismo Análisis ideológico de los ministros del Régimen.* Barcelona: Euros.

Diamandouros, Nikiforos, Richard Gunther, and Hans J. Puhle, eds. (1995). *The Politics of Democratic Consolidation in Southern Europe in Comparative Perspective.* Baltimore: Johns Hopkins University Press.

Diamond, Larry (1999). *Developing Democracy: Toward Consolidation.* Baltimore: Johns Hopkins University Press. Chapter 2.

Diamond, Larry, Jonathan Hartlyn, Juan J. Linz, and Seymour Martin Lipset, eds. (1999). *Democracy in Developing Countries: Latin America.* 2nd ed. Boulder: Lynne Rienner.

Diamond, Larry, Juan J. Linz, and Seymour Martin Lipset, eds. (1988). *Democracy in Developing Countries: Africa.* Boulder: Lynne Rienner.

—— (1989). *Democracy in Developing Countries: Asia.* Boulder: Lynne Rienner.

Di Palma, Giuseppe (1990). *To Craft Democracies: An Essay on Democratic Transitions.* Berkeley: University of California Press.

—— (1995). "Totalitarian Exits." In Houchang Chehabi and Alfred Stepan (eds.), *Politics, Society and Democracy: Comparative Studies.* Boulder: Westview Press. Pp. 233–245.

Djilas, Milovan (1983). "Disintegration of Leninist Totalitarianism." In Irving Howe (ed.), *1984 Revisited: Totalitarianism in Our Century.* New York: Harper and Row. Pp. 136–148.

Ekiert, Grzegorz (1996). *The State Against Society: Political Crises and Their Aftermath in East Central Europe.* Princeton: Princeton University Press.

Elster, Jon, ed. (1996). *The Roundtable Talks and the Breakdown of Communism.* Chicago: University of Chicago Press.

Ferry, Luc, and Evelyne Pisier-Kouchner (1985). "Théorie du totalitarisme." In Madeleine Grawitz and Jean Leca (eds.), *Traité de Science Politique,* vol. 2, pp. 117–159.

Friedheim, Daniel V. (1993). "Regime Collapse in Democratic Transitions: The East German Revolution of 1989." *German Politics* 2 (April): 97–112.

Fontaine, Pascal (1977). "L'Amérique latine à l'épreuve des communismes Cuba: L'interminable totalitarisme tropical." In Stéphane Courtois et al., *Le livre nóir du communisme,* pp. 707–725.

Furet, François (1999). *The Passing of an Illusion: Communism in the Twentieth Century.* Chicago: University of Chicago Press.

Geiger, Theodor (1954). "Die Legende von der Massengesellschaft." *Acta Sociologica* 1, 1: 75–79.

Gentile, Emilio (1975). *Le origini dell'ideologia Fascista (1918–1925).* Rome: Laterza.

—— (1986). "Fascism in Italian Historiography: In Search of an Individual Historical Identity." *Journal of Contemporary History* 21: 179–208.

———— (1989). *Storia del partito fascista.* Rome: Laterza.

———— (1995). *La via italiana al totalitarismo: Il partito e lo stato nel regime fascista.* Rome: La Nuova Italia Scientifica.

———— (1996). *The Sacralization of Politics in Fascist Italy.* Cambridge, Mass.: Harvard University Press.

———— (1997). "Il Fascismo e le Via Italiana al Totalitarismo." In V. Balducchi and B. Corbellini Andreotti (eds.), *Sudditi Cittadini.* Manduria: Piero Lacaita Editore.

Giner, Salvador (1976). *Mass Society.* New York: Academic Press.

Gleason, Abbot (1995). *Totalitarianism: The Inner History of the Cold War.* New York: Oxford University Press.

Goldhagen, Daniel Jonah (1996). *Hitler's Willing Executioners: Ordinary Germans and the Holocaust.* New York: Alfred A. Knopf.

Graham, Lawrence S., and Harry Makler, eds. (1979). *Contemporary Portugal: The Revolution and Its Antecedents.* Austin: University of Texas Press. Includes chapters by Philippe C. Schmitter, Manuel de Lucena, and Howard J. Wiarda on the Salazar-Caetano regime.

Grawitz, Madeleine, and Jean Leca, eds. (1985). *Traité de Science Politique,* vol. 2, *Les régimes politiques contemporaines.* Paris: Presses Universitaires de France.

Gregor, A. James (1979). *Italian Fascism as Developmental Dictatorship.* Princeton: Princeton University Press.

Griffin, Roger (1991). *The Nature of Fascism.* London: Pinter.

Gross, Jan T. (1988). *Revolution from Abroad: The Soviet Conquest of Poland's Western Ukraine and Western Belorussia.* Princeton: Princeton University Press. Pp. 225–240.

Hadenius, Axel, ed. (1997). *Democracy's Victory and Crisis: Nobel Symposium No. 93.* New York: Cambridge University Press.

Hamilton, Richard F. (1995). "Some Difficulties with Cultural Explanations of National Socialism." In Houchang Chehabi and Alfred Stepan (eds.), *Politics, Society, and Democracy.* Boulder: Westview Press. Pp. 197–216.

Henke, Klaus Dietmar, ed. (1999). *Totalitarismus.* Dresden: Hannah-Arendt Institut für Totalitarismusforschung an der Technischen Universität Dresden.

Hermet, Guy (1985). "L'autoritarisme." In Madeleine Grawitz and Jean Leca (eds.), *Traité de Science Politique,* vol. 2, pp. 269–312.

Hermet, Guy, ed. (1984). *Totalitarismes.* Paris: Economica.

Herz, John H., ed. (1982). *From Dictatorship to Democracy: Coping with the Legacies of Authoritarianism and Totalitarianism.* Westport: Greenwood Press.

Higley, John, and Richard Gunther, eds. (1992). *Elites and Democratic Consolidation in Latin America and Southern Europe.* Cambridge: Cambridge University Press.

Hobsbawn, Eric (1994). *Age of Extremes: The Short Twentieth Century 1914–1991.* London: Michael Joseph.

Hoffmann, Peter (1979). *Widerstand, Staatsstreich, Attentat, Der Kampf der Opposition gegen Hitler.* 3rd ed. Munich: R. Piper.

Hölderlin, Friedrich (1970). "Hyperion." In Grünter Mieth (ed.), *Sämtliche Werke und Briefe.* Munich: Carl Hanser. Vol. 1, p. 607.

Hollander, Paul (1981). *Political Pilgrims: Travels of Western Intellectuals to the Soviet Union, China and Cuba.* New York: Harper Colophon Books.

Hough, Jerry F. (1977). *The Soviet Union and Social Science Theory.* Cambridge, Mass.: Harvard University Press.

Howard, Marc (1999). "Demobilized Societies: Understanding the Weakness of Civil Society in Post-Communist Europe." Ph.D. dissertation, University of California, Berkeley.

Howe, Irving, ed. (1983). *1984 Revisited.* New York: Harper and Row.

Huntington, Samuel P. (1994). *The Third Wave: Democratization in the Late Twentieth Century.* Norman: University of Oklahoma Press.

———— (1996). *The Clash of Civilizations and the Remaking of World Order.* New York: Simon and Schuster.

Janos, Andrew C. (1982). *The Politics of Backwardness in Hungary, 1825–1945.* Princeton: Princeton University Press.

Jerez Mir, Miguel (1982). *Elites politicas y centros de extracción en España 1938–1957.* Madrid: Centro de Investigaciones Sociologicas.

Jesse, Eckhard, ed. (1996). *Totalitarismus im 20. Jahrhundert: Eine Bilanz der internationalen Forschung.* Baden-Baden: Nomos.

Jowitt, Kenneth, ed. (1997). *Social Change in Romania, 1860–1940: A Debate on Development in a European Nation.* Berkeley: Institute of International Studies, University of California.

Kalyvas, Stathis N. "The Logic of Violence in Civil War." Unpublished manuscript.

Kasza, Gregory J. (1995). *The Conscription Society: Administered Mass Organizations.* New Haven: Yale University Press.

———— (1999). "Fascism from Above? Japan's Kakushin Right in Comparative Perspective." Unpublished manuscript.

Kershaw, Ian (1993). *The Nazi Dictatorship: Problems and Perspectives of Interpretation.* London: Edward Arnold.

Kershaw, Ian, and Moshe Lewin, eds. (1977). *Stalinism and Nazism: Dictatorships in Comparison.* Cambridge: Cambridge University Press.

Klemperer, Victor (1995). *Ich will Zeugnis ablegen bis zum letzten.* Berlin: Aufbau Verlag.

Kluge, Ulrich (1984). *Der oesterreichische Ständestaat, 1934–1938.* Munich: Oldenbourg.

Krämer, R. (1993). "Der alte Mann und die Insel: Kuba auf dem Weg zu einem spätsozialistischen Caudillo-Regime." *Berliner Debatte INITIAL,* Nr.2.

———— (1995). "Democratization and Imperial Power: The Case of Cuba." *Welt Trends,* Nr.7 (June).

Kraushaar, Wolfgang (1977). "Von der Totalitarismustheorie zur Faschismustheorie-Zu einem Paradigmenwechsel in der bundesdeutschen Studentenbewegung." In Alfons Söllner et al. (eds.), *Totalitarismus,* pp. 267–283.

Kronenberg, Volker (1998). "Rückblick auf das Tragische Jahrhundert: Furet, Nolte und die Deutung des totalitären Zeitalters." In Uwe Backes and Eckhard Jesse (eds.), *Jahrbuch Extremismus a Demokratie.* Baden-Baden: Nomos. Pp. 49–80.

Kuper, Leo (1981). *Genocide: Its Political Use in the Twentieth Century.* New Haven: Yale University Press.

Laqueur, Walter, ed. (1976). *Fascism: A Reader's Guide.* Berkeley: University of California Press.

Larsen, Stein Ugelvik, Bernt Hagtvet, and Jan Petter Myklebust, eds. (1980). *Who Were the Fascists: Social Roots of European Fascism.* Bergen, Norway: Universitetsforlaget.

Lepsius, Rainer M. (1993). "Strukturbedingunges vor der nationalszialistischen Machtergreifung." In *Demokratie in Deutschland: Soziologische-historische Konstellationsanalysen.* Göttingen: Vanderhoeck 2 Ruprecht. Pp. 51–74.

Liddle, R. William (1996). *Leadership and Culture in Indonesian Politics.* Sydney: Allen and Unwin.

Lieven, Anatol (1993). *The Baltic Revolution: Estonia, Latvia, Lithuania, and the Path to Independence.* New Haven: Yale University Press.

Linz, Juan J. (1973) "Opposition in and Under an Authoritarian Regime: The Case of Spain." In Robert A. Dahl (ed.), *Regimes and Opposition.* New Haven: Yale University Press.

―――― (1976). "Some Notes Toward a Comparative Study of Fascism in Sociological Historical Perspective." In Walter Laqueur (ed.), *Fascism*, pp. 8–121.

―――― (1978a). *Crisis, Breakdown and Reequilibrium.* Baltimore: Johns Hopkins University Press.

―――― (1978b). "Non-competitive Elections in Europe." In Guy Hermet et al. (eds.), *Elections Without Choice.* New York: Wiley/Halstead. Pp. 36–65.

―――― (1980). "Political Space and Fascism as a Late-Comer: Conditions Conducive to the Success or Failure of Fascism as a Mass Movement in Inter-War Europe." In Stein Ugelvik Larsen et al. (eds.), *Who Were the Fascists,* pp. 153–191.

―――― (1991). "La crisis de las democracias." In Mercedes Cabrera, Santos Juliá, and Pablo Martin Aceña (eds.), *Europa en crisis.* Madrid: Editorial Pablo Iglesias.

―――― (1992a). "Staat und Kirche im Spanien: Von Bürgerkrieg bis zur Wiederkehr der Demokratie." In Martin Greschat and Christoph Kaiser Jochen (eds.), *Christentum und Demokratie im 20. Jahrhundert.* Stuttgart: W. Kohlhammer. Pp. 60–88.

―――― (1992b). "Types of Political Regimes and Respect for Human Rights: Historical and Cross-national Perspectives." In Asbjørn Eide and Bernt Hagtvet (eds.), *Human Rights in Perspective: A Global Assessment.* Oxford: Blackwell.

―――― (1993). "Religión y política en España." In Rafael Díaz-Salazar and Salvador Giner (eds.), *Religión y sociedad en España.* Madrid: Centro de Investigaciones Sociológics. Pp. 1–50.

―――― (1997a). "Der religiöse Gebrauch der Politik und/oder der politische Gebrauch der Religion, Ersatzideologie gegen Ersatzreligion." In Hans Maier and Michael Schäfer (eds.), *Totalitarismus und Politische Religionen.*

―――― (1997b). "Totalitarianism and Authorianism: My Recollections on the Development of Comparative Politics." In Alfons Söllner et al. (eds.), *Totalitarismus,* pp. 141–157.

Linz, Juan J., and Alfred Stepan (1996). *Problems of Democratic Consolidation: Southern Europe, South America, and Postcommunist Europe.* Baltimore: Johns Hopkins University Press.

Löwenthal, Richard (1983). "Widerstand im totalen Staat." In Karl Dietrich Bracher et al. (eds.), *Nationalsozialistische Diktatur 1933–1945.* Also the essays of Detlev Peukert, Klaus Gotto et al., and Armin Boyens.

Lyttelton, Adrian (1987). *The Seizure of Power: Fascism in Italy, 1919–1929.* Princeton: Princeton University Press.

Maier, Hans (1996). "Politsche Religionen-ein Begriff und seine Greuzen." *Jahresbericht Görres-Gesellschaft 1996.* Pp. 5–21.

Maier, Hans, and Michael Schäfer, eds. (1997). *Totalitarismus und Politische Religionen.* Paderborn: Ferdinand Schöningh.

Maravall, José María (1997). *Regimes, Politics and Markets: Democratization and Economic Change in Southern and Eastern Europe.* Oxford: Oxford University Press.

Marcou, Lilly, ed. (1982). *L'U.R.S.S. vue de gauche.* Paris: Presses Universitaires de France.

Merkel, Wolfgang (1999). "Defekte Demokratien." In W. Merkel and A. Busch, *Demokratie in Ost und West: Für Klaus von Beyme.* Frankfurt: Suhrkamp. Pp. 361–381.

——— (1999). *Systemtransformation: Eine Einführung in die Theorie und Empirie der Transformationsforschung.* Opladen: Leske and Budrich.

Merkel, Wolfgang, and Hans-Jürgen Puhle (1999). *Von der Diktatur zu Demokratie.* Opladen: Westdeutscher Verlag.

Meuschel, Sigrid (1999). "Totalitarismustheorie und moderne Diktaturen: Versuch einer Annäherung." In Klaus Dietmar Henke (ed.), *Totalitarismus,* Pp. 61–78.

Mommsen, Wolfgang J. (1997–1998). "Krieg und Kultur: Künstler, Schriftsteller und intellektuelle im Ersten Weltkrieg." In Wissenschaftskolleg zu Berlin, *Jahrbuch 1997–98.* Pp. 261–276.

Mosse, George L. (1964). *The Crisis of German Ideology: Intellectual Origins of the Third Reich.* New York: Grosset and Dunlap.

——— (1985). *Toward the Final Solution: A History of European Racism.* Madison: University of Wisconsin Press.

Mujal-León, Eusebio, and Jorge Saavedra (1977). "El posttotalitarismo carismático y el cambio de régimen: Cuba en perspectiva comparada." *Encuentro* 6/7 (Otoño–Invierno): 115–123.

Müller, Klaus (1997). *East European Studies: Neo-Totalitarianism and Social Science Theory.* Berlin: Papers des Wissenschaftszentrum Berlin für Sozialforschung.

Nolte, Ernst (1987). *Der europäische Bürgerkrieg 1917–1945: Nationalsozialismus und Bolschewismus.* Frankfurt: Berlin Propyläen Verlag.

O'Donnell, Guillermo, and Philippe Schmitter (1996). *Transitions from Authoritarian Rule: Tentative Conclusions about Uncertain Democracies.* Baltimore: Johns Hopkins University Press.

O'Donnell, Guillermo, Philippe Schmitter, and Lawrence Whitehead, eds. (1986). *Transitions from Authoritarian Rule: Prospects for Democracy.* Baltimore: Johns Hopkins University Press.

Offe, Claus (1994). *Der Tunnel am Ende des Lichts: Erkundungen zu Transformation im Neuen Osten.* Frankfurt: Campus Verlag.

——— (1997). *Varieties of Transition: The East European and East German Experience.* Cambridge: MIT Press.

Ost, David (1990). *Solidarity and the Politics of Anti-Politics.* Philadelphia: Temple University Press.

Özbudun, Ergun (1995). "Parameters of Turkish Democratic Development: The Struggle Between the Military-Bureaucratic Founders of Democracy and

New Democratic Forces." In Houchang Chehabi and Alfred Stepan (eds.), *Politics, Society, and Democracy*. Boulder: Westview Press. Pp. 297–310.

Payne, Stanley G. (1987). *The Franco Regime, 1936–1975*. Madison: University of Wisconsin Press.

—— (1995). *A History of Fascism, 1914–1945*. Madison: University of Wisconsin Press. The bibliography and footnotes are an invaluable resource for scholars.

—— (1999). *Fascism in Spain, 1923–1977*. Madison: University of Wisconsin Press.

Pérez-Stable, Marifeli (1999). *The Cuban Revolution: Origins, Course and Legacy*. New York: Oxford University Press.

Perlmutter, Amos (1981). *Modern Authoritarianism: A Comparative Institutional Analysis*. New Haven: Yale University Press.

Petersen, Jens (1997). "Die Geschichte des Totalitarismus Begriffs in Italien." In Hans Maier and Michael Schäfer (eds.), *Totalitarismus und Politische Religionen*, pp. 15–35.

Peukert, Detlev (1984). *Alltagsgeschichte der NS-Zeit: Neue Perspektive oder Trivialisierung?* Munich: Oldenbourg.

—— (1987). *Inside Nazi Germany: Conformity, Opposition and Racism in Everyday Life*. New Haven: Yale University Press.

Pipes, Richard (1984). *Survival Is Not Enough*. New York: Simon and Schuster.

—— (1990). *The Russian Revolution*. New York: Vintage Books.

Pisier-Kouchner, Évelyne, ed. (1983). *Les interprétations du stalinisme*. Paris: Presses Universitaires de France.

Preston, Paul (1994). *Franco. A Biography*. New York: Basic Books.

Przeworski, Adam (1991). *Democracy and the Market: Political and Economic Reforms in Eastern Europe and Latinamerica*. Cambridge: Cambridge University Press.

Ramírez, Manuel, et al. (1978). *España 1939–1945: Régimen politico e ideología*. Barcelona: Guadarrama-Labor.

Roy, Olivier (1994). *The Failure of Political Islam*. Cambridge: Harvard University Press.

Rubenstein, Diane (1990). *What's Left? The Ecole Normale Supérieure and the Right*. Madison: University of Wisconsin Press.

Rueschemeyer, Dietrich, Evelyne Huber Stephens, and John Stephens (1992). *Capitalist Development and Democracy*. Chicago: University of Chicago Press.

Rupnik, Jacques (1984). "Le totalitarisme vu de l'est." In Guy Hermet (ed.), *Totalitarismes*, pp. 43–71.

Sartori, Giovanni (1993). "Totalitarianism, Model Mania and Learning from Error." *Journal of Theoretical Politics* 5 (1): 5–22.

Scalapino, Robert A. (1953). *Democracy and the Party Movement in Prewar Japan*. Berkeley: University of California Press.

Schmädeke, Jürgen, and Peter Steinbach, eds. (1985). *Der Widerstand gegen den Nationalsozialismus. Die deutsche Gesellschaft und der Widerstand gegen Hitler*. Munich: Piper.

Schmitter, Philippe C. (1979). "The 'Regime d'Exception' that Became the Rule: Forty-Eight Years of Authoritarian Domination in Portugal." In Lawrence S. Graham and Harry Makler (eds.), *Contemporary Portugal*, pp. 3–46.

Schoeps, Julius H., ed. (1996). *Ein Volk von Mördern? Die Dokumentation zur Goldhagen Kontroverse um die Rolle der Deutschen im Holocaust.* Hamburg: Hoffmann and Campe.

Shain, Yossi, and Juan J. Linz, eds. (1995). *Between States: Interim Governments and Democratic Transitions.* Cambridge: Cambridge University Press.

Söllner, Alfons, Ralf Walkenhaus, and Karin Wieland, eds. (1997). *Totalitarismus: Eine Ideengeschichte des 20. Jahrhunderts.* Berlin: Akademie Verlag.

Staniszkis, Jadwiga (1984). *Poland's Self-limiting Revolution.* Princeton: Princeton University Press.

Stepan, Alfred, ed. (1973). *Authoritarian Brazil: Origins, Policies, and Future.* New Haven: Yale University Press.

———— (1978). *The State and Society: Peru in Comparative Perspective.* Princeton: Princeton University Press.

———— (1988). *Rethinking Military Politics: Brazil and the Southern Cone.* Princeton: Princeton University Press.

———— (2000). "The World's Religious Systems and Democracy: Crafting the 'Twin Tolerations.'" In Alfred Stepan, *Arguing Comparative Politics.* New York: Oxford University Press.

Sternhell, Zeev (1978). *La droite révolutionnaire, 1885–1914: Les origines françaises du fascisme.* Paris: Editions du Seuil.

———— (1986). *Neither Right nor Left: Fascist Ideology in France.* Berkeley: University of California Press.

Stokes, Gale (1993). *The Walls Came Tumbling Down: The Collapse of Communism in Eastern Europe.* New York: Oxford University Press.

Thompson, Mark R. (1995). *The Anti-Marcos Struggle: Personalistic Rule and Democratic Transition in the Philippines.* New Haven: Yale University Press.

———— (1998). "Weder totalitär noch autoritär: Post-Totalitarismus im Osteuropa." In Achim Siegel (ed.), *Totalitarismustheorie nach dem Ende des Kommunismus.* Cologne: Böhlau Verlag. Pp. 209–339.

Turner, Henry A. (1989). *Geissel des Jahrhunderts: Hitler und Seine Hinterlassenschaft.* Berlin: Corso bei Siedler.

Turner, Henry Ashby, Jr. (1999). "Victor Klemperer's Holocaust." *German Studies Review* 22: 385–395.

Tussell, Javier (1988). *La dictadura de Franco.* Madrid: Alianza.

———— (1992). *Franco en la guerra civil.* Madrid: Tusquets.

Viver Pi-Sunyer, C. (1978). *El personal politico de Franco (1936–1945). Contribución empirica a una teoría del régimen franquista.* Barcelona: Vicens Vives.

Wiarda, Howard J. (1977). *Corporatism and Development: The Portuguese Experience.* Amherst: University of Massachusetts Press.

Winckler, Edwin A. (1999). *Transition from Communism in China: Institutional and Comparative Analyses.* Boulder: Lynne Rienner.

Wippermann, Wolfgang (1997). *Totalitarismustheorien: Die Entwicklung der Diskussion von den Aufängen bis heute.* Darmstadt: Primus Verlag.

Wynot, Edward D., Jr. (1974). *Polish Politics in Transitions: The Camp of National Unity and the Struggle for Power, 1935–1939.* Athens: University of Georgia Press.

Zaslavskaia, Tatiana (1984). "The Novosibirsk Report." *Survey* 28 (1): 88–108.

1

INTRODUCTION

Variety and Prevalence of Nondemocratic Regimes

We all know that governments are different and that it is not the same thing to be the citizen or subject of one or another country, even in matters of daily life. We also know that almost all governments do some of the same things, and sometimes we feel like the pure anarchist, for whom all states, being states, are essentially the same. This double awareness is also the point of departure of our intellectual efforts as social scientists.

We obviously know that life under Stalin or Hitler, even for the average citizen but particularly for those occupying important positions in their society, was different than for citizens living in the United Kingdom or Sweden.[1] Without going to such extremes, we can still say that life for many people—but perhaps not that many—is different in Franco's Spain than in Italy. Certainly it is for a leader of the Communist party in either country. As social scientists we want to describe in all its complexity the relationship of people to their government and to understand why this relationship is so different in different countries. Leaving aside consideration of personal documents—the memoirs of politicians, generals, intellectuals, conspirators, and concentration camp inmates—and the literary works inspired by the human experience of man confronting power, often brutal and arbitrary power, we will consider the work of social scientists who have, by observation, by analysis of the laws, the judicial and administrative decisions, the records of the bureaucratic activities of the state, by interviews with leaders and sample surveys of the population, written excellent monographs on politics in many societies, trying to describe and explain how different political systems work.

Political theorists have given us the framework to ask relevant questions. However, we cannot be satisfied with even the best descriptive studies of political life in a particular society at a particular time. We, like Aristotle when he confronted the diversity of constitutions of the Greek polis of his time, feel the need to reduce the complexity to a limited number of types sufficiently different to take into account the variety in real life but also able to describe those elements that a certain number of polities share. Such an effort of conceptualization has to ask why these polities share some characteristics and, ultimately, what difference it makes. The classification of political systems, like that of other aspects of reality—of social structures, economic systems, religions, kinship structures—has been at the core of social science since its origins. New forms of political organizations, of creating and using power and authority, and new perspectives derived from different values have inevitably led to new classifications. The intellectual task is far from easy, confronted as we are with the changing political reality. The old terms become inadequate. As Tocqueville noted when he wrote about "a kind of oppression which threatens democratic nations that will not resemble any other form previously experienced in the world": "It is something new, I must therefore attempt to define it for I cannot name it." Unfortunately, we have to use names for realities that we are just attempting to define. Worse even, we are not alone in that process, since those who control political life in the states of the twentieth century also want to define, describe, and name their political system—or at least to define it according to what they want it to be or what they want others to believe that it is. Obviously the perspectives of scholarship and of political actors will not always coincide, and the same words will be used with different meanings. This makes the need for conceptual clarity even more imperative. In addition, societies differ not only in the way they organize political life but in the relations of authority in spheres other than politics. Certainly those who consider dimensions of society other than government more important for the life of people would prefer a conceptualization of the variety of societies in which politics would be only one and perhaps not a very important dimension. Our concern here is, however, the variety of political systems as a problem in itself.

One of the easiest ways to define a concept is to say what it is not. To do this obviously assumes that we know what something else is, so that we can say that our concept is not the same. Here we shall start from the assumption that we know what democracy is and center our attention on all the political systems that do not fit our definition of democracy. As Giovanni Sartori (1962a, pp. 135–57) noted, as he was reviewing the use of terms like totalitarianism, authoritarianism, dictatorship, despotism, and absolutism which over time had been opposed to democracy, in modern times it has become more and more difficult to know what democracy is not. We feel, however, that the work of many scholars has at least provided us with a definition of democracy that fits a large number of political systems sufficiently similar in the way of organizing political life and the relationship between citizen and government to be described by a single definition. We shall therefore deal here with the political systems that share at least one characteristic, that of not being like those we shall describe with our definition of democracy. Thus, we shall deal here with nondemocratic political systems.

This basic duality has been described traditionally with terms like "polycracy" and "monocracy," "democracy" and "autocracy." In the eighteenth century "absolutism" and "despotism" became the descriptive and ideological terms to describe governments that were free from restraint *(legibus solutus),* even when there was an ambivalence such as the term "enlightened despotism" reflects. Late in the nineteenth century and early in the twentieth century, after constitutional governments had been established, at least on paper, in most Western countries and liberalism and the *Rechtstaat*—"state of law"—had become the symbol of political progress, the new autocratic forms of rule were generally called dictatorships. In the twenties Mussolini adopted Giovanni Gentile's neoidealist conception of the state as an "ethical" and "totalitarian" state, and as he said: "The armed party leads to the totalitarian regime. . . . a party that governs totalitarianly a nation is a new fact in history."[2] Only shortly later the term would find echo in Germany, more among the political scientists like Carl Schmitt (1940), writing in 1931, than among the Nazi leadership. The success of the word was easily linked with the famous work by General Ludendorff (1935), *Der Totale Krieg,*[3] which turned around the old Clausewitz conception of "war as a continuation of politics with other means" to conceiving of peace as a preparation for war, politics as continuation of war with other means. An influential writer, Ernst Jünger (1934), at that time also coined the phrase *"Totale Mobilmachung."* Soon this idea of total mobilization would enter the political discourse and even legal texts like the statutes of the Spanish single party with a positive connotation. Already in the thirties, political scientists like Sabine (1934) would start using it for the new mobilizational single-party regimes, fascist and communist. Robert Michels (1928, pp. 770–72) already in 1928 would note the similarity between the Bolshevik and the fascist parties. Trotsky (1937, p. 278) in 1936 would write: "Stalinism and fascism, in spite of a deep difference in social foundations, are symmetrical phenomena. In many of their features they show a deadly similarity." And many fascists, particularly left fascists, would feel strongly the affinity between their ideals and those of a national Russian communism led by Stalin.[4] It was therefore not left to the liberal critics of the fascist powers and the Soviet Union to discover those affinities and the usefulness of a concept that would cover these two novel political phenomena. As we shall see, only recently a reaction has set in against the overextension and misuse of the concept, as well as its intellectual fruitfulness. Already in the thirties, however, some theorists who favored authoritarian, antidemocratic political solutions but were hostile to the activist mobilizational conceptions of the totalitarian state and were concerned about the autonomy of the state from society, even a society mobilized by a single party, formulated the contrasts among the authoritarian state, the totalitarian state, and what they called the neutral liberal democratic state (Ziegler, 1932; Voegelin, 1936). Those formulations did not find echo in political science after World War II. With the cold-war transition to democracy of some authoritarian regimes like Turkey and Brazil and the initial democratic form taken by the new independent nations, it appeared as if the dichotomy between democracy and totalitarianism could serve to describe the universe of political systems or at least the polar extremes toward which other systems would tend. It was at this point that the regimes that could not be classified either as political democracies or totalitarian systems tended to be conceived of either as tutelary democracies, that is, as regimes that have adopted the formal norms of a democratic polity and whose elites have as a goal the democratizing of their polities even though they might be unclear as to the requirements, or as traditional oligarchies surviving from the past (Shils, 1960). Even so, the regimes that found themselves between these two types, oriented either toward a democratic future or a traditional past, required the formulation of the type of modernizing oligarchies. Significantly, in that case the description focused more on the goal of economic development than on the nature of the political institutions to be created or maintained.

Only a few years later the great hopes for democracy in Latin America, particularly in the more developed republics of South America and those created by the apparently successful transfer of British and French democratic constitutions to former colonies that became independent, were disappointed. On the other hand, authoritarian regimes like Spain and Portugal unexpectedly survived the defeat of the Axis. Political scientists would discover that such regimes could not be understood as unsuccessful totalitarian regimes, since many, if not all, of their founders did not share a totalitarian conception of society and the state; they functioned very differently from Nazi or Stalinist regimes; and their rulers, particularly in the Third World, did not keep up the pretenses of preparing the nation for democracy with temporary authoritarian rule. They increasingly rejected explicitly the liberal democratic model and often pretended to mutate the Leninist model of the vanguard party for building the new states or nations. Soon social scientists would discover that the ideological pronouncements and the organization charts of the parties and the mass organizations in almost all cases did not correspond to any reality, as in the past the pseudofascism of Balkan, Eastern European, and Baltic states had not corresponded to the German or even the Italian model. Inevitably those developments would lead to the formulation, with one or another emphasis, of the idea of a third type of regime, a type *sui generis* rather than on a continuum between democracy and totalitarianism. On the basis of an analysis of the Franco regime, particularly after 1945, we (Linz, 1964) formulated the concept of an authoritarian regime distinct from both democratic governments and totalitarian systems.

Our analysis here will focus on totalitarian and authoritarian regimes that share at least one characteristic: they are nondemocratic. Therefore we shall start with a brief statement of an empirical definition of democracy that will allow us to delimit the subject of our research. We shall turn to the rich theoretical and empirical research on totalitarian political systems over the last decade as well as to the recent critiques of that concept in order to delimit the types of regimes that we shall call authoritarian by what they are not. However, those three types do not exhaust fully the types of political systems existing in the twentieth century. There are still a number of regimes based on traditional legitimacy whose nature we would misunderstand if we would classify them together with the modern authoritarian regimes established after the breakdown of traditional legitimacy or after a democratic period. We also feel that it would not be fully fruitful to consider certain types of tyrannical, arbitrary rule exercised by an individual and his clients with the help of the praetorian guard, without any forms of organized participation in power of institutional structures, with little effort of legitimation of any sort, and in pursuit of more private than collective goals, in the same category with more institutionalized authoritarian regimes in which the rulers feel that they are acting for a collectivity. We therefore decided to deal with this type of regime separately, calling it "sultanistic," even when it shares some characteristics with those we have called authoritarian. The case of dual societies, in which one sector of the society imposes its rule on another, by force if necessary, while allowing its members to participate in political life according to the rules of political democracy except for excluding from discussion the issue of the relationship to the dominated group, supported by a wide consensus on that issue, poses a special problem. We have labeled that type of regime "racial democracy," conveying the paradox of democracy combined with racial domination. Recent developments in Eastern Europe after de-Stalinization and even some trends in the Soviet Union have raised the question of the nature of the post-Stalinist communist regimes. We have found that the emerging regimes in Eastern Europe have many characteristics in common with those we have described as authoritarian, but their more or less recent totalitarian past and the commitment of their elites to some elements of the totalitarian utopia makes these regimes quite distinct. We shall discuss them as a particular case of authoritarian regimes: as post-totalitarian.

The two main dimensions that we shall use in our definition of the authoritarian regime—the degree or type of limited political pluralism under such regimes and the degree to which such regimes are based on political apathy and demobilization of the population or limited and controlled mobilizations—lead us to distinguish a number of subtypes. Those subtypes are based fundamentally on the type of participants in the limited pluralism and on the way in which they are organized, as well as on the level and type of participation. We shall distinguish: bureaucratic-military authoritarian regimes; those forms of institutionalization of authoritarian regimes that we shall call "organic statism"; the mobilizational authoritarian regimes in postdemocratic societies, of which the Italian Fascism was in many ways an example; postindependence mobilizational authoritarian regimes; and finally the post-totalitarian authoritarian regimes. Certainly these ideal types in the Weberian sense do not fully correspond to any particular regime, since political systems are built in reality by leaders and social forces with contradictory conceptions of the polity and subject to constant changes in emphasis and direction. Regimes are the result of contradictory manifest and latent tendencies in different directions and therefore are all mixed forms. However, some regimes approach more one or another type. In that sense it would be difficult to locate precisely each country even in a particular moment in time within the boxes of our typology. Therefore our table and figure in this paper have to be taken as suggestive of a political attribute space in which regimes can be placed.

Social scientists have attempted to classify the independent states of the world using some operational criteria (Shils, 1960; Almond and Coleman, 1960; Almond and Powell, 1966; Huntington, 1970; Huntington and Moore, 1970; Moore, 1970b; Lanning, 1974).[5] Political change, particularly in the unstable states of the Third World, obviously has quickly dated many of those classifications. In addition there has been little consensus on the few theoretical efforts to classify political systems into any more complex typology, largely because there are few systematic collections of data relevant to the dimensions used in formulating the typologies and because the politics of many countries has not been the subject of scholarly research. There is, however, considerable consensus on the countries considered by Dankwart Rustow to be democratic systems and by Robert Dahl to be polyarchies and those characterized as competitive by the contributors to the 1960 review of *Politics of the Developing Areas*. Many of those studies show that only between one-fourth and one-third of the political systems of the world at any time were political democracies. Robert Dahl, Richard Norling, and Mary Frase Williams (Dahl, 1971, Appendix A, pp. 231–49), on the basis of data from the *Cross Polity Survey* and other sources on eligibility to participate in elections and on the degree of opportunity for public opposition using seven indicators of required conditions, scaled 114 countries into 31 types. On the basis of those data, gathered around 1969, they classified 29 as polyarchies and 6 as near-polyarchies. The list of Dankwart Rustow (1967), which coincides with that of Dahl except for Mexico, Ceylon, Greece, and Colombia, included 31 countries. Both lists omit a few microstates that would qualify as polyarchies.

Among the 25 countries whose population in 1965 was over 20 million people only 8 at the time were considered polyarchies by Dahl and one, Turkey, a near-polyarchy, to which the list of Rustow would add Mexico.[6] If we consider that among those 25 countries Japan, Germany, and Italy for a considerable part of the first half of this century were under nondemocratic governments and that among the 5 largest states in the world only the United States and India have enjoyed continuously democratic rule since their independence, the importance of the study of nondemocratic political systems should be obvious. In fact, in some parts of the world even fewer are democracies. Only 7 countries, mostly small ones, of the 38 African nations that gained independence since 1950 remain multiparty states in which elections are held and parties can campaign. Seventeen of those 38 nations by 1973 had a military chief of state and 64 percent of the 266 million inhabitants in them were under military rule (Young, n.d.). Even in Europe, excluding the USSR and Turkey, only 16 of 28 states were stable democracies, and 3, Portugal, Greece, and Cyprus, face at this moment an uncertain future. Of the European population west of the Soviet Union, 61.5 percent live under democracies, 4.1 percent live under unstable regimes, and 34.4 percent live under nondemocratic political systems.

There is certainly considerable diversity among democracies—diversity between those like the United States, where there have been continuous popular elections since 1788, and those like the Federal Republic of Germany, established in 1949 after twelve years of Nazi totalitarianism and foreign occupation; between states based on majority rule, like the United Kingdom, and those based on complex arrangements among ethnic religious minorities which combine competitive politics with the unity of the state, as in Lebanon; between highly egalitarian societies, as in Scandinavia, and a country with the inequality of India. Despite all those differences, the political institutions of these countries have many similarities that allow us to consider them democracies. That basic similarity becomes apparent when we consider the heterogeneity in the list of the 20 largest nondemocratic countries. No one would doubt that the Soviet Union, Spain, Ethiopia, and South Africa are politically more different from each other than are the United States and India, to take extreme cases, or to stay within Europe, Spain and East Germany. It shall be our task in this chapter to attempt a conceptualization that will allow us to make some meaningful distinctions among that great variety of political systems that no stretching of the concept would allow us to consider competitive democracies and under which at least half of humanity lives.

Certainly the richest countries, the 24 whose gross national product per capita around 1965 was over 1,000 U.S. dollars, were democracies—with the exception of Czechoslovakia, the Soviet Union, East Germany, Hungary, and the special case of Kuwait; but already among the 16 ranking behind them with over $500 per capita only 7 could be considered stable democracies. We are not therefore dealing only with poor, underdeveloped countries or with countries arrested in their economic development, since among 36 countries whose growth rate was above the mean of 5.1 percent for the period 1960–65 only 12 appear on Dahl's list of 35 polyarchies or near-polyarchies. If we were to take only those with a high per capita growth rate for the same period, that is, over 5 percent, only 2 of 12 countries would be on that list of Dahl.

Therefore, in spite of the significant relationship discovered between the stability of democracy in economically developed countries and the higher probability that those having reached a certain level of economic and social development would be democracies, there is a sufficient number of deviant cases to warrant a separate analysis of types of political systems, social systems, and economic systems. There is no doubt that certain forms of political organization, of legitimation of power, are more likely in certain types of societies and under certain economic conditions than others and that some combinations are highly unlikely. We feel, however, that it is essential to keep those spheres conceptually separated and to formulate distinct typologies of social, economic, and political systems. Unless we do so, important intellectual questions would disappear. We would be unable to ask, What type of social and economic structure is likely to lead with greater probability to the establishment of certain types of regimes and their stability? Nor could we ask, What difference does it make for the social and economic structure and its development to have one or another regime? Is there a greater likelihood of the society and perhaps the economy to develop under one or another type of political system?

Certainly there is no one-to-one relationship between those different aspects of social reality. Democratic governments are certainly compatible with a wide range of social and economic systems, and the same is true for the variety of autocratic regimes. In fact, in only the recent past German society has been ruled by the unstable Weimar democracy, Nazi totalitarianism, and the stable Bonn republic. Undoubtedly the social and economic structures were considerably affected by those different regimes, in addition to other factors, but the political differences were clearly greater than those in the economic and even the social structure. It is for this reason that we shall center our attention on the variety of political systems without including in our conceptualization dimensions more directly relevant for a typology of societies or of economic systems.

We cannot emphasize enough how important such an analytical distinction is for raising meaningful questions about the relationship between polity, society, and economy, to which we should add a fourth aspect, the cultural and religious realm.

Democratic Governments and Nondemocratic Polities

It is relatively easy to define democratic government without implying that the social structure and social relations in a democratic state should enter into the definition.[7] We shall call a political system democratic when it allows the free formulation of political preferences, through the use of basic freedoms of association, information, and communication, for the purpose of free competition between leaders to validate at regular intervals by nonviolent means their claim to rule; a democratic system does this without excluding any effective political office from that competition or prohibiting any members of the political community from expressing their preference by norms requiring the use of force to enforce them. The liberal political rights are a requirement for that public contestation and competition for power and for the expansion of the right to participate in elections for an ever increasing number of citizens an inevitable consequence. The requirement of regular intervals excludes from the definition any system in which the rulers at one point in time might have derived their legitimacy from support in a free contest but refuse to be accountable at a later date. It clearly excludes certain plebiscitarian authoritarian regimes, even if we should accept the honesty and freedom of choice in the original plebiscite. The requirement that all effective political offices should be directly or indirectly dependent on the election by the citizens excludes those systems in which a traditional ruler, through inheritance, retains powers not controlled or mediated by a popularly elected assembly or in which nonsymbolic offices are for life, like Franco as head of state or Tito as president of the Republic. A wide range of political freedoms that guarantee the freedom of minorities to organize and compete peacefully for the support of the people are essential, even when there are some legal or even de facto limits, for us to state that certain systems are more or less democratic (Dahl, 1971). Nondemocratic regimes, however, not only impose de facto limits on minority freedoms but establish generally well-defined legal limits, leaving the interpretation of those laws to the rulers themselves, rather than to independent objective bodies, and applying them with a wide range of discretion. The requirement that no citizen should be excluded from participation in elections, if that exclusion requires the use of force, takes into account the fact that the expansion of citizenship has been a slow and conflictual process from censitary suffrage to universal male suffrage and finally to the inclusion of women and young adults, as pressures developed from those sectors demanding the expansion of suffrage. Systems that at one point in time allowed more or less restricted participation but refused, using force, to expand it to other groups would be excluded on that count. South Africa would be a prime example of a political system that decades ago might have qualified as a democracy but by excluding permanently and in principle the blacks from the electorate and even depriving the Cape Town Coloured of their vote has lost that characteristic. Whatever element of democratization the development of internal party democracy in a single-party regime might represent, the limitation of "citizenship" to the members of a single party, that is, to those agreeing with certain basic political preferences and subject to party discipline and exclusion from it, would not qualify the regime as democratic. Certainly a system with internal party democracy is more democratic than one without it, one in which the party is ruled by the *Führerprinzip* or "democratic centralism," but the exclusion from participation of citizens unwilling to join the party does not allow us to classify the political system as democratic.

In our definition we have not made any reference to political parties, because in theory it is conceivable that the competition for power could be organized without them, even though we know of no system without political parties which would satisfy our requirements. In theory, competition for leadership could take place among individuals within narrow constituencies, without organizations of some permanence committed to particular principles, aggregating a wide range of issues across many constituencies, which we call parties. This is the *theory of organic or corporative democracy*, which holds that representatives should be elected in primary social groups where people know each other and share common interests, presumably eliminating the need for political parties. In a later section on organic statism we shall discuss in detail the theoretical and empirical difficulties in the creation of a free competition for power in so-called organic democracies and the authoritarian character of such regimes. Therefore, the freedom to form political parties and of parties to compete for power and not a share in power offers a prima facie test of the democratic character of the government. Any system in which a party is de jure granted a special constitutional and legal status and its offices are subject to special party courts and granted special protection by the law, in which other parties have to recognize its leadership and are allowed to participate only insofar as they do not question that preeminent position or have to commit themselves to sustain a certain social-political order (beyond a constitutional framework in which free competition for power at regular intervals can take place by peaceful means), would not qualify. It is fundamental to keep clear the distinction between de facto predominant parties obtaining overwhelming support, election after election at the polls, in competition with other parties, from hegemonic parties in pseudo-multiparty systems. It is on this ground that the distinction between democratic and nondemocratic regimes cannot be made identical with single and multiparty systems. Another criterion often advanced for the distinction between democratic and nondemocratic regimes is that alternation in power provides a presumption of democracy but is not a necessary condition (Sartori, 1974, pp. 199–201).

The criteria mentioned allow an almost unequivocal classification of states as democracies without denying democratic elements to other states or the presence of de facto ademocratic or antidemocratic tendencies in those so classified. Only in a few cases has disagreement among the scholars about the facts about the freedom for political groups and competition among them lead to doubts.[8] Further evidence for the validity of the distinction is the resistance of nondemocratic regimes that claim to be democracies to introducing just the elements listed here and the ideological contortions into which they go to justify their reluctance. The fact that no democracy has been transformed into a nondemocratic regime without changing one or more of the characteristics listed is further evidence. Only in rare cases has a nontraditional regime been transformed into a democracy without constitutional discontinuity and the use of force to remove the incumbents. Turkey after World War II (Karpat, 1959; Weiker, 1963 and 1973), Mexico (if we accept the arguments of those who want to classify it as a democracy), and perhaps Argentina after the 1973 election are cases in point. The borderline between nondemocratic and democratic regimes is therefore a fairly rigid one that cannot be crossed by slow and imperceptible evolution but practically always requires a violent break, anticonstitutional acts, a military coup, a revolution, or foreign intervention. By comparison, the line separating totalitarian systems from other non-democratic systems is much more diffuse, and there are obvious cases in which systems lost the characteristics that would allow us to define them as totalitarian in any meaningful sense of the term without becoming democracies and in a way that does not allow the observer to say exactly when and how the change took place. Despite our emphasis on the importance of retaining the distinction of totalitarian and other nondemocratic types of polity, these have more in common with each other than with democratic governments, justifying nondemocratic as a more general comprehensive category. It is those regimes that constitute our subject.

A Note on Dictatorship

One term often used to designate nondemocratic and nontraditional legitimate governments, both in the literature (Sartori, 1962b), and common usage, is "dictatorship." From its historical origins in Rome as *dictator rei gerundae causa,* designating an extraordinary office limited and foreseen in the constitution for emergency situations—limited in time to six months, which could not be extended, or in function to carry out a particular task—the term "dictatorship" has become a loosely used term of opprobrium. It is no accident, as Carl Schmitt (1928) and Sartori (1962b, pp. 416–19) have noted, that even Garibaldi and Marx should still have used it without that negative connotation.

If there is a point in conserving the term for scientific usage today, it should be limited to describe emergency rule that suspends or violates temporarily the constitutional norms about the accession to an exercise of authority. Constitutional dictatorship is the type of rule that is established on the basis of constitutional provisions for situations of emergency, especially in the face of widespread disorder or war, extending the power of some offices of the state or extending their mandate beyond the date it should be returned to the electorate through a decision taken by constitutionally legitimate authority. Such an extraconstitutional authority does not necessarily have to be anticonstitutional, that is, a permanent change of political institutions. But it might well serve to defend them in a crisis situation. The ambivalent character of the expression "constitutional dictatorship" has led Sartori and others to prefer the term "crisis government" (Rossiter, 1948). In fact, the revolutionary committees that have assumed power after the breakdown of traditional rule or authoritarian regimes with the purpose of calling free elections to restore democratic regimes, as long as they have remained provisional government without the ratification by an electorate, can be considered dictatorships in this narrow sense of the term. Many military coups against traditional rulers, autocratic governments, or democracies in the process of breaking down, due to efforts to assure a fraudulent continuity in power through manipulation or delay of elections, gain broad support on the basis of the commitment, initially honestly felt by some of the leaders, to reestablish free competitive democracy. The difficulty in the extrication process of military rule, so well analyzed by Samuel Finer (1962) and Huntington (1968, pp. 231–37), accounts for the fact that more often than not such military rule creates authoritarian regimes rather than assures the return to democracy. Overt foreign *domination* for the purpose of establishing the condition for democracy by ousting from power nondemocratic rulers would be another very special case. Japan, Austria, and West Germany after World War II would be unique examples, since certainly the Allied High Commanders and Commissioners were not democratic rulers of those societies (Gimbel, 1968; Montgomery and Hirschman, 1968). But their success might also have been due to quite unique circumstances in those societies not likely to be found everywhere. In this restricted sense we are talking only about those dictatorships that Carl Schmitt (1928) has called *"Kommissarische Diktatur"* as distinct from the ones he called "sovereign dictatorships."

In the world of political realities, however, the return to constitutional democracy after the break with democratic legitimacy, even by so-called constitutional dictatorship or by the intervention of monarchs or armies as moderating power in emergency situations, is uncertain. One exception is perhaps national-unity governments in case of war, when all major parties agree on postponing elections or avoiding real electoral competition to assure almost unanimous support to the government to pursue a united war effort. Dictatorship as extraordinary emergency power limiting civil liberties temporarily and/or increasing the power of certain offices becomes hard to distinguish from other types of autocratic rule when it lasts beyond a well-defined situation. The political scientist cannot ignore the statements of those assuming such powers even when he or she might have doubts about their honesty or their realism in their expectations of devolving power to the people, because those statements are likely to have permanent consequences for the legitimacy of nondemocratic rule so established. The political scientist cannot decide *a priori* but only *ex post facto* that the rule of an individual or group was actually a dictatorship in this narrow sense of the term as derived from its historical Roman meaning. Dictatorships of this type are more often than not bridges toward other forms of autocratic rule, and it is no accident that the kings of the Balkan states that broke with constitutional rule should have been considered royal dictatorships rather than a return to absolute monarchies. Once the continuity of traditional legitimacy has been given up for democratic forms, the return to it seems to be impossible. Dictatorship as interim, extraordinary authority all too often is perpetuated in more or less institutionalized forms of authoritatrian rule. Let us not forget that already the Roman constitutional institution was subverted and transformed into a more permanent authoritarian rule when Silla became in 82 B.C. *dictator reipublicae constituendae* and Caesar became in 48 B.C. dictator for a limited time and in 46 B.C. for ten years. Caesarism has been since then a term for the subversion of constitutional government by an outstanding leader.

We shall reserve the term dictatorship for interim crisis government that has not institutionalized itself and represents a break with the institutionalized rules about accession to and exercise of power of the preceding regime, be it democratic, traditional, or authoritarian. The temporary suspension of those rules according to rules foreseen in the constitution of a regime shall be called crisis government or constitutional dictatorship.

2

TOTALITARIAN SYSTEMS

Toward a Definition of Totalitarianism

In view of the central place in the study of modern noncompetitive democratic regimes of totalitarianism it seems useful to start with some of the already classical definitions of totalitarian systems and, after presenting them, attempt to push our knowledge somewhat further along the lines derived from the criticism they have been subject to (Jänicke, 1971; Friedrich, 1954; Friedrich and Brzezinski 1965, S. Neumann, 1942; Aron, 1968; Buchheim, 1968a; Schapiro, 1972a, 1972b; Seidel and Jenkner, 1968). Carl Friedrich has recently reformulated the original descriptive definition he and Z. K. Brzezinski (1965) had formulated, in the following way:

> The features which distinguish this regime from other and older autocracies as well as from heterocracies are six in number. They are to recall what by now is a fairly generally accepted set of facts: (1) a totalist ideology; (2) a single party commited to this ideology and usually led by one man, the dictator; (3) a fully developed secret police and three kinds of monopoly or more precisely monopolistic control; namely, that of (a) mass communications, (b) operational weapons, and (c) all organizations including economic ones, thus involving a centrally planned economy. . . . We might add that these six features could if greater simplicity is desired lie grouped into three, a totalist ideology, a party reinforced by a secret police and a monopoly of the three major forms of interpersonal confrontation in industrial mass society. Such monopoly is not necessarily exercized by the party. This should be stressed at the outset in order to forestall a misunderstanding which has arisen in some of the critical commentaries

65

in my earlier work. The important point is that such a monopolistic control is in the hands of whatever elite rules the particular society and thereby constitutes its regime. (Friedrich, 1969, p. 126)

Brzezinski has offered a more essentialist definition emphasizing the ultimate end of such systems when he writes:

> Totalitarianism is a new form of government falling into the general classification of dictatorship, a system in which technologically advanced instruments of political power are wielded without restraint by centralized leadership of an elite movement for the purpose of affecting a total social revolution, including the conditioning of man on the basis of certain arbitrary ideological assumptions, proclaimed by the leadership in an atmosphere of coerced unanimity of the entire population. (Brzezinski, 1962)

Franz Neumann (1957, pp. 233–56) has provided us with a similar set of defining characteristics.

Let us stress that in these definitions the terror element—the role of the police, of coercion—is not central as, for example, in the work of Hannah Arendt (1966). In fact, it could be argued that a totalitarian system could be based on the identification of a very large part of the population with the rulers, the population's active involvement in political organizations controlled by them and at the service of their goals, and use of diffused social control based on voluntary, manipulated involvement and a mixture of rewards and fears in a relatively closed society, as long as the rulers could count on the loyalty of the armed forces. In some respects, communist China has approached this type of totalitarianism, and the Khrushchev experience of a populist rationalization of party control described by Paul Cocks (1970) would fit such a model.

Explicitly or implicitly those definitions suggest a tendency toward the destruction of the line between state and society and the emergence of "total" politicization of society by political organizations, generally the party and its affiliates. However, this dimension that differentiates totalitarian systems from various types of authoritarian regimes and particularly from democratic governments is unlikely to be fully realized and, consequently, the problem of tension between society and political system, while reduced, is far from disappearing under such systems. The shaping of the individual, the internalization by the mass of the citizens of the ideology, the realization of the "new man" of which

ideologists talk are obviously even more unlikely, even when few social systems, except religions, have gone as far in this direction as the
totalitarian systems.

The dimensions that we have to retain as necessary to characterize
a system as totalitarian are an ideology, a single mass party and other
mobilizational organizations, and concentrated power in an individual
and his collaborators or a small group that is not accountable to any
large constituency and cannot be dislodged from power by institutionalized, peaceful means. Each of those elements can be found separately
in other types of nondemocratic systems and only their simultaneous
presence makes a system totalitarian. This means that not all single-
party systems are totalitarian, that no system in which there exists a
fair competition for power between freely created parties can be totalitarian, and that no nondemocratic system without a single party, or
more specifically an active single party, can be considered totalitarian.
As Friedrich admits in his revised version, it is not essential that ultimate power or the largest amount of power should be found in the
party organization, even when it seems highly improbable that such a
single mass party and the bureaucracy controlling it should not be
among the most powerful institutions in the society, at least in relationship to its members and to the common citizen.

There are certainly dictators—Caesaristic leaders, small oligarchies like military juntas, or coalitions of elites within different institutional realms not accountable to the members of their organizations
and institutions—whose power we would not call totalitarian. Unless
their power is exercised in the name of an ideology guided to a greater
or lesser degree by some central ideas, or *Weltanschauung,* and unless
they use some form of mass organization and participation of members
of the society beyond the armed forces and a police to impose their
rule, we cannot speak of a totalitarian system but, as we shall see later,
of authoritarian regimes. Whatever its unity, infighting might exist in
the top leadership around and under the top leader and between organizations created by the top leadership. Such group politics does not
emerge from the society or take place between institutions or organizations that existed before taking of power. The conflicting men, factions, or organizations do not derive their power from structures of the
society that are not strictly political, even when those engaged in such
struggles for power might have closer links with some sectors of society than with others. In this sense it seems impossible to speak of class
conflict in a Marxist sense in totalitarian systems. The initial power

positions from which the competitors attempt to expand their base by linking with the diversity of interests in the society are part of the political system—political organizations like the party, affiliated mass organizations, regional organizations of the party, the party militia, or government and police bureaucracies. In stable totalitarian systems preexisting institutions like business organizations, the church, or even the army play a secondary role in the struggle for power, and to the extent that they participate they are brought in to support one or another leader or group within the political elite. Their leadership is not a legitimate contender for political power but only for influence on particular decisions and rarely capable of veto power. In this respect, the subordination of the military authority is one of the distinctive characteristics of totalitarian systems in contrast to other nondemocratic systems. To this day, no totalitarian system has been overthrown or changed fundamentally by the intervention of the armed forces, even when in crisis moments one or another faction might have reinforced its power by the support of the military.

Only the highly political People's Liberation Army (PLA) in China (Joffe, 1965, 1971; Pollack, 1974; Schurmann, 1968, pp. 12–13; Gittings, 1967) and the army in Cuba (Domínguez, 1974; Dumont, 1970) might have played such a role. It is only in a very relative sense that we can speak of particular leaders or factions or bureaucracies within the power structure as representing the managers, the farmers, linguistic or cultural groups, the intellectuals, and so on. Whenever leaders or groups represent to some degree the interests of such sectors of the society, they are not accountable to a constituency, do not derive their power base fundamentally from it, generally are not recruited from it, and often are not even co-opted as leaders emerging from such social groups. The destruction or at least decisive weakening of all the institutions, organizations, and interest groups existing before a new elite takes political power and organizes its own political structures is one of the distinguishing characteristics of totalitarian systems compared with other nondemocratic systems. In this sense we can speak of monopoly of power, monism, but it would be a great mistake to take this concentration of power in the political sphere and in the hands of the people and the organizations created by the political leadership as monolithic. The pluralism of totalitarian systems is not social pluralism but political pluralism within the ruling political elite. To give one example: the conflicts between the SA and the SS, the DAF (Labor Front) and the party, the four-year plan organization of Goehring and the Organization

Todt of Speer, were conflicts within the Nazi elite and between its organizations. They certainly looked for and found allies among the military, the bureaucracy, and sectors of business, but it would be a great mistake to consider any of those leaders or organizations as representatives of the pre-Nazi structures of German society. The same could probably he said about the struggles among factions within the Politbureau or the Central Committee after the death of Stalin.

However, it might be argued that in a totalitarian system that is fully established and in power for a long time, members of the political organizations, particularly the party, become identified through a process of differentiation and division of labor with particular policy areas and are likely to identify increasingly with particular economic or territorial interests and represent their aspirations and points of view in the formulation of specific policies, particularly in peacetime, when no single goal is all-important, and at the time of succession or leadership crisis. Once basic decisions about the nature of the political system have been settled, preexisting social structures destroyed or decisively weakened, and dominant leaders displaced, a transformation of the system allowing a pluralism limited in scope and autonomy is not unlikely to take place. At that point, the degree of vitality of the ideology and the party or other organizations committed to its dominance and the strength of the leaders at the top will be decisive in characterizing the system as some variety of totalitarianism or as being transformed into something different. Certainly such transformations within totalitarian systems are not without tension and strain and therefore may be characterized by cyclical changes rather than a smooth continuous evolution.

Any typology of totalitarian systems will have to take into account the relative importance of ideology, party and mass organizations, and the political leader or leadership groups than have appropriated power—and the cohesion or factionalization of the leadership. In addition, it will have to analyze how those three main dimensions link with the society and its structure, history, and cultural traditions. Different totalitarian systems or phases of the same system might be characterized as more ideological, populist, or bureaucratic, depending on the character of the single party, and more charismatic, oligarchical, or even feudal, depending on the structure of the dominant center of power. The absence of any of those three factors or their weakening beyond a certain point will fundamentally change the nature of the system. However, the variety among those three dimensions certainly allows for quite different types of totalitarian systems.

It is the combination of those three dimensions that accounts for many of the other characteristics we are more likely to find in totalitarian than other nondemocratic systems. However, some of those other characteristics are neither necessary nor sufficient to characterize a system as totalitarian and can be found in other types of political systems.

In summary, I shall consider a system totalitarian when the following characteristics apply.

1. There is a monistic but not monolithic center of power, and whatever pluralism of institutions or groups exists derives its legitimacy from that center, is largely mediated by it, and is mostly a political creation rather than an outgrowth of the dynamics of the preexisting society.

2. There is an exclusive, autonomous, and more or less intellectually elaborate ideology with which the ruling group or leader, and the party serving the leaders, identify and which they use as a basis for policies or manipulate to legitimize them. The ideology has some boundaries beyond which lies heterodoxy that does not remain unsanctioned. The ideology goes beyond a particular program or definition of the boundaries of legitimate political action to provide, presumably, some ultimate meaning, sense of historical purpose, and interpretation of social reality.

3. Citizen participation in and active mobilization for political and collective social tasks are encouraged, demanded, rewarded, and channeled through a single party and many monopolistic secondary groups. Passive obedience and apathy, retreat into the role of "parochials" and "subjects," characteristic of many authoritarian regimes, are considered undesirable by the rulers.

This third characteristic brings a totalitarian society closer to the ideal and even the reality of most democracies and basically differentiates it from most "nontotalitarian nondemocratic systems." It is this participation and the sense of participation that democratic observers of totalitarian systems often find so admirable and that make them think that they are faced with a democracy, even a more perfect democracy than one in which citizens get involved in public issues only or mainly at election time. However, the basic difference between participation in a mobilizational regime and in a democracy is that, in the former, in each realm of life for each purpose there is only one possible channel for participation and the overall purpose and direction is set by one center, which defines the legitimate goals of those organizations and ultimately controls them.

It is the constant feedback between the dominant, more or less monistic center of decision making, undergirded by the ideological commitments that guide it or are used or manipulated by it, and these processes of participation for those ideological purposes within those controlled organizations that characterizes a totalitarian system.

It should be possible to derive other characteristics frequently stressed in describing totalitarian systems from the three we just sketched, and we shall do so in discussing in more detail some of the main scholarly contributions to the study of specific totalitarian systems. Here we might give a few basic examples. The tense relationship between intellectuals and artists and the political authorities,[9] in addition to being the result of the personal idiosyncrasies of rulers like Hitler and Stalin, is certainly the result of the emphasis on an ideology and the exclusion by the commitment to it of other systems of ideas or the fear of the questioning of the values implicit in the ideology, particularly the collective and public goals versus individual and private ones. Privatized, inner-oriented man is a latent threat, and certainly many forms of aesthetic expression search for that orientation. The same is true for the exacerbation of the normal conflicts between church and state to conflicts between religion and politics.[10] The importance of ideology also has positive aspects, in the sense of making education a highly valued activity, making selective cultural efforts and their mass diffusion highly desirable. This is in contrast to most traditional autocracies, with the exception of religious indoctrination in religious autocracies and scientific and technological education in secular autocracies. Propaganda, education, training of cadres, intellectual elaboration of the ideology, scholarship inspired by the ideology, rewards for intellectuals identified with the system are more likely to be important in totalitarian than in other nondemocratic systems. If we ignore the limited content of that effort, the limitations or denial of freedom, we find here a certain convergence with democratic systems, in which the mass participation in political life requires also mass education and mass communications and assigns to intellectuals an important, even when not always welcome, role.

The concentration of power in the leader and his collaborators or a distinct group of powerholders, formed by their joint participation in the struggle to gain power and create the regime, their socialization in the political organizations, or their co-optation from other sectors (keeping in mind criteria of loyalty and/or identification with the ideology), necessarily limits the autonomy of other organizations like industrial enterprises, professional groups, the armed forces, the intellectuals, and so on. The sharing to greater or lesser degree of the belief in the ideology, of the identification with its symbols, and the conviction that decisions should be legitimized or at least rationalized in terms of the ideology, separates this group from those more skeptical or disinterested in the ideology and from those who, because of their calling, like the intellectuals, are most likely to question those ideas. However, it also brings them close to those who, without challenging their power, are willing to elaborate the ideology. The element of elitism so often stressed in the analysis of totalitarian systems is a logical consequence of this search for a monopoly of power. It is also a source of the bitterness of many conflicts within the elite and the ostracism or purge of those who lose the struggle for power. Power, more than in democratic societies, becomes a zero-sum game.

The commitment to ideology, the desire for monopolistic control, and the fear of losing power certainly explain the propensity toward coercive methods in such systems and the likelihood for continuing terror. Therefore, terror, particularly within the elite rather than against opponents or even potential opponents to the system, distinguishes totalitarian systems from other nondemocratic systems. The size of the society, stressed by Hannah Arendt, and the degree of modernization in terms of technology linked with industrialization, stressed by other scholars, are not as important as ideological zeal in explaining the drive for positive commitment rather than apathy of subjects or just external conformity of bureaucrats.

The nature and role of the single party is obviously the most important variable when we come to analyze in behavioral terms the impact of totalitarian systems on different societies. The importance assigned to the party organization, the specialized political organizations emerging from the party, and the mass organizations linked with it account for many of the basic characteristics of such systems. Foremost, their capacity to penetrate the society, to be present and influential in many institutional realms, to mobilize people for large-scale tasks on a voluntary or pseudo voluntary basis rather than just for material incentives and rewards allows such systems to carry out important changes with limited resources and therefore to serve as instruments for certain types of economic and social development. It also gives them a certain democratic character, in the sense of offering to those willing to participate (accepting the basic goals of the leadership rather than advancing alternative goals) a chance for active participation and a sense of involvement. Despite the bureaucratic character of the state and of many organizations and even the party, the mass membership in the party and in related sponsored organizations can give meaning, purpose, and a sense of participation to many citizens. In this respect, totalitarian systems are very different from many other nondemocratic systems—authoritarian regimes—in which the rulers rely fundamentally on a staff of bureaucrats, experts, and policemen, distinct and separate from the rest of the people, who have little or no chance to feel as active participants in the society and polity beyond their personal life and their work.

The party organization and the many minor leadership positions in it give many people a chance to exercise some share in power, sometimes over people who in other hierarchies of the society would be their superiors.[11] This obviously introduces an element of equality undermining other stratified structures of the society while introducing a new and different type of inequality. An active party organization with members involved in its activities also increases enormously the possibilities of control and latent coercion of those who are unwilling to join or are excluded. Many of the energies that in a democratic society are channeled into political life, but also into a myriad of voluntary associations that take an interest in collective goods, are used by totalitarian systems. Much of the idealism associated with collective orientation rather than self-orientation (idealism that in the past went into religious organizations and now in liberal democratic society goes into voluntary groups) is likely to be found in the party and its sponsored organizations, together, obviously, with the opportunism of those attracted by a variety of rewards and access to power or the hope of having it. This mobilizational aspect is central to totalitarian systems and absent in many, if not most, other nondemocratic systems. Some of the kind of people who in a totalitarian system become zealous activists on many of the tasks assigned to them by the leadership in other nondemocratic systems would be passive subjects only interested in their private narrow goals or alienated in view of the lack of opportunities for any participation in efforts directed at changing their societies. Certainly much of the attraction that the totalitarian model has comes from this participatory mobilizational dimension of the party and the mass organizations. But also much of the alienation and negative feelings about such systems are due to the absence of choice for the average citizen between alternative goals for the society and the limited freedom or lack of freedom in choosing the leadership of such organizations due to the bureaucratic character derived from norms like the leadership principle or democratic centralism.

Other characteristics often noted in describing totalitarian systems, like their expansionist tendencies, are much more difficult to derive from their more central characteristics. There is obviously an indirect relationship, since the emphasis on an exclusive ideology makes the persistence of alternative ideologies and belief systems a latent threat. However, much will depend on the content of the ideology, and certainly the character and direction of the expansionism will be shaped more by that than by other structural features.[12]

A search for conformity, a proscription of most forms of dissidence, particularly those that can reach larger segments of the population and that involve any attempt of organization, a reduction of the private realm, and considerable amount of half-free if not enforced participation are almost inevitable in totalitarian systems. The massive and/or arbitrary use of terror as we find in the concentration camps, the purges, the show trials, the collective punishments of groups or communities do not seem essential to a totalitarian system. However, we can say that it was not accidental that some of those forms appeared under Hitler and Stalin, that they were distinctive and widespread as they have not been in any democratic system, and that they should have been qualitatively and quantitatively different from other nondemocratic systems, except in their periods of consolidation in power either during or immediately after a civil war. Terror is neither a necessary nor sufficient characteristic of totalitarian systems, but there seems to be a greater probability that it should appear under such systems than under others, and certain of its forms seem to be distinctive of certain types of totalitarian systems. Some authors have rightly spoken of totalitarianism without terror.

Early studies of totalitarianism, particularly Sigmund Neumann's (1942) *Permanent Revolution,* emphasized the role of a leader. The fascist commitment to the *Führerprinzip* and the exaltation of the *Duce,* together with the cult of personality around Stalin, certainly made this an obvious element in a definition of totalitarian systems. However, in recent years we have seen systems that on many counts are still totalitarian in which we do not find such an undisputed leader at the top or a comparable cult or personification of leadership. On the other hand, there are many nondemocratic systems that would not fit into the type we have delineated above in which a single leader occupies a comparable place and the cult of personality has gone as far. Therefore we can legitimately say that the appearance of a single leader who concentrates vast amounts of power in his person, is the object of a cult of personality, and claims a charismatic authority and to a greater or lesser extent enjoys it among the party members and the populace at large is highly probable in totalitarian systems but not inevitable or necessary for their stability. Succession crises that some scholars thought threatened the stability and even survival of such regimes have not led to their downfall or breakdown even when they have been very critical for them.[13] It could be argued that the emphasis on personal leadership is characteristic of totalitarian systems of the fascist type, and this is certainly true of Italy and Germany as well as of some of the minor fascist regimes, but the role of Stalin in the Soviet Union shows that it was not a feature exclusive to fascist regimes. Obviously if we should argue, as some dissident communists and some left fascists do, that Stalin was the Russian functional equivalent to fascism, the difficulty would disappear. But this seems a sophistic solution. At this point we can say only that there is a higher probability that such leadership will appear in totalitarian systems than in other nondemocratic systems. Changes in the relationship between leadership, ideology, and organized participation are the variables likely to offer the best clue for the construction of the typology of totalitarian systems and for an understanding of the processes of consolidation, stability, and change— and perhaps breakdown—of such systems. It might be overambitious to attempt to formulate some propositions about those interrelationships among those relatively independent variables for any totalitarian system; and certainly only a theoretical-empirical analysis of particular types and even unique cases will facilitate such a theoretical effort at a higher level of abstraction. With all the risks involved, we shall attempt to sketch some directions in which such an analysis might move. Let us stress from the beginning that the relationships are likely to be two way without any of them being ever fully unidirectional, since unidirectional relationships would change decisively the nature of the system and bring into question the independent character of each of the variables, but also that the flow of influence of the variables might be stronger in one or another direction.

Ideology and Totalitarianism

As some of the scholars have noted, totalitarian systems might be considered ideocracies or logocracies, and Inkeles (1954) has developed the notion of totalitarian mystique to convey the importance of ideology as a powerful independent variable in such systems.[14] There can be no doubt that totalitarian leaders, individuals or groups, in contrast to other nondemocratic rulers, derive much of their sense of mission, their legitimation, and often very specific policies from their commitment to some holistic conception of man and society. Ideologies vary much in the richness and complexity of their content and in the degree to which they are closed, fixed, and can be action-related. The study of ideologies as systems of ideas, of meanings, and of the internal logical or emotional connections between those ideas is obviously essential to understanding different totalitarian systems. Such a study can be done from different perspectives: intellectual-cultural history, sociology of knowledge, and social psychology. The initial commitment of a ruler or ruling group to an ideology imposes constraints, excluding a greater or smaller number of alternative values, goals, and styles of thinking, and sets a framework limiting the range of alternative policies. There can be no question that an intellectually elaborate ideology like Marxism provides a more complex and heterogenous as well as rational starting point for ideological elaboration than the more simple, emotional, and less intellectually fixated elements of fascist ideology. Some of those who question the usefulness of the totalitarian approach to the study of fascist regimes and of Nazism do so because they question the ideological character of those movements reducing their ideas to those of their founders and rulers and engaging in purely pragmatic power seeking and opportunist manipulation of symbols. The existence of a printed and fixed and to some degree unambiguous corpus of writing of Marx, Engels, and Lenin, which can be doctored, partly suppressed, and reinterpreted but not fully abandoned, certainly differs from those regimes in which the leader or group in power claims identification with much less elaborate ideas or is in the process of giving ideological content to his rule. The autonomy or heteronomy in the control of ideological formulation is obviously a key to the autonomy and stability of different totalitarian systems and is one of the sources of conflict between them when they attempt to derive their legitimacy from identification with an ideological corpus. The hypothesis may be advanced that a fully autonomous totalitarian system cannot exist without almost full control over the formulation or interpretation of the ideological heritage or content. In this respect different fascist regimes found themselves in a better position in relation to the hegemonic powers in their camp than did the Eastern European communists, and the regimes of China and Cuba found themselves in a better position than those of other minor communist states. The heteronomous control of the ideological content of Catholic thought by a universal church and specifically by the Pope is one of the most serious obstacles to the creation of a truly totalitarian system by nondemocratic rulers claiming to implement Catholic social doctrine in their states. Among other factors this is one that has prevented the Austrian "clerical-fascists" and the regimes of Franco and Salazar from pursuing further the path toward totalitarianism (Linz, 1964, p. 303).

Ideologies in totalitarian systems are a source of legitimacy, a source of the sense of mission of a leader or a ruling group, and it is not surprising that one should speak of charisma of the leader or the party, for at least important segments of their societies, on the basis of that element. Many of the differences between systems or within the same system over time are to be understood in terms of the relationship of people in those positions to the ideology. However, while the ideology imposes some constraints, more or less narrow, on the rulers and their actions, the relationship is not one-sided, and much of the effort in such systems goes into the manipulation, adaptation, and selective interpretation of the ideological heritage, particularly in the second generation of rulers. Only a complete change in the relationship to the ideology—its substitution by pragmatic policy formulation and the acceptance of heteronomous sources for ideas and central policies, of evidence clearly and explicitly in conflict with the ideology—will lead to changes away from the totalitarian model. The ruling group might very well reach the conclusion that a fixed ideology limits its choices too much and that a scholastic reinterpretation of the texts can go only so far, but the fact that a simplified and vulgarized version of the ideologies has been central to the indoctrination of the middle levels of cadres of the single mass party and even the membership will certainly make it difficult to abandon certain policies and sometimes create real crises of legitimacy. The autonomy and importance of the party organization compared to the personal power of the leader or a small oligarchy is to some extent a function of the importance of the commitment to the ideology. Inversely, the constraining character of the ideological commitments for the ruling group is likely to be directly related to the active life of the party—intraparty discussion, elaboration of party thought, cadre training activities, agitprop activities, and so on. Important ideological changes rather than just manipulation of the ideology require some activation of the party structure and thereby impose pressures on the ruling group, contribute to crises within it, and might lead to important changes in its composition. Obviously, changes in the relationship between the ruling group or leader and the party organization, like those achieved by Stalin as first secretary, also make possible changes in the ideology and the displacement of those in the ruling group who had devoted their energies to the intellectual elaboration of the ideology and policies derived from it rather than to the development of an organizational base. The displacement and elimination of the original Bolshevik intellectual ideologists by the apparatchiki identified with Stalin certainly contributed to the debasement of the Marxist-Leninist ideological heritage. This process had some interesting parallels in fascist regimes, with the displacement of Rosenberg by Himmler and Bormann and of Gentile and Bottai by Starace. Such processes are not without consequences for the system, since the capacity to mobilize the loyalties of intellectuals, students, and young idealistic activists in the party and the mass organizations is to some degree a function of the capacity for creative ideological development as well as for continuity. This might account for waves of ideological fervor and with them mobilization of new members in some sectors of the regime. The intellectual elaborations sponsored by the SS, often neglected by scholars, might be a good example. The simultaneous weakening and ossification of the ideology and the party organization obviously tend to isolate the ruling group, weaken the dynamism of the society, and create a certain power vacuum that tends to be filled by more coercive bureaucratic control and the reliance on a more praetorian police. Ultimately this could lead to the transformation of a totalitarian system into other forms of authoritarianism.

The Totalitarian Party

The unique syndrome of totalitarian political systems resulting from the importance of ideology, the tendency toward a monistic center of power, and the emphasis on mass participation and mobilization finds its purest expression in the totalitarian party, its dependent organizations and affiliates, and the functions they perform in the society. The totalitarian party, as a unique type of organization, distinguishes most clearly the modern forms of autocracy from any traditional absolutist regime and from a great variety of other nondemocratic governments. Mussolini was right when he wrote: "The party that governs a nation totalitarianly is a new fact in history; similarities and comparisons are impossible" (Aquarone, 1965, p. 577).[15] In the mid-thirties Mihail Manoïlesco (1938), a Rumanian scholar and cabinet member sympathetic to authoritarian regimes, wrote one of the first comparative analyses of single parties, including, together with the fascist parties that enjoyed his sympathies, the Communist party of the Soviet Union and the Turkish Republican party. The index of his book reflects some of the permanent intellectual problems in the study of such parties: the ideological-historical context in which they are born, their functions in the process of taking power and consolidating it, in established regimes the complex relationship between party, state, and nation, their organizational characteristics, and their special legal status. At that time there were six single ruling parties. Today their number has multiplied manifold and we are conscious that there are many different types of established single-party systems. In addition, in a number of communist countries, including China, one cannot speak of one-party systems but of dominant leading parties and subordinate parties under their aegis. The theoretical model of the totalitarian party has been widely imitated, but only under very special circumstances can we say that the single party is a totalitarian party. In many democracies we find parties that more or less explicitly have the goal of doing away with party competition. Such parties often by extension have been called totalitarian but we feel this is a misleading use of the term, since only after taking power can such a party realize its ambitions. In fact, it is debatable whether a party that shares an ideology and certain organizational characteristics with totalitarian parties would not be forced to function differently if it came to power in a stable democracy and might even become a loyal opposition or a legitimate participant in democratic politics.

The concept of the totalitarian party itself reflects some of the inherent tensions and ambivalence of the term, and it is no accident that some of the parties, particularly of the fascist and nationalist type and including many Nazi theoreticians, tried to substitute the word "party" by others like "movement." Party underlines that the organization is only part of the political life, while the adjective totalitarian indicates the more or less utopian goal of encompassing the whole individual, the whole society. Communist parties based on the Leninist conception of the vanguard party have always emphasized this part character. For example, Article 126 of the Stalin Constitution:

> The citizens of the USSR are guaranteed the right to unite in public organizations, trade unions, cooperative societies, youth organizations, sport and defense organizations, cultural, technical, and scientific societies. And the most active and politically conscious citizens in the ranks of the working class, working peasants, and working intelligentsia voluntarily unite in the Communist Party of the Soviet Union which is the vanguard of the working people in their struggle to build a Communist society and is the leading core of all organizations of the working people, both societal and governmental. (Meyer, 1965, p. 107)

The party is therefore a minority, a vanguard in communist terminology, an elite in that of the fascist. In most communist countries it represents somewhat less than 5 percent of the population, and even where it is larger than that it does not get close to 25 percent.[16] Totalitarian parties fit the definition of party of Max Weber:

> The term "party" will be employed to designate associations, membership in which rests on formally free recruitment. The end to which its activity is devoted is to secure power within an organization for its leaders in order to attain ideal or material advantages for its active members. These advantages may consist in the realization of certain objective policies or the attainment of personal advantages, or both. (1968, Vol. 1, p. 284)

The goal of power within an organization highlights a major problem in the study of totalitarian parties, the relationship between party and state. In spite of all the bureaucratization of parties, the oligarchic continuity of leadership, and even the legally privileged status of its leaders and members, parties are deliberately distinct from the organization of a state, its offices and bureaucracy, whatever degree of overlap between their leadership. In the USSR ministers of the Soviet government have frequently not been members of the highest bodies of the Politbureau and even the Central Committee, and men highly placed in the party have never held government office. Fraenkel (1941), in his analysis of early Nazi rule, even when emphasizing some different aspects, spoke of the dual state. In principle, therefore, the totalitarian party retains the function of expressing the demands, aspirations, interests of the society or particular classes of society. In this sense it is a modern phenomenon, inconceivable without the duality of state and society. Despite the tendency of the totalitarian party to become a closed group, incorporated by law into the administrative staff, the formal criterion of voluntary solicitation and adherence distinguishes parties from state bureaucracies, modern or patrimonial, and from most modern armies. Membership involves whatever the psychic, social, and economic pressures to join there are, for example for civil servants, a commitment to a voluntary identification. It is no accident that a member of the Hitler cabinet would for reasons of conscience refuse even an honorary membership in the Nationalsozialistische Deutsche Arbeiterpartei (NSDAP) (Peterson, 1969, p. 33).[17] This part character contrasts with the totalitarian goal expressed in a 1958 edition of the official *Primer of Soviet Philosophy:*

> Only the party expressing the interest of the entire nation embodying its collective understanding, uniting in its ranks the finest individuals of the nation, is qualified and called to control the work of all organizations and organs of power. The party realizes the leadership of all state and public organizations through its members who work in these organizations and who enter into their governing organ. (Schurmann, 1968, p. 109)

Hitler (1924–26) in *Mein Kampf* expressed this ambition of totality of the party in this revealing text:

> Every philosophy of life, even if it is a thousand times correct and of highest benefit to humanity, will remain without significance for the practical shaping of a people's life as long as its principles have not become the banner of the fighting movement which for its part in turn will be a party as long as its activity has not found completion in the victory of its ideas and its party dogmas have not become the new state principles of a people's community. (p. 380)

Ideas valid for the whole community or a class cannot be realized without a militant organization. Significantly, the party had to conquer and retain the power in the state. The state is an indispensable means for its realization but no totalitarian leader conceives that the state could realize his utopia. It is significant that only in Italy, where the Fascists tended, after taking control of the state, to subordinate the party organization and its leaders to Fascist state officials and where the corporativist ideology offered an alternative way to organize society, the possibility of dissolving the party would be discussed briefly. Despite the constant use by the Fascists of the term "totalitarian," the Fascist conception of the party as an organization of the political administrative forces of the regime, as a voluntary civil militia, at the order of the *Duce,* at the service of the Fascist state, tended to undermine the totalitarian conception of the party and make it more comparable to the many single parties created by a ruler or ruling group from above.[18]

The totalitarian party is a mass party. It is not just an organization of officeholders based on the co-optation by a ruling group of officials, local notables, army officers in civilian garb, and perhaps some functionaries and a few office-seeking members, as many single parties in authoritarian regimes can accurately be described. It is also not an organization based on indirect membership in trade unions, cooperatives, professional associations, and so forth. Certainly, totalitarian parties have a close relationship with such functional organizations. The NSDAP, for example, made a clear distinction between the party as a cadre and membership organization, its divisions *(Gliederungen),* the Hitler Youth *(Jugend),* the SA, the SS, and the large number of affiliated organizations *(angeschlossene Verbände),* that is, professional and interest groups including the giant labor organization, the *Deutsche Arbeitsfront* (DAF) (Orlow, 1973, pp. 6–7, 92). Those organizations for the communists are transmission belts, and as Stalin put it:

> To forget the distinction between the advanced detachment and the whole of the masses which gravitate towards it, to forget the constant duty of the advanced detachment to raise ever wider strata to this most advanced level means merely to deceive oneself. (1924, p. 174)

As one *Gauleiter* (regional head of the party) representing the popular Nazi farmers organization, the *NS Landvolk,* put it, the purpose of the *NS Landvolk* is not to represent the farmers but to make National Socialists out of them (Orlow, 1973, p. 59). Membership in theory and very often in practice involves much more than paying dues, like in many democratic parties and even social democratic parties. It is no accident that the definition of party membership should have been one of the basic disagreements between Martov and Lenin, between the Mencheviks and the Bolsheviks, by requiring personal participation in one of the party organizations. The acceptance by the party member of party discipline and the intolerability of any criticism undermining or obstructing the unity of action decided on by the party, extended even to activities outside of politics in the professional sphere, even in conflict with the hierarchical authority relationships in the state or the army, characterize totalitarian parties. Admission to membership is not automatic; parties reserve for themselves the right to admit or to reject. They often establish a probationary or candidate period, formally grant different rights to new members and provide for expulsion, which means, as the statutes of the PNF *(Partito Nazionale Fascista)* stated, "The Fascist who is expelled from the party must be outlawed from public life" (Aquarone, 1965, p. 510). Deliberate planning of the composition of the membership and purges by the leadership characterize those parties,[19] and, consistent with the conception of the organization as voluntary and self-regulating, there is no recourse in the absence of other parties against the decision to any outside authority or court despite the privation of political citizenship (Rigby, 1968; Buchheim, 1958). Many positions in the state and societal organizations are formally or de facto accessible only to party members.

Totalitarian parties are bureaucratic in a way that even the most bureaucratized democratic parties are not. As Lenin stated it in *One Step Forward, Two Steps Back:*

> The party link must be founded on formal "bureaucratically" (from the point of view of the disorganized intellectual) worded rules strict observance of which alone can guarantee us from the willfulness and the caprices of the circle spirit, from the circle scramble methods which are termed the free "process of the ideological struggle." (Daniels, 1969, p. 11)

The life of the party is regulated by innumerable rules. Written norms are constantly enacted, extensive files are kept, decisions go through channels, and party officials control that apparatus. Both at the center and at the periphery there is a large number of full-time officials, who often have distinctive training and sometimes with privileged legal status and enjoy not only power but other rewards comparable to those of civil servants; in addition there are others who exercise leadership functions on a part-time basis. In the Communist party the expression "cadre" is used to designate party members who exercise leadership roles with distinctive ranks included in the *nomenklatura* (list of key job categories and descriptions used in elite recruitment) (Harasymiw, 1972). In the case of the Nazis the equivalent was the *Hoheitsträger,* the political leadership of the party from the *Gauleiters* down to the local leaders. In 1934, in Germany, the terrritorial cadre organization, *Politische Organisation,* had 373,000 functionaries for a party membership of some 2.5 in million, while the Weimar Social Democratic party, with 1 million members, needed only 10,000 (Orlow, 1973, p. 42). At that time the Hitler Youth had 205,000 functionaries and the NSDAP, including all its affiliates, had 1,017,000, not all of them necessarily party members. Jerry F. Hough (1971, p. 49), on the basis of the size of the apparatus of various city and district party committees, estimates the number of party apparatchiki in the Soviet Union between 100,000 and 125,000. A 1956 breakdown of party membership by occupation in China lists 1,039,419 "organs," which seems to refer to party members employed full-time in the party bureaucracy among the party's 10.7 million members. The penetration by the party into the society to perform the multiple functions assigned to it is achieved by a large number of functionaries close to the masses, the heads of cell and local organizations. The figures for the NSDAP in 1939 show 28,376 leaders of local groups, 89,378 cell leaders, and 463,048 block leaders, without counting those of the affiliated organizations. Obviously the degree of ideological consciousness, dedication to political activity, and willingness of these cadres to put loyalty to the party ahead of other loyalties vary enormously from party to party and over time. However, we cannot underestimate the degree to which the cadres of a party are perceived by the members as leaders and by the citizens as representatives of the power of the party, for good and evil, to help them solve many problems (like a ward heeler in urban America) or to supply information to those in power about their doings and attitudes (Inkeles and Bauer, 1959, p. 321–37). Nor can we ignore the sense of participation in politics, in a collective effort, or the petty gratifications of these leaders, which are so characteristic of totalitarian systems. It is this cadre structure that allows totalitarian parties to pursue successfully their functions, and many of the achievements in transforming the society have to be attributed to the cadres. Without them the mobilization for the large number of campaigns, actions, problems, policies, would be impossible. Even if the party did not play a decisive role, as it does in communist systems, in the management of the society and the economy, the availability at short notice of such cadres and those they can influence or control can assure a massive and visible expression of support for the regime in plebiscitarian elections and mass rallies. If we keep in mind the findings about opinion leaders as mediators between the mass media and the individual in democratic societies and the impossibility of creating any comparable network of personal influences, except in some cases the churches, we can understand the success of propaganda, the appearance of enthusiasm and support and the pervasive conformity in totalitarian systems. Many of those who in pluralistic societies devote their time and energy to diverse voluntary associations do so in totalitarian societies in the activities of the party and its affiliated organizations, often with the same motivation and sincerity. Their actions contribute to the efficacy of the system and through it to its legitimacy. It is the absence of either pluralistic or single-party forms of voluntary participation and of a complex organizational network that characterizes most authoritarian regimes (except for short periods of mobilization through single parties).

Since the totalitarian party assumes a growing number of functions of a technical character in the management of complex industrial societies, the cadres experience a slow process of transformation, not infrequently accompanied by reversals, in the course of the stabilization of totalitarian systems. Initially, the cadres are recruited from the old fighters, the people who joined the party while it was in the opposition and sometimes in the illegal underground, who often made great sacrifices for the cause. Their loyalty, except for those disappointed by the absence of a second revolution, tends to be unquestionable but their competence to manage large-scale organizations in normal rather than exceptional circumstances is often limited. If the party wants to retain its momentum and not abdicate its revolutionary ambition and become dependent on the civil service, it has to recruit and socialize those who are experts and in due time train loyal party members as experts. The creation of party schools (Orlow, 1965; Scholtz, 1967; Ueberhorst, 1968; Mickiewicz, 1967), the promotion of activists from the youth organization through educational channels and through stages in different sectors of party activity into elite positions, the efforts to commit and even to compromse in the party those with expert knowledge are some of the techniques used. The dilemma of red or expert, which has been central to the Communist parties in power, is a perfect example. In the case of communist regimes the problem is compounded by the fact that the party plays a decisive role in the management of industry, agriculture, and services. The problem of preventing red expert cadres from also becoming professionals with a less political conception of their role, particularly devoting less attention to the social and political mobilization dimension of the party, has been particularly well analyzed in the Chinese case by Franz Schurmann (1968, pp. 75–76, 163–67, 170–72; Townsend, 1972). The Italian PNF, despite some efforts to create party schools, never fully faced this dilemma, due to the limited ideological thrust of the movement, the compatibility of its authoritarian nationalism and corporativism with a reliance on the state, and Mussolini's identification with the state, whose ministries and prefectures he had taken over, leaving to the party officials a secondary role. We do not know how the Nazis would have ultimately solved this dilemma, except that the social recruitment by the party before takeover and the ideological affinity of conservative, nationalist, authoritarian experts allowed the Nazis the partification of many sectors of the society. Even so, the men in the administration of the party felt unhappy about the situation and made generally unsuccessful attempts to train the Nazi elite in special schools. The irrational, romantic, anti-intellectual, militaristic, genetic, and racist components of the ideology were an obvious obstacle for the training of party men as experts. The SS as an elite within the party, with its pseudoreligious, pseudofeudal, semisecret, and terroristic character, opted for a process of co-optation and compromise in the "order"; these were men who had made their career not in the street fights and propaganda activities of the party before 1933, but in the establishment (Krausnick, 1968; Höhne, 1969). We do not know how a stable Nazi regime, victorious in the war, would have handled this problem. We know, however, how the Soviet Union and other communist countries have, in the course of their longer and more stable, peaceful development, moved toward combining *partiinost* ("partyness") with expertise. What we do not know exactly is the answer to the question raised so well by Jerry F. Hough (1971, pp. 47–92) of to what extent the apparatchiki of the contemporary Soviet Union in their multiple functions and career lines, with their professional education and expertise, their frequent shifts from state administration to party work, share a distinctive ideological outlook, and have common interests, have a different party perspective than their counterparts in the governmental and economic hierarchies. As he writes:

> It would certainly simplify the comparative study of political systems if we could assume that the elite members of the institutional groups which comprise "the gigantic bureaucracy party organizational complex" in a country such as the Soviet Union represent essentially their own interests and not those of farmers, workers, and clerks whom they supervise. (Hough, 1971, p. 89)

Franz Schurmann, in the context of his analysis of the Cultural Revolution in China, has suggested the need to make a distinction between professional and expert when he writes:

Expertise means a technical capacity (e.g., in science, technology, or administration). Professionalism means commitment to an occupational position. I have noted that two elites appeared to be developing in China, the body of organizational leaders with political status deriving from ideology and the professional intellectuals with status deriving from education. If occupational position gives rise to status, then professionalism will lead to the formation of elites. The accusations directed against "the authoritarian clique following the capitalist road" have aimed at the elite status, and not at the expertise. That has also been at the root of the attacks on the tendencies for a professional officer corps to develop. The intellectuals are the men of expertise in China, its scientists, technicians, and administrators. There are, have been, and undoubtedly continue to be tendencies toward the formation of an expert elite. However, since the brunt of the attack of the Cultural Revolution was on the Party, of gravest concern to Mao Tse-tung and his followers was the emergence of a professional red elite—that is, an elite whose power and status derived from Party position. (Schurmann, 1968, p. 565)

The commitment in a totalitarian society to the ideology of "politics takes command," to the control and preferably guidance of the society by a group of dedicated people committed to collective interests and to a utopian vision (however muddleheaded it is), accounts for the basic ambiguity in the role of the cadres of a party. It might well be that what starts as total politicization through the mobilization of a party might end, except for permanent revolution against the party or within the party, in the administration of a post-totalitarian society with its limited bureaucratic pluralism.

Party Leadership

Many scholars in their analysis of totalitarian parties have emphasized as the ultimate key to our understanding the role of the leader, be it the *Duce, Führer,* or First Secretary, and the unique concentration of power in his hands and the cult of personality, *Führerprinzip,* the distorted interpretation of democratic centralism that from the top down permeates the party (Schapiro, 1972a; Tucker, 1965; Vierhaus, 1964).[20] Others go even further and find the explanation in the unique personalities of men like Hitler and Stalin.[21] It would be an obvious mistake to ignore those factors, but the question will still remain, Why were those men capable of exercising such power and how did those principles emerge and become accepted by their staff and many party members? Michels (1962; originally published 1911) in his sociology of the modern party lists many of the factors that account for the exercise of such power, which are far from absent in competitive democratic parties but do not have the same consequences due to the pluralism of parties. Rosa Luxemburg in 1904 already noted that "the ultra centralism advocated by Lenin is not something born of the positive creative spirit but of the negative sterile spirit of the watchman" (Daniels, 1969, p. 12), and Trotsky felt that Lenin would have the party and its prescribed theology substitute for the mass movement in order to force the pace of history, concluding prophetically:

> These methods lead, as we shall yet see to this: the party organization is substituted for the party, the Central Committee is substituted for the party organization, and finally the "dictator" is substituted for the Central Committee. (Daniels, 1969, p. 13)

He concludes that the complicated task of cleaning out deadwood and bourgeois thinking "cannot be solved by placing above the proletariat a well-selected group of people, or still better one person and with the right to liquidate and demote." Those tendencies toward an all-powerful leader and the destruction even of a collective leadership are perhaps, as recent trends show, not inevitable in a communist party. They were, perhaps, in fascist parties, given some of their basic ideological orientations—the voluntarism, irrationalism, and appeal to emotion so congruent with the appeal to charisma, the admiration of military organization and leadership, the appeal of the great man in history idea, and in the German case the romantic yearning for a saviour with particular virtues based on a fascist, feudal, or Germanic imagery. However, it should be noted that fascist party statutes provided for elected leadership and that one of the few changes in *Mein Kampf* from the first edition was a radical formulation of the *Führerprinzip*.[22] The commitment to an indisputable ideology that expresses inexorable laws of history with substantive rather than procedural content makes the emergence of that kind of leadership more likely. Such commitment can easily justify the search for unanimity and the outlawing of any opposition within the party. The degree of free discussion before reaching a decision and the tolerance for loyal support of dissenters not convinced in such a context would depend on the personality of the leader or leaders rather than, in a more relativist conception of politics, based on normative limits of authority and pragmatic skepticism. The leadership principle, the charismatic demand of obedience, and the truly charismatic or pseudocharismatic loyalty of the followers are congruent with the totalitarian party but perhaps not inevitable. The model of concentration of power in a rational bureaucratic organization, the creation of a single center of decision making, is often used in describing such regimes. In fact, the contrary is true, and Franck, the Nazi governor of Poland, was right in stressing the anarchy in Hitler's rule. No centers of power challenging the authority of the leader are allowed to emerge, but the struggle for power between subleaders and organizations is one of the central characteristics of totalitarian systems, tolerated, if not encouraged, by the leader, following a policy of divide and rule. In a pure totalitarian system that struggle takes place mainly within the party and its affiliate organizations, which seek alliances with pretotalitarian structures or the emerging social interests of complex societies. As Orlow (1973, pp. 7–12) has noted, Hitler subcontracted (with the understanding that the contract could be terminated at will) segments of his authority to his individual agents, rather than to officers or institions, on the basis of intensely personal relationships. Since, on the same principle, those agents developed strong power bases with different interests and goals and with poorly defined areas of competence, conflicts between them were endemic and required either arbitration by the *Führer,* or by those able to speak in his name, or efforts of coordination by creating complex interdependencies between agencies, new organizations under someone the rivals could agree on, or the like. The system, despite the appearance of monocentrism, could not be further from rational bureaucratic organization principles, and only arbitrary interventions of the leader or his spokesmen could disentangle it. In the German case the importance of certain ideological elements derived from the romantic idealization of the Middle Ages and the hostility to law contributed to giving it, as Robert Koehl has noted, a feudal aspect (Koehl, 1972), understanding by feudalism, in the words of Coulborn, a system in which "the performance of political functions depends on personal agreement between a limited number of individuals . . . since political power is personal rather than institutional, there is relatively little separation of function" and in which "a dispersal of political authority amongst the hierarchy of persons who exercise in their own interests powers normally attributed to the state, which are often in fact derived from its breakup." In other systems in which the emotional bond between the leader and most of his followers was less stable than in the case of Hitler, the political process approached more the model of court politics in a degenerate patrimonial regime. Sometimes the withdrawal of direct intervention of the leaders leads to stalemates, greater bureaucratization, and rationality, but as long as the leader retains legitimacy and/or control of coercion he can impose his will without being restrained by norms or traditions. This is one among the many factors accounting for the unpredictability so often noted in the analysis of totalitarian politics. It is also one of the factors that ultimately may account for the instability of pure totalitarianism and the emergence of post-totalitarian patterns, the rejection of the cult of personality and the emergence of collective leadership, and the search for greater rationality in the allocation of competencies by the leadership that has experienced working with such a leader. It accounts for an effort to institutionalize the charisma of the leader in the party as a corporate body.

Functions of the Party

The totalitarian party, however, is defined not only by its unique structure but by its functions. Functions obviously change from one period in the development of the regime to another. They are different in the stage of creating a power vacuum in a previous regime, particularly a democratic one, in the takeover phase, the phase of consolidation (often combined with considerable tactical compromises with the existing power structure, social interests, and pretotalitarian institutions in a two-step-forward, one-step-backward pattern to neutralize them), in the phase of purging itself from those co-opted in that consolidation process, in the renewed efforts of mass mobilization followed by more stable domination of an atomized society (Kornhauser, 1959; Dallin and Breslauer, 1970), to a final phase of administering society without basis for principled opposition but facing complex policy decisions heading to a moderate degree of pluralism among decision makers even within the party. The scholarly literature focusing on politics in totalitarian regimes rather than on the process of their establishment, particularly in the case of Nazi Germany, and the more monographic work on particular policy areas make us more conscious of those phases and the very different functions performed by the party and its organization in each of them. It is impossible to summarize here in a comparative perspective these problems, and therefore we have to describe the functions of the party without taking into account the high and low tides in their performance (Orlow, 1973).

Foremost among its functions is the politicization of the masses, their incorporation in-cadration, integration, conscientization, and conversion, and their reciprocals, the detachment from other bonds, the destruction of the autonomy of other organizations, uprooting of other values, and desocialization. This process is achieved by a mixture, which is very different in various totalitarian systems, of propaganda, education, and coercion. It is here where the different styles of totaitarian systems become most visible. There is an abyss between the brutal regimentation of the Nazis in their mass organizations and the sophisticated combination in China of coercion in the land reform and the "speaking bitterness," the small groups organized by party cadres and activists for thought reform, propaganda, and coercion, in very different proportions in different phases (Townsend, 1972; Schurmann, 1968). This function of integration and conscientization also accounts for the importance assigned in such parties to the youth organization as the recruiting ground for future leaders and to counteract the socializing influences of family and church (Brandenburg, 1968; Klönne, 1957; Kassof, 1965; Germino, 1959). The in-cadration of masses not ready to join the party and participate in its many activities is to be achieved by the many functional organizations to which people have to belong to achieve other ends. In the case of Nazi Germany, this, given the large number of organizations and their high rate of penetration into their constituencies (which contrasts within the theory of mass society of Kornhauser, 1959, as Lepsius, 1968, has noted), required either the destruction or the infiltration and *Gleichschaltung* of those organizations. An example: the *Doppolavoro* and *Kraft durch Freude* organizations of leisure time in Italy and Germany show how even the free time can, by voluntary participation on apolitical grounds, be used for political socialization. In the case of less developed countries one of the great achievements of totalitarian parties is to create such functional organizations that can serve as transmission belts. It is important to stress that participation is not passive but involves active engagement in campaigns for the benefit of community, from welfare to beautification, sports to culture, and, in developing countries, for production on the basis of moral incentives. Organizations like a voluntary or compulsory labor service, *Arbeitsdienst,* capture motivations such as in the United States led young people to join the Peace Corps. Brigades of volunteers also serve as a recruiting ground of activists and future leaders. In fact, one of the threats to the totalitarian ideological socialization is that many participants become more interested in the substantive functions of such organizations and activities than in ideological schooling (Pipping, 1954, pp. 324–25). In a stabilized totalitarian society the careful screening and indoctrination of educators obviously lowers the saliency of these socialization functions of the party and probably weakens the responsiveness of those tired of indoctrination.

The integrative function explains the importance assigned to elections and plebiscites in totalitarian systems and their use to test the effectiveness of the party and its mass organizations in their success of getting out the vote.[23] Voting is not just a duty but an opportunity to express publicly, visibly, and preferably joyously the identification with the regime. Many types of authoritarian regimes less concerned with democratic legitimation and ideological conversion just put off elections or tolerate apathy as long as their candidates get elected.

The second central function of the totalitarian party is the recruitment, testing, selection, and training of the new political elite. This is obvious in the phase of the struggle for power in opposition, underground, revolution, and civil war. In the process of consolidation, co-optation into the party of experts and people of the establishment swells its ranks, often leading to the closure of admission and even purges of the newcomers (Rigby, 1968, pp. 178–81; Aquarone, 1965, pp. 379–81; Orlow, 1973, pp. 202–5; Buchheim, 1958). Ideally, once the party has consolidated itself in power, the recruitment should take place through socialization in the youth organizations, a so-called *leva fascista,* literally "fascist draft," by which those who graduate from the youth organizations are admitted into the party. The compulsory or at least mass character of those youth organizations, however, limits their effectiveness as a selection mechanism, and more stringent and specialized systems of recruitment tend to be devised. The dilemma of expert versus red and the search for the red expert often leads to lateral entry, particularly through active participation in party-affiliated mass organizations. Success of the party ultimately depends in a stabilized totalitarian system on its capacity to attract people in different sectors of society who are loyal to the regime but uninterested in political activism, contact with the masses, and political responsibilities. Recruitment and cadre selection in a stabilized totalitarian system finds itself between the Scylla and Charybdis of professionalization, with the consequent loss of representativeness by emphasizing educational requirements, and the promotion of activists without qualification with the risk of incompetence. The efforts to combine a broad recruitment, particularly in communist systems from the working class in the factories, with rapid and intensive training in party programs in organizational and managerial skills reflect this dilemma (Rigby, 1968, pp. 115–25; Ludz, 1964 and 1970). In communist systems the important role of the party in the management of production and economic planning makes this problem central. It also accounts for the more rapid routinization of totalitarianism in advanced industrial communist societies.

One major function of totalitarian parties is to control a variety of specialized functions that can become independent, nonpolitical centers of power. The party is a recruiting ground for the political commissars in the army (Kolkowicz, 1967 and 1971), and in this respect it is interesting to remember that the Nazis in the last period of their rule were moving to partify the army (Orlow, 1973, pp. 460–62). The importance of coercion of opponents in the struggle to gain power, the tradition of secrecy developed in the period of illegality under repressive regimes, the international tension that has often surrounded the new regime, and the emergence of many of them in a civil war lead to an almost projective fear of subversion, conspiracy, and aggression, and consequently to a propensity for terror. Since a defense of order involves political considerations, a strictly professional police is largely inadequate, and therefore the politicization of police forces and the creation of party militias are characteristic of totalitarian systems. The organizations involved tend to be heavily recruited through party channels.

However, the main function of the party is to be present in the many sponsored organizations and those that have been taken over— trade unions, cooperatives, professional and interest groups. In a socialized economy this control function acquires a special sense. There is a great variety in the way of conceiving this "leading and guiding function" of the party, and volumes have been written on the shifting conception of the relationship between party and society, both in ideology and practice, particularly in communist countries.

Even among the Nazis, as Orlow (1973, pp. 14–16) has pointed out, two conceptions of the role of the NSDAP emerged, identified with Hess, the "representative of the *Führer*," and Ley, the head of the Party Organization Office and the Labor Front. The key terms in the differing approaches were "control" and *"Betreuung"* ("welfare, taking care"), signaling two different ways of responding to a complex, sophisticated, industrialized society, ways that largely remained intact during the years of struggle for and after the seizuire of power. According to Ley, the synthetic party community, *Gemeinschaft,* created in the course of the struggle, should merge with the remaining, now politicized segment of the German social organism and form a *Volksgemeinschaft,* a people's community, through *Betreuung* ("taking care of the needs of the people through a politically motivated welfare state"), emphasizing less the elite status of membership and the cadre organization by ultimately fusing the party with the Labor Front into a single mass organization. His opponents felt that far from becoming a *Volksgemeinschaft,* Germany should remain a society *(Gesellschaft)* in which the key activity of the party was controlled through a tightly knit centralized organization with an elite co-opted membership and a fanatic but technically and administratively competent functionary corps. Neither of the two conceptions won the endorsement of Hitler, but basically the regime was closer to the second alternative.

State and Party

The important role of the party in providing leadership to many affiliated or sponsored organizations that control other institutions should not lead us to forget that the main function of the party is to fill political offices at all levels of government through elections or appointments. Since the officeholders in totalitarian systems, in contrast to competitive political systems, are assured their position as long as they enjoy the confidence of the party, basically the party has its own extensive and often specialized bureaucracies and the relation between government and party is central to these systems. The extent to which the party in government is or is not independent from the party as an organization, attempts to subordinate or ignore the party, or the party organization attempts to give orders to its representatives at all levels of government is perhaps the most interesting question in the study of totalitarian parties. Only when the party organization is superior or equal to the government can we speak of a totalitarian system.[24] Without that tension the system degenerates into bureaucratic authoritarianism, losing its linkage with the society and much of its mobilization and dynamic potential. Mao's statement that the party is the instrument that "forges the resolution of the contradiction between state and society under socialism" is a very exact formulation of this novel phenomenon (Schurmann, 1968, p. 112). The superiority of the state apparatus even when manned by party members characterizes a pretotalitarian phase of the regime, a failure of the totalitarian drive, as in the case of Italy, or the transition to a post-totalitarian system. It is fundamental to remember that in the Marxist ideological tradition there is no legitimacy in the postcapitalist society for the state apparatus and that ultimately the utopian stage will represent the withering away of the state. What is less known and almost deliberately forgotten is that Hitler in *Mein Kampf* expressed his hostility to the state and the traditional German *Staatsgläubigkeit.* As he writes:

> It is therefore the first obligation of the new movement standing on the ground of the folkish world view to make sure that the conception of the nature and purpose of the state attains a uniform and clear character.
> Thus the basic realization is: that the state represents no end but a means. It is, to be sure, the premise for the formation of higher human culture, but not its cause, which lies exclusively in the existence of a race capable of culture. . . . thus the precondition for the existence of a higher humanity is not the state but the nation possessing the necessary ability . . . of course as I have said before, it is easier to see in state authority the near formal mechanism of an organization, than the sovereign embodiment of a nationality's instinct of self preservation on earth. (1924–26, p. 391)

The chapter goes on from here into a rambling discourse on race, biological selection, and a socialization informed by those values. The radical community is basically counterposed to the state, particularly a state like the German that does not coincide with that community. As Hannah Arendt (1966, pp. 257–66) rightly noted, the totalitarian movements cannot be understood without reference to the hostility to the state, and to conventional patriotism and the substitution by a loyalty to a larger social unit. She rightly links totalitarianism with the pan-movements that appeared in Central and Eastern Europe, where state and national boundaries did not tend to coincide like in the West. Hitler, born Austrian, deserter from the Imperial Army, serving in that of his adopted country, Germany, clearly reflects this disjunction between state and broader social community. The international proletariat and the identification of socialism in one country with leadership of a world political movement beyond its borders is the Marxist equivalent. In this context the ideological and organizational development in Italy and in Mussolini's mind put inherent limits to a totalitarian development. Hitler's confused idea in the second book of *Mein Kampf* of a distinction between subjects and citizens of the state, which found its legal expression in the Nuremberg racial laws, differentiates his regime from both the civic culture of democracies and traditional and authoritarian conceptions of the state.

The Party in Theory and Reality

The description of both manifest and latent functions of the party we have presented is based largely on the ideological conception, programatic statements, ideal typical descriptions, and research on the overlap between parties and other institutions. The question is, To what extent do party cadres, particularly at the middle and lower levels, and party members behave as expected? There are obvious variations from one totalitarian system to another, from one period or phase to another, which monographic research, particularly studies of regional and local life under such regimes, is revealing every day.[25] The research points out that, for a variety of reasons, there is considerable degree of policy diversion, that is, alteration of policies from within the power structure in directions not wanted by the rulers. It also shows that particularly on the periphery the local organs of the party, far away from the centers of ideological infighting at the top, might concentrate their attention on a function that appears in the theory of totalitarian parties but tends to be less emphasized, to represent the interests of the constituencies before higher-up party, and government, bureaucracies. This point has been particularly emphasized by Jerry F. Hough (1969) for the Soviet Union, but a reading of literature on Nazi local party activities would probably show the same pattern, even when in a more limited sphere, in view of the function of the Soviet party in the economy. The representation of the interests of territorial communities (perhaps facilitated because of a relatively centralized system with a national policy and monocentrism for major decisions) by the local party organizations, is not unlike democratic parties and democratically elected lower government units. Less divided over and involved in overall policy formulation and resource collection, they can agree on demanding as much as possible from the center for the benefit of their constituents. Successful, influential, old-time party leaders can act as mediators between a variety of local, special, and even private interests and the higher bureaucratic structures, and this, as in democratic government, is obviously an opportunity for corruption and for diversion of policy.

Somewhat similarly, the ideologically assigned functions of a party at the higher levels become often secondary to those of bureaucratic infighting between organizations, both in the party and in the government controlled by party officials, interested, like their civil servants, in protecting the autonomy of the organization from the party. Totalitarian politics, despite its mobilizational component, very often gets clogged down in endless bureaucratic infighting, which in the German case, given the very personal direct relations of many of the top leaders with Hitler, led to feudal infighting and court politics and consumed most of the energies of the elite. Thus the limited span of attention of the top levels of leadership, even their work habits, the shifting goals and policies often hastily decided, run counter to any image of totalitarian politics as an efficient machine frictionlessly transmitting decisions from the top to the bottom. However, a superficial reading of Edward Peterson's book (1969) *The Limits of Hitler's Power* should not lead us to forget that many, and particularly the really important, wishes of the *Führer* were ultimately implemented without the possibility of any effective opposition to them, and that the "rule of anticipated reactions" made the whole system responsive to decisions congruent with the image of his power and his basic policies, or of those close to him. In a sense, an image of an all-powerful leader making all the decisions is empirically false, but in another sense it is true, since the men chosen by him or tolerated around him will act in such a system largely as they think he expects them to do. In this sense, contrary to finding in the total power of the leader an alibi for the party and other organizations, they have to share in the responsibility for decisions (Speer, 1971, pp. 649–50). Without them there cannot be even the attempt to create a totalitarian society, nor can there be the attempt without the responsiveness to their expectations of a large number of middle and lower cadres, party members, and citizens whatever the motivation, even if as minimal as the security of the individual and his or her family. The lesser commitment of many of the top leaders to such a total control for the sake of certain utopian goals of social mobilization, and as a result the lesser commitment throughout the structure of the state, explains that Italian Fascism never reached the level of control and mobilization that the pronouncements of the *Duce* and the legal enactments would lead us to expect. This in turn might have been a reflection of the degree to which Italians felt more strongly other loyalties and interests, even particularistic ties embedded in the culture, than loyalty to the PNF. In our discussion of the conditions for the emergence of totalitarianism we shall note some of the social, economic, cultural, and psychological conditions that make it possible for a totalitarian organization to approach even remotely its utopian self-image that has served us to construct the ideal type. We have seen, however, that it is dangerous to lose sight of the degree to which a limited number of political systems, in particular historical phases, approach the totalitarian utopia, both for evil and for good.

Communist and Fascist Parties

There are many important differences between communist and fascist totalitarian parties, not only in the ideology and policies, as we noted before, but in the organizational structure. The most important difference is the emphasis in the fascist parties on the *Führerprinzip* (Vierhaus, 1964; Nyomarkay, 1967; Horn, 1972), specifically in the Nazi case, which contrasts with the democratic component of democratic socialism, whatever similarities emerged in practice in the Stalinist period. The different ideological and formal principle is of central importance. Some degree of internal party democracy is possible in communist parties and there is ideological basis for those who want to move in that direction, while there was none in the National Socialist case.

Another major difference between the national socialist totalitarian party and Stalinist parties is the formal institutionalization of paramilitary organizations like the SA and the SS. Already the Italian Fascists had attempted, with the creation of the *Milizia volontaria per la sicurezza nazionale* (MVSN), to absorb the more unruly elements of the party *squadrismo* and to give a legal and institutional basis to the repression in support of the regime. In Italy its subordination to the head of the government and the coordination with the army for the appointment of officers did not allow it to become a real political army. The evolution of the SA (Werner, 1964) and particularly the SS (Höhne, 1969; Krausnick et al., 1968), which in the course of the war became a real party army, parallel to the army of the state but not subject to its control and influence, was one of the basic differences with Italy that assured the turn toward totalitarianism of the Nazi regime. There have been similar tendencies in communist countries, but the total control by the political leadership of the regular army and its politicization, as well as the politicization of the police, have prevented the emergence of organizations of violence as part of the party and distinct from those more professional organizations. The difference, while congruent with the ideological romanticization of violence in fascism and the nationalist admiration for the armed forces, can also be explained by the different process of takeover of power. The fascist parties emerged in liberal democratic societies that allowed the opponents a large degree of freedom of organization and tolerated, if not indirectly encouraged, for a variety of reasons (reaction to communist revolutionary attempts or fear of a highly organized and mobilized working class, illegal rearmament in violation of the Versailles treaty), the emergence of paramilitary organizations and armed party groups. Once the fascist leadership had taken over a state thanks largely to the violence and the threat created by those organizations, it was not ready to disband them even when they were forced to compromise with the establishment, particularly the military, which was suspicious of them. Such a compromise and fear of a second revolution led in Germany to the bloody purge of the SA in 1934, which, however, initiated the rise of the SS and, contrary to formal promises to the army, broke the monopoly of armed forces (Mau, 1953). Those organizations based on a voluntary recruitment attracted a strange mixture of violence-prone persons—fanatical idealists, mercenaries, and sadists—who nonetheless could feel, on the basis of elaborate rituals, the comradeship of the barracks; the romantic, pseudofeudal rhetoric of "loyalty is mine honour" plus their rejection by civil society produced a sense of being the vanguard of the movement, a mixture of monastic and chivalry order. It was this organization that implemented the most monstrous aspects of the totalitarian utopia. As Himmler said:

> These measures could not be carried out by a police force consisting simply of officials. A body which had merely sworn the normal official oath would not have the necessary strength. These measures could only be tolerable and could only be carried out by an organization consisting of the staunchest individuals, of fanatical, deeply committed National Socialists. The SS believes it is such an organization, considers that it is fitted for this task and so has assumed this responsibility. (Buchheim, 1968b, p. 366)

In the communist countries the party was born in secrecy without opportunity to organize freely—and even less so its strong arm. The takeover of power took place either in societies in which the existing establishments had disintegrated or under the sponsorship of the Soviet army. In most cases the takeover required a more or less prolonged civil war often mixed, like in China or Vietnam, with a national independence struggle. In such circumstances the party acted as a core organizing element of a new army, the Red Army, the People's Liberation Army, and in the areas controlled by the revolutionaries the party was able to establish its own police, the *Cheka,* and its successor organization staffed by loyal party members. Neither the army nor the police had to compete with organizations created before the takeover, with their distinct professional status and self-conception and therefore perceived as unreliable from a political point of view. Even though there is evidence of idealization of the role of the *chekist,* there was no need to develop a distinctive ethos for the instruments of coercion and make them elitist, voluntary, ideological organizations (Barghoorn, 1971). It was possible to conceive of them as part of the state apparatus, intimately coordinated with the party but never equal or potentially superior to the party mass organization. It is no accident that the revolutionaries in the SA would have preferred a militia type of army in which they would have played a leading role and that a segment of the SS, the Waffen SS, showed tendencies to drift apart from the more terroristic *Verfügungstruppe* and were less interested in ideology, seeking ultimately the respectability of the armed forces. In authoritarian regimes with totalitarian tendencies, particularly with a fascist party, the failure to build an independent armed militia to challenge the monopoly of force in the hands of the army and traditional police corps is one of the best signs of the limit to the total politicization and control of the society.

Excursus on Terror

The claim of the modern state to monopolize the use of force is one of its defining characteristics, but certainly regimes differ widely in the amount, type, and ways of using coercion. Totalitarian systems, at least in some of their phases, have been characterized by massive coercion—police acting unrestrained by any outside controls, concentration camps and torture, imprisonment and executions without proof of guilt, repressive measures against whole categories of people, the absence of public trial and even any opportunity for defense, the imposition of penalties totally out of proportion to the actions of the accused, all on a scale without precedence in recent history (Solzhenitsyn, 1973).

Political terror, defined by Dallin and Breslauer (1970, p. 7) as "the arbitrary use, by organs of the political authority of severe coercion against individuals or groups, the credible threat of such use or the arbitrary extermination of such individuals or groups," has certainly characterized totalitarian rule. This has led Hannah Arendt (1966, p. 474) to define totalitarianism as "a form of government whose essence is terror and whose principle of action is the logicality of ideological thinking." However, it is undeniable that the forms of coercion we have mentioned and political terror can be found in political systems that otherwise, without stretching the term, could not be called totalitarian (Chapman, 1970). Certainly, nondemocratic systems not characterized by "the logicality of ideological thinking" have shown their capacity for terror and the violation of the most elementary human rights. We only have to think of the rule of Trujillo in the Dominican Republic, where the arbitrary terror exercised by one man did not have or need ideological justification and was not characterized by modern forms of political mobilization.

On the other side, we can conceive regimes with the characteristics we have used in defining totalitarianism, and which distinguish them from those we characterize as authoritarian, without political terror. Certainly in such regimes we cannot expect the political freedoms enjoyed by a citizen of a democracy, but we can expect limits on the arbitrary power of the police, certain legal, particularly procedural, guarantees, and a return to the principle of *nullum crimen sine lege,* which makes it possible for those not willing to take the risk of violating the laws to enjoy a modicum of security. Even with laws that punish behavior considered legal in other societies, like publishing criticism of the government, associating for political purposes or the defense of interests, participating in strikes, etc., the definition of such acts as crimes, the exclusion of retroactive application of the law, combined with a mininium of procedural guarantees for the defendant, independence of the judiciary from direct intervention of the authorities, and restraints on the police, would allow the citizen who does not contest the regime to live without fear. A regime with those characteristics could still be highly monopolistic in its power structure, be guided by ideological commitment, and demand and reward active participation in its organizations. It would be, in our view, totalitarianism without terror. Its legal system would be repressive rather than liberal but certainly different from Stalinism or the rule of the SS under Hitler. The Soviet Union in recent years, with the introduction of what is called "socialist legality," is moving in this direction (Barghoorn, 1972, Chapter 10; Lipson, 1968; Weiner, 1970; Berman and Spindler, 1972).

To summarize our argument, while terror acquired a unique importance in totalitarian systems, many of its manifestations are not absent in regimes that lack many of the characteristics used by most authors to characterize totalitarianism, and we can conceive of particularly stabilized systems with all the characteristics of totalitarianism except widespread and all-pervasive terror. It is for that reason we have not included terror in our definition of totalitarianism.

We cannot ignore, however, the distinctive forms and scale of repression under totalitarianism and have to raise the question: Was the terror that accompanied it, without being a necessary consequence, a likely result of that type of regime rather than of the personality of men like Stalin and Hitler? We would argue that the system made those leaders possible but not inevitable. We also have to ask if and why terror in those systems had some characteristics not found elsewhere. Does the terror of different totalitarian systems differ? Which were functions and consequences of terror? Can we distinguish different types of terror, corresponding to different phases in those regimes? These and other questions would bring us closer to an answer to the question, How was it possible? In addition we shall ask the question, What forms does terror and coercion take in authoritarian regimes? Are they different, and if so, can we link the differences to the characteristics defining totalitarian and authoritarian regimes?

Coercion in totalitarian systems has shown the following characteristics: (1) its unprecedented scale, (2) its use against social categories without consideration of guilt for specific acts, (3) the disregard for even the appearance of legal procedures, the formalities of the trial, and the opportunity for some kind of defense, in imposing penalties, (4) the moral self-righteousness and often the publicity surrounding it, (5) the extension of the terror to members of the elite, (6) the extension to members of the family of the accused not involved in the crime, (7) the emphasis on the intent and social characteristics of the accused rather than on his actions, (8) the use of organizations of the state and/or the party rather than of so-called uncontrolled elements, and the size and complexity of those organizations, (9) the continuing and sometimes growing terror after the consolidation of the regime in power, and (10) the nonexclusion of the leadership of the armed forces from the repressive policy.

In addition, with the all-important position of the party in the society, a new form of sanction emerges: the exclusion from party membership, the purges that affect decisively the life chances of people and their social relations.

The scale in number of lives lost, man-years in concentration camps, and people arrested and subject to limitations of freedom of movement not resulting from strictly military operations is unique in modern repressive societies. While there can be debates about the exactness of statistical estimates, the magnitude is beyond discussion. Conquest (1968) has brought together the scattered evidence on the number of arrests, executions, and prisoners and death in camps and the estimates that can be derived from population census data. The estimate for executions in the late 1930s runs into around 1 million persons. Calculations for the number of inmates in camps around 1940 range between 6.5 and 12 million, depending on the year and the method of estimate. Taking the conservative figure of an average over the period 1936–1950, inclusive of an 8 million population of the camps and a 10 percent death rate per annum, we get a total casualty figure of 12 million dead. Adding to them the million executions of the period, the casualties of the pre-Yezhov era of Stalin's rule (1930–1936), those sent to camps who died, and the 3.5 million victims of the collectivization, Conquest reaches the figure of 20 million dead in 23 years of Stalin's rule. The figures for China in the consolidation phase are lower, but Mao admitted in February 1967 that in the first five years of communist rule some 800,000 "enemies of the people" had been killed, while others estimate the number between 1 and 3 million, that is, between $1/3$ and $1/2$ of 1 percent of the population (Dallin and Breslauer, 1970, p. 55). Reitlinger (1968, pp. 533–46) estimates that the number of victims of the Nazi "final solution of the Jewish problem" ranges between 4.2 and 4.5 million persons, with a total loss of Jewish life estimated at 6 million. It Italy, despite strong tendencies toward totalitarianism, terror except in the struggle for power and the short-lived Republic of Salo period was more limited. The Special Tribunal for the Defense of the State sentenced over the years 33 persons to death, of whom 22 were executed, and tried 5,619, sentencing 4,596 to an average of five years (Aquarone, 1965, p. 104). Undoubtedly the scale of repression in a number of regimes approaching far less the totalitarian model than Italy has been greater.

As significant, if not more, than the scale of the terror in some totalitarian systems has been its use against whole categories of people irrespective of any evidence of guilt or even intention of threatening the political system. The deprivation of human rights, wholesale arrests, and extermination as a result of deliberately formulated government policy by the agents of the state or the party of those identified, in the case of the Nazis, as Jews, gypsies (Döring, 1964), members of religious sects, biologically unfit, certain prisoners of war, or sectors of the population of occupied territories (Institut für Zeitgeschichte, 1958) and, in the case of communist countries, as belonging to certain social categories that could be labeled counterrevolutionary, like landlords, the clergy, and kulaks, and as members of ethnic groups on the basis of collective guilt (Conquest, 1960), have been unique in modern times. In those cases, the victims did not need to be personally guilty of any acts against the state or the social order, nor did their persecutors have to attempt to make a case against them based on any charges, trumped up or real, nor could they represent in many cases any real threat even if they had wanted to do so. Their fate was the result of ideological preconceptions, often, like in the case of Hitler, formulated before coming to power, which deprived those people of their human character and linked the creation of a better society with their destruction. The holocaust was in the eyes of a Himmler (Bracher, 1970; Krausnick et al., 1968) a painful duty at the service of historical tasks for which future generations would be grateful.

In every political system there are miscarriages of justice, violations of procedural guarantees, obstacles to an adequate defense, biased courts, unfair trials, as well as illegal violence against political opponents ordered or condoned by those in power. But the systematic, large-scale, formally organized imposition of penalties, including death, without even the semblance of an adversary procedure and in the absence of an emergency situation, has been characteristic of totalitarian systems. The power of the special boards of the Ministry of Internal Affairs in the Soviet Union, on the basis of the 1934 statute, effective until 1953, to sentence people in absentia and without trial or counsel to labor camps is only one example. The executions ordered by the *Führer* without intervention of any regular or extraordinary courts that began with the purge of the SA leadership and other opponents in "the night of the long knives" in 1934, legalized by a law as emergency defense of the state, officially of 77 persons but perhaps three times as many, was only the beginning of the legalization of lawlessness (Bloch, 1970; Bracher, 1970; Mau, 1953). The terror of totalitarianism is not only the perversion and misuse of justice in the courts or the unofficial tolerance for illegal acts of the authorities that we find in many authoritarian regimes, and sometimes in democracies, but the normative institutionalization of such practices and their ideological justification sometimes even in the learned commentaries of jurists. The writing of Soviet and Nazi legal theorists, sometimes men of intellectual distinction—like Carl Schmitt—reflect and articulate that break with a long legal tradition. When Vyshinsky, the attorney general of the USSR, wrote in 1935,

> The formal law is subordinate to the law of the revolution. There might be collisions and discrepancies between the formal commands of laws and those of the proletarian revolution. . . . This collision

must be solved only by the subordination of the formal commands of
law to those of party policy (Berman, 1963, pp. 42–43),

he was expressing a thought that we will not find so frequently and
authoritatively stated in any authoritarian regime.

The most striking characteristic of terror under totalitarianism and
perhaps the explanation for its pervasiveness and scope is the moral
self-righteousness with which it is justified by the rulers and their supporters, sometimes publicly, other times in the inner circle. Often it
even conflicts with more pragmatic goals of the system. The nonpurely
instrumental character of the terror derived from the passion for unanimity, the ideal of conflictlessness, the need to eradicate totally social
groups defined as evil as a historical task, the explicit rejection of traditional moral standards that would make other men hesitate or feel
guilty, and the demand of abdication of personal responsibility constitute some of the unique characteristics of totalitarian terror (Arendt,
1963; Cohn, 1966; Jäger, 1967; Barghoorn, 1971; Dicks, 1972). They
ultimately are derived from the strength of ideological commitments.
They also explain why many of the agents of terror could be otherwise
normal men in their daily life, rather than psychologically defective
persons. Let us not forget that Khrushchev in his secret speech of February 1956 concludes, after his appalling revelations and his negative
portrayal of Stalin's personality, saying:

> Stalin was convinced that it was necessary for the defence of the in-
> terests of the working class against the plotting of the enemies and
> against the attack of the imperialist camp. He saw this from the posi-
> tion of the working class, the interests of the working people, the in-
> terests of the victory of Socialism and Communism. We cannot say
> that these were the deeds of a giddy despot. He considered that this
> should be done in the interests of the Party, of the working masses, in
> the name of defence of the revolution's gains. In this lies the whole
> tragedy. (Conquest, 1968, p. 66)

Another unique feature is the extension of the terror to members of
the elite, in fact, the harsher punishment particularly under Stalin of
those who had made the revolution with him and those who had positions of responsibility and whose loss of favor or trust in other systems
would lead to their demotion, return to private life, and often to power-
less but well-paid or prestigeful sinecures. In the case of Stalin, the victims were not only Soviet citizens but the leaders of foreign Communist

parties living in the USSR and the satellite countries (Kriegel, 1972; Oren, 1973). Few data could tell the grim story of political terror better than those of Weber (1969, pp. 36–37) on the fate of the 504 leading cadres of the German Party (KPD) before Hitler: of the 136 who died violently, 86 (17 percent) were victims of the Nazis and 43 (9 percent) of Stalinist and East German purges. Members of the elite that lose in the struggle for power, even when they cannot represent a real threat, are to be destroyed, dishonored, and under Stalinism made to confess crimes they did not commit and to become nonpersons even in the writing of history (Leites and Bernaut, 1954; Brzezinski, 1956; Kriegel, 1972; Levytsky, 1974). As a result of the subordination of the military to the political leadership and the capacity of the party or police units to challenge the monopoly of force of the army, even the military leadership cannot escape political repression and a nonmilitary jurisdiction. The figures given by Conquest (1968, p. 485) for the Stalinist purges—3 of the 5 marshalls, 14 of the 16 army commanders Class I and II, 60 of the 67 corps commanders, 136 of the 199 divisional commanders, and about half of the officer corps, some 35,000 either shot or imprisoned—are testimony of that capacity. In the case of Germany, 20 generals of the army executed among 675 do not represent comparable figures, particularly considering the actual involvement in the plot of July 1944 against Hitler, but show the capacity to punish even in wartime the high command (Zapf, 1965, p. 164). Another unique characteristic is the extension of legal responsibility to the members of the family of the accused irrespective of complicity in their acts, both in the Nazi *Sippenhaft* (arrest of the family) and in the provisions of Article 58 (i.c.) of the criminal code of the RSFSR that punished "in the event of flight abroad of a member of the armed forces, the adult members of his family if they assisted him . . . or even if they knew about the crime but failed to report," and made "the remaining members of the family, and those living with him or dependent on him at the time of the commission of the crime liable to exile to the remote areas of Siberia for a period of five years" (Conquest, 1968, p. 558). The Nazi taking away the children of those involved in the 20th of July plot and the praise given to members of the youth organizations ready to denounce their parents are examples of the disregard for family bonds under totalitarian terror.

The ideological basis of totalitarian coercion leads to a rejection of legal formalism even in the definitions of crime, in the formulation of the accusation by the prosecutors, the argumentation of the judges of their sentences, and the variations in the punishment. Rather than strict laws and draconian but clearly established penalties, the tendency is to introduce subjective considerations, diffuse standards, and unpredictable sentences more dependent on who the defendant is than on his legally typified actions. Even the harshest military summary justice, by contrast, tends to be formalistic and even legalistic, paying little attention to the motive and not trying to justify its decisions except on the basis of repressive legislation and inarticulated, pragmatic considerations. Political justice in totalitarian regimes tries to show the base motives of the actor, to punish his intention rather than just his acts. The punishment is to reflect substantive ideological criteria, like the *gesunde Volksempfinden* ("the healthy sense of the people") or "socialist legal consciousness," and the pedagogical and exemplary rather than retributional aspects. The emphasis on the actor and his motive rather than the act itself is closely linked with the consideration given to the social background of the defendant and the ideological characterization of entire social groups. This explains the paradox that legal positivism in authoritarian settings serves the repressive state and in totalitarian systems is substituted by a sociological conception of law with legal positivism becoming an obstacle to the desires of the rulers (Schorn, 1959; Staff, 1964; Johe, 1967; Weinkauff, 1968).

Another tendency is the greater implication of the whole society in the repressive process, which is not left in the hands of a professional police and the courts but tends to involve actively or passively many members of the society through participation in the party and its formations, typically commanding those among high-status groups who had joined the SS to a tour of concentration camp duty, by making party members informers on their neighbors, by widespread publicity of selected political trials, and particularly in China through participation of the whole community in the process of repression—the "speaking bitterness" against landlords and efforts toward "thought reform" with the participation of the work group or the community. The Moscow show trials, the great purge, and the trial before the *Volksgerichtshof*—People's Court—of those involved in the plot against Hitler and their propagandistic exploitation are examples of this pattern without many parallels in authoritarian regimes (Travaglini, 1963). This does not exclude on the other hand the utmost secrecy surrounding other manifestations of the terror. Without accepting the thesis of Hannah Arendt that terror under totalitarianism increases with the consolidation of the regime and the weakness of its opponents, we can say that it certainly is not limited to or greatest in the takeover stage, as it tends to be in most authoritarian regimes. Perhaps because terror is not just instrumental in the way that Lenin and Trotsky conceived it when the latter wrote:

> The question as to who is to rule . . . will be decided on either side not by references to the paragraphs of the constitution, but by the employment of all forms of violence . . . war like revolution is founded upon intimidation, a victorious war generally destroys only an insignificant part of the conquered army intimidating the remainder and breaking their will, the revolution works in the same way, it kills individuals and intimidates thousands. (Dallin and Breslauer, 1970, p. 77)

That type of terror in the takeover stage would be found in most authoritarian regimes, particularly when confronted with a well-organized opponent whose defeat is not assured, as in the case of Spain after the Civil War or in Chile today.

Totalitarian terror acquires its unique character from the centrality of ideology for many of those participating in it. As Hitler had remarked, "Any violence which does not spring from a firm spiritual base will be wavering and uncertain, it lacks the stability which can only rest in a fanatical outlook." However, it would not be possible without the organizational resources provided by the cadres and activists of a party committed to the defense of the regime. Without those factors it would not reach the intensity and scope or the systematic character that it can but does not necessarily reach under totalitarianism. Terror under some authoritarian regimes can be widespread, and under those that we shall call sultanistic, equally if not more arbitrary, but as we think we have shown it is likely to be very different.

In accounting for that difference one major factor is that in most authoritarian regimes the repressive function is left to the armed forces, which, while far from reluctant to use violence and expeditious methods of justice, tend to have a bureaucratic mentality emphasizing rules and procedures and none of the interest of intellectually more sophisticated men in motives and ideological justifications and little desire to explain their actions to the people and to gain their support. Unfortunately, we have no comparative analysis of political trials under different types of political systems to capture the different styles of the proceedings under totalitarianism and authoritarian regimes. A reading of the reporting in the mass media and systematic observation would certainly reveal some of the basic differences.

In totalitarian systems the independence of the regular courts is likely to disappear and their politicization to be the goal of the regime (Wagner, 1968), while most authoritarian regimes tend to leave to the regular judiciary its traditional degree of independence while they shift the politically relevant cases to special courts, generally the military justice (Toharia, 1974). We find here another example of the breakdown of the differentiation between state and society, politics and administration under totalitarianism.

There are undoubtedly major differences in the forms of repression under different totalitarian systems that should not be ignored but that we cannot fully develop here. It is not always clear to what extent those differences are due to national culture and legal traditions, to the idiosyncrasies of the leadership, to the patterns of behavior acquired in the process of takeover of power, and last but not least to a learning process based on the experience of similar regimes preceding them. Nazi and communist terror are certainly different in many respects, and despite many similarities between communist regimes, Stalinist and Chinese methods differ in many fundamental respects. In Cuba the possibility of emigration (estimated to be 7.1 percent of the population) to Spain and the United States probably limited the need for repression (Fagen, Brody, and O'Leary, 1968). The Nazis, having come in to power in a society whose institutional order had not been destroyed, initially relied much more on manipulated spontaneity and uncontrolled but planned actions than on the normal machinery of the state, which they only slowly transformed to serve their purposes. It also meant the emergence of a dual state and ultimately a parallel state of the SS, as well as a much greater secrecy surrounding their actions. The Nazis never developed the same urge to have the victims confess their guilt and to recognize the rightness of those in power. The self-criticism of the victims of the purges under Stalin has no parallel in Germany. Undoubtedly the communist conception of man as perfectable and the biological determinism underlying the Nazi ideology account in part for the difference. The Chinese, with their idea of the recuperability through "thought reform" and "coercive persuasion" even of class enemies, tend toward a "voluntarism" and "activism" and an emphasis on consciousness that substitutes a sophisticated assault on the individual's identity through self-criticism, confession, self-degradation, punishment, and rehabilitation for strictly physical punishment (Lifton, 1968; Schein, 1961; Townsend, 1972; Vogel, 1967). In this the Chinese carry to the ultimate consequences certain tendencies implicit in the Soviet party. The contrast between Soviet Stalinism and the Chinese communists might also reflect the different process of conquest and consolidation in power, the different relationship to the rural masses in both systems. The patterns of behavior acquired during the revolution and the civil war by the *chekists* could be extended under Stalin to the kulaks by basically urban cadres and created the habits of brutality that would be institutionalized in the *Yezhovshchina*. Perhaps the Chinese also became aware of the fact that certain forms of terror provoke hostility that only terror can repress, that is, of the dysfunctional consequences of terror. Finally, the experience of Stalinist terror accounts for the efforts of the post-Stalinist leadership in the Soviet Union to do away with his excesses, to introduce forms of "socialist legality" while maintaining patterns of coercion very different from those in most authoritarian regimes through the creation of comrades courts and other forms of popular participation in enforcing social and political conformity (O'Connor, 1963; Lipson, 1967). The Committees for the Defense of the Revolution in Cuba, with their multiple social functions, also represent a system of collective vigilance capable of arresting those threatening the political order (Fagen, 1969). Undoubtedly, the 110,000 CDR, with 2 million members, represent a capacity of political integration, socialization, and organizational implementation of various programs that goes far beyond the vigilance activities for which they initially were created to face the counterrevolutionary challenge in the 1960s, but their presence in each neighborhood and work place contributes to providing the coercive organs of the state and party with information it would otherwise not have. In the last analysis, the compliance and efficacy of consolidated totalitarian systems is likely to depend more on such a penetration of the society and the coercive atmosphere it can provide than on the police and indiscriminate terror. It could be argued that initially the Stalinist form of terror was the result of the loss of revolutionary enthusiasm combined with low capacity to satisfy demands and the lack of penetration of the Communist party in many rural areas. Paradoxically, it could be argued that coercive compliance under totalitarianism is more likely to be achieved by the penetration of the party and its mass organizations in the whole society along Chinese lines than the excesses and the surplus of Stalinist police terror.

The great question on the prison walls and one that has no easy answer is, Why? Why did terror take the forms it took, how was it possible to create the machinery to implement it, and why was no one able to stop it? Dallin and Breslauer (1970), those who have written about the great purges (Leites and Bernaut, 1954; Brzezinski, 1956; Conquest, 1968; Gliksman, 1954; Kriegel, 1972), and those who have written on Nazism and the SS (Bracher, 1970; Arendt, 1963, 1966; Cohn, 1966; Krausnick et al., 1968; Höhne, 1969; Dicks, 1972) have all asked these questions. The answers, sometimes conflicting, cannot be discussed in detail here. Undoubtedly terror and its different manifestations have to be explained differently in the variety of systems and historical situations. Any political system established by a minority or even a majority against the will of others who decided to use force to oppose its consolidation will turn to a greater or lesser extent to terror. The greater the conviction of those involved in the conflict and the weaker the support in the whole political community in the absence of a normative framework regulating conflict accepted by both sides, the more coercion. Violence has its legitimate place in revolutionary thought and tends to go with a takeover of power as "measures of suppression and intimidation towards determined and armed counter-revolution," to use Trotsky's words, and "the scientific concept of dictatorship means nothing else but power based directly on violence unrestrained by any laws, absolutely unrestricted by any rules," to use Lenin's expression (Dallin and Breslauer, 1970, pp. 10–11). Without theorizing as much about it, any counterrevolutionary would agree within those formulations substituting the word counterrevolution by revolution. The takeover phase directed at breaking the backbone of the opposition and punishing those collaborating with it, particularly in a civil war, leads to mass violence without concern of hurting innocents. The weakness of the minority attempting to impose a new order is likely to heighten its repression. Terror in turn leads to counterterror and the consequent spiral of violence. The justifications then formulated create the "habit of violence" among those involved in the repression. At this stage the terror can be seen as purely instrumental, even when many of its manifestations go far beyond such a "means-end" relationship to become ends in themselves, as a purifying act carried out by idealists or as a source of gratification of the base motives of its agents. But terror continues and even in many political systems, particularly totalitarian ones, it seems to increase to become more rationalized and bureaucratically controlled when the regime seems most consolidated and counts on at least a passive compliance of most of the population. Dallin and Breslauer (1970) and many others have attempted to explain the continuity and rise in terror by describing its functions for the regime in this new phase, in which the regime attempts to achieve a decisive breakthrough toward critical goals. The more a regime attempts to transform the social order to create the "new man," to change the values of the people, and the greater the speed with which it attempts to achieve those ends, the greater the perception of the resistance to those changes, the more terror. They describe this period as a mobilization phase. The fewer the positive incentives in terms of rewards and the greater the deprivations required to implement the policies of the ruling elite, the greater the terror in the mobilization phase. We find this type of analysis among those who argue that the rapid industrialization of the Soviet Union, which required the transformation of the rural economy and society and consequently deprivations for the peasantry, was at the root of Stalinist terror. In such a view terror is still instrumental and rational, at least for those who accept the goals of the rulers and their timetable as valid and cannot conceive alternative ways to achieve the same goals. Those assumptions undoubtedly do not remain unchallenged and are not easy to prove or disprove. It is certainly difficult to argue that the goals achieved justified the cost in human misery, but it is possible to think that rulers could feel the need to sacrifice one generation for the sake of goals highly valued. Here the ideology, "the spiritual base," of which Hitler spoke, becomes decisive in the fanatical implementation through terror, and we can find here the root of the high probability of terror in totalitarian systems. In this context the emphasis has been on the functions of terror in establishing the monopoly of authority and organization, eliminating all autonomous subgroups, destroying physically and morally not only actual but potential opponents, creating an atomized society in which individuals feel unable to trust others, disrupting even the most elementary solidarities like the family and friendship, creating a widespread sense of personal insecurity leading to compliance and even overcompliance (Moore, 1954). Terror is conceived as social prophylaxis (Gliksman, 1954) and as educational—"unfreezing" the individual's perceptions, assumptions, and attitudes, particularly in the Chinese conception of "thought reform," with a combination of public accusation, confession, and reeducation in small groups. Significantly Kriegel (1972) subtitles her book *La Pédagogie infernale*. It is no accident either that the imagery used in describing the victims so often refers to the opponents as carriers of sickness; we have only to think of the expressions used by Hitler (Jäckel, 1972) to describe the Jews and Mao Tse-tung's view of "the citizen as a patient in need of treatment."

In one case the cure required the destruction of its carrier, in the other a complex process labelled "coercive persuasion." In either case the victims are not considered normal members of the community. The "passion for unanimity" that follows from the commitment to a single belief system, a single hierarchy, and the concomitant definition of orthodoxy and heterodoxy requires the use of coercion within the elite and particularly against intellectuals. Since the right policy goals are presumably linked to the orthodox political beliefs, that kind of terror becomes presumably functional to their implementation. A latent function that often is neglected in the analysis but has been noted particularly for the SS state is that of compromising those connected with the terrorist system and even many ordinary citizens, to assure ultimately their loyalty as fearful accomplices.

The emphasis on those functions runs the risk of making the whole process far too rational and purposive, ignoring that it has a dynamics of its own that cannot be explained by the alleged functions in the mobilization phase. First of all, one cannot ignore the carryover of the habit of terror from the revolutionary takeover period among policemen and activists, nor can one ignore the personal grievances and vendettas and just plain human nastiness that find a now-legitimate outlet. The bureaucratic apparatus itself ends having to justify its existence, and compliance and overcompliance with directives from above produce more and more victims. The assignation to the labor camps of certain economic functions ends creating the need to supply more inmates (Dallin and Nicolaevsky, 1947). The criticism, the hatred, the resistance created by terror and the fear that they arouse in its agents in turn spiral the wave of terror. Finally the Khrushchev speech reminds us of the personality of the top leader and the obedience he can find as a major factor in initiating and maintaining a system of terror. In view of all those noninstrumental reasons for widespread terror we should not overestimate the extent to which it is a prerequisite for the deep social transformations that totalitarian systems want to achieve. That is why we can conceive similar totalitarian systems and comparable social transformations with very different amounts, degrees, and forms of terror, and the same would be true for authoritarian regimes. A frightening and rationally difficult to explain characteristic of Nazi and Stalinist terror was the degree to which it was unnecessary and even dysfunctional for the achievement of the goals those systems had set themselves, the extent to which it had become an evil end in itself (Nove, 1964). This also accounts for the fact that the "decompression" of terror could be introduced relatively easily in the post-Stalin era without serious threats to the system, except in its Eastern European periphery, without a radical change in the nature of the political and socioeconomic system and probably with considerable gains in legitimacy. Certainly the introduction of calculated rather than arbitrary forms of coercion allows for new and before-unknown expressions of dissidence (Tökés, 1974) and with it the need for renewed coercion, but it should not be forgotten that those manifestations of dissidence were made possible by the end of terror. Undoubtedly, as Dallin and Breslauer (1970, p. 90) note, terror may generate alienation, and the abandonment of terror may paradoxically permit the expression of such alienation in the form of organized resistance or revolt, or more mildly in various forms of dissidence. This is why the phase of decompression is a dangerous one for totalitarian and authoritarian regimes that have been highly coercive and not able to create stable bases of legitimacy. Often, if it were not for the fears of the members of the elite of becomming themselves victims of terror and probably for the loss of faith in the ideological commitment, we would expect an increase in coercive measures after such a liberalization phase.

The Internal Dynamics of the Totalitarian System

A systematic analysis of the relative independent contribution of ideology, party, and ruling group or leader to the legitimacy, the formulation of policies, and the mobilization of the population in different totalitarian systems might be one way to conceptualize different types of totalitarian systems and to understand better the processes of change within them. Without ignoring the significance of the other factors we might then distinguish ideological totalitarian systems, power-centered ones, of which those in which the leadership principle becomes dominant would be a specially important subtype, and party-centered ones, which might vary from more bureaucratic to more populist-participatory. We might suggest very tentatively that the dynamics of such regimes move from a highly ideological phase, in which often there is a spectre of a second revolution of those ideologically committed but disappointed with the compromises the leadership had to make with reality in the process of consolidation of power, to more personalized leadership or oligarchic control. In a second phase a more instrumental attitude toward ideology, despite protestations to the contrary, is likely.

In a later one the staff of the ruling group, to assure its continuity, safety, and a certain degree of predictability, tries to limit the power of the leader or ruling group and institutionalize it within the party organization by various attempts of rationalization of the party along a variety of strategies, from populism to an emphasis on technical expertise, and ultimately to the development of more reciprocal links between the middle levels of the party organization and the larger society and its differentiated structures. The more remote the ideological initial thrust and commitment becomes and the more scholastic the use of the ideology, the more the system will either turn to personal power or, once the staff in a Weberian process proceeds to the routinization of charisma and its institutionalization in the party, toward a process of deideologization. This process in turn should open the way to nontotalitarian forms of autocratic rule, though sometimes the rule would be threatened by ideological revivals. This process has to some extent been described in the recent literature on "post-totalitarian" Soviet-type politics[26] as the emergence of the "administered society" by Kassof (1969), "organizational society" by Rigby, the "regime of clerks or bureaucratic politics" by Brzezinski, less descriptively as post-totalitarian by Tucker, and "populist totalitarianism" by Paul Cocks. In the same direction we find a model in which leaders in the party organization, the mass organizations, and other bureaucracies establish for the formulation of policies closer links with different interests. A model for the emergence of group politics is a limited pluralism not only of political factions and organizations but of a variety of economic and professional and even class or regional interests, which ultimately should lead to the transformation into a kind of system that would no longer deserve the name of totalitarian. Gordon Skilling in his work has very hesitantly and imprecisely described the kind of system that might emerge this way in the womb of a totalitarian system. However, there would be some serious difficulties with such a transformation, given the importance of the ultimate legitimation of the system in the absence of a linkage with the ideology or a more aggregating central political organization like the party (and in the absence of true and independent choices by the population giving a democratic legitimacy for such a mixture between technocratic and interest group power). Unfortunately, the number of cases in which we could observe and study such a life cycle of totalitarian systems is limited, due to the relatively recent instoration of a number of them, the imperfect realization of the totalitarian model due to the resistance of the society to its implementation in other cases like Fascist Italy, and the premature disappearance of the Nazi regime.

Those changes are likely to be associated also with the very different composition in terms of social, educational, and career background of the ruling elite and the middle-level cadres in such systems. They are likely to have some interesting correlation with the types of legitimacy formulated by Max Weber. After an initial phase, which in some respects we should consider pretotalitarian, in the center of ideological formulation some type of charismatic authority is likely to appear supported by a group of disciples. The weaning of the belief in the uniqueness of the leader or of his immediate successor might give rise to a combination of patrimonial bureaucratic features, which can degenerate into the sultanistic type, while the post-totalitarian phase would show a combination of patrimonial bureaucratic characteristics with the emergence of legal authority, and a distrust or fear of the reemergence of charismatic leadership together with attempts to institutionalize the charisma in the party. The institutionalization of interest or group politics might lead, as it seems to have happened in the case of Yugoslavia, to the emergence of certain forms of corporative representation on an occupational basis, for which obviously the ideology of the Soviets provides a legitimacy not available for an individualistic representation that would be closer to the model of competitive democracy. The party organization might fight back in this context by reinforcing the more plebiscitarian elements of direct mass participation. In this context it is interesting to note that even those totalitarian systems that dabbled with corporative ideological elements in their totalitarian phase were suspicious of corporative organic representation and that the party leadership rejected such tendencies to reinforce the more charismatic plebiscitarian component.

Totalitarianism of the "Left" and the "Right"

Many critics are right in noting that works using the totalitarian model tend to focus on formal similarity in the way power is organized, created, and used, somewhat like the term democracy is used to cover such different political social systems as Scandinavia, Italy, and the United States, neglecting the content of the policies formulated and implemented through institutions that in other respects might have considerable similarities. To some extent the critics are right in noting that the emphasis on how things are done tends to neglect for whom and to whom. Unfortunately the literature comparing different totalitarian systems, particularly communist and fascist, is not rich. Talmon (1961, pp. 6–8), in a few pages, has stressed some basic differences in the ideological assumptions of both totalitarianisms, and Groth (1964) has attempted a more empirical analysis of some basic differences, noting at the same time some of the difficulties for a systematic analysis. While it might sound scholastic, we cannot avoid an emphasis on some of those methodological problems that he could not fully resolve.

The first difficulty lies in the fact that fascist totalitarian systems, particularly the only one that strictly speaking can be called totalitarian, had a short life span compared to the Soviet Union. Is a totalitarian system in the process of consolidation, like that of Hitler before World War II, comparable to a regime in its second and third decade, like Stalin's Soviet Union? A second difficulty is to isolate the impact of war on the German, and to a lesser extent the Italian, society. Were certain features of the Nazi regime a result of the war? Did the war accelerate the process toward totalitarianism or was it a temporary obstacle? Would we have had to wait to see the development of the regime after the war to evaluate better its totalitarian potential?

Another series of methodological difficulties emerge from the analysis of fascism. To what extent is Nazism a very special type of fascism or a model example of fascist regimes? To what extent were the ideological commitments of fascism realizable in a complex, advanced society with a long history of institutionalization and with masses of the population, to which fascism wanted to appeal, largely preempted by previously successful political movements, particularly socialism and Catholic social movements, limiting therefore its appeal to other strata of society? The left fascists, whose ideological formulations have recently received more attention (Kühnl, 1966), were aware of this problem. Other fascist movements with the more popular and less middle-class or uppermiddle-class support, like those in some Balkan countries (Nagy-Talavera, 1970) and Peronism (Germani, 1965, 1973; Kirkpatrick, 1971), arose in societies where part of the lower classes had not developed such strong partisan loyalties. An analysis in terms of the initial social base of fascist parties limited to the Italian and the Nazis, as we find in Marxist literature, obviously ignores the possibility of a broader *Volksgemeinschaft* and a less class-bound fascist movement. There is also an ambivalence built into the analysis about the degree to which a totalitarian party in power reflects in its policy its original social composition and class appeal (Schoenbaum, 1967; Dahrendorf, 1967; Kele, 1972). Here again the length of the German experiment imposes serious limitations on the comparison.

Much of the value of the comparison depends on the narrowness or inclusiveness of the policy areas considered. It is significant that those who argue for the similarity of the systems pay special attention to the coercive aspects of the regimes, their impact on the legal systems and the role of the judiciary, their relation to education and youth, some of the impact on the family, and perhaps more than anything else on mass media, culture, and the arts, and the relation to religion. On the other hand they are very sketchy on the relationship between the national socialists and the economy, aspects like the role of owners, managers, and planners, as well as the role of the government and party-related sector, in economic policy formulation and the direction of production (Schweitzer, 1965; Mason, 1968; Milward, 1966; Eichholtz, 1969; Hennig, 1973). Even more complicated is the analysis of the impact of totalitarian systems on the distribution of income and power between social classes and particular social groups in relationship to economic decisions and daily work life (Schoenbaum, 1967; Schumann, 1958; Uhlig, 1956; Bauer, Inkeles, and Kluckholn, 1956; Inkeles and Bauer, 1959; Lipset, 1973; Lipset and Dobson, 1973). It is in this area where Groth and other authors find essential differences, arguing that fascist totalitarianism did not intend to change the class structure, while communism deliberately aimed at such a change. The argument is obviously easy to make if we consider exclusively the variable of private ownership of large enterprises but ignore the separation between ownership and control and the degree to which such control shifted into the hands of state or party-related bodies.

Given the initially different basis of the Communist party and the supporters of the Bolshevik Revolution in the Soviet Union and those supporting the rise to power of Hitler, the social composition of the elites of both regimes was very different, with the working class providing fewer of the leaders among the Nazis than among the Bolsheviks, particularly at the middle levels (Linz, 1976; Lerner, 1966; Zapf, 1965). We know how the leadership of the Soviet Union in recent years has changed considerably in its composition (Farrell, 1970b; Barghoorn, 1972), but we cannot know what that of a second generation Nazi elite would have been. Certainly we could have expected a certain amount of convergence of the two systems, given the greater emphasis on education and with it a certain transmission of positions within the intelligentsia in the Soviet scene, while in Germany the Nazification of the whole society would perhaps have provided for a broader recruitment of the elite and a disposessing of some of the traditional strata whose values and style were in conflict with the Nazis.

The question of the elite composition, however, has to be kept quite separate from that of distribution of income and other advantages among major social strata like managers, employees, workers, and farmers as well as nonproductive groups like youth and the old. Such a comparison in societies in which many advantages are not distributed through wages and salaries is particularly difficult, and much research needs to be done in the comparison of political and social systems, holding constant economic development levels, the business cycle, and relations of international dependency even within ideological blocs. Undoubtedly such differences cannot be deduced simply from the social composition of the political elite or from the continuity in certain positions of the old elite. Nor are such differences in a modern economy exclusively dependent on the distribution of property.

The fact that the Soviet Union was built on a war-ravaged country after a revolution that had often physically destroyed the old social structure obviously contrasts with the composition of Nazi rule on a society that acquiesced in its taking of power and therefore did not need to be restored and rebuilt to the same extent.

An obvious difference between communism and fascism is the latter's almost insane commitment to nationalism, even pan-nationalism, against the state when its frontiers do not coincide with the nation, in contrast with the ideological internationalism of the Bolsheviks and the formal commitment to federal, multinational states. In practice, however, this rigid ideological distinction, which served the fascists to attack communism even while admiring many aspects of it, is not such a neat criterion to distinguish the two types of totalitarianism. Totalitarian Russia and China have not given up the appeal to national loyalties and traditions, particularly in the Stalinist patriotic war, and the Soviet leadership has not neglected its national interest in relation to other communist countries, which in turn have increasingly strengthened their legitimacy, like Rumania (Jowitt, 1971), by turning to nationalism without either democratization or liberalization. On the other side, in the original fascist movements, particularly in some of the German left National Socialists, some strains of Italian Fascism, and in the ideologists of the SS, we find elements of internationalism (Ledeen, 1972; Kluke, 1973).

Obviously the racism in Nazism was a crucial difference between its totalitarianism and that of the Soviet Union, but the emphasis on the Nordic or Aryan race was latently in conflict with the traditional conception of nation. Fascism in a number of its manifestations was not racist or even anti-Semitic, except the Hungarian Arrow Cross and the Rumanian Iron Guard. Fascist leaders were even capable of identifying with non-Western fascist movements (Kühnl, 1966). In fact, fascism was not exclusively European. The lack of success of Japanese fascists (Maruyama, 1963; Morris, 1968) confronted with the bureaucratic, military, authoritarian state and the failure of Chandra Bosse's Indian fascism as well as of Latin American fascism of the Brazilian *Integralistas* (Trindade, 1974), have obscured this fact. Even when communist anti-Semitism under the label of anti-Zionism and anticosmopolitanism is not racist and is a minor feature in its politics—and some of the appeals to non-Western races by the Chinese are more a part of political-economic conflict—those secondary strains show how the apparently neat distinction on this ideological dimension between the two historical antagonists is not so neat.

A major difference in the ideological formulations of both movements can be found in the emphasis on elitism and the leadership principle, with its charismatic connotation in fascism from its beginning in contrast to the fundamentally democratic commitments of communism, even in the form of democratic centralism. However, the Stalinist version of cult of personality led to considerable convergence but its ultimate ideological illegitimacy was important for the reforms of Khrushchev. The "vanguard" notion of the party in turn introduced an important elitist element reinforced by the special education of party schools. In making this important contrast we should, on the other hand, not forget that leadership in the fascist doctrine and party statutes initially had a democratic legitimation rather than a purely traditional one, even when democracy was to be limited to the party. The elitism of race, party, and followers of the leader ultimately was based in fascism on an idea of identity with the nation, the *Volksgemeinschaft*. This ultimately introduced into traditional status- and class-based societies certain egalitarian features, like the use of the second person in its familiar form among party members irrespective of rank, the subversion of traditional status and class differences by a new hierarchy in the party, and the sense of solidarity across class lines expressed symbolically. Actually, fascist regimes, given their social base and the unrevolutionary way in which they generally took power, did not fully activate those commitments and therefore in reality the two systems were very different. Both ideologies ultimately pursued, by different ways, a classless society rather than an institutionalization of class conflicts as it has become characteristic of societies under democratic governments. The critics of totalitarianism have seized on this aspect, stressing the negative side of a mass society undifferentiated, subordinated, and manipulated by the rulers, but in doing so have neglected the appeal that this renewed sense of community had for those living in societies in which class conflicts had become bitter, societies in which it was obvious that the dictatorship of the proletariat was not to be, in the sense of Marx, the dictatorship of the majority but of the minority, since important segments that Marx would have considered proletarian, like the white-collar workers, did not want to consider themselves proletarians.

The contrast between communism and fascism highlights both the importance of certain ultimate social and philosophical assumptions that differentiate them and also certain common responses to modern society and the strains it imposes with its pluralism, conflict of interests, absence of a shared comprehensive system of values after secularization. Those ultimate differences in intellectual origins, however, became crucially important for the different development of both systems and the basis of immanent critique. In turn, the relationship between the ideology and the realities of the society in which it was to be implemented politically, as well as the way in which the two movements came to power, made for very different consequences for different social strata. The realities of fascist and communist rule cannot be confused, whatever affinity at some level of analysis we might find in the ideological assumptions. However, some of those ideological assumptions were very important for the way of organizing political power and thereby to the common totalitarian features: the role of ideology, the concentration of power in a ruling group, the role of the party, and the emphasis on mobilization.

For a better understanding of both systems, however, it is interesting to compare specifically how those three aspects differ between the Soviet Union and Nazi Germany.

Probably the most important difference between communism and fascism can be found in the nature of the ideology and the way in which it affected the political process. We do not accept the position of those who deny to fascism the character of an ideology and reduce it exclusively to the arbitrary pronouncements of the leadership adapting ideas to Machiavellian power seeking. Recent work on fascism, particularly Gregor, Mosse, Nolte,[27] has again delineated clearly the difference between fascism and other political ideologies. The reader of fascist ideology and literature, party programs, and slogans can certainly distinguish them from other ideologies like conservatism or Catholic corporativism, to mention two of a certain affinity (Schmitter, 1974; Wiarda, 1973a, 1973b, 1974), the same way that he can distinguish a Marxist-Leninist formulation from the variety of African socialism and similar ideologies of the Third World. The fact that fascism is a late-comer on the political scene and therefore defines itself largely in negative terms as antiliberalism, anticommunism, anticlericalism, anti-internationalism, antiproletarianism, etc., should not obscure the fact that there was a distinctive style, rhetoric, and sensibility that had a positive appeal in its time. The argument that an antirationalist conception and emphasis on action and emotion rather than intellectual and scientific thought cannot constitute an ideology ignores the fact that much of modern and respected philosophy and thought has an irrationalist strain. A more serious difference is that communism links with the work of Marx, who in addition to being a man of action was a philosopher and a learned social scientist. Despite the use by fascists of the name and the ideas of a number of philosophers, thinkers, and writers, none achieved similar importance for them and therefore no thought formulated before and independently of taking power became equally binding as a source of legitimacy and criticism within the movement. This, together with the irrationalist emphasis on action, not fully absent from Leninism, allowed infinitely wider scope to political opportunism and therefore made fascist totalitarianism much less an ideocracy and more the rule of a leader and his loyal followers, more often than not without ideas. Totalitarianism in both cases meant manipulation of the ideological heritage, in the case of Stalin even the elimination of the intellectuals in the movement, like Bukharin, in the case of Hitler the loss of influence of Rosenberg, or in that of Mussolini, of Gentile. The enshrinement of Marx and Lenin and of their printed work, however, ultimately allows some intellectual criticism and further elaboration of communist thought and thereby of vitality of the ideology. The ultimate ideas underlying both ideological movements are a lasting part of our intellectual heritage and respond to some needs of modern man, but undoubtedly Marxisms, being closer to a modern science of society and economy, offers a better basis for the formulation of rational policies. Even when some outstanding intellectuals could feel a temporary sympathy or affinity with fascism (Hamilton, 1973), fewer could explain away its negative aspects; and the absence of a corpus of thought like that of Marx ultimately limited its appeal beyond committed followers and party hacks. The fact that Marx could be interpreted in a noncommunist-democratic and even liberal-humanist direction makes it possible for the non-Marxist-Leninist and particularly for the non-Stalinist to appreciate the ideology of communist systems. This in turn can be and has been a stimulus for ideological evolution, polycentrism (Labedz, 1962; Laqueur and Labedz, 1962; Drachkovitch, 1965; Shaffer, 1967; Triska, 1969), and therefore tension with a strict totalitarianism. In Nazism the combination of social Darwinism and totally unscientific racism with an irrationalist voluntarism in the hands of an uneducated autodidact led to a parochial and crude ideology whose implementation brought out the worst potentialities of ideological totalitarian rule. This makes it difficult to conceive a post-Hitler evolution.

The difference between the two totalitarianisms is based not on the fact that one has an ideology and the other does not but on the different quality of the two ideologies. This allows us to separate communism from its worst manifestations under Stalin but makes it almost impossible to separate national socialism from Hitler and his final solution. The fact that the fate of non-Nazi fascism became tied during the war to the leader of the fascist camp in a way that communism after Yugoslavia, China, and Cuba is not tied to the Soviet Union and Stalin is decisive for the future of both ideologies. We are likely to find fascist ideological elements in many nondemocratic regimes, but it is doubtful that we will find a true fascist regime and even less a true fascist totalitarianism. The lack of success of neofascist parties cannot be explained only by military defeat and discrimination against its representatives.

In spite of important similarities in the conception and organization of the totalitarian parties in communist and fascist systems, there are important differences between them that should not be neglected, differences that are not exclusively a result of the different social composition of the membership and/or elite and the different social, economic, political, and historical contexts in which they came to power. The organizational conception of the Bolsheviks, after all, emerged out of the mass socialist parties more or less linked with the trade union movement of nineteenth-century Europe; and the Leninist conception of an elite of professional revolutionaries was an adaptation to the particular circumstances of czarist autocracy, even when it became rationalized in terms of incapacity of the working class masses to go beyond trade union consciousness (Schapiro, 1965; Daniels, 1969; Meyer, 1957). Fascist parties, in contrast, emerged out of the experiences of World War I and/or as a response to the success of communist parties. The war experience of the *arditi,* the *Frontkämpfer,* was the basis of the emphasis on military models of organization and discipline, the "community" of elite units, and the love of uniforms and symbols, exalted by the ideology. Reinforced by organizational forms and social composition, including the young and the veterans, the movement turns from instrument into an end in itself. The romantic element of the *Bund,* a sociological category invented by Schmalenbach to distinguish a type of group from both *Gesellschaft* ("association") and *Gemeinschaft* ("community"), is characteristic of fascist parties (Duverger, 1963, pp. 124–32). The ideological concern for personalized relations based on a search for meaning, a rejection of individualism, etc., reflects the concerns of the secularized bourgeoisie for a modern society without its insecurities (Merkl, 1975). It leads in the Nazi case to emphasize the pseudoreligious and therefore the ritual, the indoctrination, the style, the creation of a feeling of membership. A distinction, in military terminology, between a first and a second line, between the active militant member of the fascist squad and the regular party member, introduces into the party the elitist element and is the source of the characteristic heterogeneity of organizations in fascist totalitarianism. In Germany, with the pseudoreligious groups of the *völkisch* movement, with its romantic, mystic images of peasant-military democracy, medieval teutonic knights, and its semilegal or illegal paramilitary *Kampfbünde,* combined with Hitler's hate-love attitude toward the Jesuits, this tendency reaches it paroxysm (Gamm, 1962). There is nothing comparable in communist countries to the plurality of organization, with distinctive uniform styles and outlook—the party, the SA, the SS, and ultimately the internal divisions within the SS—that we find in Germany. The Red Guard always remained basically instrumental rather than an elite of the party superior to the regular member. This plurality of organizations introduces into Nazi totalitarianism an element of heterogeneity and thereby of feudal rather than bureaucratic characteristics (Koehl, 1972). The infighting of the elites is not only of individuals but of political organizations, not of factions necessarily identified with different sectors of the society or the administration but of political organizations tied together only by their identification with the leader. Another consequence was that the terror became even more directly tied with the party with the strange fusion between the police and a party elite, the SS.

Ideological components reflected in organizational forms reinforce the fundamentally antidemocratic and antipopulist character of Nazism. They also reinforce the cult of masculinity, which, separating men and women, has a latent homosexual component. Without using the Nazi exaggeration, this style element also explains why in none of the fascist parties women would play a prominent role compared to some of the communist movements. The organizational form of the militia party organization also made it difficult for fascist parties to maintain their drive when they were out of power, to become electoral opposition parties, and accounts for the urgency they felt to gain power rather than to disintegrate. This kind of activism of the SA man or the *squadristi* could not be maintained in the same way as could the loyalty of party members and voters of a communist party. The organizational form of the militia party organization also accounts for the initial collaboration of army officers, their active involvement in fascist parties, but also for the suspicions and even hatred by the army of some fascist movements, reflected for example in the suppression of the Iron Guard by Marshall Antonescu. The exclusivist character of such paramilitary political organizations also accounts for the very different way the fascists and communists handled membership in the party of army officers in active service; the communists drove to affiliate officers with the party (Weinberg, 1964; Berghahn, 1969; Messerschmidt, 1969), while Franco went to the opposite extreme, making all officers party members. It is also at the root of the emergence of a party army like the Waffen SS, which cannot be compared to the special NKVD (People's Commissariat of Internal Affairs) troops under Beria, since such units did not have an equally ideologically justified status in the communist system. The multiorganizational structure of Nazism and the elitism within the elite movement led to a multiplication of channels of recruitment and an internal differentiation, which contrasts with the model of monolithic authority of some descriptions of totalitarians. Nazi career lines took place not within the party and through missions of the party in different organizations but within the feudal structure of party organizations, in turn characterized by identification with different subleaders. However, this multiplicity, which some have likened to feudalism and others have described as a quasi-anarchy, while menacing the unit of the ruling group during the period of Hitler (who benefitted from playing one off against the other) and particularly after Hitler, did not imply the kind of pluralism we find in authoritarian regimes, or even the type of group politics that Skilling and others want to see in posttotalitarian communism. The articulation of these leader-follower structures and bureaucracies with the rest of the society was quite different. It was based not on functional specialization and a division of labor like that of party workers with experience in agriculture or industry but on personal linkages and affinities of style, cutting even more across the social structure than do factions in the communist party. The comparison between totalitarian and semitotalitarian parties shows how organizational principles are related to the ideology and interact constantly with it.

The characteristics of the ruling group and particularly the role of the leaders are probably the most important differentiating variables between totalitarian systems but also the least theoretically relevant. Historical context, particularly the process of taking power and consolidating it, and personality factors stand out more. These obviously are less susceptible to generalizations, more idiosyncratic, and to certain extent accidental. It is difficult to say to what extent the patterns of interaction between Stalin and his intimate collaborators and that of Hitler were a reflection of the ideology and the organizational forms or of their personalities. The fact that Stalin had been only one among the initial leaders of the Bolshevik Revolution, far from loved by many of his peers who he wanted to make subordinates, accounts for the deep-seated suspicions in the relations and for the fact that purges affected much of the leadership of the politbureau (Schueller, 1966; Levytsky, 1974). In contrast, Hitler over a number of years in the opposition had been able to shape the party, and the departure of the dissidents had left only the loyal comrades; even so he felt the need to purge Roehm and his SA leaders. Where the difference between the two ruling groups might become more apparent is in the relationships between the top leader, his lieutenants, and the rank and file. Those relationships obviously depend very much on the process of growth of the party and the leadership group, as the works of Orlow (1973) and Nyomarkay (1967), the description of the relationship of the *Gauleiters* with Hitler by Peterson (1969), and the works on communist elites in Eastern Europe and in China (Farrell, 1970b; Barton, Denitch, and Kadushin, 1973; Beck, 1970; Lewis, 1963; Scalapino, 1972) show. The date of joining the party, the shared experiences like jail, the international brigades, or regional party organizations, guerrilla versus underground activity in the cities, fusion of related parties or organization, etc., become important factors in understanding the internal life of movement parties. They are—and this shows the importance of the political socialization and organizational experiences—generally more important than elites. They also account for the different climates and styles of different totalitarian systems within the communist camp as well as among the fascists.

As Groth has stressed, the alliances made in the process of taking power have considerable impact on the system at least until its full consolidation and maturity. The fact that the fascists and Nazis came to power through a silent revolution under pseudolegal forms (Linz and Stepan, 1978), with the support of institutions and parties that hoped to use them for their own purposes and with a passive support or at least submission of many potential antagonists, accounts for a more complex relationship with the pre-takeover social structure than in communist systems that gained power by revolution, civil war, or support of the Soviet army (Seton-Watson, 1967; Gripp, 1973, pp. 19–39). Many of the differences between totalitarian systems, both communist and noncommunist, can be explained by how they gained power and their strength and cohesion before gaining power (Huntington, 1970, p. 14). The type of society in which they took over the government and the circumstances under which they did so also account for the more or less totalitarian character of their rule and, in cases like Italy and Spain, for the failures to establish a fully totalitarian regime despite the ambition of many fascist leaders. The coexistence between fascist and prefascist or pseudofascist, if not antifascist, elements naturally affected the ideology, the organization, and the character of the party and its affiliates and many of its policies in the process of consolidation in power. The relative ease with which fascists gained power in contrast to the Russian, Chinese, Yugoslav, and even Cuban communists accounts for the much greater range of policy diversion even under the Nazis, so well described by Peterson (1969). We could establish some interesting parallels in Eastern European communist countries, particularly in the case of Poland, where the relative weakness of the Communist party and the strength of the Church led to patterns very different from those of Hungary. Azrael (1970a) in his analysis of the varieties of de-Stalinization, Zvi Gitelman (1970) in his "Power and Authority in Eastern Europe," and Roger W. Benjamin and John H. Kautsky (1968) in their "Communism and Economic Development" have convincingly shown how the background of the society and the process of taking power and consolidating it have modified the nature of communist regimes. For our comparative purposes, however, we do not have a communist regime created by a silent revolution taking power by semi- or pseudolegal processes within a competitive democracy and once in power transforming its rule into a nondemocratic control except Czechoslovakia (Korbell, 1959). It would be interesting to see if in such a system there would develop some forms of cooperation between the preexisting institutions and elites in the Church and the managers and the military that would lead to a less total transformation of the social structure than other communist regimes have carried through. In the case of fascist regimes and particularly Nazism it is always difficult to distinguish the coincidence of interests between pre-takeover institutions and groups, the shared ideological commitments, the co-optation and corruption of those institutions by the yielders of political power, and the cooperation obtained by the coercion and fear. Certainly those factors all operated at one time or another, and the differences between totalitarian systems often are based on focusing on one or another phase of such systems. The persistence of pre-takeover social structures, institutions, and interests and the conservative character of the system, which Groth rightly stresses, would be true for the early years of Nazi rule and perhaps the first years of the War but not after July 20, 1944, and it might have disappeared after victory in World War II or under a Himmler or Bormann succession of Hitler and the elimination of other leaders like Goering.

As in all macrosociological phenomena, generalizations are made difficult by the fact that previous experiences are known. Scholars studying Chinese communism, Eastern European collectivization, terror in the Soviet Union and China, etc., all note how the knowledge of the Stalinist period has led communist rulers elsewhere to modify their tactics and attempt to avoid some of the worst features of Stalinism, to invent other methods of social control emphasizing, for example, voluntarism and thought control rather than police terror (Schurmann, 1968, pp. 311–13). In this sense it becomes dangerous to overgeneralize from any historical experience, and certainly no totalitarian system will be fully identical to any that has preceded it in time except when it is, like some Stalinist Eastern European systems for a short time, a dependent system. In this sense every totalitarian system—every political process—carried out by people who know about the recent past will not be identical to a previous one. No attempt of model building can ignore the historicity of macrosocial phenomena.

The Critiques of the Concept of Totalitarianism and Some Suggested Alternatives

In recent years important contributions have been made to the critique of the writings using the term "totalitarianism" and suggestions have been made to replace it by other concepts. With the exception of the use of the term "mobilization regimes" or "parties," none of the latter has gained equal acceptance. The critique has many valid points that should be extremely fruitful in a more careful elaboration of the model of the totalitarian system and even more so in advancing our knowledge of the variety of totalitarian systems in time and space. A somewhat systematic exposition of the many critiques and a sifting of their valid contributions and their less useful negative aspects seems to be a first step in preparing the ground for future thinking and research by those who want to retain the term.

Explicitly or implicitly many of the critics stress that the concept was formulated and gained acceptance in the context of the cold war with a pejorative evaluative connotation and that its polemic significance makes it intellectually useless (Barber, 1969; Curtis, 1969; Spiro, 1968; Burrowes, 1969). However, this could be said about many of the most important concepts in political science, and the alternative would be to renounce all the terms that have entered the political discourse and struggle and to formulate a distinctive formal terminology, which would lead to the opposite accusation of being scholastic and ivory-towerish and difficult for the layperson to understand. Another alternative would be to use the terminology used by the actors to describe their systems with their evaluative connotations and to describe the realities so often covered up by those terms. Neither of those solutions seems adequate. The critics, in addition, forget that the term "totalitarian" was formulated before the cold war (Jänicke, 1971) and that many scholars and politicians—and not only liberal democrats—had discovered the common elements between fascist and communist systems: Robert Michels is just one distinguished name among the scholars, and on the political scene there are the left wings of a number of fascist movements and some dissident communists. The critics also forget that the term "totalitarian" was formulated and accepted without negative connotation by many fascists. Therefore the critique is rather, Can the same term be used to describe certain common features of fascist and communist regimes rather than to be limited to fascism, in which case we might not need the term? Certainly the concept has become associated, particularly in some definitions, with some of the most negative aspects in the evaluation by most people of those regimes, specifically terror, neglecting those that can be considered more positive from a variety of value perspectives. It is no accident that Hannah Arendt should practically limit the use of the term to the rule of Hitler and Stalin. If, however, it should turn out that a number of political systems in addition to those two share a sufficient number of characteristics to distinguish them from other autocracies, we should be allowed to retain the term. Ultimately, much hinges on the interpretation of the rule of those two men as being the result either of their idiosyncratic personalities or of the possibilities that the particular form of organization of political life and the ideological assumptions justifying it offered them.

The critics are on solid ground when they reject the indiscriminate use of the term to describe all nondemocratic systems or at least all those the author does not like, a critique that also would deprive us of any scholarly use of the term "fascism." Certainly if the term has any use it is to describe a very specific type of autocracy and not to serve as a synonym for dictatorship, despotism, or just nondemocratic regimes. There are certainly regimes we would not in any meaningful use of the term call totalitarian which from most value perspectives would be considered equally or more negative than the rule of Hitler, especially the rule of Trujillo.

Another argument of revisionists is to stress that some of the features used in characterizing totalitarian systems are also found in societies under different political systems, including advanced Western democracies. Similarly, the work of Barrington Moore (1965, pp. 30–88) on totalitarian elements in preindustrial societies has shown the usefulness of the concept totalitarian beyond the study of the political systems we would call totalitarian. Certainly a distinction between totalitarian political systems and totalitarian elements in other systems is a fruitful one, but does not invalidate characterizing as totalitarian those systems in which totalitarian elements are dominant and central to the political system. The recent critique of liberal democracy by the new left certainly introduces confusion in the use of the term "totalitarian" but indirectly is evidence of its usefulness (Marcuse, 1964, 1969).

Another criticism is that totalitarianism refers only to a reality that has been metamorphosized by time. Regimes that have been vanquished to the realm of historical controversy and others that have undergone fundamental changes seem to relinquish the term to the field of historical scholarship, like those of feudalism, absolute monarchy, enlightened despotism, and the police state. In that case the question would be: Is the study of such systems only of historical interest, or are they close enough to our own political life and reality to be significant in understanding contemporary political systems in a way quite different from the concept of feudalism (using the term in a strictly historical sense)?

Much of the criticism justifiably centers on the number, different character, and lack of precision of the definitions. Unfortunately that criticism can be directed against most concepts in political science dealing with complex phenomena. Certainly the different definitions and descriptions have contributed to our knowledge by highlighting different dimensions of the phenomena and probably providing elements for further conceptualization, distinguishing types of totalitarian systems that share only a limited number of crucial common characteristics. The effort of Benjamin R. Barber (1969) to classify the phenomenological and essentialist definitions is useful but somewhat scholastic. Most such definitions underline some of the qualitative or quantitative dimensions on which the political systems that are to be subsumed are different from a variety of others. Certainly the more descriptive rather than essentialist definitions make it easier to identify empirically a particular system as totalitarian, or at least as more or less totalitarian. Certainly most of the scholars have not gone very far in operationalizing the dimensions to the extent that would allow an empirical researcher to make an unambiguous decision that a system at any particular point in time is or is not totalitarian or to transform an attribute space into a continuum allowing measures of totalitarianism using some qualification of a series of indicators. This has been and certainly is one of the great obstacles in the use of the concept. One possibility, naturally, is to conceive totalitarianism as an ideal type, which will not correspond exactly to any concrete historical reality. In fact, some of the essentialist's definitions include normative elements in the minds of the leaders of totalitarian parties and the ideologists of what a totalitarian political system and a society dominated by it should be, rather than what it is likely to be. As we have seen and Giovanni Sartori (1962a) has stressed, this is also true for the concept of democracy and perhaps is inherent to many political science concepts. To some extent our insights into the nature of totalitarian systems will come from an analysis of these tensions between the ideal type and the reality it partly describes. It is no accident that some of the essentialist concepts would be acceptable to the leaders that have shaped those systems and often, from their value perspective, do not involve a negative connotation as some of the more descriptive concepts almost inevitably do.

A much more substantial criticism is that the term "totalitarian" attempts to cover too much, to characterize political systems that on many important aspects are fundamentally different. The burden of proof must be on those who advocate the term to show the extent to which some communist systems, at least in some of their phases, share a sufficient number of important characteristics with the Nazi system to warrant the inclusion under a common concept, to show that both subtypes respond to some similar preconditions in their emergence, and that the use of the concept allows us to understand better the way they handle some invariant problems of political life. It is also the burden of advocates of the concept to show that the systems so characterized share characteristics that differentiate them from other types of autocracies which would not be highlighted without the use of such a concept. Much of this has been and can be done, but it also demands as a counterpart more thorough analysis of the basic differences between totalitarianism of the Stalinist era and that of the National Socialists or Fascists. This has unfortunately not been done systematically in the literature.

A more thorough analysis of the subtypes of totalitarianism—communist, fascist, and perhaps nationalist—and of stages of development of totalitarian systems and the modification of soviet totalitarianism in different social contexts, especially the USSR, China, some of the Eastern European communist states, and perhaps Cuba, should lead us to a more elaborate typology of totalitarian systems. It also should bring the term "totalitarianism" down from its fairly high position on the ladder of abstraction to produce middle-range theories (Sartori, 1970a). The most general and abstract construct of a totalitarian system should serve as a point of reference to understand and describe better the various subtypes of communist and fascist systems and to contribute to a theory about the processes leading to the consolidation and establishment of a totalitarian system and those leading to their transformation, like the recent efforts by Azrael (1970a) to understand types of de-Stalinization, or post-totalitarian systems in communist countries.

A serious limitation of some of the definitions of totalitarianism has been the static and rigid character of many of the conceptualizations, which ignored the dynamic element, the tensions inherent in the ideal and almost normative models, the resistance that societies offer to the full development of the totalitarian system, and therefore the stages, phases, degrees, of totalitarianism. A central theme on the agenda of the study of totalitarianism has to be the study of change in and of them. Unfortunately for the scholar, the limited time that the most pure totalitarian fascist system existed and the fact that there was no successor regime to Hitler, in contrast to the long period of Soviet rule and the variety of communist systems, make it difficult to formulate generalizations about the processes of change in totalitarian systems rather than only within communist totalitarian systems.

A very different type of criticism is one we might label "historicist," which underlines the unique social or cultural preconditions and traditions of the country in which regimes we labelled totalitarian emerged. The "Slavophile" interpretation of Soviet communism[28] or the analysis of the unique German political, cultural, and social history that accounts for the rise of national socialism[29] are powerful alternatives to a political science conceptual analysis. Certainly scholars have made important contributions stressing the continuities between modern totalitarian systems and the premodern or preindustrial traditions of their societies. Others have rightly stressed how the unique personality of certain leaders accounts for some essential features of the political systems they created or shaped. Some would go so far as to argue that without those leaders those systems would never have emerged, particularly in the cases of Mussolini and Hitler, to which we certainly could add the role of Lenin in the victory of bolshevism. However valid such an approach might be to a point, it is certainly not fruitful to reduce such a complex historical phenomenon as national socialism or Stalinism to their personalities and to treat them as accidents not requiring explanation by social scientists. In this respect the Marxist or Marxist-Leninist inability to explain in general categories, in their case sociological/economic, the phenomenon of Stalinism stands in clear contrast to their scientific ambitions. Obviously it should be the task of any in-depth analysis of the systems under the rule of these men to attempt to describe the impact of their personal leadership on the system and to separate the more structural components from the more idiosyncratic ones. Probably the specific form that terror took under Stalin cannot be fully explained without reference to his personality. However, the historicist critique of totalitarianism as a conceptual approach is implicitly a critique of any effort of social science conceptualization of ultimately unique historical phenomenons. While such a critique can moderate the illegitimate claims of social scientists, it cannot be accepted without loss of knowledge and of understanding of social phenomena.

A more fruitful criticism comes from those scholars who have studied carefully the reality of totalitarian rule, particularly at the local level and due to the openness of the archives in Germany. Those scholars have rightly stressed, as has Edward N. Peterson (1969), the limits of Hitler's power, the heteronomy rather than monism of power, the changing role of the party and other organizations struggling for power, the diversion of decision making, the survival of opposition in and under the system—the islands of separateness, as Inkeles called them. These are facts that are incompatible with some of the more simplistic and overdrawn characterizations of totalitarian systems. But those scholars who emphasize them risk losing sight of the forest for the trees, missing the more central tendencies that differentiate the systems from other autocracies. The work of Skilling (1973a) stressing the group politics element in communist systems, particularly after Stalin, is a welcome corrective of overstatements of the monism of such regimes, as long as it does not fall into the pitfall, stressed by Sartori, of neglecting the essential difference between such relatively pluralistic group politics within the framework of a totalitarian or even an authoritarian system and analogous processes in democratic regimes.

The theories of convergence between the Soviet Union and the United States, summarized by Alfred G. Meyer (1970), more or less explicitly question the usefulness of the totalitarian category. By pointing out common tendencies and problems in advanced industrial societies, particularly the Soviet Union and the United States—the similarity in bureaucratic organizations, large-scale economic units, certain types of economic decision making and military organization, the similar impact of such societies on common people and the resulting psychological attitudes of conformity, powerlessness, etc.—these theories represent a welcome corrective of a tendency to make black and white contrasts between societies. However, much of the writings in this direction focus more on the similarities in social structure than in political institutions. Ideological motives are not absent, nor are the desires to overcome the cold war or, particularly among some new-left critics, to question both advanced, industrial, democratic and communist societies from a distinct value perspective. These analyses, while discovering the similarity in certain key decision-making processes at the top—the kind of processes analyzed by Mills in his *Power Elite*—and certain similarities in the daily life of common citizens in their factories or in their dealings with bureaucracies, tend to ignore some of the fundamental differences in a whole middle range of decision making, institutions, and roles in different political systems.

Undoubtedly the most serious challenge to the construct of totalitarianism comes from the difficulty of defining in clear operational terms the difference between totalitarian systems and other types of autocracy, particularly in empirical terms, because of the difficulty of documentation. The problem is much more complex than the problem of defining the boundaries between competitive democracies, as we define them, and various transitional authoritarian regimes. It is certainly more difficult because the changes are more likely to be matters of degree and generally do not involve the discontinuities created by revolutions, coups, or foreign intervention which with rare exceptions have characterized the transition between democracy and authoritarian regimes or totalitarian systems.

The critique of theories of totalitarianism has not been limited to questioning those theories; there are some attempts to offer alternative conceptualizations. In some cases it is difficult to distinguish clearly the alternative concepts from the old definitions of totalitarianism. Others, like Tucker's (1963) concept of "mobilization regimes," seem to us to fall into some of the same difficulties that the critics of the loose use of the term "totalitarian" have noted, specifically, covering too wide a range of autocracies and ignoring important differences among them. In addition, the term "mobilization," as Azrael (1970a, pp. 136–37) has noted, is in itself ambiguous, is used as a distinctive criterion rather than as one of a number of dimensions to characterize political systems, and is very difficult to use empirically. Other attempts of conceptualization, like Meyer's (1967) "administrative totalitarianism," "totalitarianism without terror," or "rationalization" and "populist totalitarianisms" describing certain features of post-Stalinist Russian political life, are more fruitful but do not imply a rejection of the broader category of totalitarianism. Other conceptualizations, like that offered by Rigby (1969) of "traditional market and organizations societies," seem to deal more with social and economic systems than with political systems. Certainly the alternative concepts offered in recent years have not gained as wide an acceptance as the old concept of totalitarianism.

The efforts of the critics have not led us to give up some concept of totalitarianism, even though we might accept the suggestion of finding another term less loaded with the connotations that have become attached with it through the rule of Hitler and Stalin, which might be considered quite unique. The critics have, however, made evident that the term should not be used loosely if it is going to be of any use, that a theory of totalitarianism or totalitarianisms does not exhaust the understanding and description of particular historical political systems, that there is urgent need for careful systematic comparison between totalitarian systems to discover their common and their differential elements, that we need a typology of totalitarian systems, and that the theory has to include a more dynamic analysis of change within and of totalitarian systems rather than, as up to now, theories about the origin of totalitarianism. Certainly much of our thinking and research has been centered on the rise of totalitarian movements and the takeover of power after the breakdown of democracies, particularly the rise of fascism. Even in the case of the Soviet Union there has been little theorizing about how the system evolved from the February Revolution to the dominance of the Bolsheviks, the displacement of other radical parties (Schapiro, 1965; Daniels, 1969) from Lenin to Stalin, and at what point we can consider the system totalitarian and why it should have become so. A comparative study of the rise to power of autochthonous communist movements in the Soviet Union, China, Cuba, and North Vietnam would certainly tell us more than some of the more abstract models like Kornhauser's *Politics of Mass Society* (1959). The military defeat of fascism and particularly Nazism has prevented scholars from analyzing change in totalitarian systems after succession crises, but since the death of Stalin and de-Stalinization an analysis of the dynamics of change in and of totalitarian systems has become imperative. In addition, more monographic research and theoretical conceptualization of nondemocratic regimes that cannot be meaningfully labeled totalitarian should help us in conceptualizing more precisely different types of autocracy. The discovery of multiple dimensions that distinguish types of totalitarianism and clarify the distinction between totalitarianism and other nondemocratic regimes should also allow us a more complex evaluation of such regimes. Certainly totalitarian systems must have many positive features that make them attractive to people who are not ignorant of some of their worst features. The ultimate result of the criticism should be a more complex theory of totalitarianisms rather than the initial model of a totalitarian system. In the same way, contemporary political science is beginning to think about types of democracies and the internal dynamics of democratic regimes rather than of a single type (identified preferably with one or another of the great Anglo-Saxon democracies).

The Conditions for Nondemocratic,
Particularly Totalitarian, Systems
in Modern or Modernizing Societies

A superficial analysis would suggest that the absence of the conditions making competitive democracies possible and stable[30] would be the first answer to the question of what conditions must exist for nondemocratic regimes and more specifically for totalitarianism. However, this might not be true even for nondemocratic regimes, since those, as the critics have noted, have appeared in countries that according to many analysts should have had a high probability of having democratic regimes. Obviously the introduction of the time dimension, analyzing the conditions that existed when the regimes were installed rather than at any specific point in time, would have eliminated some apparent exceptions. If we accept the distinction between a variety of nondemocratic regimes and the totalitarian systems, we still have to answer the question, What are the specific conditions for totalitarianism? A more fruitful accounting scheme would require answers to the questions that follow.

1. A first step in the analysis would be to specify the conditions leading to the crisis and final breakdown of pretotalitarian regimes, distinguishing various types of nondemocratic regimes and democracies, since at least one of the most outstanding models of totalitarianism emerged in a former democracy. It is perhaps this aspect that has been studied best by scholars, particularly the outstanding work of Bracher and his collaborators Sauer and Schulz on the rise to power of Hitler (Bracher, 1957; Bracher, Sauer, and Schulz, 1960), the works on the crisis of Weimar democracy (Matthias and Morsey, 1960; Eschenburg, 1966; Conze and Raupach, 1967; Kaltefleiter, 1968; Lepsius, 1968, 1971; Jasper, 1968), as well as the excellent study of the process at the local level by Allen (1965). The less theoretical but richly informative studies on the rise of fascism in Italy (De Felice, 1965, 1966b, 1968), the origins of the Spanish Civil War,[31] the end of party government in Japan (Scalapino, 1953), the decline of constitutional democracy in Indonesia (Feith, 1962), and some of the studies of the fall of Latin American democracies, particularly Brazil in 1964 (Schneider, 1971; Stepan, 1971), should allow the formulation of some model or theory of the breakdown of democracies (Linz and Stepan, 1978). However, the analysis of the crisis and the breakdown of democracy does not tell us what kind of regimes will emerge or what conditions will make for

its consolidation and stability. In fact, ignoring the cases of reequilibration of democracy, like France in 1958, in only one of the cases
mentioned was the outcome a pure totalitarian system and in another
an incipient one. Breakdown of democracy therefore is not identical
with the establishment of totalitarianism, but it can be one of the conditions. It should not be forgotten, however, that the other outstanding
model of totalitarian system did not result from the breakdown of a relatively stabilized democracy, since the regime born in the February
Revolution of 1917 in Russia can certainly not be considered a mini-
mally institutionalized democracy.

2. A question that coincides in part with that of the crisis and
breakdown of democratic regimes is the analysis of the conditions
leading to the emergence and growth of antidemocratic mass parties.[32]
Since such parties have appeared and gained widespread support in a
number of democracies without having been able to provoke or contribute decisively to their breakdown, the study of the emergence of
fascist and communist parties and their appeal, organization, leadership, policies, legal and illegal activities, etc., can contribute only one
element to the causal chain. In fact it might be misleading to speak of
totalitarian parties, since the term can refer only to the type of political system such parties might intend to create, and we know that a
number of them have been unable even after the breakdown of democracy to create totalitarian systems. Some parties committed to ideologies and to some degree to models like the Soviet Union, which would
lead us to label them totalitarian, in democracies of sufficient stability
over long periods of time might undergo a process of change that could
in the long run make them legitimate participants in a democratic political system.[33] The case of Italy in the near future might be particularly interesting from this perspective (Blackmer, 1968; Blackmer and
Tarrow, 1975).

3. If the breakdown of democracy and even the existence of a party
committed to an ideology and having many of the organizational characteristics that should make it the single party of a totalitarian regime
are not sufficient to establish such a regime, we have to ask an additional question: Which are the conditions that lead to the establishment
of a more or less totalitarian system rather than to other forms of nondemocratic government once a democratic regime has broken down?
Given the definition of totalitarian system, it is highly unlikely that
such a system will be created in a short time, and therefore we can
expect a period of transition of nondemocratic rule that does not be-

come fully institutionalized and leads to the emergence of a totalitarian system. In this sense it is more difficult to date the establishment of totalitarianism than the breakdown of democracy. Therefore the most important and specific question that has to be raised is: How does a nondemocratic situation or regime develop the specific features we have identified as totalitarian? How do the ruling groups conceive totalitarian institutions or is it an accident that they should have developed such a model of society? What factors make some of them successful and prevent other groups from transforming their political systems and societies into truly totalitarian systems?

4. What accounts for the stabilization and persistence of totalitarian systems over longer periods of time? In this context it is important to note that to this day no totalitarian system has been overthrown by force internally, but those that have lost some of their distinctive totalitarian characteristics have done so by a complex process of transformation.

5. Is totalitarianism a stable type of political system like democracy or many traditional forms of autocratic rule? And if not, which are the factors leading to transformation into other forms of nondemocratic rule?

The first two questions are not specific to the problem of totalitarianism but to the problem of the breakdown of democracies and the emergence of potential leaders and parties that could, under favorable circumstances, become the core of a totalitarian system. It seems difficult to conceive an analysis of the conditions making for the emergence of the more specific features of a totalitarian system without reference to the particular subtypes, most importantly by the communist and fascist ones. In addition it becomes difficult to analyze those conditions without explaining why in some situations in which there were many elements favoring the establishment of a totalitarian system this was not possible. In this respect the comparison of the evolution of the Nazi regime and that of Mussolini would be extremely revealing, as would be a comparison of the evolution of the different communist systems, particularly in the Stalinist phase. Many of the analyses of these processes were written at the time or shortly after the event and therefore could assume that certain conditions were unique to the societies under study, when events years later would show that some similar processes would be possible in very different societies. In this respect it is interesting to see how the initial interpretation of the rise of fascism and the consolidation of Mussolini in power looked for distinctive characteristics of Italian society and history, and interpretations of a number of relatively underdeveloped countries of Eastern Europe and Turkey asserted that similar developments would not be possible in advanced industrial societies and particularly in Germany, in spite of the strength of the National Socialist party (Borkenau, 1933; Matossian, 1958). The literature derived from the experience of Germany and the Soviet Union, in turn, underlined certain characteristics of industrial society that would seem irrelevant in the case of China. Perhaps it would be better to proceed through the analysis of particular cases of successful and unsuccessful drives toward totalitarianism, and only after the variables most relevant in each case have been analyzed to attempt a generalization at a higher level of abstraction.

Just as the analysis of the conditions for the instoration of democracy, has to face the problem of endogenous processes as distinct from exogenous factors, so does the analysis of totalitarianism.[34] We cannot forget the external imposition of democratic systems in the case of Italy, Germany, and Japan after World War II, even when there were many endogenous factors favorable for the success of the regime so instored (Dahl, 1971, pp. 189–201). In the case of Stalinist totalitarian or semi-totalitarian systems we also have to be aware of such exogeneous factors like the presence of the Soviet army. Those cases, however, show how important the endogenous factors were for the full consolidation of such a regime when we consider the later evolution of the different Eastern European countries.

Cutting across many of the questions we have raised, we encounter different intellectual perspectives, the contribution of different disciplines, and a variety of theoretical approaches, which, unfortunately, have not been applied to all cases but only to some so that it is impossible to test their validity for others. For example, in the literature on the origins and the development of Nazi totalitarianism we have a number of studies that emphasize psychological variables, culture, personality, even psychoanalytical perspectives (Greenstein, in the original *Handbook,* Vol. 2), but relatively few studies have applied the same perspective to the rise and consolidation of power of Stalin. Marxism has provided the students of fascism with many of their hypotheses, but few have applied a Marxist theoretical perspective to Stalinism. Most of the theoretical orientations and hypotheses developed for the cases in which totalitarian systems consolidated themselves in power have not been tested, *a contrario,* in those cases where the drive toward totalitarianism was unsuccessful or only partly successful. We shall deal with those theories in other sections in accounting for the emergence of a variety of types of authoritarian, but not totalitarian, regimes, which should complement our review of the theories on the origins and conditions for totalitarianism.

Two Historico-Sociological Analyses: Wittfogel and Barrington Moore

Some of the analyses of totalitarianism, rather than focusing on the particular historical crisis that led to the breakdown of a predecessor regime, the concurrent social disorganization, and the rise to power of a new elite with a totalist commitment, place the problem in a macro-historical context of basic socioeconomic and organizational structures resulting from a long evolution. Outstanding works in this tradition are Wittfogel (1957) and Moore (1966). For Wittfogel, *Oriental Despotism,* as a form of total power resulting from the requirement of a bureaucratic rule to regulate the use of water in the societies he calls hydraulic—described by Marx as the "Asiatic mode of production"— serves as a basis for despotic institutions. Societies in which "the state is stronger than society" limit the development of autonomous secondary groups of political significance and lead to the development of a stratification system based on political control rather than property, that is, bureaucratic capitalism and landlordism. Significantly, in his view, communist scholars have ignored Marx's analysis of this type of society, presumably because it could serve to interpret contemporary realities in the communist world. The theory has not remained unchallenged, particularly by Eberhard with respect to the role of the Chinese gentry (for a review see Eisenstadt, 1958).

More directly linked with contemporary political realities—though in my view there are important missing steps—is the thesis of Moore (1966) about alternative paths to modernity in his *Social Origin of Dictatorship and Democracy,* significantly subtitled: *Lord and Peasant in the Making of the Modern World.* The first path has been the great revolutions and civil wars that led to the combination of capitalism and Western democracy. The second route has also been capitalist, but culminated during the twentieth century in fascism. Germany and Japan are the obvious cases, called the capitalist and reactionary form, revolution from above due to the weakness of the bourgeoisie. The third route is communism, exemplified in Russia and China, countries in which the great agrarian bureaucracies inhibited the commercial and later industrial impulses, even weaker than in Germany and Japan. The then-large remaining peasantry provided the destructive revolutionary force that overthrew the old order under communist leadership, which later made the peasants its primary victims. The ways in which the landed upper classes and the peasants reacted to the challenge of commercial agriculture were the decisive factors in determining the political outcome.

The fusion of peasant grievances with those of other strata has been decisive for revolutions, but the success of revolutions has been negative for peasants although decisive in creating new political and economic conditions. Those revolutions have been the result of the absence of commercial revolution in agriculture led by the landed upper classes and the survival of peasant social institutions into the modern era, with consequent stresses particularly when traditional and capitalist modes of pumping surplus out of the countryside were added to each other. This and the loss of functions of the landlord with the growth of centralized monarchy was the cause of revolutions. One outcome was conservative modernization and fascism, with a separation of government from society and modernization from above at the expense of the lower classes after unsuccessful attempts at parliamentary liberal democracy. In it the landed upper class will use a variety of levers to hold down a labor force on the land.

Moore's effort—to whose richness in specific analyses, complexity, and limitations we cannot do justice—by offering an explanation of the conditions for democracy, fascism, and communism, places the problem of nondemocratic politics in an ambitious historical framework worth testing and refining (Moy, 1971). In our view the neglect of the smaller European democracies that did not undergo the great revolutions, the equation of Japanese authoritarian rule with Nazi totalitarianism under the common label "fascism," and the ambiguous answer to the question Why democracy in India? pose serious problems to his analysis. Even greater are the problems raised by the time gap between the agrarian developments in Germany in the nineteenth century and the rise of Nazism to power in the thirties, the neglect of the tensions created within urban industrial society with the rise of an organized working class, and the impact of World War I and its aftermath on the middle classes. The same would be true for the impact of war and defeat on the semitraditional agrarian societies of Russia and China in making possible the rise to power with opportune peasant support of communist revolutionaries, a process not explainable exclusively in terms of socioeconomic structure and labor repression.

3

TRADITIONAL AUTHORITY
AND PERSONAL RULERSHIP

Introduction

The main types of modern political systems—democratic, totalitarian, and authoritarian—are at the center of our attention in this chapter. There are, however, still political systems that would not fit, by any stretching of concepts, into those three main types, particularly various forms of traditional authority (sometimes combined, it is true, with more modern bureaucratic-military elements). Traditional rule of more or less patrimonial or feudal character still enjoys considerable legitimacy, even though its future is in doubt. Those traditional elements are even more important at the regional and local level in many countries in the Maghreb, Southeast Asia, and Subsaharan Africa. On the periphery of the modern Western world, particularly Latin America after independence, under formally democratic constitutions, forms of non-strictly traditional personal rulership emerged: *caudillismo* and the oligarchic rule of local notables, landowners, and *políticos*, sometimes in alliance with a more modern center, a system known as *caciquismo*. In fact, the combination of traditional and modern elements in economically underdeveloped countries with an unmobilized population (sometimes ethnically and culturally distinct like the Andean and Middle American Indians) and with limited civil liberties made possible what we might call "oligarchic democracies," often alternating with more open authoritarian rule (for example in Peru, see Bourricaud, 1967). In a few societies relatively unique circumstances allowed the emergence of more centralized, in some respects more modern forms of personal rulership (to use the expression of Guenther Roth, 1971) not based on tradition, or charisma, or organized corporative institutions, or a modern single party. We shall discuss this type of highly arbitrary personal rule as "sultanistic," borrowing the term from Max Weber.

The regimes just mentioned—*caudillismo, caciquismo,* oligarchic democracy, sultanistic—show many similarities with those we label authoritarian (*strictu sensu*). The coercion and fear under sultanistic regimes reminds one of totalitarianism but the roots and function of the regimes are radically different. All this leads us to discuss these types of political systems separately in the next few pages.

Traditional and Semitraditional Legitimate Authority

It is beyond our scope to review the extensive literature on premodern political systems, except for brief references to the few states still under traditional rule and to the persistence of traditional elements, legitimation, and institutions in partly modernized systems. Political anthropologists, particularly the students of African politics, have significantly broadened our understanding of how the state and primitive political systems emerge.[35] Historians, and in their footsteps sociologists, have made major advances in the systematic typological and comparative study of a multiplicity of political forms—from gerontocracy, patriarchalism, and patrimonialism to kingship in different societies, from ancient city-states like the Greek polis in its various manifestations to the medieval city-states of the Renaissance.[36] Feudalism in the West, in Japan, and elsewhere, the evolution of representative institutions and estate societies in the West and the centralized traditional polities (particularly the bureaucratic empires), and the emergence of the modern state have been the object of historical and social science scholarship for decades. The great political and legal thinkers, moralists, and churchmen throughout the ages have added their perspectives. Thus many disciplines have contributed to our understanding of that variety of *premodern, predemocratic political forms* which with few exceptions were autocratic and devoid of a free and peaceful competition for power among all the members of the political community, even less among all the inhabitants of a political unit.

That scholarship has crystallized, notably in the work of Max Weber, in a series of typological and analytical concepts of more than historico-descriptive value for the social scientist, concepts that are of great use in understanding contemporary political systems, particularly those in transition from tradition to modernity in the non-Western world. The historico-sociological scholarship has also contributed much to our understanding of the historical, institutional, and legal conditions for the emergence of representative institutions and, with them, of liberal democratic regimes. The persistence of traditional political culture, most evident in the great non-Christian civilizations, and the role of religious values and institutions in many societies make the understanding of the traditional political culture essential in the study of diverse regimes.[37] Authoritarian rule outside of communist countries, and perhaps even in them, in non-Western and largely rural societies cannot ignore the traditional elements in their politics. These elements are apt to be strongest at the local community level, and scholars focusing on the authoritarian structures at the center—single parties, military establishments, bureaucracies—risk underestimating the extent to which government and politics take place in traditional or mixed institutions according to traditional values, legitimated by religion and tradition, through traditional channels, and at the margin or outside the controls of central authorities. The growing body of scholarship on politics at the local, tribal, community, or regional level in those countries is likely to correct or, more exactly, to complement the description of both democratic and authoritarian governments in many parts of the world.

The small and diminishing number of Third World traditional political systems whose rulers enjoy continuing legitimacy and govern through patrimonial bureaucracies, feudal authoritative structures, tribal organizations, or some combination of traditional forms should be distinguished from those in which such elements have been mixed with nontraditional, generally Western institutions, often in uneasy coexistence. Some of those relatively pure traditional politics have shown considerable stability as compared with semimodern states, though it is difficult to say if it is the persistence of traditional legitimacy beliefs, the traditional or premobilized social structure, or isolation and economic underdevelopment (or in the Middle East disproportionate wealth) that accounts for the stability of the regimes, for example, of the emperor of Ethiopia (Perham, 1947; Hess and Loewenberg, 1964; Levine, 1965; Abraha, 1967; Hess, 1970), and the king of Nepal (Rose and Fisher, 1970), or some of the kings, emirs, and sheiks on the Arabic peninsula. Even after their formal overthrow or abdication such rulers may continue to exercise power under pseudomodern forms copied from the West. Yet Thailand (Wilson, 1962; Riggs, 1967) and

Iran (Binder, 1962; Zonis, 1971), two Asian countries never subject to colonial rule, have commingled modern authoritarian or democratic forms and the remnants of traditional legitimacy to sustain apparently stable social orders without undergoing radical breaks with tradition. Malaysia too is proof that such partial continuity with the past is not fully incompatible with the introduction of democratic institutions (Milne, 1967), even when the number of semitraditional regimes with bureaucratic-military-authoritarian governments seems to be growing. Traditional authority of monarchs and their patrimonial bureaucracies has and can facilitate the introduction of modern political institutions, a process with historical precedents in Japan in the Meiji restoration or the more recent institution of democracy under the American occupation.[38] Traditional authority can persist in mixed political systems but there is no evidence that it can be fully restored once elements of discontinuity have appeared. Attempts at restoration may only lead to various forms of neotraditional authoritarian rule, often, as in the case of Morocco,[39] with considerable instability.

The societies of the Maghreb exemplify very well how a historical heritage of a traditional, precolonial political and social structure and its transformation under different patterns of colonial rule, in turn partly a response to preconquest structures, can affect political developments after independence. The excellent study by Elbaki Hermassi (1972) comparing national development, both political and economic, in Morocco, Tunisia, and Algeria explains how the dominance of the monarchy, the party, and the army in each case is the result of structural factors and elite development, elite coalitions, and cleavages resulting from that historical background, precolonial and colonial. Hermassi shows how the Moroccan monarchy proved too powerful to be weakened by the political parties and too entrenched to allow expansion of the political system. He notes, following Samuel Huntington, three possible strategies open to the monarchy: to reduce its authority and promote movement toward a modern constitutional monarchy, to combine monarchical and popular authority in the same political system, or to maintain the monarchy as the principal source of authority and minimize the disruptive effects on it by the broadening of political consciousness (Huntington, 1968, pp. 40–91). The king attempted the third by assuming personal command of the army and the police and placing the ministry of interior in the hands of a former head of his private cabinet. This solution has led to a quasi-vizierial system without having opted initially for a purely vizierial or purely ministerial system.

This unstable arrangement based on a council dominated by nonparty technicians, not responsible before political groups—which could make their work impossible—and not committed by collective responsibility for the government, ultimately forced Mohammed V and his successor, Hassan II to vizierial governments with their members separately designated and individually responsible to the king, to use the description of Zartman (1971).

The rejection of the second strategy—direct monarchical rule leavened by some popular participation, for example, by the *Istiqulal* party and a variety of organized interests represented in the National Assembly—led to the split of the nationalist movement and the formation of a new opposition to the regime. To play off this new opposition the king summoned counterelites, such as the supporters of the rural Berber cause and the advocates of pluralism (who argued that the complexity of Moroccan society made one-party rule unworkable and a royal arbitrator a necessity). After the elections under a constitution promulgated in 1962 gave the monarchical forces only 69 seats of 144, the king suspended the constitution and reverted to government through his ministry of interior, first under a state of emergency and later under a new fundamental law that legalized his absolute power. The regime, as the repeated attempts to overthrow it and its ineffectiveness in economic policy making show, finds itself largely isolated from the political elite. It is an interesting example of the impossibility of return to stable traditional rule after a period of considerable political mobilization. In the Moroccan case the situation was compounded by the absence of success in economic development due largely to the constraints imposed by the limited power basis of the regime.

Hermassi's analysis of the historical development of Morocco before independence exemplifies well the kind of conditions that can lead to the stalemate of neotraditionalism. Colonial rule often reinforces traditional social structures and institutions at the same time as it produces the mobilization of new social forces in a struggle for independence. In the nineteenth century the Maghrebi states were all characterized by patrimonialism—private appropriation of army and administration, total discretion in appointments of officers, dynastic appropriation of the land, and imitation of the same traits in the provinces. Even so, the personal exercise of power was to greater or lesser extent circumscribed by religious and traditional restraints. Another constraint on the patrimonial domination emanated from the tribal grounding of the rural society, which created constant problems in territorial and social unification for the state apparatus. In Morocco the state remained dependent on armed tribes until the middle of the nineteenth century, and the establishment (*Makhzen*) remained a rudimentary organization dependent for its effectiveness on the existence of a venerate personage, an institution unto himself, the sultan. Patrimonial rule faced the almost unsolvable problem of maintaining in a quasi-subsistence economy a taxation system capable of meeting the needs of the bureaucracy and the army. The resultant rebellion of the notables and the grand chiefs in the marginal zones left the sultan no other recourse but to make use of French assistance to maintain his empire. Thereafter, colonization interrupted any autonomous form of political and economic development, whether feudalistic, capitalistic, or whatever.

The French, entering each of the three Maghreb societies at different times with different methods, manipulated the existing tensions to their advantage, maintaining and at the same time changing the traditional social structure. While in Tunisia the Berber element had almost disappeared and in Algeria had continued to be 30 percent of the population, with half of those Berbers being rural, it represented 40 percent of the Moroccan population and two-thirds of the total rural population. The nineteenth century was a period of change in which the sultan attempted to stabilize his control over the tribes using firearms, his religious monopoly, and the conflict between *Bled el Makhzen,* or "land of government," and *Bled es-Siba,* or "land of dissidence." This territorial conflict, in which the intensity of tribal connections, difficulties of communication, and the oscillation between nomadic and sedentary forms of life had sheltered marginal populations from the central power, eventually evolved from a twofold to a threefold cleavage. This change came about with the institutionalization of intermediary powers of chiefs, who presented themselves to the regime as integrators of anarchical tribes and to the tribes as an ultimate resort against a fatal submission. Those chiefs eliminated local, more or less democratic institutions and substituted a personal despotic patrimonial form of government. The sultanate had to limit the arbitrariness of its notables and encourage intermediary chiefs to face dissident units without letting their power become strong enough to be a temptation to disloyalty in times of crisis. In doing so the sultanate seized on traditions of political legitimacy in Islam, meeting the aspirations of rural Muslims by emphasis on individual charismatic authority of a descendant of the prophet and gaining urban legitimation by seeing that no investiture was actually carried out without the notables and religious scholars (*Ulama*) assenting and making binding arrangements in the name of the community. As Geertz (1968) has noted, the Alawites in Morocco managed to combine in their sultanate principles of political and religious organization that remain antithetic in most parts of the Muslim world. The religious legitimacy extended even to the marginal population officially considered politically dissident.

In Morocco the French administered neither directly nor through a partial control, as in Tunisia, but by a complicated administrative structure that dissociated the symbols of legitimacy, the loci of power, and the instrument of authority. The monarchy was preserved; administration lay in the hands of Europeans, who acted in the name of the monarchy, and a body of qaids formally appointed by the sultan. The French protected the Berber qaids and their tribal solidarities, encouraging chieftaincies and keeping alive the old Marabout confraternities. In contrast to Tunisia, Morocco did not continue in the process of centralization of government, due to the absence of tribal segmentation and dissent. Nor did the French destroy the existing administration, as in Algeria, where they had arrived much earlier and erased all existing signs of Algerian sovereignty in the name of an ideology of integration, making the indigenous population a dust of individuals. The protectorate policy in Morocco was based on using the ancient ruling cadres instead of dissolving them. The greater functional weight of the Moroccan monarchy compared with the Tunisian dynasty led the French to undertake the modernization of the sultan's administrative apparatus. The tribes, which for a long time had refused to submit to France, were willing to surrender to the French-supported sultan, bringing the unexpected benefit of unification of the society, to the advantage of the monarchy. The traditional religious universities of Morocco and Tunis were left undisturbed, and the learned strata of the old turban cities continued to exert leadership in a way that was impossible with the deculturation of Algeria. The homogeneity and openness to cosmopolitan influences in Tunisia and the greater historical weakness of the bey compared with the sultan of Morocco undermined the bey's authority and permitted the creation of a secular one-party state engaged in considerable mobilization. In Morocco the Berber Dahir of 1930, which attempted to isolate the Berber rural society through the maintenance and restoration of customary law and legalization of the dual conception of the land of government and the land of dissidence, thus structuring the divisions between Berbers and Arabs, led against their goals to the emergence of modern nationalism. The protest movement expressed the liberals' fear of partition of their society but also enlisted the support of politico-religious leaders, who, with the backing of urban bourgeois families and in the name of primordial Islam, clustered their energies around the restoration of integral power in the hands of the monarch. French-sponsored educational institutions for the sons of urban bourgeois families and Berber students, a military academy oriented to the children of rural notables, and the persistence of traditional Islamic education further divided the elite. The nationalist movement, *Istiqlal,* was led by a coalition of heterogenous elites, whose aims were approved by the sultan. Simultaneously accused of capitulation by some nationalists and of obstructionism by the French, reproached by Chief El Glawi of being the king only of the *Istiqlal* and the marginal elements of turban society, Mohammed V became allied with the national elites. This led to counteralliances from the apparently civic to the fundamentally primordial, particularly around the rural notability. To counteract the growing turban opposition, the French attempted to ruralize politics by expanding the suffrage. Within the boycott of the elections by the *Istiqlal,* the French began a policy of reactivation of tribal dissidence combined with the repression of the urban elite. Mobilization of religious chiefs and qaids, and through them of traditional masses, against the sultan effected his deposition and exile. Nothing better might be imagined to bring together such diverse factions as the Marxists and the *Ulama* for the restoration of the monarch in place of the broader goals of independence, forcing even the sultan improvised by the French to demand the return of the legitimate ruler. Through this complex process the monarchy emerged as the major beneficiary of independence, with the national elite forced to a secondary role, and the unitary party drowned in a morass of pluralistic tendencies. As Geertz notes (1968, p. 78), "there is probably no other liberated colony in which the struggle for independence so centered around the capture, revival, and renovation of a traditional institution." At the same time the rapidly expanding state power undermined the traditionalist, scripturalist, Islamic forces.

The Moroccan case well exemplifies trends found in different degrees and forms in many transitions from colonialism to independence, trends sometimes masked by semi- or pseudomodern authoritarian forms. The particular historical development in the colonial policy of segmentation, traditionalism, and praetorianism, the structural incapacity of the elite to undertake rural mobilization, and the functional weight of the monarchy resulted in the unstable and ineffective semitraditional system we have described above. Unfortunately, we cannot extend ourselves in the comparative analysis that Hermassi develops with Tunisia, one of the most stable and successful mobilizational single-party systems, and with Algeria, where the colonial rule, most destructive of indigenous society due to its direct rule, the large white settlement, and the deculturation, probably created the difficulties of political institutionalization that have led to the rule by the army. His analysis shows how important a thorough understanding of the historical background, precolonial and colonial, is to a grasp of the diversity of authoritarian regimes emerging in non-Western societies. The example of Morocco should indicate how superficial some of the typological efforts to understand such regimes can be. It also shows, considering the degree to which the countries of the Maghreb share a common Islamic culture and common European influences, the limits of a cultural interpretation underlying so many area approaches to comparative politics and the importance of structural, social, historical, and economic factors.

Sultanistic Regimes

We encounter a few regimes based on personal rulership (Roth, 1971) with loyalty to the ruler based not on tradition, or on him embodying an ideology, or on a unique personal mission, or on charismatic qualities, but on a mixture of fear and rewards to his collaborators. The ruler exercises his power without restraint at his own discretion and above all unencumbered by rules or by any commitment to an ideology or value system. The binding norms and relations of bureaucratic administration are constantly subverted by personal arbitrary decisions of the ruler, which he does not feel constrained to justify in ideological terms. In many respects the organization of power and of the staff of the ruler is similar to traditional patrimonialism as described by Weber (1968, pp. 231–32). But the lack of constraint derived from tradition and from continuing traditional legitimacy distinguishes it from the historical types of patrimonial rule. The staff of such rulers is constituted not by an establishment with distinctive career lines, like a bureaucratic army or civil servants, recruited by more or less universalistic criteria, but largely by men chosen directly by the ruler. They are neither "disciples" nor old fighters of a movement party or conspiratorial group. They are often men who would not enjoy any prestige or esteem in the society on their own account but whose power is derived exclusively from the ruler. Among them we very often find members of his family, friends, cronies, business associates, and men directly involved in the use of violence to sustain the regime. The army and the police play a prominent role in the system, but assassination, attacks, and harassment against opponents are often carried out privately with the knowledge of the ruler but without using the police or the courts. Certainly such arbitrary use of power and the fear of it can also be found in the worst phases of totalitarianism. However, there is an essential difference between these regimes and totalitarian systems: the lack of ideological goals for the society on the part of the ruler and his collaborators as well as of any effort of mobilization of the population in a mass single party. The personalistic and particularistic use of power for essentially private ends of the ruler and his collaborators makes the country essentially like a huge domain. Support is based not on a coincidence of interest between preexisting privileged social groups and the ruler but on the interests created by his rule, the rewards he offers for loyalty, and the fear of his vengeance. The boundaries between the public treasury and the private wealth of the ruler become blurred. He and his collaborators, with his consent, take appropriate public funds freely, establish profit-oriented monopolies, and demand gifts and payoffs from business for which no public accounting is given; the enterprises of the ruler contract with the state, and the ruler often shows his generosity to his followers and to his subjects in a particularistic way. The family of the ruler often plays a prominent political role, appropriates public offices, and shares in the spoils. It is this fusion between the public and the private and the lack of commitment to impersonal purposes that distinguishes essentially such regimes from totalitarianism. The economy is subject to considerable governmental interference but not for the purposes of planning but of extracting resources.

The position of the officials derives from their purely personal submission to the ruler, and their position vis-à-vis the subjects is merely the external aspect of this relation, in contrast to bureaucracies, both civil and military. Even when the political official is not a personal dependent, the ruler demands unconditional administrative compliance, for the official's loyalty to his office is not an impersonal commitment to impersonal tasks that define the extent and content of his office, but rather a servant's loyalty based on a strictly personal relationship to the ruler and an obligation that in principle permits no limitation. In this description we have paraphrased some of Weber's description of patrimonial officialdom. Those officials enjoy little security; they are promoted or dismissed at will and enjoy no independent status. They may even, in extreme cases, be subject to dishonor and persecution one day and return to the graces of the ruler the next. The legal and symbolic institutionalization of the regime is pure facade and likely to change for reasons external to the system, like the availability of models enjoying legitimacy abroad.

Such regimes are obviously dependent on the economic situation, since the rewards the ruler can offer to his staff depend on it, and opposition to his regime is likely to come from disappointed members of the staff rather than from social strata, institutions, or political organizations of the regime. The sudden collapse of such regimes as well as their equally sudden reestablishment manifest the fundamental instability of such domination based on force.

Such regimes are unlikely to be established in advanced industrial societies but are compatible with an agrarian economy with commercial and some industrial enterprises. Their stabilization and continuity require a certain degree of modernization of transportation and communications as well as of the military and police organizations, to provide the funds to sustain the rule and to prevent threats to it from the periphery. The isolation of the rural masses, their lack of education, and their poverty are probably necessary to assure their passive submission, which results from the combination of fear and gratitude for occasional paternalistic welfare measures made possible by a modicum of economic development. The rulers' policies are likely to encourage certain types of capitalist enterprise, particularly commercial and plantation types, but can be a serious obstacle to rational calculability, required by enterprises with heavy investments in fixed capital and oriented toward a consumer market. It is also probable that a small-sized country with few urban centers might facilitate this type of rule, making difficult the emergence of alternative elites and of uprisings in the periphery. Certainly the regimes of Trujillo (Wiarda, 1968; Galíndez, 1973; Crassweller, 1966) and Duvalier (Rotberg, 1971; Diederich and Burt, 1969; Fleischman, 1971), which in many ways fit this model, were made possible by the fact that the Dominican Republic and Haiti are on an island, which, combined with their economic dependence on export crops, facilitated both the control of resources like trade and the isolation from external threats.[40] Outside of underdeveloped economies and societies, sultanistic regimes, like some traditional autocracies, have a chance of survival only when they can dispose of considerable economic resources produced by enterprises that do not require a modern industrial labor force and entrepreneurial class, a modern administration, urbanization, expansion of education, etc. Obviously, easily exploitable natural resources whose production is in the hands of one or few enterprises with high profits can provide the resources for such a regime. In the case of Trujillo,[41] the limited modernization of the country under his longtime rule facilitated both the appropriation of resources and the use of some modern techniques of control that most nineteenth-century Latin American *caudillos* could not count on, making their rule so often unstable and often contested by other *caudillos*. The discovery of oil in Venezuela certainly made possible the consolidation of the rule of the *caudillo* Gómez and later of Pérez Jiménez, even when at that point Venezuelan society had already reached a level of complexity that ultimately made his rule impossible despite some populistic components. The plantation economy of some Central American republics has also served as a basis for such regimes. However, it would be a mistake to consider such regimes as the inevitable result of the economic structure, ignoring many other factors contributing to their emergence and stability, including the interests in "order" of foreign investors that have established stable "business" relations with the ruler.

This type cannot be always neatly distinguished from other types of authoritarian regimes, particularly those without a real single party. But certainly any student of the Dominican Republic or Salazar's Portugal, to take just two relatively small countries, becomes immediately sensitive to the fundamental difference between two types of authoritarianism. The rule of a Stalin or Hitler would never have produced the admiration and loyalty of the masses, and even of intellectuals and foreign observers identified with very different types of regimes, if they had not put their rule at the service of impersonal purposes. Under totalitarianism, even when some of the members of the ruling group like a Göring enjoy life and when corruption is not absent, the rule of a Stalin or a Hitler was not directed at the personal enrichment of the ruler and his family, nor was power exercised simply in the benefit of the ruling group. In fact, under such a sultanistic system what is at stake is the maintenance and futherance of the privileges, not of the social class or stratum, but of a group of power holders, often by exploiting even the privileged landowners, merchants, or foreign capitalists who buy their peace in that way.

Obviously, the costs of such a regime fall mainly on the masses of the population, since the privileged are likely to revert their contributions to the maintenance of the system back onto the masses, who lack of any organization to resist exploitation due to the atomization created by the autocratic rule and whose only recourse is to turn to the benevolent paternalism of the ruler. Sometimes the ruler, out of status resentment and to consolidate his power against economically or socially privileged oligarchies or institutional groups like the army officers, might combine his rule through patrimonial officials and mercenaries with populistic gestures. This seems to have been the pattern of Duvalier in Haiti in his exploitation of racial and social tensions.

The overthrow of sultanistic authoritarian regimes without considerable prior social and economic change is not likely to lead to anything but another sultanistic regime or at best to more rational authoritarian rule with the support of the privileged oligarchies. However, with outside support it is not impossible that a revolutionary regime, which might have some totalitarian features, could emerge, while the transition to a stable democracy seems extremely difficult. Batista's Cuba is a very special case, since it shared many of the characteristics of the model just described, even though it also had some of those of the authoritarian regime, combining the rule of the military with that of politicians and interest groups (Solaún, 1969). The fact that Batista was ruling over a country with many modern characteristics in its urban sector contributed to its basic illegitimacy and its ultimate downfall when its military could not suppress the Castro rebellion. The unwillingness of the establishment of Cuban society—parts of the judiciary, the Church, etc.—to support Batista's rule made his overthrow and his flight possible without a real civil war, which is more likely to accompany revolutionary challenges against traditional autocratic rule, like in Yemen, or nonsultanistic authoritarian regimes.

Caudillismo and Caciquismo

In nineteenth-century Latin American politics the disintegration of larger political units and the difficulties of establishing a new type of legitimate rule led to the rule of *caudillo*—"chieftain"—politics. *Caudillaje* politics has been defined by Eric Wolf and Edward Hansen by the following four characteristics:

(1) the repeated emergence of armed patron-client sets, cemented by personal ties of dominance and submission, and by a common desire to obtain wealth by force of arms; (2) the lack of institutionalized means for succession to offices; (3) the use of violence in political competition; and (4) the repeated failures of incumbent leaders to guarantee their tenures as chieftains. (Woolf and Hansen, 1967, p. 169)

It was a system that emerged with the broad diffusion of military power among wide strata of the population, as it could not be found in modern Europe, and that deranged the predictable interplay of hierarchical class relations. Its base was the traditional *hacienda*, the labor and economic dependencies based on it, the social ties of kinship and friendship, and a personal capacity for the organization of violence (Gilmore, 1964). It was an essentially unstable system, due to the limited resources to impose one's rule, the competition among *caudillos*, the instability of personal loyalties. This instability and changes in the international economic situation as reflected in Latin America led to "order and progress" dictatorships, exhibiting many *caudillo* features but achieving greater centralization, more stable relations with certain social forces, and international links, of which the Mexican Porfiriato (1876–1911) was a prototype. The "order and progress" dictatorship was on the boundaries between the sultanistic and the military-bureaucratic authoritarian regime. However, at the local level the power structures that served as the basis of *caudillaje* became the support of *caciquismo, coronelismo* systems (Kern, 1973), which were based on alliances between central power holders and those at the local level who "delivered" the votes in exchange for patronage, pork barrel, or just exemption from interference in their arbitrary or paternalistic authority over laborers, tenants, and local government.

Caciquismo has been defined by Kern and Dolkart (1973, pp. 1–2) "as an oligarchical system of politics run by a diffuse and heterogenous elite whose common denominator is local power used for national purposes." Its base is predominantly agrarian but not exclusively so, since professionals, merchants, industrialists, and urban bosses of political machines are often involved. The basis has been "strong local power organized pyramid-fashion so that the 'boss' systems or 'chiefdoms'— *cacicatos*—interlock with one another to form the political infrastructure in many Luso-Hispanic states," with a restricted oligarchy of nationally influential men at the top connected consciously through social ties, formal and informal, with the local *caciques*.

Such structures, through constant transformations,[42] have survived under both authoritarian and semidemocratic regimes at the center up to our days. Sultanistic authoritarianism reproduces at the national level some of the worst features of local nineteenth-century *caciquismo,* perhaps due to the absence of some of the social controls by a local community.

4

AUTHORITARIAN REGIMES

Toward a Definition of Authoritarian Regimes

In an earlier essay we attempted to define a variety of nondemocratic and nontotalitarian political systems as authoritarian if they were

> political systems with limited, not responsible, political pluralism, without elaborate and guiding ideology, but with distinctive mentalities, without extensive nor intensive political mobilization, except at some points in their development, and in which a leader or occasionally a small group exercises power within formally ill-defined limits but actually quite predictable ones. (Linz, 1964, p. 255)

This definition was developed by contrasting those systems both with competitive democracies and with the ideal type of totalitarian systems (Linz, 1964, 1970a, 1973a, 1973b). It implies clear conceptual boundaries with democratic polities but somewhat more diffuse ones with totalitarianism, since pre- and post-totalitarian situations and regimes might also fit the definition. A further delimitation is the exclusion of traditional legitimate regimes, on account of the different sources of legitimacy of the leadership, or oligarchies ruling authoritarianly. The type of regimes we have labelled sultanistic-authoritarian regimes have much in common with those we intend to cover with our definition of authoritarian but differ from them in the importance in sultanistic-authoritarian regimes of arbitrary and unpredictable use of power and the weakness of the limited political pluralism. For other reasons we find it convenient to exclude from our definition the nineteenth-century semiconstitutional monarchies, which were halfway between traditional

159

legitimate and authoritarian rule (with monarchical, estate, and even feudal elements mixed with emerging democratic institutions), and the censitary democracies, where the restricted suffrage represented a step in the process of development toward modern competitive democracies based at least on universal male suffrage. The oligarchic democracies that, particularly in Latin America, have resisted pressures toward further democratization through the persistence of suffrage limitations based on illiteracy, control or manipulation of elections by *caciques,* frequent recourse to the moderating power of the army, undifferentiated parties, etc., find themselves on the borderline between modern authoritarian regimes and democracy. They are closer to democracy in their constitutional and ideological conception but sociologically more similar to some authoritarian regimes. Our delimitation by exclusion still leaves us with a large number of contemporary political systems fitting our definition and therefore requiring, as we shall see, the characterization of a number of subtypes.

Our concept focuses on the way of exercising power, organizing power, linking with the societies, on the nature of the belief systems sustaining it, and on the role of citizens in the political process without, however, paying attention to the substantive content of policies, the goals pursued, the *raison d'être* of such regimes. It does not tell us much about the institutions, groups, and social strata forming part of the limited pluralism or about those excluded. The emphasis on the more strictly political aspects exposes the concept to some of the same criticism of formalism advanced against a general concept of totalitarianism, or for that matter of democracy. We feel, however, that by characterizing regimes independently of the policies they pursue we tend to deal in a distinctive way with problems faced by all political systems, for example, the relationship between politics and religion and the intellectuals. The conditions for their emergence, stability, transformation, and perhaps breakdown are also quite distinct. The general and abstract character of our definition makes it even more imperative to go down on the ladder of abstraction into the study of the variety of subtypes, as we shall do here.

We speak of authoritarian regimes rather than authoritarian governments to indicate the relatively low specificity of political institutions: they often penetrate the life of the society, preventing, even forcibly, the political expression of certain group interests (as religion in Turkey and in Mexico after the revolution, labor in Spain) or shaping them by interventionist policies like those of corporativist regimes.

In contrast to some analysts of totalitarianism, we speak of regimes rather than of societies because the distinction between state and society is not fully obliterated even in the intentions of the rulers.

The pluralistic element is the most distinctive feature of these regimes, but it cannot be strongly enough emphasized that in contrast to democracies, with their almost *unlimited* pluralism, their institutionalized political pluralism, we are dealing here with *limited* pluralism. In fact, it has been suggested that we could also have characterized these regimes as of limited monism. In fact, these two terms would suggest the fairly wide range in which those regimes operate. The limitation of pluralism may be legal or de facto, implemented more or less effectively, confined to strictly political groups or extended to interest groups, as long as there remain groups not created by or dependent on the state which influence the political process one way or another. Some regimes go even so far as to institutionalize the political participation of the limited number of independent groups or institutions and even encourage their emergence without, however, leaving any doubt that the rulers ultimately define which groups they will allow to exist and under what conditions. In addition, political power is not legally and/or de facto accountable through such groups to the citizens, even when it might be quite responsive to them. This is in contrast to democratic governments, where the political forces are formally dependent on the support of constituencies, whatever de facto deviations the Michelsian "iron law of oligarchy" might introduce. In authoritarian regimes the men who come to power reflecting the views of various groups and institutions derive their position not from the support from those groups alone but from the trust placed in them by the leader or ruling group, which certainly takes into account their prestige and their influence. They have a kind of constituency; we might call it a potential constituency, but this is not solely or even principally the source of their power. A constant process of co-optation of leaders is the mechanisms by which different sectors or institutions become participants in the system, and this process accounts for the characteristics of the elite: a certain heterogeneity in its background and career patterns and the smaller number of professional politicians, men who have made their career in strictly political organizations, compared with the number of those recruited from the bureaucracy, technically skilled elites, the army, interest groups, and sometimes religious groups.

As we shall see, in some of these regimes an official or a single or privileged party is one more-or-less important component of the limited pluralism. On paper such parties often claim the monopolistic power of the totalitarian parties and presumably perform the same functions, but in reality they have to be kept clearly distinct. The absence or weakness of a political party often makes lay organizations sponsored by or linked with the Church, like Catholic Action or the Opus Dei in Spain, a reservoir of leadership for such regimes not too different from their function in the recruitment of elites of Christian democratic parties (Hermet, 1973). The single party more often than not is what the Africans have called a *parti unifié* rather than a *parti unique,* a party based on the fusion of different elements rather than a single disciplined body (Foltz, 1965). Often such parties are a creation from above rather than from the grass roots, created by the group in power rather than a party-conquering power like in totalitarian systems.

In the definition of authoritarian regimes we use the term "mentality" rather than "ideology," from the distinction of the German sociologist Theodor Geiger (1932, pp. 77–79). For him ideologies are systems of thought more or less intellectually elaborated and organized, often in written form, by intellectuals, pseudointellectuals, or with their assistance. Mentalities are ways of thinking and feeling, more emotional than rational, that provide noncodified ways of reacting to different situations. He uses a very graphic German expression: mentality is *subjektiver Geist* (even when collective); ideology is *objektiver Geist.* Mentality is intellectual attitude; ideology is intellectual content. Mentality is psychic predisposition, ideology is reflection, self-interpretation; mentality is previous, ideology later; mentality is formless, fluctuating—ideology, however, is firmly formed. Ideology is a concept of the sociology of culture, mentality is a concept of the study of social character. Ideologies have a strong utopian element, mentalities are closer to the present or the past. Ideological belief systems based on fixed elements and characterized by strong affect and closed cognitive structure, with considerable constraining power, important for mass mobilization and manipulation, are characteristic of totalitarian systems. In contrast, the consensus in democratic regimes is based on a procedural consensus, the commitment to which acquires some of the qualities of ideological beliefs.

The utility and validity of the distinction between mentality and ideology has been questioned by Bolivar Lamounier (1974). He notes that as an actual political variable, as cognitive forms of consciousness actually operative in political life, particularly in the communication process, they are not really that different. He feels that the distinction implies a hasty dismissal of the ruling ideas of authoritarian regimes as an object worth study. Nothing could be further from our intent. He rightly notes the effectiveness of symbolic communication, the multiplicity of referential connections between symbol and social reality, in authoritarian regimes.

Much of the argument hinges on the philosophical assumptions about the definition of ideology, an aspect into which we shall not go. Both ideologies and mentalities as characterized above are part of a broader phenomenon of ideas leading to action-oriented ideas—which are an aspect of the institutionalization of power relationships for which Lamounier prefers to use the term "ideology."

The important question is, Why do ideas take a different form, different coherence, articulation, comprehensiveness, explicitness, intellectual elaboration, and normativeness? On those various dimensions ideologies and mentalities differ. Those differences are not without consequences in the political process. It is more difficult to conceive of mentalities as binding, requiring a commitment of the rulers and the subjects irrespective of costs and of the need of coercion to implement them. Mentalities are more difficult to diffuse among the masses, less susceptible to be used in education, less likely to come into conflict with religion or science and more difficult to use as a test of loyalty. The range of issues for which an answer can be derived from them, the degree of precision of those answers, the logic of the process of derivation, and the visibility of the contradictions between them and policies are very different. Their constraining power to legitimate and delegitimate actions are very different. The student of an authoritarian regime would be hard pressed to identify explicit references to ideas guiding the regime in legal theorizing and judicial decisions in nonpolitical cases, in art criticism and scientific arguments, and would find only limited evidence of their use in education. He or she certainly would not find the rich and distinctive language, the new terminology and esoteric use of an ideology, all difficult to understand to the outsider but important to the participants. Nor would he or she find in the libraries stacks of books and publications of an ideological character elaborating endlessly and in a variety of directions those ideas.

Let us admit that the distinction is and cannot be clear-cut but reflects two extreme poles with a large gray area in between. Certainly bureaucratic-military authoritarian regimes are likely to reflect more the mentality of their rulers. In others we are likely to find what Susan Kaufman (1970) has called a programmatic consensus and in others a set of ideas derived from a variety of sources haphazardly combined to give the impression of being an ideology in the sense we have described in the totalitarian systems. Certainly the authoritarian regimes on the periphery of ideological centers feel the pressure to imitate, incorporate, manipulate dominant ideological styles. This can often lead scholars to serious misunderstanding of such regimes, to misplaced emphases. The real question to ask is, What power arrangements seem to prevent ideological articulation in such regimes? In our view the complex coalition of forces, interests, political traditions, and institutions—part of the limited pluralism—requires the rulers to use as symbolic referent the minimum common denominator of the coalition. In this way the rulers achieve the neutralization of a maximum of potential opponents in the process of taking power (in the absence of the highly mobilized mass of supporters). The vagueness of the mentality blunts the lines of cleavage in the coalition, allowing the rulers to retain the loyalty of disparate elements. The lack of an assertion of specific, articulated, and explicit commitments facilitates adaptation to changing conditions in the nonsupportive environment, particularly in the case of authoritarian regimes in the Western democratic sphere of influence. The reference to generic values like patriotism and nationalism, economic development, social justice, and order and the discreet and pragmatic incorporation of ideological elements derived from the dominant political centers of the time allow rulers who have gained power without mobilized mass support to neutralize opponents, co-opt a variety of supporters, and decide policies pragmatically. Mentalities, semi- or pseudoideologies reduce the utopian strain in politics and with it conflict that otherwise would require either institutionalization or more repression than the rulers could afford. The limited utopianism obviously is congruent with conservative tendencies.

Such regimes pay a price for their lack of ideology in our sense of the term. It limits their capacity to mobilize people to create the psychological and emotional identification of the masses with the regime. The absence of an articulate ideology, of a sense of ultimate meaning, of long-run purposes, of an a priori model of ideal society reduces the attractiveness of such regimes to those for whom ideas, meaning, and values are central. The alienation of intellectuals, students, youth, and deeply religious persons from such regimes, even when successful and relatively liberal compared with totalitarian systems, can be explained in part by the absence or weakness of ideology. One of the advantages of authoritarian regimes with an important fascist component was that this derivative ideology appealed to some of those groups. But it also was one of the sources of tension when the disregard of the elite of the regime for those ideological elements became apparent.

In theory we should be able to distinguish this content of ideas of the regime, including its style, from the ideas guiding or influencing the political process as an actual political variable. It could be argued that the first aspect, to which we will be looking for the objectivization, is ultimately less central than the subjective appropriation, the various forms of consciousness actually operative in political life. However, we feel that the distinction between mentality and ideology is not irrelevant for the way in which they affect activities and communication processes in politics and society. The complex interaction between both levels of analysis precludes any a priori statement about the direction in which the relationship operates. Probably in totalitarian systems the actual political processes are more deeply affected by the content of the ideology, while in authoritarian regimes the mentalities of the rulers, not having to be equally explicit, might reflect more the social and political realities.

The elusiveness of mentalities, the mimetic and derivative character of the so-called ideologies of authoritarian regimes, has limited the number of scholarly studies of this dimension of such regimes. Only interview studies of the elites and surveys of the population, of great sophistication given the limited freedom of expression and the obstacles in the communication processes, make this an important dimension in the study of such regimes. The typology of authoritarian regimes we will present relies more on the character of the limited pluralism and the degree of apathy or mobilization than on an analysis of types of mentalities.

* * *

In our original definition we emphasized the actual absence of extensive and intensive political mobilization but admitted that at some point of the development of such regimes there could be such mobilization. The characteristic of low and limited political mobilization is therefore a factual characteristic on which such regimes tend to converge, for a variety of reasons. As we shall see in the discussion of the subtypes, in some regimes the depoliticization of the mass of the citizens falls into the intent of the rulers, fits with their mentality, and reflects the character of the components of the limited pluralism supporting them.

In other types of systems the rulers initially intend to mobilize their supporters and the population at large into active involvement in the regime and its organizations. Their public commitments, often derivative ideological conceptions, push them in that direction. The historical and social context of the establishment of the regime favors or demands such a mobilization through a single party and its mass organizations. The struggle for national independence from a colonial power or for full independence, the desire to incorporate into the political process sectors of the society untapped by any previous political leadership, or the defeat of a highly mobilized opponent in societies in which democracy had allowed and encouraged such a mobilization lead to the emergence of mobilizational authoritarian regimes of a nationalist, populist, or fascist variety. In reality there is a likelihood of convergence of regimes starting from such different assumptions following quite different routes. That convergence should not, however, obscure many important differences derived from those origins in terms of the type of pluralism emerging, the legitimacy formulae chosen, the response to crises situations, the capacity for transformation, the sources and types of opposition, etc.

Ultimately the degree of political mobilization and with it the opportunities for participation in the regime of those among the citizens supporting it are a result of the other two dimensions used in the definition of authoritarian regimes. Mobilization and participation ultimately become difficult to sustain unless the regime moves in a more totalitarian or democratic direction. Effective mobilization, particularly through a single party and its mass organizations, would be perceived as a threat by the other components of the limited pluralism, typically the army, the bureaucracy, the churches, or interest groups. To break through those constraining conditions would require moves in the totalitarian direction. The failure to break through those conditions and the limited pluralism standing in the way to totalitarianism has been well analyzed by Alberto Aquarone, who quotes this revealing conversation of Mussolini with an old syndicalist friend:

> If you could imagine the effort it has taken me to search for a possible equilibrium in which I could avoid the collision of antagonistic powers which touched each other side by side, jealous, distrustful one of the other, government, party, monarchy, Vatican, army, militzia, prefects, provincial party leaders, ministers, the head of the Confederazioni [corporative structures] and the giant monopolistic interests, etc. you will understand they are the indigestions of totalitarianism,

in which I did not succeed in melting that "estate" that I had to accept in 1922 without reservations. A pathological connecting tissue linking the traditional and circumstantial deficiencies of this great, small, Italian people, which a tenacious therapy of twenty years has achieved to modify only on the surface. (Aquarone, 1965, p. 302)

We have described how the maintenance of equilibrium between those limited pluralisms limits in reality the effectiveness of the mobilization to a single party and ultimately has to lead to the apathy of the members and activists, since such a party offers limited access to power compared with other channels. Underdevelopment, particularly of a large rural population living in isolated areas and engaging in subsistence agriculture, often linked with traditional or clientelistic power structures integrated into the unified party, despite the ideological pronouncements, the organization charts, and the machinery of plebiscitarian elections, does not create a participatory political culture, not even controlled or manipulated participation.

As we shall see in more detail, the authoritarian regimes that emerge after a period of competitive democratic participation that created an unsolvable conflict in the society opt for depoliticization and apathy, which is felt by many citizens as a relief from the tensions of the previous period. Initially this is the apathy of those defeated by the new regime, but in the absence of a disciplined totalitarian mass party and its mass organizations combined with terror, little effort will be made to integrate them to participate in the system. As the tensions and hatreds that produced a mobilization for the system diminish, the supporters are also likely to lapse into apathy, which often the rulers might welcome to avoid pressures to make good the promises they made in the process of mobilization.

The absence of an ideology, the heterogeneous and compromise character, and often mimetism of the guiding ideas, and above all the mentality of the rulers, particularly military elites, bureaucrats, experts, and co-opted politicians of pro-regime parties, are serious obstacles in the process of mobilization and participation. Without an ideology it becomes difficult to mobilize activists for voluntary campaigns, regular attendance at party meetings, face-to-face propaganda activities, etc. Without an ideology with utopian components it is difficult to attract those interested in politics as an end in itself rather than a means for more pragmatic and immediate interests. Without ideology the young, the students, the intellectuals are not likely to get involved in politics and provide the cadres for politicization of the population.

Without the utopian element, without the appeal to broader constituencies that would require a participatory pluralism rather than the limited, controlled, and co-opted pluralism of elites, the appeals based on a consensual, nonconflictive society, except in moments of upsurge of nationalism or of danger to the regime, tend to reduce politics to administration of the public interest and to the de facto expression of particular interests.

The limited pluralism of authoritarian regimes and the different share that the tolerated pluralistic components have in the exercise of power in different moments lead to complex patterns of semiopposition and pseudoopposition within the regime (Linz, 1973a). There is semiopposition by groups that are not dominant or represented in the governing group and that engage in partial criticism but are willing to participate in power without fundamentally challenging the regime. Without being institutionalized such groups are not illegitimate, even when they lack a legal framework in which to operate. They might be highly critical of the government and some aspects of the institutional order, but they distinguish between these and the leader of the regime and accept the historical legitimacy or at least necessity of the authoritarian formula. There are groups that advocate different emphases and policy, groups that join in supporting the establishment of the regime but in the hope of achieving goals not shared by their coalition partners. There is dissidence among those who initially identified with the system but did not participate in its establishment, typically the Young Turks of the regime, and among those within the regime who want to work for goals that are not illegitimate, like the restoration of a previous regime initially announced but never realized. There are those who had stronger ideological commitments but accepted seeing them postponed to gain power against an enemy, those with a foreign model and/or even loyalty from which the rulers attempt to distance themselves, and in the late stages of such a regime those who oppose its transformation, specifically its liberalization and the abandonment of its exclusionary character. Semiopposition is likely to appear among men of the older generation who joined in the establishment of the regime to pursue goals they had already formulated before the takeover. But it also appears among the intellectuals and the young, particularly students who have taken seriously the rhetorical pronouncements of the leadership and who in addition find that there are no effective channels for political participation. Not infrequently the semiopposition within the regime becomes an alegal opposition. It has given up hope of transforming the regime from the inside but is not yet ready to move into illegal or subversive activities and finds intermittent tolerance sometimes based on the personal ties established in earlier years. The weakness of the efforts of political socialization and indoctrination in authoritarian regimes also accounts for the fact that when the third generation, never incorporated in the regime, discovers politics it might turn to an alegal opposition. The autonomy left by the regime to certain social organizations, the limited efforts of liberalization and increased participation in the regime organizations, and the relative openness to other societies create opportunities for the emergence of an alegal opposition, which sometimes serves as a front for an illegal opposition that is ready to infiltrate the organizations of the regime, rejecting the moral qualms about participating in it held by other opponents. Opposition is often channeled into formally apolitical organizations of cultural, religious, or professional character. In multilingual, multicultural societies, where the regime is identified with one of the national groups, cultural manifestations such as the use of languages other than the official language become an expression of opposition. The special position of the Catholic Church in many societies under authoritarian rule and the legal status of many of its organizations in the concordats between the Vatican and the rulers allow priests and laymen a certain autonomy to serve as a channel for opposition sentiments of social classes, cultural minorities, generational unrest, etc., and for the emergence of new leaders. In the case of the Catholic Church the transnational character, the moral legitimation of the relatively wide range of ideological positions by the refusal on the part of the Pope to condemn them, the legitimacy for moral prophetic indignation against injustice, particularly after Vaticanum II, together with the concern of the hierarchy for the autonomy of religious organizations and the freedom of priests account for the role of religious groups in the politics of authoritarian regimes. Paradoxically, the Church has provided the regimes through its lay organizations with elites but has also protected its dissidents and occasionally played the role described by Guy Hermet (1973) as tribunicial against the regime by being witness of moral values against abuses of power. The Church as an institution that will outlast any regime, even those with which it becomes identified in the particular historical moment, is likely to disidentify and regain its autonomy when signs of crisis appear. The same is true for other permanent institutions that might have retained considerable autonomy under authoritarian rule, like the judiciary or even the professional civil servants.

Let us emphasize here that the semioppositions—the alegal but tolerated opposition, the relatively autonomous role of various institutions under conditions of semifreedom—creates a complex political process of far-reaching consequences for the society and its political development. The liberalization of authoritarian regimes can go far, but without a change in the nature of the regime, without the institutionalization of political parties, is likely to be quite limited. The semifreedom under such regimes imposes on their opponents certain costs that are quite different from those of persecution of illegal oppositions and that explain their frustration, disintegration, and sometimes readiness to cooptation, which contribute to the persistence of such regimes sometimes as much as does their repressive capacity. The ambiguity of opposition under authoritarian regimes contrasts with the clear boundaries between regime and its opponents in totalitarian systems. However, let us emphasize that the limited pluralism, the process of liberalization, and the existence of the tolerated opposition, in the absence of institutional channels for political participation and for the opposition to reach the mass of the population, allow a clear distinction between authoritarian and democratic regimes.

Before closing our general discussion of authoritarian regimes we want to call attention to one difficulty in their study. In a world in which the great and most successful powers are and have been either stable democracies or communist or fascist political systems, with the unique attraction given to them by their ideologies, their organizational capacity, their apparent stability, their success as advanced industrial nations or in overcoming economic backwardness, and their capacity to overcome international second-rank status, authoritarian regimes are in an ambiguous position. None of them has served as a utopian model for other societies, except, perhaps for special historical reasons, Nasser's Egypt in the Arab world. Possibly Mexico, with its combination of the revolutionary myth and the pragmatic stability of its hegemonic party regime, could serve rulers as a model. None of the authoritarian regimes has fired the imagination of intellectuals and activists across the borders. None has inspired an international of parties supporting such a model. Only the original solutions attempted by the Yugoslavs have created a noncritical interest among intellectuals. Under those circumstances authoritarian regimes and their leaders have felt constrained to take the trappings of the appealing totalitarian models, avoiding or unable to incorporate the substance of the model. Only the thirties, as we shall see, with the ideology of corporativism combining a variety of ideological heritages and linking with Catholic conservative social doctrine, seemed to offer a genuine nontotalitarian and nondemocratic ideological alternative. The visible failure of such systems, the fact that no major power followed that route, the diffuse boundaries between conservative or Catholic corporativism and Italian fascism, and, finally, the disengagement of the Church from its commitment to organic theories of society have ultimately undermined this third model of politics. Authoritarian regimes, whatever their roots in the society, whatever their achievements, are ultimately confronted with two appealing alternative models of polity, which limit the possibilities of full and self-confident institutionalization and give strength to their opponents (Linz, 1973b).

The Problem of a Typology of Authoritarian Regimes

The social science literature offers many ideas for developing typologies of such regimes: Almond and Powell's (1966) distinction of conservative, modernizing, and premobilized authoritarian systems, of which respectively Spain, Brazil, and Ghana would be examples, and the many inchoate typologies in the chapters of Samuel Huntington and Clement Moore (1970) in their analysis of the dynamics of established one-party systems, particularly Huntington's distinction between exclusionary and revolutionary one-party systems and between revolutionary and established one-party systems. Nor should the pioneer effort of Edward Shils (1960), distinguishing tutelary democracies, modernizing oligarchies, and traditional oligarchies, be forgotten. Giovanni Sartori, in an unpublished study of political parties, with his unexcelled ability to make clear logical distinctions has differentiated the variety of party state systems, that is, noncompetitive-party systems, distinguishing one-party and hegemonic-party systems and, further down on the ladder of abstraction, totalitarian and authoritarian parties, single or hegemonic parties, and finally ideological and pragmatic parties (Sartori, 1970b). The four-fold typology of single-party ideologies of Clement Moore follows. (See Table 4.1.)

It is based on a distinction between instrumental and expressive functions, whose operationalization seems to offer certain difficulties. The distinction resulting between totalitarian and chiliastic systems is particularly hazy, and it is not fully clear why the tutelary should be considered instrumental and the administrative expressive (Moore, 1970b).

It is, however, far from our intention to dismiss or ignore such typologies that highlight certain aspects of authoritarian regimes and that might be particularly valuable for the analysis of such regimes in the new and old states of the non-Western world or certain cultural areas like Africa south of the Sahara.

Since many authoritarian regimes have been founded by military coups and are headed by military men, it would seem that a typology distinguishing military and nonmilitary authoritarian regimes would be fruitful, distinguishing further the political nature and purpose of the military intervention in assuming power. Certainly the writers on military in politics like Finer (1962) and the many specialists on Latin America and the Middle East have made valuable contributions to our understanding of authoritarian regimes. However, a category of military authoritarian regimes would include too many, quite different regimes, as the mention of the names of Ataturk, Pétain, Franco, Perón, Nasser, Odria, Medici, and Cárdenas suggests. Military regimes, with some significant and interesting exceptions, undergo a process of civilization, if they are stable, and the military origin or military background of the head of state does not tell us enough about their nature. Military men can carry out a deep cultural revolution like Ataturk, important social and economic changes like Nasser, displace traditional regimes like they did or prevent a continuing process of change toward democracy and perhaps social revolution after a break

Table 4.1   Transformation Goals

Functions	Total	Partial
Instrumental	Totalitarian	Tutelary
	Stalinist Russian, Maoist China, Nazi Germany, "Stalinist" East Europe	Tunisia, Tanzania, Yugoslavia, Ataturk's Turkey
Expressive	Chiliastic	Administrative
	Fascist Italy, Nkrumah's Ghana, Mali, Guinea, Cuba, Ben Bella's Algeria	Mexico

within tradition with a counterrevolutionary intent, like Franco. Certainly the military mentality of men at the top would give such regimes certain common features, which, however important, are not sufficient for any meaningful typology.

Scholars are likely to be confused in studying authoritarian regimes because of the frequent inauthenticity of their claims. Since the founding group or leader has no or few ideological commitments before taking power except some vague ideas about defending order, uniting the country, modernizing the nation, overthrowing a corrupt regime, or rejecting foreign influences, they find themselves without ideological justification, without ideas attractive to the intellectuals, removed from the mainstream of international ideological confrontations. In that vacuum the rulers will search for acceptable symbols and ideas to incorporate them into their *arcana imperi.* Those ideas are likely to be the ones dominant at the time and congruent within the "march of history." It is no accident that Ataturk should have chosen progressive, secularist, democratic ideas and symbols; that the Eastern European royal dictators, bureaucrats, and officers, and Franco, should have mimicked fascism; that contemporary authoritarian regimes should claim to be socialist and to introduce "democratic centralism" or "participatory democracy" and "workers' councils" rather than corporativism. No scholar should accept such claims at face value—not that the claims are irrelevant, since such initially vague commitments largely condition the international response to such regimes and influence their later development, opening certain possibilities and excluding others (Linz, 1973b). However, it would be dangerous to base our classifications on those claims. Actual policies and the operation of political institutions might be very similar despite such pseudoideological differences, and the similarity in mentality of the rulers might make possible an understanding and affinity between leaders of systems apparently dissimilar.

The ideological elements used, far from central to the understanding of such systems, would allow us to distinguish the following main types.

1. Authoritarian regimes claiming to carry out basic processes of modernization, particularly secularization and educational reforms, to create the preconditions for constitutional democracy like that of the more successful Western nations. Regimes born in the eve of World War I, like Turkey and Mexico, were committed to such a pattern, which was reflected in the institutional rules, ignored in practice, but ultimately is making possible an evolution in that direction.

2. Fascist- or semifascist-nationalist authoritarian regimes.
3. Authoritarian regimes that we shall characterize as "organic statism," attempting to link with the Catholic corporativist social doctrine mixed with fascist elements but distinct from the fascist-populist-nationalist totalitarian conceptions. Often these types of regimes that attempt to institutionalize a particular type of pluralism have been confused with fascism, and the term "clerical fascism" reflects both the bias of the observers and the ambiguity of that type of authoritarianism in the late twenties and early thirties.
4. The authoritarian regimes born in the aftermath of World War II in the newly independent states claiming to pursue a different national way toward participation, including a single party or subordinating the existing parties, characterizing their regimes as tutelary democracies, like Sukarno in Indonesia, or institutionalizing "basic democracies" in Pakistan.
5. More recently, African new nations and Islamic countries rejecting traditional religious conceptions of authority, impressed by the success of communist countries and sometimes searching for their sympathy, have claimed to be socialist, to build mass parties and to reject Western individualism for a new sense of community based on identification with the leader and the party. In the case of Islamic countries an attempt has been made to link those ideological imitations with a genuine national cultural tradition, the Islamic notion of community, sometimes fusing modern ideas with traditional religious conceptions. It is no accident that some political scientists like James Gregor should have noted some of the similarities between African socialism (and similar ideologies) and fascism in semideveloped agrarian societies in the thirties (Gregor, 1968 and 1974a).
6. Communist post-totalitarian authoritarian regimes, described by Gordon Skilling as "consultative authoritarianism, quasi-pluralistic authoritarianism, democratizing and pluralistic authoritarianism and anarchic authoritarianism."

Despite the usefulness of the six types briefly delineated above, except for the sixth one, I would argue that this is not the most fruitful approach to the development of a typology of authoritarian regimes as defined above.

Toward a Typology of Authoritarian Regimes

If our definition is useful, it should also allow us to develop subtypes of such regimes. The limited pluralism, as opposed to the tendency toward monism, should lead us to typologies taking into account which institutions and groups are allowed to participate and in what way, and which ones are excluded. If rejection of mobilization along totalitarian lines or failure to achieve such mobilization distinguishes such regimes from totalitarianism, the reasons for and the nature of the limited mobilization should provide another dimension of a typology. Since mentalities in contrast to ideologies are elusive to study, that dimension, particularly due to the importance of mimicking of ideologies, should turn out in practice to be less helpful. Even when in theory it should provide important elements for typologies. (See Figure 4.1.)

The limited pluralism of authoritarian regimes takes a variety of forms, and within it different groups or institutions take a more or less preeminent place. The participation of groups in political power is

Figure 4.1 Typology of Authoritarian Regime

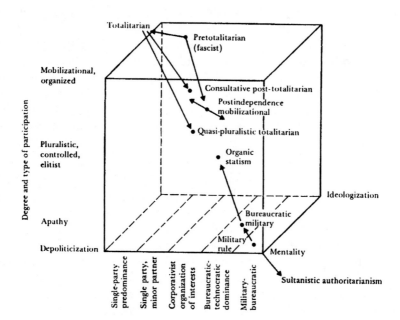

controlled by certain social forces and channeled through different organizational structures. On that account authoritarian regimes range from those dominated by a bureaucratic-military-technocratic elite that preexisted the regime, to a large extent, to others in which there is a privileged political participation and entry into the elite through a single or dominant party emerging from the society. In other regimes we find that a variety of social groups and institutions defined by the state are created or allowed to participate in one or another degree in the political process under the forms we shall call "organic statism," which often is ideologically described as corporatism not organic democracy. A very special case of limited pluralism is the one in which a large part of the society is excluded from organized participation in influencing major decisions on the basis of an ascriptive characteristic like race or ethnicity while other citizens enjoy the political freedoms of democracy, except insofar as advocating the inclusion into the body politic of the excluded segment of the society. We shall discuss this very special type of authoritarian regime under the paradoxical label of "racial democracies."

If we turn to the other dimension of our definition of authoritarian regimes—the limited participation, the controlled participation, the tendency toward political apathy of most citizens and the toleration or encouragement of such apathy—we find that in bureaucratic-military-technocratic regimes there are few, if any, channels for participation of the mass of the citizens and that the rulers have no particular interest in even manipulated participation. On the other hand we have regimes that attempt to mobilize the citizens to participate in well-defined, more or less monopolistic channels created by the political leadership, most characteristically through a mobilization of single or dominant party and its dependent mass and functional organizations. Insofar as such a single party is not conceived to exclude other organizations and institutions from a limited political pluralism and does not thoroughly penetrate them, we are dealing with an authoritarian regime. Such regimes would then be characterized as mobilizational authoritarian regimes and in this respect would be different from both bureaucratic-military-technocratic regimes and those we have labeled organic statism. They would also be different from the much freer political pluralism within the privileged racial community of the racial democracies.

Taking into account the circumstances under which such relatively mobilizational authoritarian regimes have appeared historically, we have two main types. In the first type the mobilizational single party or dominant party has emerged from the society in the course of the struggle for independence from foreign domination and has established in the process of taking power a dominant position, which it will protect from any competitors that might emerge either by outlawing the political freedoms that would lead to the emergence of other parties or by co-opting or even corrupting the leaders of such potential competitors. Initially such regimes are based on a considerable mobilization and, under conditions different from those of postcolonial underdeveloped societies, could move in a totalitarian direction but, for reasons to be analyzed later, become authoritarian regimes in which the originally mobilizational party becomes one important component in the structure of power. The second main type of mobilizational authoritarian regimes can be found in postdemocratic societies, in which a purely bureaucratic-military rule or one based on the representation of a well-defined, limited number of social groups and institutional interests in organic statism is not feasible because of the expectation of a large part of the society of some form of opportunity for participation for the average citizen. In addition, such regimes emerge when the struggle to exclude from the political process particular sectors of the society, to destroy the organizations of those sectors, has required something more than a coup d'état, when a mobilization was necessary to proceed with the exclusion of those sectors by the creation of a mass party, a variety of mass organizations, and even coercive organizations beyond the bureaucratic structures of the police or any army. This kind of exclusionary mobilizational authoritarian regime in postdemocratic societies was one of the outcomes of the fascist mobilization of a variety of interests and ideological and emotional commitments among the citizens of the democracies in crisis in the Europe of the interwar years. To the extent that such mobilizational authoritarian parties and movements aimed at a totalitarian monopoly of power and *Gleichschaltung* of a variety of social groups, interests, and organizations and a total political neutralization of others like the churches and armed forces, but did not succeed in so doing, we can speak of defective or arrested totalitarian systems. Since the process of establishing a truly totalitarian system is not achieved the day of takeover of power, we can also characterize as an authoritarian situation the pretotalitarian phases of certain political systems.

Finally, the way in which the limited pluralism in certain political systems emerges after a period of totalitarian rule leads us to speak of the post-totalitarian societies as a very distinct type. In such systems the dominant position of the party has not fully disappeared. The limited pluralism of other institutions, groups, and interests that share or influence political power is to a large extent emerging out of the social and political structure created by the new regime rather than from the preexisting society, politics, and history. To the extent that these groups are not simply parts of the single-party, controlled political structure and that the competition for power among them is not simply the result of bureaucratic or factional infighting within the elites and the institutions of the system but links with broader segments of the society, we are dealing with post-totalitarian authoritarian regimes. However, the legacy of organizational patterns, political culture, and memories of the past of the totalitarian period makes such regimes distinct from those listed before.

It would be surprising if the types we have derived from our analysis of the nature of the limited pluralism and the degree and type of participation or apathy would not also have some affinity with different ways of articulating ideas to legitimize the system. Certainly such ideas are least articulated intellectually in the case of the bureaucratic-military rule; it is in those cases that we can speak mostly of mentalities of the rulers and should pay least attention to the ideological formulations offered, which are likely to be simple and often derivative. In contrast, the mobilization of authoritarian regimes, particularly when they assign an important role to the single or dominant party and attempt to encourage the participation of at least a certain number of citizens in that party, is likely to rely on ideological formulations. Those ideological formulations, while they do not play a role comparable to the role of ideology in totalitarian systems, are an important factor in the political process. However, it is their relative lack of articulation and complexity and often their derivative character that contribute to the relatively rapid decay of the mobilizational component, that is, of the role of the party and of mass participation. This process was particularly visible in many of the African one-party states, that initially appeared as regimes based on an ideology and moving in a direction that would have placed them closer to the totalitarian systems that some of their leaders might have thought as a model. The outcome has been obviously to bring many mobilizational authoritarian regimes closer to either the bureaucratic-military type or the organic-statism type. Only in the mobilizational-postdemocratic-exclusionary authoritarian regimes in Western societies with a fascist party that had become an important political force before taking power did ideology remain an important independent factor that could not be fully reduced to what we have described as mentality. This is even truer for the post-totalitarian systems, for those we have called defective or arrested totalitarianism systems, and the pretotalitarianism phase of some regimes.

In the following pages, therefore, we will describe in some detail the characteristics of a variety of types of authoritarian regimes, the conditions for their emergence, some of the consequences of the political processes, and the lives of citizens of those types. Let us note here that they have not been logically derived from the dimensions of our concept of authoritarian regimes, but derived largely inductively from an extensive descriptive literature on such regimes, which did not offer a comparative typological conceptualization. We feel, however, that the types inductively derived fit our definition of authoritarian regimes and that the salient differences used to characterize them are found along the dimensions of the definition.

Congruently with our emphasis on the relatively well defined boundary between nondemocratic and democratic systems, in terms of our definition, only those systems we have conceptualized as racial or ethnic democracies could at one point or another have been considered democratic, that is, as long as they did not need to use considerably repressive force to prevent the excluded racial group from demanding participation and do not increasingly have to do so with the members of the privileged racial community who would advocate such an extension of political rights. On the other hand, the boundary between authoritarian regimes and those approaching the ideal type of a totalitarian system is much more difficult to operationalize. This fact is reflected in the need we felt to describe as types of authoritarian regimes post-totalitarian political systems, the defective or arrested totalitarian regimes, and the pretotalitarian phases of another set of regimes.

To some extent the bureaucratic-military authoritarian regimes, which have developed neither a more complex institutionalization of the limited pluralism in the form of organic statism or a single party contributing to the recruitment of the top-level elite serving as an instrument of control and as a channel for participation of citizens so motivated, are in some ways the paradigmatic authoritarian regimes. They are those furthest removed from any similarity to democratic political systems but also from modern totalitarianism. The question might be raised: Which of the other types more closely approach the model of democratic politics? In some respects it might be argued that the opportunities for participation in political life and through it access to positions of power in mobilizational authoritarian regimes bring those closer to the ideal type of democratic politics. On the other hand such mobilizational organizations like the single party and the various mass organizations controlled by it are an obstacle for the survival and political influence of the pluralism in the society, and to that extent will run counter to the freedom of organization for social and political purposes that characterizes democratic policies in societies. On the other hand, organic statism, by institutionalizing, even when in a controlled form, the existing social pluralism and incorporating it into the political process without creating or granting a monopoly to a single political organization, is closer to the social pluralism that develops spontaneously within a free society but at the cost of broader opportunities for participation of average citizens in contrast to various elites. In this respect organic statism is further removed from the idea of citizen participation than are the more mobilizational regimes. On one or another count both mobilizational authoritarian regimes and organic statist regimes are therefore clearly distinct from democratic regimes and societies. Even more difficult to answer is the question to what extent either of these types has potential to transform itself into a competitive democracy. It could be argued that the organic statism leaves more freedom for the articulation of specific interests and more autonomy to institutions, makes less effort to politicize in a particular direction the mass of the citizens, and therefore creates a society that is better prepared to accept the unlimited pluralism, the multiple and conflicting leadership of democratic politics. However, within the framework of organic statism, the privileges granted to the recognized organizations and institutions are likely to lead their leadership to perceive the opportunities for political mobilization of citizens through political parties as particularly threatening and therefore to cling to the authoritarian framework to defend them. In contrast, a mobilizational authoritarian regime, if it feels that the single or dominant party has penetrated the society sufficiently to be assured, even in a more competitive framework created by the extension of political freedom of its dominant position might be tempted to explore the possibility of retaining its power within such a framework. In fact, an initial chance of retaining its dominant position might encourage, given the legitimacy of competitive democracy, a slow transformation in that direction. In the long run or by a miscalculation such a move could ultimately lead to the installation of competitive democracy. A mobilizational authoritarian regime also retains institutionally and ideologically the principle of direct participation of individual citizens in the political process, a principle that is essential to competitive democracies. In view of this we can understand that the Turkey of Ataturk, in which a bureaucratic-military regime had become a single-party, moderately mobilizational authoritarian regime, could transform itself after World War II into a competitive democracy. The same would be true to some extent for the transformation of Estado Novo in Brazil into a populist democracy in which the elites of the preceding authoritarian regime could continue playing an important role. Mexico would be another case in point.

Some observers have placed considerable hope on the development of internal democracy within single parties in mobilizational authoritarian regimes and particularly in post-totalitarian regimes. We feel that the possibilities of transformation into competitive democracies of such regimes are more dubious than those observers have thought, since ultimately that participation through the single dominant party assumes a commitment to the party, its program and ideology, and the exclusion of any opportunity for alternative competing political conceptions that would be a requisite for competitive politics and that could always be rejected on the basis that there are opportunities for political participation within the boundaries of the party and its mass organizations.

Unfortunately we cannot develop at any length, with the information available and the space given to us, an analysis of the many regimes that are on the borderlines between the ideal types we have described. Many of the regimes combine in a more or less planned or accidental way elements from the different types, giving more or less importance to one or another in different phases of their history. It would seem that many authoritarian regimes are established as bureaucratic-military but after consolidating themselves in power explore the other alternatives and attempt with more or less success to transform themselves into organic-statist regimes and, generally unsuccessfully, into mobilizational regimes. On the other side many regimes that start as mobilizational authoritarian, either postindependence or postdemocratic, seem to drift into a combination of bureaucratic and organic statism, when they are not overthrown by a combination of military and bureaucratic power that soon rules with the help of technocratic elites and attempts to institutionalize some degree of organic statism. Each phase in the development of authoritarian regimes, from their emergence of the preauthoritarian society, their installation, their search for legitimate models to imitate, their hesitant efforts of institutionalization, is likely to leave an imprint on the system. Authoritarian regimes in reality, therefore, are likely to be complex systems characterized by heterogeneity of models influencing their institutionalization, often contradictory models in uneasy coexistence. It is this that accounts for the difficulty to subsume particular regimes under the types we shall describe here. Certainly many of the regimes, being nondemocratic, at one or another point in time would be closer to one or another of the types described. This fact is to some extent neglected in our emphasis on the analysis of the developmental aspect, the genesis of such regimes, and their location on a particular point in time in relationship to the preceding or subsequent regime. It is no accident that years after having been established such regimes are still, in the view of their rulers, in a constituent stage, that constitutional law after constitutional law is being enacted, and that the political edifice remains unfinished for a long time, giving hope to a variety of political forces of building it according to their particular blueprints. Paradoxically, democratic regimes seem to have a shorter period of constitution making, which prejudges in many, often unexpected, ways the future development of the regime. Paradoxically, the phase of installation of a new democracy offers to the democratic elites the temptation to use their power to constitutionalize their political preferences, with the result that social forces weak at that point in their organization in competing for political power might later be placed in the situation of having to challenge the constitutional order using the freedoms that democracy grants them. The rationalistic streak in Jacobinic democracy in this respect contrasts with the often very pragmatic way of creating political institutions in authoritarian regimes. Perhaps here we might find one of the clues to the relative stability of many authoritarian regimes despite considerable change in the regime and the instability of newly established democracies in the same societies.

Our effort to conceptualize and understand the variety of authoritarian regimes—strictly defined—encounters considerable difficulties due to the tendency to study political systems, outside of both the Western democratic world and communist systems, within the framework of geographic cultural areas like Latin America, the Middle East, Southeast Asia, and Africa rather than using analytical categories.[43] On the other hand, the tendency of scholars to group the Eastern European communist countries for comparative analysis and to specialize in the study of communist politics has led them to ignore potential comparisons with noncommunist authoritarian regimes.[44] Similarly, the dominant attention to Nazi Germany in the study of interwar fascist Europe has led to the neglect of the authoritarian regimes of the twenties and thirties as a distinct type of polities, leaving us mainly with excellent historical accounts but few systematic studies. In that context the neglect of Portugal, the most long-lived authoritarian regime in a Western society, is striking.[45] On the other hand, the analysis of many authoritarian regimes has been limited by the perspective introduced by a one-sided emphasis on the origins of such regimes as cases of military intervention in politics without further analysis of their functioning after having been established by a coup. The lack of a broader comparative perspective has been particularly damaging in the case of Latin America, where a regional grouping on the basis of certain cultural, historical, and international politics has prevented scholars from potentially fruitful comparisons with Latin-European politics, for example, the comparable economic and social development of some of the more advanced Latin American countries and those of Europe and the important ideological influences coming from Europe.

More recently the overemphasis on sociological categories, very often based on relatively simple indicators of economic development, and even more recently simplified Marxist analyses have led to a neglect of the most distinctively political variables in the study of many political systems of the Third World. The same is true for the emphasis in the literature on grand theories of political development or modernization, often at a high level of abstraction, which do not build bridges between the descriptive case studies and empirical comparative research, focusing on particular variables and their interrelationships. Lately the quantitative global studies based on the data, of dubious quality for these types of political systems and societies, accumulated in the data banks have tended to ignore the differences between types of political systems by treating them all on a single continuum of social-economic development, political development, and democratization used in a very loose sense of the term, leading to findings of specious scientific accuracy.

These various intellectual perspectives certainly have not encouraged scholars to undertake systematic comparative studies of a limited number of political systems with middle-range theoretical problems, or paired comparisons, or the systematic collection of hard data for comparisons.

We would argue that such a middle-range comparative analysis of authoritarian regimes in different cultural and geographic areas and under the influence of different ideological systems should allow the scholar to identify more clearly the distinctive impact of cultural traditions as well as of ideological models rather than attributing to both or either of them patterns that might be found in a great variety of systems where those variables might not be present.

Obviously there is considerable overlap between the study of authoritarian regimes and of the processes of political development, particularly in the so-called Third World of economically underdeveloped societies and new states, since so many of them are neither competitive democracies nor communist totalitarian systems. Since there is a chapter in the [original] *Handbook* (Chapter 1) devoted to political development, we have deliberately neglected this fruitful perspective.

I. Bureaucratic-Military Authoritarian Regimes

Authoritarian regimes in which a coalition predominated by but not exclusively controlled by army officers and bureaucrats establishes control of government and excludes or includes other groups without commitment to specific ideology, acts pragmatically within the limits of their bureaucratic mentality, and neither creates nor allows a mass single party to play a dominant role are the most frequent subtype. They may operate without the existence of any parties, but more frequent is the creation of an official government-sponsored single party, which, rather than aiming at a controlled mobilization of the population, tends to reduce its participation in political life even in a manipulated form— to use the fortunate expression of Schmitter (1974), "to occupy political space." In quite a few cases such regimes allow a multiparty system but make sure that the elections do not offer an opportunity for a free competition for popular support, even among the limited range of parties allowed, and attempt by a variety of manipulations, going from cooptation and corruption to repression, to assure the collaboration, subservience, or ineffectiveness of such parties (Janos, 1970a).

In the more polemic literature such regimes tend to be labeled fascist, particularly since in the years between the two World Wars they adopted some fascist slogans, symbols, and style elements and when possible co-opted some of the more opportunist elements of the fascist movements in their countries. Some countries in Eastern Europe were led by geographical and foreign-policy imperatives to align with the Axis powers, who often preferred them to more sincere, and therefore nationalist, fascist movements like the Iron Guard in Rumania. The essentially pragmatic character of such regimes allowed some of them to be allied with the Western democracies against their rising fascist neighbors (Seton-Watson, 1967). The prominent role of the army as a supporter of the regime and the fact that many officers played an important role in those regimes in which the army as an institution did not assume power lead other authors to describe them as military dictatorships. Some of them were born as military dictatorships, and the military continued in a few of them to play the dominant role, but it would be a mistake to ignore the much more complex political structure and the important role of civilian leaders, mainly higher civil servants but also professionals and experts as well as politicians of the precoup parties, in such regimes (Janos, 1970a; Roberts, 1951; Tomasevich, 1955; Cohen, 1973; Macartney, 1962). In many of them traditional institutions like the monarchy and to a much lesser extent the Church, or premodern social structures like large landowners, aristocratic or bourgeois, played an important role, but it would be a mistake to describe such systems as traditional. To start with, the traditional legitimacy of the monarchy in the countries with such regimes with a few exceptions was and is relatively weak (Clogg and Yannopoulos, 1972). In a number of them it had been established only a few generations back and the kings came from an alien royal house. In one case, that of Iran, the dynasty has been established by a successful general after a coup. It is very doubtful that in most of these regimes any significant sector of the population gave its allegiance to such rule, on account of the sacredness of tradition, of a belief in the divine right of kings, or strong loyalty to a dynasty like that of feudal retainers. Even the traditional social structures like the aristocratic landholders were often more the beneficiaries of the rule of more modern elites recruited from other social strata, who generally exercised political power and often attacked some of the symbolic privileges of the traditional ruling strata that often saw their power limited to the rural communities. In the typology proposed by Edward Shils, and let us not forget it, formulated mainly for non-Western developing nations, such regimes would logically fall into the category of traditional oligarchies. While the borderline between the type of regime we are describing and the more traditional oligarchies and the purely traditional political systems is somewhat difficult to define, it should not be forgotten that a large number of the powerful leaders of such regimes do not come from the families of the traditional oligarchy and have no strong ties with them. Their policies, while not attacking seriously the privileges of the traditional oligarchy, serve a much greater variety of social groups.

In terms of the Weberian types of legitimacy, such regimes tend to be very mixed. Very few of their supporters think of the man heading the government, or of the single party, as a unique personality endowed with a mission and as having a personal attraction that would deserve the label of charismatic leadership. More often than not the personalities at the head of the government are, in their own style, their own conception of their task, and in the appeal they have to their supporters, acharismatic if not the opposite from charismatic, or sometimes pseudocharismatic. While we find many features in the exercise of their rule that we could call patrimonial or characteristics of a patrimonial bureaucracy, the element of traditional legitimacy is too weak to fall into the pure type of traditional authority in the Weberian sense. Redefined in the sense of personal rulership, as has been done in the work of Guenther Roth, quite a few would fit that characterization. Despite the many arbitrary elements in the exercise of authority not only in relationship to an illegal opposition or just opponents and critics of the system, such regimes made and make a considerable effort to operate within a legalistic framework: enacting constitutions modeled after the Western liberal democratic type, holding on as long as possible to pseudoconstitutional parliamentary forms, using and abusing legal procedures and the courts, and above all demanding obedience from civil servants and officers not on the ground of an identification with their policies, programs, or charisma but on the basis of legal authority. This legalism, congruent with the training of many of those holding power—civil servants and politicians of a previous, more liberal democratic period—often leads to odd contradictions in such regimes. It assures surprising areas of individual freedom but also accounts for some of the more outrageous misuses of power, like political assassination, the execution of opponents while "attempting to escape" (rather than after a trial or, like in totalitarian systems, a show trial), and the use of private violence with the connivance of the authorities. Rather than "revolutionary legality," we find the distortion or perversion of legality.

In the typology offered by Shils these regimes would sometimes, if we were to trust some of their programmatic statements, appear as tutelary democracies. But probably the majority would fit the type of modernizing oligarchies that he proposes, particularly when they make their appearance in preindustrial societies with a low development of the urban bureaucratic, professional, and commercial middle classes. In other cases it would be misleading to speak of modernizing except in a relative sense. Certainly some of the men who take control of such systems are higher civil servants, quite often experts in fiscal matters, committed to tax reforms, a certain degree of government intervention in the economy, and encouragement of industrialization without, however, creating a large-scale public sector (Janos, 1970a, pp. 212–16). Their policies are pragmatic and responsive to business cycles and the international economic system and therefore are likely to use a variety of measures often not too dissimilar from those of countries with other political systems.

Such regimes have appeared in societies that had an incipient industrialization and not highly modernized agriculture and consequently had a large rural population, generally of poor peasants and/or farm laborers or tenants. They have appeared in those societies that, despite their now low level of economic development, generally were characterized by considerable urbanization, particularly in a capital city, by an expansion of education beyond what we could expect in terms of economic development, and therefore by the growth of a stratum of middle-class professionals seeking government employment or dependent directly or indirectly on government activities, a stratum in which we would find both intelligent upwardly mobile persons and others who were downwardly mobile trying to hold on to their social status. While other social groups might have been the beneficiaries of the policies of such regimes, particularly some of the wealthier rural strata or the few well-connected business sectors, the main support for the regime and the recruiting ground for the elites of the system were found largely in what the students of Eastern European societies like Seton-Watson (1967) called state bourgeoisie and Linz and De Miguel (1966a) in the study of Spanish society have called *clases medias,* in contrast to bourgeoisie with its connotation of a stratum linked with a modern economy. The middle-class coup of José Nun (1968) would also fit to some degree into this model.

Politically such regimes made their appearance in societies in which liberal democratic institutions, particularly parliamentary institutions, had been introduced but no true party system attracting the loyalties of the population had emerged and/or the parties were unable to produce stable governments. The incapacity of the parties to mobilize democratically the population outside of a few urban centers reflected the persistence of landlord power in some parts of the country, the low level of education of the masses, and clientelistic politics at the local level. However, in contrast to the nineteenth century, they had been sufficiently mobilized to create a threat to a system of traditional oligarchic rule through parties of notables.

In Eastern Europe the peasant parties that emerged as powerful political movements after World War I, stimulated by mobilization in the war, the hopes and results of agrarian reform, the expansion of suffrage, the self-consciousness of the peasantry when confronted with what

they perceived as the wickedness of urban life particularly of a bourgeoisie oriented toward foreign life styles, appeared as a threat to the
crown, the old liberal political oligarchies tied with landlords, fi-
nanciers, large merchants, and a few industrialists. In some cases (like
Croatia) such parties also threatened the state-supporting ethnic-cul-
tural community (like the Serbs). The leaders of the peasant parties,
when confronted with the world depression and its impact on the farmers, could not find satisfactory solutions. Their support failed, and in
some cases more aggressive fascist movements competed for their constituency and contributed with their violence to the crisis atmosphere.
The bind of agricultural countries in the process of industrialization in
relation to advanced industrial nations created unsolvable problems
(Roberts, 1951). The moral intransigence of peasantist leaders did not
contribute to consensual solutions. The outcomes were the royal dictatorships and an alternation between elections allowing participation of
all parties but assuming the victory of some, the outlawing of some and
toleration for others, and sometimes the creation of a single national
party with the participation of many politicians of the old parties and
some co-opted from the opposition parties, peasantist or fascist. Ultimately the tensions led to military takeovers, in the case of Rumania
first incorporating the Iron Guard and later brutally suppressing it.

In the more economically, socially, and culturally advanced societies the dislocations produced by war and/or the model of foreign
revolutions created pockets of protest and in crisis moments revolutionary attempts condemned to failure or waves of terrorism and counter-
terrorism. The experience of a revolutionary threat gave to many of the
systems a strong counterrevolutionary and reactionary character.

The purpose of such regimes is to exclude from independent, uncontrolled opportunities to participate in power and to organize to that
effect the masses demanding a greater share in the goods of the society,
particularly workers, farm laborers and underprivileged peasants, and
sometimes religious, ethnic, or cultural minorities. Such systems allow
more or less pluralism within other sectors of society and assure a
prominent role to the military and the bureaucrats capable of enforcing that exclusion and implementing policies that will prevent the excluded strata from exasperation. In that process they are unlikely to introduce major structural changes in the society, but often they will also
limit the power, organizational capacity, and autonomy of privileged
elites: business, professional groups, foreign capitalists, even the

churches, and in rare cases the army. Some quotations of a study by Manuel Lucena (1971) of the Portuguese regime selected by Philippe Schmitter (1973a) reflect the ambivalent relation of such systems, even of one of the most conservative and least "populistic" ones, with the class and economic structure. He writes, for example:

> The State, in the course of this (evolutionary) process, dealt with capitalists with a velvet but heavy hand. Using capitalism it remained ahead (but not brilliantly) of most capitalists. It assisted the most powerful, but it also obstructed them. It captured all of them, large and small in the thickest of regulatory nets. Finally, it is itself, a large entrepreneur, against the wishes of its founder, but in agreement with the imperative laws of the economic system. . . . One must never forget that, especially in its beginnings, this (corporatist) system was a creature of the State. It was not created by the dominant class which had to be carefully reassured. . . . Portuguese corporatism controls the sphere of labor without, however, obeying that of capital. It is the State which created *de toutes pieces* their forced agreement which benefited capital. The latter had neither unity nor clear ideas. And, it does not always show itself properly appreciative. . . . The New State has been the avant garde of a bourgeoisie that did not support it. (Lucena, 1971, pp. 56, 75bis, 126, 292)

Such regimes generally emerge after a period of liberal democracy has allowed a more or less high level of mobilization of the underprivileged strata. They will vary in the degree of autonomy they are ready to grant the more privileged, in social economic terms, strata, in view of the threat that dominance of those strata might represent for those who have assumed the task of protecting the regime and themselves from the revolutionary radical claims of the underprivileged. Depending upon the strength of the regime, traditional notables would be allowed a share in power. Economic development will determine to what extent those controlling the means of production will be allowed a place in the coalition or dominant influence. The degree of preauthoritarian regime mobilization of the underprivileged will largely determine the degree to which those committed to the maintenance of the system—bureaucrats and military—will play a dominant role and the extent to which they will attempt to incorporate them through controlled organizations for the underprivileged, official trade unions, corporative organizations, or populist or fascist-type parties. We will discuss those types of authoritarian regimes later. Despite their initially

reactionary purpose and the conservative character of many of their supporters, they are not unlikely to engage in social welfare and economic
development policies, thereby often threatening or limiting the interests
of the economically privileged and powerful. As Philippe Schmitter has
shown in his use of the Bonapartist model as developed by Marx, such
authoritarian regimes can go far in making the state itself completely independent and breaking the political power of the middle class, daily
anew, protecting at the same time the material power of those strata.[46]
Obviously, where there is a politically unmobilized or secure and con-
tented peasantry, such a stratum provides much support to such regimes.
The limits imposed on the economically privileged strata and the obstacles placed on the free articulation of the interests of most of the middle
class, particularly its intellectually most sophisticated sectors and sometimes including sectors of the bureaucracy and the army, lead to the
paradox that such regimes are more threatened in their stability by the
strata that brought them to power and that largely benefit of their rule
than by those excluded from the limited pluralism.

Another problem that many of the liberal democratic regimes had
been unable to solve were the deep-seated ethnic and nationality cleavages, particularly in Eastern Europe, where every country had its irredenta abroad and its more or less oppressed minorities at home, sometimes loyal to a neighboring country. Such nationality conflicts
reinforced chauvinistic nationalism and the political role of the army.
As Janos (1970a) and Nagy-Talavera (1970) have shown, the social position of the Jews in a number of Eastern European societies, particularly their overrepresentation among those with university education in
societies with large-scale intellectual unemployment, created strong
feelings of anti-Semitism. The important role of the Jews in the financial and business elite in some of the countries contributed to the popular anti-Semitism, while on the other hand it favored secret coalitions
that corrupted political life.

It is no accident that in Hungary and Rumania the true fascist
movements, with a populist ideology attempting a mobilization of the
masses and succeeding like the Arrow Cross in gaining the support of
many workers in Budapest and the Iron Guard mobilizing peasants of
the least developed areas of Rumania, should have been the most active
and dangerous opposition movements to those bureaucratic authoritarian regimes. The fact that in both Hungary and Rumania some of the
more dispossessed social groups had not become identified with a
Marxist protest movement before the establishment of an authoritarian

regime allowed the fascists to appeal to them, something they could not do in some of the more socially and economically advanced and integrated countries, like Spain. Therefore, the co-optation of fascism into the authoritarian regime depended more on the external situation, its own weakness, and a desire to share in power rather than to present the oligarchic structure with the challenge of a national fascist revolution. It is no accident either that some of the fascist leaders would come from an ethnically marginal background and that some of the fascist movements would be appealing to nationalities that were not part of the ruling oligarchical authoritarian elite, like the Croats in Serb-dominated Yugoslavia.

Andrew Janos has very well summarized some of the factors that account for

> the survival of pluralism in the face of totalitarian tendencies inherent in the ideology of the single party. If and when revolutionary movements seize power in an insufficiently mobilized society, or in a society in which the commitments of the mobilized strata of the population are sharply divided, the new elite may be forced to seek at least temporary accommodations with autonomous groups and organizations. Thus the emerging one party state will often be totalitarian in ideology and form, but not in reality. On the other hand, the precepts of the revolutionary ideology will militate against bargaining, compromise and reconciliation, and the development of institutional mechanisms for the resolution of conflict. In such political contexts (the term "system" appears to be inappropriate here) tensions between ideology and structure will produce considerable randomness in the political process and may result in recurrent attempts by competing groups to eliminate one another from the political scene. These types of party state are pluralistic *de facto* but not by custom or by explicit agreement. This is pluralism by default and not by design. If one may borrow a term from the vocabulary of administrative theory, they are neither pluralistic nor monolithic but "prismatic." By definition these prismatic configurations of political forces are unstable and they best be conceived of as representing a transitional stage in the process of political change. The prismatic condition of a polity may lead to full-fledged totalitarianism, intraparty institutionalization, a multiparty system, or further and complete disintegration, to mention only some of the possible alternatives. (Janos, 1970a, p. 233)

As we will see later, in more complex societies, with higher levels of social mobilization, a Catholic intellectual tradition, and less concern about complex links between foreign and internal policy, stabilized military-bureaucratic authoritarian regimes moved further in their institutionalization, in the explicit break with liberal-democratic constitutional forms, and in the incorporation of the old political elite. Some opted for various mixes between what we shall call organic statism and experimentation with mobilizational single parties of fascist inspiration. This was the case of Spain in 1926, Portugal in the early thirties, Austria in 1934, Brazil under Vargas, 1937–1945, and Spain under Franco.[47]

The victory of the allied powers in World War II provided countries faced with the task of nation building and the crisis of modernization with two basic political models: Western competitive democracies and movement regimes after the Soviet model. Those two powerful paradigms seemed to exclude the bureaucratic authoritarian pattern developed in the interwar years in the then new nations of Eastern and Southeastern Europe. Initially only Portugal appeared as the survival of the bureaucratic authoritarian reactions to the failure of democracy in interwar Europe. The defeat of fascism had discredited any mobilizational single-party authoritarian regime not based on the model of the Communist vanguard party. Certainly the Franco regime,[48] with its mixture of bureaucratic authoritarianism with weakened fascist-single-party-mobilizational elements and the later (1942) developments of organic statism, survived ostracism by the United Nations. Argentine nationalism, reacting to foreign pressures and to the opportunities created by a new working class emerging from industrialization due to wartime import substitution, led to the transformation of a military-oligarchic regime into a populist authoritarianism with some fascist components in the form of Peronism. That model was not without attractiveness to young Latin Americans dissatisfied with unsuccessful or oligarchic democracies, but for some time political scientists could predict that with economic development, social and cultural modernization, the professionalization of traditional armies, and the shift of the Church from a democratic corporativism to Christian democracy, the countries of the Western hemisphere would move toward competitive democracy. The successful transfer of democratic institutions in India led those unaware of the long and complex historical process leading to the creation of Indian political institutions by the Congress party (after all, the party was founded in 1885 and participated in representative semisovereign institutions since 1937) to hope for a similar transfer in the other areas being decolonized by Britain. The initial deviations from that transfer model were sometimes interpreted as transitional stages that would ultimately prepare society for democracy as tutelary democracies. However, two decades later those hopes would be shattered in a few places by a successful revolution, like in Cuba, or by a combination of a national struggle for independence and social revolution, first in China and particularly in North Vietnam, and by the attempt to create mobilizational single-party regimes in Africa and Arab countries.

More unexpectedly, the optimistic model of social-economic developments increasing political pluralization and as a result of it the likelihood of political democracy was to be disproved in two of the most advanced Latin American countries. Guillermo O'Donnell (1973), building on the earlier work of Stepan (1971, 1973) on Brazil, on the basis of a case study of Argentina in recent decades has advanced an alternative model linking a higher state of economic and social development with the emergence of bureaucratic authoritarianism aimed at excluding activated popular sectors, particularly urban working classes, on the basis of the coalition between a new type of military elite—the incumbents of technocratic roles in the public and private sectors, in the more dynamic and efficient sectors—with the support of social strata threatened by mobilization. As Stepan has shown, technocratic roles in the military, the bureaucracy, and the modern enterprises share a common view of the requirements for development, particularly the need to exclude and deactivate the popular sector, and have international linkages with similar elites in advanced industrial societies, which have led them to a favorable assessment of their combined social-problem-solving capabilities and to a greater control of crucial sectors of their societies. Their emerging coup coalition will aim at reshaping the social context in ways envisioned as more favorable for the application of technocratic expertise and for the expansion of the influence of social sectors that they have most densely penetrated as a result of modernization.

O'Donnell notes with some hesitation the similarities between this model and that of the developing societies on the periphery of the industrial heartland of Europe in the interwar years, but the relative weight of the experts, technocrats, and new managers, with their emphasis on development rather than economic stability and protectionism, would suggest some important differences. They might be characterized as military-technocratic-bureaucratic authoritarian regimes in contrast to the more bureaucratic-military-oligarchical authoritarian regimes of Eastern Europe. There are other differences not stressed by O'Donnell but worth notice, like the absence in the former type of regime of even a weak monarchical legitimacy capable of shifts in policy in crisis situations (particularly as in Rumania and Yugoslavia, but also Spain under Primo de Rivera). Another difference is the absence of nationality, linguistic, and cultural conflicts, which both strengthened and weakened Eastern European and Balkan authoritarian regimes. However, in our view a basic difference is the absence of fascist coalition partners or models to mimic that on occasion gave a legitimacy to those regimes among intellectuals, students, and youth. The crisis of Catholic corporativist ideology compounds the problem of institutionalization of the new bureaucratic authoritarian regimes in Latin America. Both authoritarian responses share the fear of revolution from below, stimulated by radicalized intellectuals, a fear that was stimulated in Europe by the Russian and Hungarian communist revolutions, the peasant populist mobilization in Bulgaria, and isolated revolutionary or pseudorevolutionary outbreaks in other European countries. In Latin America in the mid-60s the Cuban Revolution and the minor efforts of guerrilla or peasant mobilization stimulated by it, particularly by Che Guevara, contributed to that fear. More realistically, important segments of the more advanced Latin American societies were concerned about the pressures coming from a popular sector, initially mobilized from above by preceding populist authoritarian regimes that had created organized forces like trade unions and parties linked with them capable of expressing their demands in democratic or quasidemocratic political systems after the fall of the Estado Novo and Peronism. In our view O'Donnell neglects to emphasize the impossibility of controlled mobilization by modernizing elites after fascism had been discredited and in societies in which populist authoritarian regimes had (perhaps incorporating fascist elements) achieved a nationalistic, more or less antioligarchical mobilization. The demobilization of those forces required coercion, like in Brazil, or produced an unstable authoritarian regime, like in Argentina, where the costs of coercion as well as those of an open society seemed too high, leading to a constant experimenting between exclusion and co-optation, particularly in the quasi-democratic stage that preceded the coup by General Onganía in 1966 and that was resumed in the last stages of bureaucratic military rule before the recent election that brought the Peronistas to power.

O'Donnell has described at length and documented carefully the structural constraints at a particular level of economic development in the specific Latin American international economic-dependency relation and their social consequences that lead to an unsolvable problem and what he calls (following Apter) a "ceiling effect," which seems to leave no other way out than bureaucratic authoritarianism. We cannot summarize here his dynamic model in all its richness, which can serve as an example of how the analysis of the conditions and processes leading to the emergence of authoritarian regimes should be done, combining economic, sociological, and political analysis. Nor can we present his comparative analysis of the conditions contributing to the instability of that solution in the Argentine case and its temporal stability and success in Brazil. Space also excludes an analysis based on the work of Alfred Stepan (1973) of the factors accounting for the different types of authoritarian institutionalization achieved by the military that took over power in Brazil in 1964 and in Peru in 1968. Their analyses, those by a distinguished group of Brazilian scholars, and the recent study by John S. Fitch III (1973) of the variety of patterns of military intervention in Ecuador have advanced our knowledge of the conditions leading to authoritarian regimes under the leadership of the army far beyond the traditional literature, with its liberal perspective of "generals versus presidents," and beyond the cultural-historical interpretations of Latin American politics. The model of O'Donnell tends to overemphasize the structural constraints and to underestimate the possibilities of political engineering (to pick up an idea of Giovanni Sartori, 1968). He also underestimates the possibility of responsible democratic leaders preventing the crisis situation that crystallized the coup coalition, gave it an apparent legitimacy, and broadened its initial basis of support. Alfred Stepan's brilliant analysis of the fall of Goulart (Stepan, 1971) and the comparison with several crises preceding it that did not lead to a change of regime is complementary and in part corrective of the macropolitical, social, and economic model of O'Donnell.

A sophisticated documented and reasoned analysis of modernization of South America, examining critically the indicators and the internal heterogeneity of societies and the degree of modernization in centers, suggests that the higher and lower levels of modernization are associated with nondemocratic political systems, while political democracies are found at the intermediate level of modernization, with the exception of Peru. Argentina and Brazil, contrary to the expectations of many analysts, have moved toward bureaucratic authoritarianism in a period that Venezuela and with some reservations Colombia moved toward democracy, while Chile, despite economic difficulties, still seemed to be holding on to its embattled democracy.

Brazil and Argentina moved in the mid-60s to exclude the already-activated urban popular sector (working class and segments of the lower middle class) from the national political arena by refusal to meet the political demands made by the leaders of this sector and denying its leaders access to positions of political power from where they could have direct influence on national decisions. Exclusion can be achieved by direct coercion and/or by closing the electoral channels of political access. Those attempts have varying degrees of success. At one extreme the political deactivation of an excluded sector may be achieved; it becomes politically inert through destruction of its resources (especially its organizational basis). At the other extreme this deactivation might not be achieved. These countries moved from an incorporating political system that purposefully attempted to activate the popular sector and allowed it some voice in national politics in a period of populism and horizontal industrialization, to exclusion. They were countries in which the world crisis of the thirties and World War II accelerated the emergence of domestic industry and an urban working class, which changed the distribution of political power away from the nationally owned agrarian areas producing exportable goods and the largely foreign-owned network of financial and export intermediaries. The basis of that process was a broad populist coalition, led by powerful leaders like Vargas and Perón, against the old oligarchies and the highly visible foreign-owned firms mediating the international-domestic market and the traditional policies of free trade. The coalition favored industrialization and the expansion of the domestic market. Socially it meant the broadening of the functions of the state and providing employment for many middle-class, white-collar workers and technicians. Nationalism and industrialization appealed to the military, benefitted the urban workers, fostered migration to the urban centers, extended the market economy, raised consumption levels, and increased unionization and benefits for the domestic-consumption-oriented agrarian sectors. The traditional export-oriented sector, provider of international currency, lost its traditional hegemony and the government extracted a significant portion of its income to redistribute for the benefit of domestic expansion and consumption. The economic importance of exports, however, allowed this sector to retain political influence disproportionate to its decreasing share in the gross national product. Nationalistic-populist policies never went much further than recurring deprecation of the oligarchy and expropriation of the more visible symbols of foreign presence. Industrialization was horizontal or extensive, and few inroads were made into the production of intermediate and capital goods; a consequence was a heavy dependence on imports of those goods as well as of technology. After an exhaustion of the easy stages of industrialization based on substitution for imports of finished consumer goods, import substitution proved to be an import-intensive activity in a period of erratic prices for exports that aggravated the poor productivity of the export sectors, which were paying the bill for the populist policies. This led to severe foreign exchange shortages. At the same time, Vargas and Perón encouraged workers' unionization as the basis for allegiance and to facilitate governmental control over newly incorporated segments of the popular sector. Even though union leaders were dependent on those leaders, the urban popular sector was given its first chance to have an effective weight in national politics and to bargain within the populist coalition, developing a high degree of organization. Initially all participants in the populist coalition were receiving payoffs roughly proportionate to their expectations in a period of exultation and hope for takeoff into sustained growth. However, the economic dynamics, described before, led to an end of the expansion. Horizontal industrialization left a schedule of supply, which included a disproportionate share of consumption and luxury items as well as a myriad of small producers coexisting with a few big firms, under an umbrella of minimum competition and maximum state protection. Consumption expectations consolidated, and vertical industrial projects became more dependent on capital and technology transfers from abroad and an increasing penetration of technocratic roles, which consolidated linkages of dependency with originating societies from which such roles had been transplanted. A new need for a high degree of stabilization and predictability in the social context was perceived with growing modernization. After reaching in this way the high point of modernization of their centers, new problems emerged that led to the breakdown of populist or developmentalist alliance. The need to clear the market of marginal producers, eliminating restrictions on the more technologically advanced or more capital intensive and financially powerful enterprises, combined with appeals to nationalism and preservation of the social peace, led to opposition to expert advice, stabilization plans, and the interests of more powerful producers. This issue had special significance for the military and *técnicos* in strategic points for national economic planning and decision making. In more open democratic political systems, like those that succeeded Vargas, with distributionist-populist economic policies, the electoral weight, the capacity to strike, demonstrate, and disrupt, and intensified political activation were perceived as profoundly threatening by most other social sectors. As a result, most propertied Argentine and Brazilian sectors agreed that the popular sectors' demands were excessive, both in terms of consumption and power participation, and that capital accumulation would be impossible if they were not controlled. The class component of the polarization led to the acceptance of a political solution that supposedly would eliminate such threats, which became particularly (we might say disproportionately) salient with the spector of socialist revolution that arose with the Cuban Revolution. The changed mentality of the officer corps, as the result of antisubversive training in the United States, and the impact of French military thinking on political-warfare and civic-action doctrines led to the national-security doctrines that included socioeconomic development as a response to internal subversion. The deterioration of the income of the large salaried middle class during the years preceding the 1964 and 1966 coups led to their disaffection from a formally democratic system and their response to a law and order appeal. The popular sector, suffering from unfavorable income redistribution, engaged in increasing political activation to obtain decreasing returns. The demands-performance gap and the differentiation-integration gap led to the situation that Samuel Huntington described as "mass praetorianism" (Huntington, 1968, pp. 192–343). Political institutions, partisan parliaments, which had never been particularly strong, were further weakened and the executive became the primary focus of a flood of demands. Governments were victimized by and collaborated in "praetorianism." The situation became a stalemate, with high levels of unrestrained conflict; sharp differences in demands, the weakness of government preventing the implementation of any policy, and concern for survival in office led to sequences of policies designated to placate the more threatening political actors with little concern for general problem solving. Competition was increasingly zero-sum, gains were precarious, and the threshold for a definitive crisis was reached when most of the political actors focused on changing the rules of the political game altogether instead of trying to obtain gains within the existing rules. The existing political system had reached its ceiling.

The process of modernization in a variety of sectors had led to the emergence of technocratic roles, particularly in larger organizations of persons trained in techniques of production, planning, and control. The incumbents of those roles have expectations derived from role models of the "originating" societies. This new group has been particularly important in the discussion by Brazilian social scientists of social change, some of whom speak of a techno-bureaucracy. Their consciousness and their expertise convince them that by molding the social context to serve their own aspirations they would at the same time improve the social situation. Potential planners and civil servants yearn for governments that will follow their advice and grant them effective decision-making power. In addition—and in this development Latin America in the sixties probably differed from the European developments in the twenties and thirties—these elites met in a new context, new business schools and advanced military schools like the *Escola Superior de Guerra* in Brazil, and new opinion-making publications emerged. As Stepan (1973) has shown, a new mentality appeared. The training of these elites emphasized technical problem solving, a rejection of emotional issues, a perception of the ambiguities of bargaining, of politics as hindrances to rational solutions, and a definition of conflict as dysfunctional. A common technical language, or jargon, facilitated communication, and the density of interaction of this group despite the small numbers led them to play a dominant role in the new coup coalition rather than, like in less modernized contexts, to withdrawal from political involvement. High confidence in their capabilities for governing led to their crucial influence in the 1964 Brazilian and the 1966 Argentine coups.

In a highly modernized context, the attempt to exclude and eventually deactivate the popular sector in the absence of the possibility of offering psychological or economic payoffs inevitably required strong and systematic coercive measures. Bureaucratic authoritarianism—eliminating political parties and elections and the political personnel sensitive to the demands of the popular sector, domesticating labor unions by co-optation, if not by coercion, and attempting to bureaucratically encapsulate most social sectors to maximize control—was the answer. Bargaining and interest representation would be limited to leaders at the top of these organizations, and spontaneous modes of demand formulation as well as dissent would have no legitimate place.

O'Donnell links his model with that offered by Barrington Moore (1967) as the third historical path toward industrialization, in addition to the bourgeois and communist revolutions, a path that involves the coalition of the public bureaucracy and the propertied sectors (including a subordinate industrial bourgeoisie) against the peasantry and an emerging proletariat. It is a conservative reaction to the strains of advancing industrialization and to a weak push toward parliamentary democracy and the entry of the masses into the political scene. Such regimes attempt to consolidate traditional forms of domination in the rural areas and accelerate industrialization, minimizing the chances of social revolution. Incidentally, we might note that here Barrington Moore and O'Donnell converging with him coincide with the insightful analysis by Franz Borkenau (1933) of the conditions for the rise of fascism. Borkenau characteristically linked fascism with the problems of semideveloped societies reaching the point of industrialization as latecomers and therefore combining the natural tensions created by change from rural to urban society, from small to modern enterprise with its new type of discipline, with the diffusion of socialist political demands, which threatened the development of national capitalism in a way that it did not in the early industrializing societies.

After developing this general model O'Donnell analyzes the differences between Brazil and Argentina after the successful military coups, particularly the different degrees of coercion applied. For him the difference can be found in the fact that in Argentina the level of activation was higher than in Brazil, even though the rate of increase in the precoup period was lower. While in Argentina the impulse came mainly from below, with the governing Radicales not encouraging it, in Brazil the inducement for political activation came from above in the Goulart government. The Peronista allegiance was perceived by established sectors as relatively less threatening than the suggestion of socialist tendencies among Brazilian governing personnel, a perception that fostered an initially tighter degree of cohesion in the ruling coalition as well as an increase in the influence of its more *antisubversive* and *"efficientist"* members. The hostility of the Radicales in power against the Peronistas led the unions and Peronistas to welcome the 1966 coup for a short period before the policy implications of the new political system were spelled out, a factor that delayed and lessened the degree of coercion, while in the Brazilian case the initial antagonistic position of the populist sector led to a more coercive response. The result was the success in the deactivation of the popular sector in the Brazilian case and the retention of the relatively high level of political activation in the Argentine modern area and accounts for the different degree of consolidation of the two systems.

In bureaucratic authoritarian regimes the incumbents of technocratic roles tend to emphasize those aspects that their socialization has best taught them to measure and deal with. Reality may be confounded with hard data indicating performance, like growth in GNP, diminished inflation, and fewer strikes, neglecting hard-to-decode information coming from noisier channels for the expression of popular preference and the fact that those achievements have been made at the cost of repression, income redistribution, elimination of national entrepreneurship, liquidation of political institutions, increased poverty of the urban and rural popular sectors, and alienation of intellectuals and students. However, if the indicators to which those elites are sensitive show satisfactory performance, the political rule will be easily rationalized, the assessment of their capabilities for solving problems reinforced, and the coalition consolidated. This accounts for the hardening and *continuismo* in the Brazilian system and the fact that in the Argentine case influential members of the original coalition seem willing to attempt a return to democracy in view of the blatant failure of the system using the set of indicators preferentially monitored. The coups that deposed Generals Onganía and Levingston and the election that the Peronists won after the interregnum of Lanusse are a reflection of the different success, in the opinion of the ruling elites, of the postcoup regimes in Brazil and Argentina. This does not mean that the effort of extrication of the military and the democratizing of bureaucratic authoritarian rule are assured success. Nor does the relative success in certain respects of the Brazilian military-technocratic-bureaucratic authoritarian regime imply that it has found a stable institutional form and legitimacy (Linz, 1973b). The strains caused by recent developments do not exclude the possibility that some military officers might appeal to domestic entrepreneurs and organized labor, using nationalistic pleas and promises of protectionist and more distributionist policies, in their efforts to reconstruct the political system along populist lines, even when in O'Donnell's opinion the chances for such solutions are slim.

He recognizes that his model stresses unidirectional effects, produced by socioeconomic factors on the political side, and the need for further research on the effects that political action can have on socioeconomic factors. Our feeling is that his analysis, while rightly underlining the negative political consequences of bureaucratic authoritarianism, tends to underestimate the broader social impact that success in economic development of the technocratic elite can have through a trickling-down process from the initial beneficiaries to larger population segments, and the possibility for such regimes to selectively implement welfare policies through the expansion of social security and enforced company paternalism, particularly in favor of critical urban working-class sectors, once an initial accumulation stage has been achieved. Even Marxist critics admit that this has been the case in

Spain, and survey data show that large segments of the society (except significantly in the most modern and highest-income regions) show a feeling of improvement, which, however, might result in heightened expectations and tensions at a later date but which also carries with it a change in the pattern of social and class relations.

On the basis of my analysis of the Spanish case I would argue that the problems of stabilized bureaucratic authoritarianism are likely to be derived more from its ambiguous legitimacy and the difficulties of political institutionalization than from economic constraints and their impact on the society. I would particularly emphasize that in the Western world, in the absence of an ideological single party, important elites use either the competitive liberal democracies or the dynamic single-party mobilizational regimes as ideals assuring participation of citizens. The international linkages with stable democratic advanced industrial societies, while contributing through the linkages of the technocratic elites to the emergence and/or success of those regimes, at the same time also constantly undermine their legitimacy through the critique to which they subject them and through the cultural influences that conflict with their values. While contributing to the basis of their success, they in the same process contribute to the basis for future crises; while justifying their existence on technical and economic grounds, they every day contribute to undermining their legitimacy by offering to their citizens an alternative political model and by encouraging them not to give their full allegiance to the authoritarian regime, not to give up hope for a democratic political development. Even with considerable achievements, bureaucratic authoritarian regimes in the West might not be assured the same stability as post-totalitarian authoritarian regimes in Eastern Europe, partly due to the different nature of their linkage with a hegemonic power in whose sphere of influence they find themselves.

Excursus on military intervention in politics. Our analysis of authoritarian regimes with a military component could be misleading without a reference to other aspects of the military in politics. First of all, not all interventions are aimed at the creation of such regimes, nor do they all lead to their establishment. Secondly, it would be wrong to derive the motives of the officers and the circumstances leading to the overthrow of a democratic regime from the nature and politico-social functions of the regime, established with the military's help, ignoring "internal," specifically military, factors—the mentality of officers, institutional interests, organizational problems—that shaped the military's response to the actions of political leaders. It is because of this that it often is difficult to predict the course to be followed in political, economic, and social matters by a military junta after taking power. Thirdly, we should not forget that more often than not it is the civilians who call at the barracks for support either to overthrow or defend constitutional government, and that in many societies the civilian and "democratically" enacted constitutions attribute to the military a "moderating" power that "legitimizes" their intervention. Ultimately, even weak democratic governments in crisis situations become dependent on military support. Fourthly, the role of the military in internal politics does not exhaust the topic of civilian-political-military relations, since there is the whole problem area of the role of the military in international affairs and the pressures for military and political considerations and leadership in the conduct of war, so brilliantly formulated by Clausewitz (1911; originally published 1832) which will not concern us here. Nor can we devote the attention it merits to the question of the relation between different regimes and their armed forces (Huntington, 1956, 1964), or to the complex process of extrication from power and civilization of the military after interventions in politics. All these themes would certainly deserve another chapter.

The analysis of military intervention has shifted between two perspectives: one emphasizing the characteristics of the military establishment motivating and facilitating its intervention, with little concern for the actions of other actors in the political and social system; the other emphasizing that the most important causes are not military but political and reflect not the social and organizational characteristics of the military establishment but the political and institutional structure of society (Fitch, 1973). There is also a difference in emphasis between those who center their attention on the level and type of social and political development and the importance of certain cultural traditions—sometimes summarized under the label of "political culture"—and those who turn to a more careful analysis of the particular historical crisis leading to a specific intervention—the process of formation of a coup coalition, the broadening of its support and neutralization of potential opponents—and the distinctive political outcome of the intervention. Others tend to ignore or dismiss the explicit justifications and pronouncements of the participants, searching for the "real" interests of the military—as a social group or as an "instrument" or "representative" of social and economic interests. Another difference found in the literature is between those who stress the political strengths of the military and those who note their political weaknesses. In addition, the increasing importance of global political conflict—the cold war and patterns of international dependency, the links established between the military of different countries (through training, military missions, expeditionary forces, supply of weapons, diffusion of military doctrines)—leads to increased emphasis on the role of foreign influences (Einaudi, 1969; Pauker, 1963). In part those differences reflect the fact that much of the literature is centered on the role of the military in particular parts of the world or countries, but there are also differences between comparative and sometimes quantitative analyses (Schmitter, 1973a; Nordlinger, 1970; Putnam, 1967) and case studies, as well as ideological and cultural preconceptions. The scarcity of systematic, theoretically oriented empirical case studies has often led to premature generalizations. Certainly all the perspectives noted should be taken into account even when one or the other might be more fruitful in the study of particular cases.[49]

The different dimensions of the problem are also likely to be of different importance in different phases of the process: the period preceding the formation of a conspiratorial group, the phase of the expansion of its appeal, the crucial period of the decision to act, the immediate aftermath of a coup, and the political process in the months and years after taking power. In fact, the main actors—within the military—at each of those stages might be quite different persons reflecting different outlooks. It is important to realize that it is difficult, if not impossible, to explain why any particular coup occurred by reference to the propositions advanced by cross-national statistical analyses in order to answer the question why some countries have higher incidence of coups than others. In the analysis of a set of variables in which the meaning of any detail depends on its relation to the whole context of which it is a part we are confronted with a higher degree of complexity than can be easily dealt with by cross-national regression analysis.

It would be risky to say that any state is immune to overthrow and even more so to a change of government under pressure of the military, but certainly political systems have quite different probabilities of maintaining subordination of the armed forces to the political leadership. In serious political, social, or economic crises, defeat in war or loss of prestige, irrespective of types of regime the military are likely to play a more influential role. With wars, or the possibility of war, as well as any potential internal disorder, it will probably increase. Different parties or factions are likely to find greater sympathy among officers, and the interests of the armed forces are likely to find a more or less responsive ear among them. However, in certain societies the political role will not easily go beyond the threshhold of insubordination, while in others that point will easily be reached. Among the models, based on different patterns of value congruence and/or control mechanisms, that have assured a high probability of subordination we find the aristocratic, the liberal, the traditional professional, and the communist, formulated by Huntington (1956, 1964).

There are, however, two models that involve a high probability of military intervention in politics and with it the establishment of authoritarian regimes, described by Alfred Stepan (1971, 1973) as the moderating pattern of civil-military relations and the new professionalism. Neither of them represents a deviation from a well-established pattern of subordination of military to political authority resulting from exceptional crisis situations in the body politic but an institutionalized response that is likely to be successful when a broad consensus develops among the leadership of the armed forces that the circumstances are such as to legitimize their intervention. To Stepan's two models we might add a third, attentivism, in which the military stand outside the political process without an explicit commitment to any regime, as a neutral power, making their loyalty or support of governments in crisis situations conditional and avoiding any support that would divide the armed forces. This was the position of von Seckt under the Weimar Republic (Carsten, 1967; Vogelsang, 1962) and of Franco in the thirties (Payne, 1967), a position that undermines the authenticity of democratic regimes and indirectly can contribute to their breakdown.

The liberal model based on objective civilian control is impossible as long as civilian groups are unwilling simply to accept a politically neutral officer corps and as long as there are multifarious civilian groups anxious to maximize their power in military affairs. It is also unlikely when the professional goals of the military as an instrument in international conflict are questioned or are of limited relevance. Under those circumstances the moderating pattern appears. In it the norms encourage a highly political military whose political acts are nonetheless limited to certain boundaries. The key components in this pattern of civil-military relations have been summarized by Stepan (1971, p. 64) as follows:

1. All major political actors attempt to co-opt the military. A politicized military is the norm.

2. The military is politically heterogeneous but also seeks to maintain a degree of institutional unity.
3. The relevant political actors grant legitimacy to the military under certain circumstances to act as moderators of the political process and to check or overthrow the executive or to avoid the breakdown of the system, especially one involving massive mobilization of new groups previously excluded from participation in the political process.
4. Approval given by civilian elites to the politically heterogeneous military to overthrow the executive greatly facilitates the construction of a winning coup coalition. Denial by civilians that the overthrow of the executive by the military is a legitimate act conversely hinders the formation of a winning coup coalition.
5. There is a strong belief among civilian elites and military officers that while it is legitimate for the military to intervene in the political process and exercise temporary political power, it is illegitimate for the military to assume the direction of the political system for long periods of time.
6. This rough value congruence is the result of civilian and military socialization via schools and literature. The military doctrine of development is also roughly congruent with that of parliamentary groups. The military officers' social and intellectual deference facilitates military co-option and continued civilian leadership.

In this model, found frequently in Latin America in the past and even formalized in constitutional provisions about the role of the army, the propensity to intervene is not pathological, as it would be if the agreed model were the liberal one, but normal. That propensity correlates with the cohesion of the relevant political strata; the propensity is high when civilian cohesion is low, low when civilian cohesion is high. The success of the coups is related to the degree of public legitimacy ascribed to the executive and the military. A typical situation of low cohesion of relevant political strata is given by the frequent conflicts between the president and the legislature, heightened in recent decades by the different electoral and popular bases of support for populist national leaders and legislators with local bases of power. Under the circumstances the attitudes of pro-regime strata toward executive become decisive. Good indicators of that lack of cohesion of relevant civilian strata are the low percentage of votes of winning candidates, the absence of a broad consensus on a compromise candidate, the belief in the legitimacy of the institutions (particularly of the executive and the conformity of his actions with the constitutional provisions) and in the personal qualifications of the president, the trust in his willingness to abide by legal or conventional rules, for example the exclusion of *continuismo,* his respect for the autonomy of institutions including the armed forces, which becomes decisive for the response of the armed forces in a crisis situation (Fitch, 1973; Solaún, 1973). In a context in which the military activists, for or against the government, are always in the minority, that minority needs to convince the great majority of officers who are either strict legalists or simply nonactivists. Activists do not wish to risk bloodshed or military splits, so they wait until a consensus has developed. Public opinion, or at least some form of expression of public opinion (as reflected for example in the editorials of leading independent newspapers), and the position of influential social groups become decisive to convince the military itself. The success or failure of attempted coups is closely correlated with that legitimation. The moderating pattern is dependent on the belief in the constitutional forms of government itself, on a military confident that the crisis could be effectively resolved by returning the government to civilian control, and on the belief that the military had no legitimacy to rule in comparison to civilians. Under such circumstances the military do not create or at least aim to create a new regime but an interim regime of exception, which has a lot in common with the Roman concept of dictatorship. The leniency with the opponents, both civilian and military, not joining in the coup and the readiness of those defeated to abandon office without resistance allowed in the past the moderating pattern to function without a permanent discontinuity in regime legitimacy.

In the last decade some of the conditions that made the moderating pattern possible have disappeared. The degree of mobilization that populist presidents, democratic or semiauthoritarian, had achieved and with it the real or misplaced confidence in their capacity to challenge the moderating role of the military have increasingly prevented the bloodless coup and the easy extrication from power. The prolonged ineffectiveness of civilian leadership, the emergence of increasingly difficult-to-solve problems, the growing social unrest and problems of public order characteristic of what Huntington has called praetorian politics, which give encouragement or tolerance to the articulation of demands that cannot be satisfied by the system operating within the constraints of the institutions, have all led to the emergence of a new pattern of intervention. A new professionalism, very different from that of the military in advanced stable societies with major foreign-policy responsibilities, has emerged. The success of revolutionary warfare techniques against conventional armies and the subsequent diffusion of ideas of counterrevolutionary internal warfare created a new type of social and political consciousness among the military. Confronted with the need or the possibility of having to fight against internal subversion that articulated demands that appeared just and could not be satisfied by the civilian authorities and whose suppression required political skills, the military expanded the scope of their preoccupations. Criticism of the uselessness of costly military establishments led to the involvement in civic action projects that made officers aware of the problems created by underdevelopment. A new type of training in military educational institutions changed the scope of attention and professional capacity of the military. That training, contact with other societies, and interaction with other elites, particularly experts and managers, led to the new professionalism in internal security and national development. The consequent role expansion led the military, when they perceived failure of civilian leadership, not to intervene in the moderating pattern but, once they believed in their capacity to rule and distrusted the politicians, to assume power *sine die.* In addition, their perception that the political leadership was mainly an instrument of special interests, of well-organized groups be they latifundia owners, exporters and foreign investors, or the trade unionists and activist intellectuals, led them to feel that their duty was to assume power to objectively serve the national interest. The new professionalism has led to the establishment of authoritarian regimes that in response to different national contexts pursue quite different policies, as the cases of Brazil and Peru exemplify, but in both cases do so in response to similar assumptions about the role of the army in societies in crisis.

2. Organic Statism

Authoritarian regimes pursuing quite different policies in terms of class interest and organization of the economy have attempted to go beyond the bureaucratic-military-technocratic authoritarian rule by a controlled participation and mobilization of the society through "organic structures." The rejection of the individualistic assumptions of liberal democracy, combined with the desire to provide an institutional channel for the representation of the heterogeneity of interests in modern or modernizing societies, while rejecting the model of class conflict, has led to a great variety of theoretical-ideological formulations and attempts to implement them through political institutions. Such attempts have been conceived as an alternative to the mobilizational single party, as an instrument or complement to single party rule, or even as a way to link a single party with society.

In competitive democracies political parties serve to articulate and aggregate a wide range of interests rather than serving as a channel for very specific interests. Political parties aiming at holding power have an inevitable tendency to search for a majority, either by representing a cross section of society agreeing at least *pro tempore* on certain goals, like the modern catchall parties, or maximizing their support in a social class or otherwise numerous sector of a society. Only parties with limited access to power identify with specific interests, as Max Weber noted for the parties in Imperial Germany, except for minor parties in a fragmented multiparty system, which generally act as minor allies of major parties. Single parties in this respect are, once again, closer to the assumptions underlying democratic politics. It is therefore not surprising that authoritarian conceptions born in a climate of rejection of political parties, of the bitterness of ideological partisan conflict in unstable democracies but in societies of some degree of economic and social complexity and having reached a certain level of political mobilization, should turn to corporativist solutions.

The ideological heritage of nineteenth-century counterrevolutionary conservatism, with its rejection of both individualistic liberalism and state absolutism and its ideological identification with the Middle Ages—the response of preindustrial strata like artisans, peasants, and sometimes even professionals to advancing industrial and financial capitalism—gave rise to a variety of corporativist ideologies (Schmitter, 1974; Manoïlesco, 1936; Elbow, 1953; Bowen, 1947; Pike and Stritch, 1974). The antiliberal, anticapitalist, and antistatist—specifically of the secularizing state—response of the Catholic Church in encyclicals like the *Rerum Novarum* was another stream contributing to its appeal (Azpiazu, 1951; Vallauri, 1971). The syndicalist tradition in the labor movement, which rejected the authoritarianism of Marxism; the persistence of the state as an instrument of oppression; and the cooptation of the social democratic labor movement by participation in electoral and parliamentary politics also contributed to the search for formulas of participation through independent councils of producers at the factory and community level which would freely agree, through pacts that could be revoked, to create larger organizations. Even some democratic liberals, fearful of the growing power of the state and of the anomie of lonely isolated individuals as a result of the growing division of labor and the crisis of traditional institutions, felt that corporative professional organizations could serve social control (Durkheim, 1902). The availability of conservative antirevolutionary, Catholic, syndicalist, and liberal solidarist traditions had its fruits in the crisis of the twenties and thirties. Italian and other fascists, in theoretical formulations, laws and learned legal commentaries, and efforts of institution building, made corporativism an influential political-ideological current.[50]

It is conceivable in theory that corporativism would have offered an alternative way to organize free and spontaneous participation to that through election of individuals or candidates of parties to a national parliament on the basis of territorial constituencies. Actually, "organic democracy" in contrast to individualist "inorganic democracy" of parties has in every case been combined with authoritarian imposition and lack of accountability of the rulers to the ruled. The reality of corporativism has been defined by Philippe Schmitter (1974) as

> a system of interest representation in which the constituent units are organized into a limited number of singular, compulsory, noncompetitive, hierarchically ordered and functionally differentiated categories, recognized and licensed (if not created) by the state and granted a deliberate representational monopoly within their respective categories in exchange for observing certain controls on their selection of leaders and articulation of demands and supports. (p. 93)

In ideal-type terms he contrasts this system with the pluralism in democracies described as

> a system of interest representation in which the constituent units are organized into an unspecified number of multiple, voluntary, competitive, non-hierarchically ordered, and self-determined (as to type or scope of interest) categories which are not specially licensed, subsidized, created or otherwise controlled . . . by the state and which do not exercise a monopoly of representational activity within their respective categories. (p. 96)

Obviously, in reality we do not find these pure ideal types; interest pluralism in democratic societies often takes corporativist characteristics, and the reality of corporativism in authoritarian regimes has some tolerance for unfettered pluralist tendencies, particularly for business and professional interests.

Why should corporativism have become identified with authoritarian regimes, become, as Alfred Stepan has aptly characterized it, organic statism? Three reasons seem to account for it: first, logical and practical difficulties in organizing political life exclusively as an expression of "corporate" interests; secondly, the socio-political purpose pursued in the particular historical-social context in which such solutions have been implemented; and thirdly, the nature of political community and the state as well as the intellectual and legal traditions on which the idea of the state is based.

The theoreticians of organic democracy all emphasize that people are naturally members of numerous groups based on primary social relations, at the work place, farmers' cooperatives, professional associations, universities, neighborhoods, parishes, etc., in contrast to artificially created larger groups, like political parties, which divide people in those primary contexts and lead to the emergence of professional politicians, party bureaucrats remote from the life of the citizen. Why not organize representation on the basis of such primary units? Obviously the representatives of such more or less face-to-face groups would be close to the people and subject to their daily control. Social science research has shown that contrary to the expectations of those theories, private governments are characterized by strong oligarchic tendencies and membership apathy.[51] Leaving this aside, the question arises, How can participation in larger units of decision making, required in urban industrial societies with large-scale organizations interacting with other large social, economic, and political units, be organized on this basis? The theory responds with multi-tier, that is, indirect, elections within a series of constituencies based on grouping such primary units up to a national chamber of corporations (Aquarone, 1965; Fraga, 1959; Fernández-Carvajal, 1969, pp. 77–124; Esteban, 1973, pp. 127–255) or a series of specialized chambers. In principle it should be possible to organize a national democratic polity on this indirect democracy basis, even when accountability of the national leadership to the individual citizen would seem difficult to achieve. However, a number of false assumptions make the model questionable: foremost, that such primary units share common interests rather than being internally conflictual; secondly, that there should be no cleavages crosscutting on a national level those units of greater saliency than the common interest of their members—that neighbors should have more interest in local problems than in, let us say, secularization versus clericalism, or war and peace, and those issues would not divide the society and require representation. If such broader issues would exist in the society, we could assume that ultimately, particularly at the national level, parties based on the aggregation of a large number of issues would emerge without the corporatively elected representatives having any basis to make their decision and without having been chosen on account of their position on them.

Even more serious is the problem of delimiting in a rational way the constituencies and the share in representational power to be attributed to them. To recognize spontaneously emerged, preexisting organizations would show the very unequal organizational mobilization of various interests, and therefore the state inevitably assumes the task of defining noncompetitive and functionally predetermined categories by certifying them or licensing them and granting them a representational monopoly. Even more difficult is the decision of what weight to assign in the decision making to the variety of organized interests. There are no obvious criteria for such a decision. The number of members would make impossible the representation of functionally important groups of numerical insignificance. The weight in the economy (a criterion used in assigning seats in the Yugoslav chamber system) again disenfranchises numerically important but economically weak sectors, like agriculture in semideveloped societies. There is no easily defensible criterion to assign representation to noneconomic, nonoccupational interests, and ultimately even the best decisions would be subject to constant revisions with changes in the economic and social structure which would make the conflicts about reapportionment in inorganic democracies children's play. The authoritarian decisions by the state, that is, by bureaucrats and/or ruling political groups, would in all cases predetermine the nature and composition of the decision-making bodies, which would then be anything but an organic outgrowth of the society. Whatever deviations from fair representation almost inevitably exist in democracies based on population and territorial constituencies (except for a single national constituency with strict proportional representation), they are incomparably smaller than those that even the most rational and equitable corporative system of representation would produce.

Sociologically, as Max Weber (1968) noted in a short section on "representation by agents of interest groups," any such system has as a latent function to disenfranchise certain strata.[52] As he notes, it is possible for such a system to be extremely conservative or radically revolutionary in its character. It can be the former by distributing mandates among the occupations and thus in fact disenfranchising the numerically superior masses, or the latter by openly and formally limiting suffrage to the proletariat and thus disenfranchising those strata whose power rests on their economic position (the case of a state of soviets). It is this that has recommended corporative representation to authoritarian regimes, particularly in societies in which the masses of workers, farm laborers, and peasants are a potentially majority support for mass class parties. This and the opportunity for electoral manipulation with indirect, multi-tier, elections accounts for the realities of political systems based on such principles. In addition, interests are often highly antagonistic and hence majority voting among elements that in status and class affiliation are highly heterogeneous is exceedingly artificial. The ballot as a basis of final decision is characteristic of settling and expressing the compromise of parties. It is not, however, characteristic of occupational interest groups. In addition, on many issues representatives of interests would have no reason to have an opinion and therefore they would be logically willing to exchange their vote on most issues for measures favoring their narrow specific interests. In such a context power ultimately ends up in a ruling group that organizes the system, delimits its constituencies, assigns the share in representation, arbitrates conflicts between interests, and decides all those issues on which the representatives have no basis for choice. Even in systems ideologically committed to organic democracy, the realities can be better described as "state organicism," with bureaucratic-military-technocratic elites and/or the leaders of a single party having the largest share of power. The corporative structure at best becomes one element in the limited pluralism of such authoritarian regimes. However, even weak corporative structures represent a limit, particularly at the grass-roots level, to the monistic ambitions of a disciplined political elite attempting to mobilize a society for its utopian purposes. It is therefore no accident that there should have been in the fascist regimes ambivalence and tension on how far those institutions should have been developed at the cost of the power of the single party, and that the Nazis, with their perception of plebiscitarian, classless *Volksgeminschaft,* should have rejected early the corporativist ideas of German conservatism (Rämisch, 1957).

No political system has made the highest and most powerful decision-making bodies—the cabinet and head of government—accountable to its corporative-type legislatures (Aquarone, 1965; Fraga, 1959; Fernández-Carvajal, 1969). In our sense of the term there has not been any democracy without political parties, even though in pure theory popular participation could be organized through corporative constituencies and elections rather than parties.

Once the ideas of institutionalized or tolerated class conflict and of a classless society in its utopian ideological versions of Marxism or Nazi *Volksgemeinschaft* are rejected, the idea of building political institutions through corporate interest representation becomes an obvious alternative. It is one that is particularly tempting for bureaucratic, military, and technocratic elites that reject the idea of open conflict and believe in a rational, ultimately administrative solution of conflicts of interests but are not guided by a utopian vision of society but by pragmatic considerations. It should allow the expression of the heterogeneity of interests, of the pluralism of society, but also serve to limit the conflictual expression of that heterogeneity, particularly in the form of class conflict. De facto the emergent systems had many elements of class imposition.

It is no accident that the National Socialists, impelled toward a more totalitarian model of society, after toying with corporativist ideas of a *Ständestaat* should have rejected it, and that democratic parties, inclined to create second chambers based on corporative principles like the *Reichswirtschaftsrat* or the *Conseil Economique et Social,* ultimately never infused real life into those bodies. In all political systems we find some elements of corporativism, of institutionalized and regulated representation of interests, particularly economic and occupational, but only in authoritarian regimes has a serious effort been made to organize a political regime according to a corporativist ideology. In reality those authoritarian regimes claiming to be corporativist have ultimately been bureaucratic, technocratic, or single-party mobilizational authoritarian regimes. However, corporativism—organic democracy— has served as an important ideological alternative to competitive democracy. It has been an important component of the institutional pluralism of regimes ruling over a society that had reached a level of social and economic complexity and social and political mobilization that could not be managed by sheer administration, and thus needing to provide for some opportunity for political participation but unable to create or sustain an ideological mass party led by a politically conscious elite or vanguard. It was also a solution particularly congruent with an economic system that rejected a free-market, entrepreneurial capitalism but also public ownership of all the means of production and centralized planning. The disillusion in a number of European and Latin American societies with liberal democracy and a pure capitalist economic system was fertile ground for the acceptance by many groups, including business elites, of corporativist solutions.

There have been and exist a significant number of authoritarian regimes that have turned to ideas of organic democracy to legitimize their rule and to organize a more or less limited participation of carefully delimited and weighted sectors of the population. Theoretically the Portuguese Estado Novo built by Salazar, with its weak single party created from above, is the purest case of such a regime (Schmitter, 1973a). There, as in Austria (Voegelin, 1936; Diamant, 1960; Busshoff, 1968) between 1934 and 1938 under Dollfuss (Bärnthaler, 1971), and in Spain under Franco after a pretotalitarian fascist period,[53] the rulers, using a Catholic ideological heritage combined with the Italian Fascist experience, created systems with a component of organic democracy. Mussolini, linking originally with the syndicalist tradition, reinforced by the intellectual heritage of rightist nationalists, and searching for the approval of Catholics, built a corporativist superstructure that served conservative interests well by disenfranchising a highly mobilized working class and providing a channel for the complex interest structure of a relatively developed society. The strong pretotalitarian tendencies of many Fascist leaders and the conception of an "ethical state" above interests derived from an idealistic tradition, however, created an uneasy balance between the corporativist and the single.party mobilizational components of the regime.[54] Authoritarian regimes in Latin America, particularly of the populist variety, found corporativist policies particularly congenial (Wiarda, 1973a, 1974). The absence of widespread political mobilization of a large working class organized by socialists or other independent labor movements before the assumption of power allowed rulers like Vargas (Schmitter, 1971), Cárdenas, and to some extent Perón to use corporativist interest representation, including powerful trade unions in their authoritarian regimes. The Mexicans, through the sector organization of the party and its reflection in candidate selection for legislature and other offices, have also incorporated into a dominant party structure corporative elements (Scott, 1964). Nowadays the military in Peru are attempting an interesting experiment of the same character by encouraging the creation of the *Sinamos (Sistema Nacional de Apoyo a la Mobilización Social,* "national system of support to social mobilization") in several spheres like (Cotler, 1972;

Palmer, 1973; Malloy, 1974): the *pueblos jóvenes* and urban slums; rural organizations; youth; labor organizations (trade unions and labor communities); cultural; professional; and economic (cooperatives, self-managed enterprises). In an initial phase after the Russian Revolution the ideas of soviets (councils of workers or of workers, peasants, and soldiers) had considerable attraction for revolutionaries who rejected the Marxist social democratic party, which had been ready to participate in parliamentary democratic regimes, as a method to disenfranchise other sectors of society and to provide a particularly effective arena to revolutionary activists ready to displace the leadership of other leftist parties and movements (Kool, 1967). However, ultimately the vanguard party dispensed with this form of participation. Yugoslavia, with workers' management and local self-government, has also created a system of chambers of corporative character, which complement the political structure based on the party and its functional organizations and the revolutionary oligarchy.

It is important to emphasize that many pluralistic systems with competitive democratic political institutions and parties institutionalize or encourage directly or indirectly corporative arrangements to handle particular problems, especially in the field of management and labor relations. Many have attempted to complement the political chambers with advisory corporative chambers, but they generally have lacked vitality when interest groups were divided along political, ideological, or religious lines. Only in the Scandinavian democracies (Rokkan, 1966) and in some of the consociational smaller European democracies, particularly Austria, have these institutions gained a considerable share in power. This has, perhaps, been possible because of the high degree of overlap of a moderate, centripetal, multiparty system with the basic interest cleavages in the society and the integration between party system and interest-organization system. However, we should not forget the basic difference between the presence of corporative tendencies in systems based on the political pluralism of parties and in systems claiming to organize the political process through corporative structures. Nor should we ignore the differences between such organizations having grown out of the society, even when often encouraged and privileged by the state, and those authoritatively created by the state. The first development is the result of a liberal period, sometimes historical continuity, and a culture and economic development encouraging the "art of association"; the other is a result of imposition in the absence of those factors or of control of them by one sector of society holding authoritarian power.

In spite of all the ideological emphasis on corporativism and organic democracy, none of the regimes identifying themselves as "organic" has renounced to a single party, which often results from a fusion of a variety of antidemocratic organizations and/or is created from above. Those single parties in Europe—with the exception of Fascist Italy—were weak organizations, while in Latin America, perhaps because of the oligarchic character of previous political systems, the new officially created parties—often closely linked with the corporative structures like "recognized" trade unions—became important institutions capable of survival after a transition to more democratic politics.

3. Mobilizational Authoritarian Regimes in Postdemocratic Societies

The Western European democratic revolution initiated in the eighteenth century spread liberal democratic institutions to societies of very different economic, social, cultural, and institutional development. In many of them there was no possibility of returning to traditional legitimate rule after political revolutions and often major social and economic changes. In a number of them the sequence of development crises—state-building legitimation, participation, incorporation of new social forces, representation in legislative organs, and ultimately share in executive power—cumulated in a short period of time. More often than not economic development did not keep pace with political change. Protest ideologies formulated in more advanced societies diffused and new movements combined demands for redistribution and participation with the hostility to the changes resulting from early industrialization and disruption of traditional economic and social patterns (Borkenau, 1933). Other countries, particularly those that had not experienced the Protestant Reformation and the disestablishment of religion that went with religious pluralism in earlier centuries, faced a crisis of secularization. Some like Italy and Germany as latecomers to statehood, whose boundaries did not coincide with those of the culture nation, experienced a heightened need for a sense of national cohesion (Allen, 1975). The success of the United Kingdom and France and to a lesser extent the Netherlands and Belgium in the colonial expansion created in other medium-sized powers the consciousness of the "proletarian nation." The loss of the last remnants of Spain's empire and the English veto of Portugal's expansion also created crises of national consciousness. The coincidence of these quite different but cumulated crises through the period of rapid political democratization, particularly in the absence or weakness of traditionally legitimate institutions and elites, prevented the successful and slow institutionalization of democratic political processes capable of incorporating the demands of new social groups awakened to class or cultural consciousness. In contrast to the Eastern European societies, those of Western Europe already before World War I had experienced the introduction of liberal freedoms, constitutional or semiconstitutional government, and an increasing importance of modern political parties, including Marxist, syndicalist, and Christian labor movements. The crisis caused by war interventions, postwar economic dislocations, and the psychological impact on the underprivileged masses of the Russian Revolution and with it the split of the socialist movement led to the delegitimation and ineffectiveness of democratic regimes in process of consolidation. In contrast to the less politically, economically, and socially developed Eastern European nations, purely bureaucratic-military-oligarchical authoritarian solutions could not be the response to the crisis. It could not be because even the oligarchic institutions of the establishment had accepted the notion that politics could not be reduced to administration and realized that a purely coercive repression was condemned to failure because in all social classes, including the privileged middle class, democratic ideas had gained considerable loyalty. In such societies the crisis of democracy would lead to new political formulas including the plebiscitarian pseudodemocratic component: the mass single party. On the other hand, those societies had reached a level of development and complexity that made it difficult for the leadership of such a single party to move in a totalitarian direction, except in the case of Nazi Germany. It is no accident that the first manifestation in Europe of a plebiscitarian, nonliberal authoritarian solution to the crisis of democracy should have been Bonapartism, considering that France was the country of Europe in which revolutionary change had brought the biggest break with traditional authority and had led to the highest political mobilization with the 1848 revolution. It is no accident that some Marxists like Thalheimer (1930) should have turned to Marx's analysis in the *Eighteenth Brumaire* to understand the novel authoritarian regimes created by fascism.[55]

The crisis of European societies at the end of World War I led to the emergence of two political movements that broke with the liberal democratic systems that seemed on the ascendancy: Leninism and fascism. Both were based on the rule by the minority, by an elite, self-appointed to represent the majority, the proletariat or the nation, at the service of a historical task. Parties led by a self-confident elite defined not by ascriptive characteristics or by professional achievements but by its will to gain power and to use it to break through social and historical constraining conditions, appealing for the support of the masses but unwilling to allow them to interfere in the pursuit of its goals. The strength of the democratic heritage of Marxism and the scientism of Marxist social science, while allowing a break with the liberal tradition, assured the persistence of an ideological commitment to democracy. Fascism as a nationalistic response to the ideological internationalism of Marxism, by linking with other ideological traditions of the nineteenth century—romantic irrationalism, social Darwinism, Hegelian exultation of the state, Nietzschean ideas, Sorelian conceptions of the role of the myth, imagery of the great man and the genius—turned explicitly antidemocratic (Gregor, 1969; Nolte, 1969; Weber, 1964). In contrast to other conceptions of authoritarianism as a modern response to the crisis of society, it searched for a new and different form of democratic legitimation, based on the emotional identification of the followers with the leader, in a plebiscitarianism that had found its first postrevolutionary manifestation in Napoleonic Caesarism. In a complex way we cannot analyze here, fascism combined and perverted many strains of Western intellectual tradition that directly or indirectly put into question the assumptions of liberal democratic pluralist society and politics.

The special circumstances of Italian society after World War I led to the emergence under the leadership of Mussolini of a new type of nontraditionalist, popular antidemocratic movement, initially carried by a small number of activists recruited among the interventionists; nationalists; the veterans of the war who found reintegration into civil society difficult; a certain type of intelligentsia heady with nationalism, futurism, and hostility for the clientelistic politics of Giolittian *transformismo* and for the selfishness of the bourgeoisie; together with revolutionary syndicalists who had discovered their national identity (De Felice, 1966a, 1969, 1970; Delzell, 1970). The poet D'Annunzio discovered a new style, new symbols for this generation of rebels (Hamilton, 1971). It was, however, the mobilization of the Italian working class by a Maximalist social labor movement, unable to implement a revolutionary takeover of power and still unwilling to follow a reformist path toward integration into democracy in the making, that created the conditions for success of this minority of activists. The red domination of the northern Italian countryside, which scared landowners and wealthier peasants, and occupation of factories in the industrial centers, particularly Torino, led a scared bourgeoisie to join and support the incipient movement (Salvemini, 1961). Its leaders, hostile to the socialists on account of their anti-interventionism and to the workers who had stayed in the factories and received with hostility the returning veterans, were ready for the alliance. The ambivalent attitude of the state and its representatives toward the terrorist activities of the *squadrismo,* the failure of the reformists to turn to support the demo-liberal state, and the tensions between the old liberal parties and both the socialists and the new democratic Christian populist party, combined with the ruthlessness and opportunism of Mussolini, led the new movement to power. A new and multifaceted ideology, a new form of political action, and a new style had been born and would find echo in much of Europe (Nolte, 1966, 1968a; Laqueur and Mosse, 1966; Rogger and Weber, 1966; Woolf, 1969; Carsten, 1967; Kedward, 1969; Hayes, 1973) and even in Latin America (Trindade, 1974) and Asia (Maruyama, 1963; Morris, 1968). Initially it was possible to conceive of fascism as a peculiar outcome of the Italian crisis (De Felice, 1966a, 1969, 1970; Nolte, 1967). Later, even as far as the 1930s, it could be interpreted as a response to the problems created by late and unsuccessful economic development and modernization (Borkenau, 1933). But with the success of Hitler it became necessary to explain it in terms of certain basic characteristics of Western society (Nolte, 1967, 1969; Gregor, 1968, 1974a, 1974b; Woolf, 1968; Turner, 1972).

In the context of our analysis of types of political systems we cannot enter into an analysis of the variety of forms the fascist antidemocratic ideology and movement took, nor an explanation of the conditions for its success (Lipset, 1960; Nolte, 1968a; Linz, 1976). The nature and definition of fascism itself is a subject of lively debate. We would characterize fascism as an ideology and movement defined by what it rejects, by its exacerbated nationalism, by the discovery of new forms of political action and a new style. The anti-positions of fascism are essential to its understanding and its appeal, but they alone do not account for its success. Fascism is antiliberal, antiparliamentarian, anti-Marxist, and particularly anticommunist, anti- or at least aclerical, and in a certain sense antibourgeois and anticapitalist; while linking with the real or imagined historical national tradition, it is not committed to a conservative continuity with the recent past or a purely reactionary return to it but is future-oriented. Those negative stances are a logical outcome of its being a latecomer on the political scene, trying to displace liberal, Marxist, socialist, and clerical parties and win over their supporters. They are also the fruit of the exacerbated nationalism that rejects the appeal to class solidarity across national boundaries and puts in its place the solidarity of all those involved in production in a nation against other nations, seizing on the notion of the proletarian nation: the poor countries against the wealthy plutocracies, which happened to be at that time also powerful democracies. Communist internationalism is defined in this context as the enemy. The latent hostility to a church that transcends the national boundaries and whose devisive effect on the national community with the struggle between clerical and secularizers interferes with the goal of national greatness, hostility that becomes bitter hatred in cases like Nazism, is another logical consequence that differentiates the fascist from other conservative antidemocratic parties. To the extent that modern capitalism is, particularly in its financial institutions, part of an international system, fascists tend to idealize preindustrial strata like the independent peasant, the artisan, and the entrepreneur, particularly the founder directing his own firm (Mosse, 1964; Winkler, 1972). Masonry, as an organization emphasizing links across nations and closely identified with the liberal bourgeois, secularized strata that created the democratic liberal regimes, is another obviouus enemy. Anti-Semitism in the Europe of the turn of the century, particularly Eastern Europe (Pulzer, 1964; Massing, 1949), had a long tradition, and wherever there were Jews fascism seized on those tendencies, stressing the anational, cosmopolitan character of the Jews and particularly of Zionism.

Those negative appeals, however, had a kind of distorted positive counterpart. The anti-Marxism is compensated by an exultation of work, of the producers of *Faust* and *Stirn,* "hand and brain," in that way appealing to the growing white-collar middle class, which rejected Marxist demands that it should identify with the proletariat (Kele, 1972). The populism of fascism leads it to support welfare-state policies and to engage in loose talk of national socialism, socialization of the banks, etc., which justifies in fascist authoritarian regimes economic interventionism and the development of an important public sector in the economy. The anticapitalism that appeals to precapitalist and petit bourgeois strata is redefined as hostility to international financial stock exchange and Jewish capitalism and as exultation of the national entrepreneurial bourgeoisie. The emphasis on a national common good, which rejects the assumptions of individualism, is easily combined with hostility to the free play of interests of economic liberalism and finds expression in protectionist and autarchic economic policies that appeal to industrialists threatened by international competition. The hostility of a secularized intelligentsia of exacerbated nationalists to clerical politics and their competition with Christian democratic parties for a similar social basis account for the anticlericalism that gets combined with an affirmation of the religious tradition as part of the national, cultural, historical tradition. Already the Action Française in secularist France had taken this path, appealing to the Catholics who rejected the secularizing, liberal democratic state. The Iron Guard, the only successful fascist movement in a Greek Orthodox country, confronted with the denationalized, secularized bourgeoisie and an influential Jewish community, was the fascism that most directly linked with religious symbolism. In the case of Germany the confused programmatic statements about positive Christianity and the identification of many Protestants with a conservative state religion were used by the Nazis, but ultimately the racist ideology became incompatible with any commitment to Christianity (Lewy, 1965; Buchheim, 1953). The antireligious stands of Marxism and particularly communism in the Soviet Union allowed the fascists to capitalize on the ambivalent identification with the religious heritage. The anticlericalism facilitated the appeal to secularized middle classes unwilling to support the clerical and Christian democratic middle-class parties, while their antiliberalism, anti-Masonic, and even anti-Semitic stands, combined with their anticommunism, facilitated the collaboration with the churches when they came to power. The antibourgeois affect, the romanticization of the peasant, the artisan, the soldier, contrasted with the impersonal capitalism and selfish bourgeois rentiers, appealed to the emotional discontent of the sons of the bourgeoisie, the cultural critics of modern industrial and urban society. The rejection of the proletarian self-righteousness and the bourgeois egoism and the affirmation of the common national interests above and beyond class cleavages exploited the desire for interclass solidarity developed among veterans of the war (Linz, 1976; Merkl, 1975) and the guilt feeling of the bourgeoisie, and served well the interests of the business community in destroying a labor movement that threatened its privileges and status. The populist appeal to community against the pragmatism of society, *Gemeinschaft* versus *Gesellschaft,* had considerable appeal in democratic societies divided by class conflict and mobilized by modern mass parties.

The deliberately ambiguous and largely contradictory appeals we have just described would have been, and were, unsuccessful in those societies in which war and defeat had not created a serious national crisis. In the defeated nations or those, like Italy, being victors, felt unjustly deprived of the fruits of their victory, an upsurge of nationalism was channeled by the new parties. The efforts to establish an international political order through the League of Nations under the leadership and to the benefit of the Western, capitalistic, plutocratic democracies became another issue in the armory of the fascists. The lack of coincidence between the national-cultural boundaries and those of the states, the irredenta on the borders, and the existence of nationalities that had not become nation-states, combined with the pan-nationalist movements, were another source of strength for fascism, particularly in the case of Nazis.

Fascist ideology had to reject totally the assumptions of liberal democratic politics based on pluralist participation, the free expression of interests, and compromise among them rather than the assertion of the collective interests above individuals and classes, cultural and religious communities. The obvious distortion of the idea of democracy in the reality of the early twentieth century and the incapacity of the democratic leadership to institutionalize mechanisms for conflict resolution provided the ground for the appeal of fascism. On a less lofty level, all the interests threatened by a powerful labor movement with revolutionary rhetoric, particularly after some of its revolutionary attempts had been defeated, could support the fascist squads as a defense of the social order. In societies that had reached the level of political, economic, and social development of Western Europe, that defense could not be left to the old institutions—the monarchy, the army, the bureaucracy, and the oligarchical political elites. In that context the fascist ideology offered a new alternative, which promised the integration of the working class into the national community and the assertion of its interests against other nations, if necessary through military preparedness and even aggression (Neumann, 1963). This position would appeal to veterans not reintegrated into civil society and army officers and would neutralize the armed forces in the course of the struggle for power.

Neither the ideological appeals nor the interests served by or expected to be served by fascism are sufficient to account for its rapid success. Fascism developed new forms of political organization, different from both the committee electoral-type of parties and the mass-membership, trade-union-based socialist parties, as well as the clerically led religious parties. It was the type of organization that, like the communist counterpart, offered an opportunity for action, involvement, participation, breaking with the monotony of everyday life. For a generation that had lived heroic, adventurous actions of war and even more for the one that had lived that experience vicariously, due to its youth, the *squadrismo* and the storm troopers offered welcome relief. Many of those who found their normal careers and education disrupted by the war and economic crisis, and probably some of the unemployed, provided the party with many of its activists, whose propaganda and direct action in support of specific grievances—of farmers to be evicted, peasants onto whom the labor unions were imposing the employment of labor, industrialists threatened by strikers—gained them support that no electoral propaganda could have achieved. This new style of politics satisfied certain psychological and emotional needs like no other party could except some forms of cultural protest and to some extent the communists.

Finally, fascism is characterized by a distinctive style reflected in the uniforms—the shirts—which symbolized the break with bourgeois convention, the individualism of bourgeois dress; and the mass demonstrations and ceremonies, which allowed individuals to submerge in the collective and escape the privatization of modern society. The songs, the greetings, the marches, all gave expression to the new myth, the hopes, and illusions of part of that generation.

This ideal-typical description of fascism as a political movement ignores national variants in ideology, appeal, social basis, and alignments on the political scene. We cannot go into the complex question of whether National Socialism, with its extreme racism, its biologic conception of man, fits into the broader category of fascism (Nolte, 1963; Mosse, 1964, 1966), particularly since many fascists felt quite critical of Nazism and many Nazis felt ambivalent toward Mussolini and his movement (Hoepke, 1968). Our view is that National Socialism, particularly the northern left wing of the movement, rather than "Hitlerism," fits into the more general category (Kühnl, 1966). Nazism did not reject the identification as fascism, but it also acquired unique characteristics making it a quite different branch of the common tree into which German ideological traditions (Mosse, 1964; Sontheimer, 1968; Lukácz, 1955) had been grafted and one that had its own distinct fruits.[56] The strength of that branch growing with the resources of German society made it an appealing competitor of the first fascist state.

The ambiguities and contradictions of the fascist utopia, combined with the inevitable pragmatic compromises with many of the forces it initially criticized, account for the failure of the model, except in Italy (to a certain point) and in Germany. To have been successful the initial nucleus would have had to gain support in all strata of the society and particularly among the working class in addition to the peasantry. However, the organizational penetration, except perhaps in Hungary, Rumania, and (if we consider Peronism as a deviant of fascism) in Argentina, of the socialist, communist, and anarcho-syndicalist (in Spain) labor movements was such that such hopes were condemned to failure. In some countries the Catholic peasantry, middle classes, and even many workers had identified with clerical and/or Christian democratic parties in the defense of religion and found in the social doctrine of the Church an answer to many of the problems to which fascism presumed to be a response. Unless deeply scared by unsuccessful revolutionary attempts, disorganized by continuous economic crises—inflation, depression, unemployment, and bankruptcies—or uprooted by war, the middle and upper-middle classes remained loyal to old parties (including, before the March on Rome, most of the Italian south) in countries like France, Belgium, the Netherlands, Scandinavia, and the UK (Linz, 1976; Kaltefleiter, 1968; Lepsius, 1968). Fascism's success in these countries was a minority, largely generational phenomenon, strengthened in nationalist border areas and gaining broader support in crisis periods. The heterogeneous basis and the failure to gain strata to which its appeal was directed, ultimately explainable by its latecomer role on the political scene, led the leaders to an unremitting struggle to gain power and to a policy of opportunistic alliances with a variety of established groups and a- or antidemocratic conservative forces, which in turn hoped to manipulate its popular appeal and youthful activist following for their own purposes. In societies that had experienced a serious crisis but no political, social, and economic breakdown comparable to czarist Russia, this meant that the way of power was open only in coalition with other forces, particularly the conservative authoritarian parties like the Partito Nazionalista in Italy and the DNVP in Germany, the powerful antilabor interest groups, and the army, and by neutralizing the churches. Such groups well entrenched in the establishment and the state could provide men more capable of governing than were the activists of the first hour. The result was the establishment of authoritarian regimes—with a seriously limited and muted pluralism—with a single party whose rule ranged from fairly dominant and active, approaching in some moments the totalitarian model, to regimes in which it was only a minor partner in the coalition of forces, or absorbed like in Portugal, or suppressed, like in Rumania. Only in

Germany would the party and its many—and competing—organizations become dominant. In all of them fascisim introduced a mobilizational, populist component, a channel for some degree and some types of voluntary political participation, a source of ideological discontent with the status quo and justification for social change, which differentiates authoritarian mobilizational regimes from other types. Even where that mobilization was ultimately deliberately demobilized, like in Spain (Linz, 1970a), the half organic-statist, half bureaucratic-expert-military authoritarian regime emerging after the 1940s would never be the same as for example the regime of Salazar, where fascisim as we have characterized it never had taken root.

The struggle against a powerful, particularly a social democratic, labor movement and the effort to undermine the authority of a democratic state exacerbated the romantic love for violence into an end in itself and generally, consciously or unconsciously, transformed the movement into an instrument of vested interests (often verbally and even sincerely denounced), transforming the "national integrative revolution" into hateful counterrevolution. The Marxist interpretation (Abendroth, 1969; Mansilla, 1971; *International Journal of Politics,* 1973; Galkin, 1970; Lopukhov, 1965[57]), while inadequate to explain the emergence of the ideology, its complex appeal, and its success in capturing the imagination of many youthful ideologists and misunderstanding the motivation of the founders and many leaders, is largely right in the analysis of the "objective" historical role played by fascism (F. Neumann, 1963). This obviously does not mean to accept the thesis that the fascists were the hirelings of capitalism based on subsidies that started coming only when the party had gathered strength and in proportion to its success relative to other anti-Marxist parties, or that fascism was the last possible defense of capitalism, or that in power it only and always served its interests. Even less does it absolve the Marxist movement of having undertaken and failed in revolutionary attempts to gain power in relatively democratic societies or of holding onto a maximalist revolutionary rhetoric that mobilizes its enemies and prevents the democratic governments from functioning effectively—a policy that prevents the government from imposing the order desired by those supporting it, while not making a serious effort to impose (at least in part) the policies favored by those movements by participating actively in democratic policymaking by either supporting or even entering government. Fascism, among other things, is a response to the ambivalence of the Marxist ideological heritage toward the importance of political institutions, toward "formal" liberal democracy, toward reform rather than revolution. Mussolini reflected this dialectical relationship when he said that if the red menace had not been there it would have had to be invented. The anti- or at least ademocratic behavior of the left made possible the more effective one of the right, even when in turn the manipulative attitude of the liberals toward democratic institutions explains the reaction of the left.

Fascist-mobilizational authoritarian regimes are less pluralistic, more ideological, and more participatory than bureaucratic-military or organic-statist regimes with a weak single party. They are further from "liberalism" and closer to "democracy," further from individual freedom from political constraint but closer to offering citizens a chance to participate, less conservative, and more change oriented.[58] Probably the greater ideological legitimacy and the greater mobilization of support made them less vulnerable to internal opposition and overthrow than other types of authoritarian rule, and in fact only external defeat destroyed them.

4. Postindependence Mobilizational Authoritarian Regimes: Theory and Reality

Mobilizational authoritarian regimes have appeared in states gaining independence from colonial rule or asserting themselves against foreign dependency. Countries in black Africa[59] and the Maghreb,[60] among the countries of the Third World, provide examples of this type. Contrary to the expectations of many political scientists, not many have proven stable over the last decade, particularly since 1964 military coups swept civilians from office in many of them (Bienen, 1968, 1974; Lee, 1969; C. E. Welch, 1970; Young, n.d.). In others a process of decline set in, leading in many places to a no-party state (Wallerstein, 1966; Potholm, 1970, pp. 272–96; Bretton, 1973).

Single-party mobilizational authoritarian regimes created by political leaders emerging from and mobilizing the grass roots, and not from above by the ruler, were possible in societies of low economic development, particularly with the relatively egalitarian peasant rural structure, where the modern economic elite was small and often composed of foreigners or members of an outside ethnic group and where the colonial rulers had not allowed or encouraged the growth of a professional middle class, a civil service with distinctive status and honor, and a professional army (Apter, 1963). In the case of sub-Saharan

Africa one might add the absence of a native hierarchically organized religious leadership. Colonial rule had often destroyed or, in the case of indirect rule, discredited traditional precolonial authorities, at least for the emerging urban-educated, more modernized sectors. In this context a new nationalist leadership emerged among those trained abroad or in the few educational institutions created by the colonial power, sometimes encouraged by the parties of the left in the metropolis as leaders of trade unions or representatives in emerging self-government institutions and stimulated by a few nationalist intellectuals and their contacts abroad (Wallerstein, 1961; Hodgkin, 1961; Carter, 1962; Coleman and Rosberg, 1964). These leaders sometimes seized successfully the representation of grievances of the native population, the workers and peasants affected by the dislocations of the traditional order resulting from economic change or the introduction of Western legal institutions and in some cases European settlement. The colonial rulers confronted with those incipient movements shifted between repression and co-optation, policies that, particularly when inconsistently applied, contributed to strengthening this emerging nationalist leadership. The desire for independence, at least initially, obscured the importance of other cleavages; the underdevelopment and the foreign character of the modern economic sector limited the importance of class politics. In the representative assemblies elected shortly before or immediately after independence the representatives of the nationalist movements obtained pluralities or majorities, which they often expanded by co-opting those representing more particularistic constituencies like tribal, religious, or traditional groups. Initially there was hope that the transfer of British or French constitutional arrangements would lead to new democratic states. However, soon after independence the actions of the opposition, or the perceptions of them by the leaders of the governing party; the governing party's conception of nation building as excluding peripheral, sectional, tribal demands (particularly in states with artificial boundaries imposed by the colonizers); the difficult economic problems; and the problems caused by new expectations of the people led those leaders to prevent, limit, or exclude free political and electoral competition. In many of the states created by decolonization, independence and statehood became symbolically identified with a leader and his party, who often claimed a charismatic authority, which was recognized by his followers. The weakness of traditional authority and the lack of understanding of the complexities of legal rational authority made the emergence of at least a semblance of charismatic leadership possible. The artificial character of many of the state boundaries, the ethnic, linguistic, and religious diversity of the population, the great difference in social development of the few urban centers and coastal areas and the rural periphery, and the weakness of administrative institutions led the leaders of the new independent states to believe that their party could serve as a nation-building instrument. Faced with the problems of national integration, the not-always loyal opposition, and the fear of foreign influences, the dominant party, in the context of a political culture that had not institutionalized liberal democratic values, soon became a single party.

Significantly, some of the leaders rejected the idea of a single monolithic party: "We are against the *parti unique*. We are in favor of a unified party [*parti unifié*]," to use the expression of Senghor (Foltz, 1965, p. 141). Many leaders of dominant parties encouraged the entry into the party of leaders with a strong regional, communal, tribal, or sectional following who initially supported the defeated opposition parties or were prominent in them. They bring into the loosely organized *parti unifié* their following and electorate.

In analyzing African one-party systems and their mobilizational capacity, we should keep in mind some facts stressed by Aristide R. Zolberg (1966, pp. 15–33) about their penetration in the society. In Ghana the first test of the strength of the Convention People's party (CPP) came in the 1951 election, two years after its founding, in which it obtained 92 percent of the votes cast in Accra, 94 percent in other municipalities where elections were direct, and 72 percent of grand electors of other areas. However, in the five municipalities, 64 percent of the qualified population registered to vote and, of these, 47.2 percent voted. Hence, the voters represented about 30 percent of the eligible population, itself somewhat smaller than the total number of adults. This was a startling achievement but one that cannot be taken as an indication of territorial saturation by the CPP. Similarly, Zolberg notes that in the Ivory Coast the organization of Houphouet-Boigny (the PDCI) in 1946 obtained 94 percent of the votes in the election to the territorial assembly, which amounted to 53 percent of the eligible electorate that had registered, but since the electorate was a very restricted one these votes represented about 6 percent of the estimated adult population. In 1952, in an election that the headers acknowledged to be fair, Houphouet-Boigny's opponents obtained only 28 percent of the votes cast and the PDCI represented only 33 percent of the enlarged electorate. A similar calculation leads to an estimation of the support for Leopold Senghor's party in Senegal, with 68 percent of the votes cast in 1951 and similarly in 1952, of perhaps 10 to 15 percent of the adult population. Certainly such voting strength is not comparable to that achieved by mass parties, democratic or antidemocratic, in critical elections preceding the breakdown of several European democracies, particularly the massive vote for the NSDAP in the early thirties. Such figures should have given pause to those who feared or hoped for a totalitarian control by a movement regime and its leaders in African states, including Ghana, where the rhetoric, the organization charts of the party, and the cult of the leader gave the impression of moving in such a direction.[61]

The single-party regimes in the newly independent nations, given the social structure and the economic development, could not extract enough resources to sustain their vision of radically transforming the society by organizational methods. The collecting of dues or taxes to sustain those organizations was unfeasible. The few politically conscious and relatively educated leaders were needed to staff the government and numerous agencies, to the detriment of the party oragnization. Primordial and personal loyalties deflected the party organization in the periphery from the tasks that the center wanted to assign to it. The discrepancies between the ideological rhetoric (Friedland and Rosberg, 1964) and the achievements and realities of politics, together with the discontent of new generations, particularly those returning from abroad and not finding positions of power commensurate to their ambitions, often created factional tension with the youth organizations, trade-union leadership, etc., which could be best avoided by placing less emphasis on the party. The ideological formulations were largely derivative, ambiguous, and in contradiction with the pragmatic policies to which the leadership felt bound by social and economic realities, and therefore did not provide clear and immediate goals to the membership. As a result, the single party, rather than becoming a totalitarian instrument of mobilization, the monistic center, became one more factor in the power structure, achieving only limited participation. Ironically, it has been argued that single parties had the best chances of survival in the least mobilized, most backward societies, like Mali (Snyder, 1965) and Tanzania (Bienen, 1970), rather than in countries like Ghana with greater resources, where, as a result, an inflationary process of demand formation is likely to develop (Zolberg, 1966, pp. 145–50). In very backward societies revolutionary blueprints affecting the modern sector of the economy caused little disruption.

Another alternative was the transformation of the single party from a disciplined, ideological mass movement into a flexible machine that maintained solidarity among its members by appealing to their self-interest while allowing for the play of factions and for recurrent reconciliation, relying characteristically on the attraction of material rewards rather than enthusiasm for political principles. Leaders who some observers and perhaps some sectors of their society had conceived of as charismatic appeared to others as political bosses. The opportunities for corruption contributed further to the crisis of the ideological single party but often cemented a machinelike organization. While the opposition and the dissidents had to be silenced, there was no need, given their numbers and their resources, for the type of paramilitary organizations developed in the advanced European societies by fascist parties. The coercion would also take the form of machine politics (Zolberg, 1966, 1969; Bretton, 1973).

Few mobilizatonal single parties retained any function only a few years after independence. Those that had not been ousted by military coups experienced considerable transformation. The typologies initially formulated (Morrison et al., 1972; Hodgkin, 1961; Carter, 1962) have been misleading because they were often based on images that the African parties wanted to convey to the world and themselves. They are based on relatively formal structures, that is, they relate to real phenomena but are limited to an account of how they would work if they worked according to the normative expectations of the elites. The people who articulated those ideologies were often not very close to the center of power within the party. However, the single party often remained as an objectified, tangible symbol of the unity of the society. From having been a means, the political monopoly becomes a self-justifying goal. As Zolberg (1966, pp. 62–63) has noted, the mood underlying the emphasis on the single party in such essentially plural societies as those of Africa is somewhat like that of the Jacobins when faced with the *Fédérés*. The faith in planning, in rational control of the economy, rather than in a complex and little visible process like the market, is parallel to and reinforces the symbolic commitment to community. Zolberg in *Creating Political Order* (1966) has noted the functions that can be performed by machine parties appealing to the self-interest of members, allowing for the play of factions and recurrent reconciliation, and providing for formal and informal representation of a multitude of relatively modern and not-so-modern groups in the society, including those based on common origin and on explicit economic and political interests. Its informal inner workings allow patterns of behavior and norms that might otherwise be dismissed as unmodern, allow participation to individuals who do not possess expert or bureaucratic skills but are interested in politics, and sustain a powerful central authority while the party remains popular, facilitating a contact between the mass and the leadership.

One hope of some single-party leaders was that they would provide a channel for democratic participation of the population without the tensions of multiparty systems in integrated societies. In this context, the attempt of Nyerere to use TANU, the Tanganyika African National Union, for the establishment of a democratic one-party state, with the sponsorship of two candidates by the party in national legislative elections, has been particularly interesting (Bienen, 1970; Hopkins, 1971). The experiment of TANU not as an elite but as a mass party through which any citizen of good will can participate in the process of government is faced with a dilemma well formulated in this official report: "To insist on narrow ideological conformity would clearly be inconsistent with the mass participation in the affairs of the party which we regard as essential" (Bienen, 1970, p. 242). On the other hand, if membership involves no political commitment of any kind, TANU would become coextensive with the nation and would cease to function as a political party in any serious sense.

Preselection of candidates within the party but competition between them should allow the people to reject an individual without appearing to reject TANU. But the initial idea of Nyerere, that TANU hold completely open elections in which patriotic individuals could run as candidates, was not accepted. In fact, tendencies have appeared demanding a more elitist and tightly organized TANU, imposing qualitative criteria for membership. In September 1965 the voters in the former Tanganyika, except in five constituencies, could choose between two candidates with the result that 22 out of 31 officeholders were unsuccessful and 16 out of 31 MPs lost. The lack of clear relationship between success or failure and the share of votes received in district preference polls in the party suggest that while only those close to the party could run, they did not enjoy oligarchic control of the outcome, in an election in which 50 percent of the adult population voted. Tanzania is an interesting experiment of combining a single-party system with a freedom of choice for the electorate (Cliffe, 1967). The open, rather than ideological and disciplined, mass-party character of TANU combined with the importance of local concerns in the electorate and the absence of deep, mobilized nationwide cleavages seem to have made it possible. However, it is dubious that any experiment of a democratic one-party state could succeed in an urban industrial or even semi-industrial society.

5. Racial and Ethnic "Democracies"

With this deliberately paradoxical concept we want to refer to regimes in which the political process among those belonging to a racially defined group, particularly a minority of the population, satisfies our definition of democracy but permanently excludes another racial group (or groups), legally or by de facto coercive means. That exclusion does not allow us to fit such regimes into our definition of democracy. The Republic of South Africa is the prime example of such a regime. In many respects regimes that exclude from a limited pluralism a large part and even a majority of population on the basis of race could be described as racial oligarchies or authoritarian regimes. On account of the importance of the ideology of apartheid and the pervasive impact of the racial caste system on the daily life of citizens, including the racial dominant minority, the level of political and social mobilization against potential dangers to its supremacy, and the actual and, even more important, the future need for coercion to maintain the status quo, those regimes could be considered pretotalitarian or totalitarian in potential. Why should we then label them as racial democracies and place them in our attribute space on the borderline with democratic regimes? This paradox is reflected in the ranking of South Africa among 114 countries, according to eligibility to participate in elections and degree of opportunity for public opposition, in scale type 14 (when the least opportunity ranks 30), far above most authoritarian regimes in the world (Dahl, 1971). The paradox is the result of the strange juxtaposition of two societies and political systems, which in the utopian ideology of the defenders of apartheid would be parallel and separate but which inevitably, due to a number of economic, social, and historical constraints, find themselves in a castelike hierarchical relation sustained politically by authoritarian and ultimately coercive domination.

This type of relation has been characteristic of colonial rule[62] and still survives in the few territories under colonial government but diverges from it in several respects. The rule is not exercised in the name of a metropolitan government through its appointed agents ideologically and legally for the benefit of the whole population but is exercised in the name and actually for the benefit of a self-governing racial minority The history of colonization in a few areas of the world led to sizable white settlements in areas where large nonwhite populations were not decimated, where racial prejudices, sometimes supported by religion and ideology and the migration of families rather than males ready to establish sexual relations with the natives, created castelike societies based on race. Those white settlers brought with them values and institutions in the mainstream of the liberal democratic tradition. In this respect they were like the societies described by Louis Hartz (1964) that resulted from fragmentation of Western European empires, particularly the United States, Australia, New Zealand, and Canada. Those traditions and their institutionalization, sometimes with the support of and other times against the metropolitan authority, could have led to the establishment of stable democracies, particularly considering the economic resources available in the case of South Africa. As long as the native population was socially nonmobilized, under traditional authority structures maintained as indirect rule, nonurban and illiterate, unexposed to Western culture, religion, and mass media, and more or less resigned to that marginal and subordinate status, the white settlers could develop representative institutions and enjoy civil liberties and the rule of law. The result was the development of a competitive party system, parliamentary government, and many of those characteristics that still in 1968, using ten characteristics of political life among the white population, place South Africa very close to the polyarchies.

However, the racism of the whites, the numerical proportions of whites and nonwhites in the population, the economic, social, and cultural inequality between the races, the fears resulting from racist prejudice and the demographic and other inequalities between the races, and the inevitable polarization resulting from the initial segregation and rejection of a policy of integration have prevented the emergence of any form of multiracial nation and consequently multiracial democratic state (Thompson, 1966; Van den Berghe, 1967; Adam, 1971; Potholm and Dale, 1972). Even the limited participation of the Cape Town Coloured in the electorate and representative institutions was slowly restricted and practically eliminated through a complex and long legal process. The metropolitan power was unwilling and/or unable (in the case of Rhodesia) to impose some form of multiracial democracy. The tensions between the large, long-time resident, Afrikaans-speaking whites and the more recent English-speaking population, based on the memories of the Great Trek and the War of 1899–1902 and the persistent differences in social structure, economic power, religion, and culture, led to the mobilizations of the white Afrikaners behind the Nationalist party and its policy of apartheid. It also accounts for the electoral weakness of moderates and the practical insignificance of the Progressive party and the enlightened minority among the elite opposing that policy. The enactment over the years of repressive legislation, culminating in the general law amendment acts of 1963 and 1965, has banned and served to destroy any African opposition to full white domination and second-class citizenship. The exclusion from the electorate of the 68.3 percent Bantus, 9.4 percent Coloureds, except for a small minority allowed to elect four representatives, and the 3 percent Asians, requiring after the Sharpeville incident an increasing use of force, places South Africa according to our definition among the nondemocratic regimes. On the other hand, the persistence of liberal democratic institutions, a wide range of civil liberties, and of parties competing for power in free elections among the white minority justifies the label "racial democracy." The political freedom among whites is based on the unity among whites, on the widespread consensus among them on the policy of racial domination, and particularly on the support by a majority of the electorate of the Nationalist party.

A racial democracy, however, is not only an authoritarian rule over the nonwhites but inevitably leads to increasingly authoritarian rule over those whites who question the policy of the majority and increasing limitations and infringements of the civil liberties and political expression of the dissidents. The Suppression of Communism Act of 1950, the Public Safety Act of 1953, the Criminal Law Amendment Act of the same year, the Prison Act of 1959, the Publications and Entertainment Act of 1963, etc., in their loose formulation include restrictions that can be and have been increasingly applied to white dissidents who protest against the law or support any campaign against it, reflecting the policy approved by the majority. Ultimately racial democracy leads to authoritarian rule with majority support regularly expressed through elections, allowing democratic political competition on nonracial issues and guaranteeing, at least for the time being, other freedoms like the equality of the Afrikaans and the English languages.

The supporter of the South African regime would argue that this description is incomplete and even distorted. He would stress that apartheid in principle, even when not perhaps in its present practice, implies the separate development of racial communities, in fact of separate nations, in their own area with their own democratic self-government.

Ignoring for the moment the difficulty of applying that model to the populations intermingled in the great urban centers without a distinct territorial basis, particularly the Asians, most of the Coloured, and a very large proportion of the Bantu population, the attempts to create democratic, nonwhite states have not and are not likely to succeed to fit our definition of democracy. The case of the Transkei, in which 400 white inhabitants were deprived of a say in local government, consistent with the ideology that non-Africans may not become citizens, does not fit. It does not fit not only because of the presence in the legislative assembly of the 4 paramount chiefs and 60 chiefs of the Transkei, among whom vacancies are filled by the regional authorities subject to the confirmation of the state president, in addition to 45 elected representatives, but because of the number of important legislative subjects excluded from its competence, among them the amendment of the Transkei Constitution enacted by the South African Parliament. The basic law is therefore similar to that of a colony under the system of dyarchy, in which the metropolitan power retains control over everything that is vital while allowing the indigenous people the qualified management of a limited range of local affairs mainly through the medium of chiefs, whom the metropolitan power can influence in many overt and covert ways.

Even ignoring that fewer than 40 percent of the African inhabitants of the republic are physically present in Bantu areas, in which, according to government policy, such black racial democracies would be established, the fact that constitutionally they would have only a share in power and no institutionalized mechanisms to participate in the decision making for the whole South African Republic would not allow us to call the African Bantustans parallel democratic political units. The development of a Coloured representative council and of an Indian representative council and the stripping of provincial and municipal authorities of many of their powers over nonwhites, considering the powers allocated to the departments of the central government and the share of power assigned to such councils and the executive committee chosen by them, show the legal and de facto limits to the experiment of a single state with segregated racial communities, whatever degree of formal self-government allowed to them. The social and economic realities in South Africa, described at greater length in the chapter by Duane Lockard (Volume 6 of the original *Handbook*), particularly the social and economic interdependence among the races in the urban economy, and the legally established inferiority of the nonwhites are even more impressive evidence of the authoritarian character of white racial "democracy."

Ultimately the political future of South Africa and Rhodesia depends on the level of political consciousness and the intensity of opposition and resistance of the nonwhite, particularly the African, majorities. That opposition by definition has to be principled and disloyal, illegal or at least alegal, and is more unlikely to be violent. Its strength and character will largely depend on the external support and the response of white South Africans. Open and violent conflict between the races, particularly with foreign support, would transform white racial democracy into a strictly authoritarian majority rule over dissident whites, which, considering the widespread support for apartheid, the strong consensus of the Afrikaners, and the support given to the policy by the Dutch Reform Churches, could lead to a totalitarian system with majority support, formal democratic institutions, and a strong component of legalism, based on a radical racist ideology.

Fortunately, the social and historical conditions that have led to the establishment of the racial democracy in South Africa are not found today in many parts of the world. Outside of Rhodesia, where the Salisbury government declaring its independence from Britain has established a similar regime, few colonies presented the combination of the large white settler population surrounded by a majority of nonwhites and having no intention or possibility of returning to the metropolitan homeland. Only Algeria, with a little over a million Europeans, many of them born there, many without roots in metropolitan France, among 8.5 million Maghrebi nationals, could have led to such a regime if the colons and the OAS had succeeded against the Algerians and the French. Perhaps in Angola could the white settler population, independent from metropolitan Portugal and under South African influence, have been tempted to establish such a regime. The American South, if it had gained its sovereignty in the war of secession, would have been another case. Undoubtedly other racially, ethnically, religiously, or culturally multinational or community societies in the non-Western world could in the future develop political forms similar to the racial democracies. But today some are experimenting with multinational democratic regimes or with a variety of authoritarian regimes with little semblance of democracy for any of the national groups. In most of them the low level of social mobilization and political organization, and consequently of coercive capacity of any group, is more likely to lead to political fragmentation and secession.

Multiethnic democracies without consensus. Paradoxically, Israel (Fein, 1967; Eisenstadt, 1967), with its democratic political culture, its democratic institutions, including proportional representation, which maximizes party pluralism, and the equal vote for all citizens, faces a future somewhat similar to the racial democracies in spite of the commitments of its leaders. It exemplifies the difficulties of creating a democratic, multiethnic, multicultural, and multilinguistic state when there is a dominant community conscious of its identity facing a demographically important minority also attached to its identity, separated by great cultural, religious, linguistic, and economic social differences. Only class and other divisions that could lead to majorities cutting across communal boundaries would make possible a democratic multinational state with real rather than formal equality of Jews, Arabs, and other minorities. Such a development in Israel, however, would run counter to the basic assumptions that have led to the creation of a Jewish state by the Zionists and of the religious characteristics introduced by the disproportionate influence of the minor religious parties in the policies of the dominant coalition since statehood. Only the cultural-ideological secularization of the state would make possible its acceptance within a democratic framework by the Arab minority and the return of the Palestinians and their loyalty to the state. It could be argued that a more federative structure that would leave considerable self-government to areas inhabited by each cultural community could, under democratic rule, facilitate such a development; but this ignores a basic presupposition of any democratic political system: the loyalty to the state and the rejection of any loyalty to another political system across its borders, any thought of secession, and any responsiveness to irredentist appeals from the outside. Those conditions do not seem likely to develop in the immediate future in Israel and in a number of other multiethnic, multicultural states whose boundaries cut across cultural, ethnic, or linguistic communities. Under such circumstances the participation of the minority in the national political process, even with full citizen rights, is likely to be partial, conditional, and suspect both to the state-sustaining majority and to those in the minority actually or potentially disloyal to it. Democratic institutions under such circumstances can work well within the majority community, particularly as long as it feels threatened, but it will be the democracy of the privileged. It could be argued that the formulas devised in those democracies not based on the strict application of majority of rule, called by Lijphart (1968a, 1968b, 1969) "consociational," should be able to handle such problems, but any reader of the now extensive literature on such systems (Daalder, 1974; McRae, 1974) is conscious of the numerous requirements for their success, unlikely to be found in many cases like that of contemporary Israel.

The case of Northern Ireland (Rose, 1971; Lijphart, 1975), with its formally democratic constitution and more or less real guarantees for political freedom for those willing to recognize its regime, is another example of the practical impossibility of making democratic processes work in divided societies without loyalty to the constitution and the regime on the part of the minority and a willingness of a large part of the majority to face the fact that a formally democratically legitimated majority rule under such circumstances becomes oppressive and has to turn to increasingly authoritarian responses.

Paradoxically, nationalism, the doctrine of self-determination of nationalities and cultural communities, born historically in the West at the same time as democratic ideals and with increasing social mobilization of the whole population, has become incompatible with democracy in many societies. The first victim of that process was a multinational Austro-Hungarian empire, which assured under autocratic rule a considerable degree of coexistence to its national components but which almost inevitably fell apart in the process of democratization. There is no easy solution within the framework of traditional democratic theory of government for the problem of permanent self-conscious minorities rejecting a common loyalty to the state and its institutions for the sake of independence or secession to join another state. The fact that in many parts of the world such communities do not coincide with any meaningful geographic boundaries, that they live interspersed in their cities or enclaves without geographical continuity, often leads to conflicts that are solved by authoritarian means or at least by the limitation of freedoms de jure or de facto for those in the minority questioning the legitimacy of a state. Their permanent frustration is likely, under certain conditions, to lead them to turn in their desperation to violence, against both members of the dominant community and those in the minority willing to participate in a democratic framework in more or less consociational formulas, reinforcing the authoritarian response of the majority. Democracy seems to have been more successful in the institutionalization of class conflicts, in the channeling through parties of economic interest conflicts and even of conflicts between religion and secularism, than in the resolution of conflicts among ethnic, linguistic, and cultural communalism. Such conflicts are one of the important factors accounting for the emergence and, paradoxically, the stability of many nondemocratic regimes (Fishman, 1968).

Racial democracy represents a theoretically interesting case of transition from democratic liberal institutions to authoritarian rule without discontinuity and by formal democratic procedures. Theoretically, other oligarchic democracies based on a restricted suffrage could have followed the same path when confronted with growing demands for expansion of political participation from the lower classes. However, the different level of social integration in racially homogeneous communities, despite other deep cleavages, and the consequent sense of community have prevented the combination of democratic liberal forms with minority rule. In such societies, inevitably, a minority of the politically privileged classes advocated the expansion of political rights and those opposed had to make concessions or give up any semblance of democratic freedoms, even within the privileged sector of the society. This provides indirect evidence for the difficulties and instability of attempts of partial liberalization and democratization within authoritarian regimes, like internal democracy in a single party. Ultimately, without a relatively rigid barrier like race defining those with the right to participate and those excluded and without an extraordinary fear of all those who deprive others of citizen rights, it becomes impossible to limit participation beyond the level of social mobilization without explicitly authoritarian institutions. However, as the case of ethnic-cultural-religious minorities shows, the extension of suffrage alone does not assure real opportunities for political participation nor real social integration and loyalty to a state needed for stable democratic politics.

6. "Defective" and "Pretotalitarian" Political Situations and Regimes

In an effort to understand the dynamics of nondemocratic political systems we have attempted to define totalitarianism fairly strictly, to keep it clearly distinct from the variety of authoritarian regimes. However, the transitions between both types do not involve the same basic discontinuity and, with rare exceptions, violent breaks, revolutions, civil wars, and military coups as do the transitions from democracy to authoritarianism. The diffuseness of the boundary is reflected in the increasing use of terms like "quasi-totalitarian," "post-totalitarian," "rationalized-totalitarian," "totalitarianism without terror," etc., to describe the gray zone between both. Our typological effort has been based on the assumption that in the process of instoration of nondemocratic governments some basic initial characteristics determine if the outcome will be closer to the totalitarian or the authoritarian pole. The analysis of the breakdown of competitive democracies (Linz and Stepan, 1978), traditional regimes, or colonial rule should tell us something about the dynamics leading to one or another outcome. We have also emphasized how the initial characteristics of the leader or group taking over power—their ideology or mentality, their organizational base in the existing social structure or in a new mass movement or conspiratorial party, and perhaps personality—prefigure, together with situational variables, the outcome. Since the complex structure of a totalitarian political system is not developed in a short time, except in societies suffering extreme disorganization after prolonged war, foreign occupation, or civil war, we can posit a stage that might be best described as pretotalitarian. We know still little about the way in which new, revolutionary rulers break through constraining conditions, to use the expression of Otto Kirchheimer (1969, pp. 385–407), and the circumstances under which they fail. We still need a theory of consolidation of new regimes. It is noteworthy that an insightful fascist politician, the Spaniard Ramiro Ledesma Ramos (1968, first printed in 1935), in a political essay comparing European one-party states, including the Soviet Union in the mid-30s, should have devoted much of his attention to the constraining conditions that, unless overcome, limited, in his view, a real totalitarian revolution. We would consider as pretotalitarian those situations in which there are important political, social, and cultural factors favorable to a totalitarian outcome; basically a situation in which there is a political group of sufficient importance pursuing a totalitarian utopia but that has not yet fully consolidated its power and given the system its institutional structure; a situation in which institutions like the armed forces, the churches, business organizations, interest groups, notables or tribal rulers, the courts, or even a monarch, not clearly committed to a system excluding all pluralisms even though largely favoring a limitation of pluralism, still retain considerable autonomy, legitimacy, and effectiveness; and a situation characterized by an uneasy balance in which predictions go one way or another, where some expect the totalitarian movement to be co-opted by the preexisting social structure, while others look forward to or fear its ultimate success.

The reader of early descriptions of the Nazi system—particularly those by Marxists, which emphasize the multiple compromises the regime made with the conservative structures of German society, particularly the bureaucracy and the military (F. Neumann, 1963) and even, in some accounts, with the churches, and the betrayal of the petty-bourgeois revolutionary ideals against modern industrial and financial capitalism, large-scale cartels, department and chain stores, etc.—should keep in mind descriptions of the Soviet Union in one of the phases of its consolidation. For example, this summary by Jeremy R. Azrael:

> After a brief period of left wing militancy, the revisionism of "Bread, Land, and Peace" gave way to the far-reaching compromises of the New Economic Policy or NEP. The free market was revived; concessions were made to foreign investors; material incentives were restored to their paramount position; and individual peasant proprietorship was actively encouraged. Similarly, "workers' control" and "workers' management" were drastically curtailed, and administrative efficiency, technical rationality, and stringent labor discipline became hallmarks of official policy. In the same vein, the regime granted more authority to holdover "bourgeois specialists" and ordered communist executives to solicit and defer to expert advice. Moreover, these developments were accompanied by definite symptoms of decay within the party itself. In particular, there was a manifest decline of "class vigilance" and revolutionary ardor among the rank and file members of the party, and the upper strata of the party showed clear signs of "regrouping" into administrative pressure groups and bureaucratic cliques. (Azrael, 1970b, p. 263)

Had the Soviet regime been destroyed at this point, the capacity of the revolutionary forces to transform Russian society and to move toward the totalitarian utopia would certainly have been questioned. It also explains that many observers at the time predicted quite different outcomes than Stalinism. The very different interpretations of Hitler's rule in early years reflect that same intermingling. The uneasy balance between such contradictory tendencies might be prolonged for many years, with moves in one or another direction, as was the case with Fascism in Italy.

A typical pretotalitarian situation is that in which a party that is bent toward more or less totalitarian control with its mass organizations and, in the fascist case, its paramilitary organizations can exercise pressures on a government in which its leaders participate in coalition with representatives of other parties.[63] Such a coalition was formed in Italy after the March on Rome and in Germany by a presidential decision under the chancellorship of Hitler, with the participation of the authoritarian-nationalist DNVP and with Papen as Vice Chancellor. The parties participating were either opposed or semiloyal to the democratic regime, or, in the case of Italy, minority representatives of other parties willing to collaborate in a compromise with the Fascists. In Germany the Enabling Act, by which the parliament, under pressure, and with the exclusion of the Communists and the opposition of the Socialists, granted the government extraordinary powers and attempted to tie those powers to the continuity of that particular coalition government as an authoritarian "presidential government." The change represented the last break with Weimar constitutionality. In Eastern Europe after 1945 the pressures of the Soviet Union, its military presence, the desire for national unity in face of the Germans, the availability of collaborationist socialists, and the compromise between Western allies and the Soviet Union led to the formation of coalition national front governments in which all antifascist parties participated according to a prearranged proportion, not necessarily reflecting their strength in the electorate and parliaments after elections (Kase, 1968; Seton-Watson, 1968; Ionescu, 1967; Oren, 1973). Such still nominally "constitutional" governments often proceed to outlaw some parties (communist or fascist, or those presumably guilty of collaborating with them), restrict civil liberties (generally with the ministry of interior in the hands of the dominant party), and co-opt some leaders of the different parties, politically neutralizing others, ending with the dissolution of all or most parties and the fusion of some—or sections of some—in the totalitarian-bent party (Korbell, 1959). The relative weight and the linkage of those co-opted elements with independent power bases is obviously decisive for the ultimate totalitarian or authoritarian outcome. In economically or militarily dependent countries, foreign influences become decisive at this stage (Black and Thornton, 1964; Triska, 1969).

In those situations the coalition partners find themselves in the position of wanting to oppose some of the policies of the totalitarian-bent party but in doing so allowing that party to question their loyalty to the government and the new regime and facilitating its goal of ousting them. On the other hand, approval or passivity in face of policies of which they disapprove contributes to legitimating the transition to every day more authoritarian rule and to preventing an active opposition by institutions or social groups still capable of it. In such situations there is much room for opportunists ready to join the stronger armies by advocating the fusion of their party with the increasingly dominant coalition partner. This was the case with many conservative authoritarian organizations in Germany and with parts of the socialist parties that fused into communist-dominated united parties, like the East German *Sozialistische Einheitspartei* (SED). In a number of communist countries this phase of national front is still reflected in a multi-party system under the leadership of the communists, with the minor parties serving to co-opt representatives of other groups and in the post-Stalinist phase serving as controlled channels for the representation of certain interests and as a legitimizing facade. A system in which the development toward totalitarianism is arrested and stabilized and in which the forces aiming at totalitarian control become one—often very important—component of the limited pluralism of the regime, their ideology affects considerable spheres of social life, and participation in their organizations is significant, might be described as "defective totalitarianism." The term "pretotalitarian," in contrast, might be reserved for the (more or less prolonged) phase leading to the instoration of a totalitarian system. Situations in which the strength of prototalitarian forces is reversed might be labelled "arrested totalitarianism."

The analysis of Spain as an authoritarian regime (Linz, 1964) has tended to emphasize the variables that led to the ultimate failure of the totalitarian tendencies within the Falangist movement, but it should be possible to reanalyze Spanish politics in the later phases of the civil war and the first years after 1939 as a defective totalitarian system. In many respects the insightful analysis by Ernst Fraenkel (1941), *The Dual State: A Contribution to the Theory of Dictatorship,* could be considered a study of the pretotalitarian aspects of the Nazi regime. The study of pretotalitarian situations and defective totalitarian regimes in connection with the theory of the process of consolidation of new regimes would be a step toward a better understanding of the uniqueness of totalitarianism and at the same time would prevent us from underestimating the totalitarian tendencies that often accompany the emergence of authoritarian regimes. Such an underestimation is perhaps one of the weaknesses of my analysis of the Franco regime as an authoritarian regime.

Historical studies like the monumental work by Bracher, Sauer, and Schulz on the Nazi *Machtergreifung,* the history of fascism in the biography of Mussolini by De Felice (1965, 1966a, 1968), Leonard Schapiro's (1965) *The Origin of the Communist Autocracy,* and Robert V. Daniels's (1969) *The Conscience of the Revolution* would be the obvious sources together with studies of systems whose totalitarian potential was weaker, like Robert Scalapino's (1953) *Democracy and Party Government in Pre-War Japan* (there are, unfortunately, few works of similar importance on the years after takeover in other nondemocratic systems). They could be the basis for a theory of emergence and consolidation of totalitarianism rather than authoritarian regimes. Such a theory would complement those analyses that focus on social, cultural, psychological, and political crises preceding the breakdown of democracy. It would also tell us the extent to which totalitarianism is not predetermined but is the result of critical choices made in such a transition period.

7. Post-totalitarian Authoritarian Regimes

The death of Stalin and the consequent de-Stalinization both in the Soviet Union and the Eastern European countries that had followed the Soviet model led to changes in those political systems which rightly made political scientists question the applicability of the classical model of a totalitarian system. Research on interest groups in Soviet politics (Skilling and Griffiths, 1971; Janos, 1970b), on specific processes of policymaking (Ploss, 1965; Stewart, 1968), on the changing composition of the Soviet elite (Armstrong, 1967; Fischer, 1968; Farrell, 1970a; Fleron, 1969, 1970; Barghoorn, 1972; Beck, 1970), on intellectual life and the expression of dissent or contestation (Barghoorn, 1973) have shown important changes from the Stalinist model despite some signs of "neo-Stalinism." The comparative study of East European Communist regimes (Brzezinski, 1960; Brown, 1966; Skilling, 1966, 1973a; Ionescu, 1967; Schöpflin, 1970) has also highlighted the increasingly differentiated development in response to national-cultural, historical, social-structural, and economic factors. The Czech spring of 1968 and the reforms proposed by and under Dubcek (Zeman, 1968; Gueyt, 1969; James, 1969; Remington, 1969; Tigrid, 1969; Windsor and Roberts, 1969; Skilling, 1970, 1973b) and before that the independent evolution of Yugoslavia from the administrative phase to self-management have raised the question of the condition and limits of change in Soviet-type political systems. The terms "liberalization" and "democratization" have been used freely, often interchangeably, and unfortunately with little precision. It is indicative of the train of thought of the discussion that the question could be raised: "Is Mexico the future of East Europe?" (Croan, 1970). It could be argued that those changes indicate a tendency in political systems that at one point in time could have been considered approaching the totalitarian model to show some of the characteristics we have used to characterize authoritarian regimes. This would be congruent with our emphasis on the relatively open and diffuse boundary between totalitarian systems and authoritarian regimes.

However, we feel it would be misleading to consider post-totalitarian authoritarian regimes as having the same characteristics as those that never were conceived by their founders to become totalitarian or that never went beyond a "defective" totalitarian stage despite the efforts of some of their founders. The totalitarian phase, even when imposed from the outside, as in some of the East European people's democracies, has left many structures—political as well as economic and social—that can be transformed but are unlikely to disappear and has created an image of a type of polity to which some of the elites still feel attached and whose "positive" aspects they might wish to retain or attain. It also has left memories, particularly of its worst features—the terror and the purges—which condition the responses of those participating in the political process and therefore affect the evolution of those systems. It is on these grounds that we find it unnecessary to consider post-totalitarian authoritarian regimes a distinct type, obviously with considerable national variations. The alternative would be to argue that the processes of change taking place after Stalin are really only a more visible manifestation of patterns already present (which would imply that totalitarianism was never as total and that the concept can be applied to the present reality too, despite changes, or that it never had any validity) or to deny any basic change. The vexing question, How much change in the system is required for change *of* the system? is obviously empirically difficult to answer, particularly when scholarship in the past might have been blind to deviations from the utopian totalitarian model and in recent years might have been too eager to see change and overestimate its importance. Unfortunately, for a more comparative analysis of what we might call "routinization" of totalitarianism—of its transformation—we are limited to communist countries, since none of the fascist totalitarian states were allowed by their military defeat to undergo such a process. There was no post-Hitler Germany, with Himmler executed, Dönitz as *Führer* displacing Bormann with a coalition of army officers loyal to the Reich, and civil servants and industrialists supporting some reasonable *Gauleiter* as head of the party.

For those who interpret Soviet totalitarianism as a reflection of Stalin's paranoic personality it is easy to consider the totalitarian phase as a passing aberration, and this might well be true for some of the most monstrous aspects of the system. This has been the official line of the de-Stalinizers. Implicit in this interpretation is a denial of a pretotalitarian character to Leninist rule and a totalitarian intent in Bolshevik revolutionary ideology. For the social scientists such an approach seems unsatisfactory or at least incomplete. They are likely to emphasize changes in the external environment, in the social-economic structure confronting the successors of Stalin: the complexity of managerial and technical decision making requiring greater rationality, decentralization, autonomy of experts, substitution of ideological *apparatchiki* by others with more education and expertise, fewer constraints with greater economic development, etc. Those writing about the convergence of postindustrial societies would certainly emphasize these factors and support the argument with reference to the role of economists and the reforms advocated by them in the process of change. Others, including some Soviet authors, would note the different international environment of a Soviet Union surrounded by allies in Eastern Europe, safe behind the atomic deterrent in a world in which the capitalist enemies find themselves challenged in the Third World and in which the mutual interests of security dictate a détente. To those factors we might add the emerging polycentrism of communism showing alternative and creative solutions linking with different national, cultural, and political traditions, which makes the original model of the first socialist state more questionable (Blackmer, 1968). The position taken by powerful nonruling communist parties toward changes in the Soviet Union and its Eastern European sphere of influence would be another factor. Certainly in the Eastern European countries the shift toward greater independence as national communist states, as the case of Yugoslavia shows, was decisive in the change. However, Rumania shows that a more nationalist policy within the bloc is not necessarily accompanied by deep internal changes (Jowitt, 1971). Without denying the decisive importance of all or some of these factors in the particular development toward post-totalitarianism in communist countries, I would agree with Gordon Skilling when he writes:

> No doubt there *are* social and economic forces at work which encourage interest group activity in the USSR. It seems clear, however, that this later development has been the consequence of certain conscious decisions of individual leaders and other participants in Soviet political life, decisions which were not necessarily pre-determined and which might be reversed in the future. The rise of group activity under Khrushchev was, in the first place, the result of an initiative from above, representing an effort by Stalin's successor to make the political system more rational in its process of decision making and more responsive to the actual needs and demands of the people, especially of the influential elites. (Skilling and Griffiths, 1971, p. 403)

The work of Max Weber provides indirectly interesting insights into the process at work. In his analysis of charismatic authority he noted that its character is specifically alien to everyday routine structures, the strictly personal character of social relationships involved. He continued:

> If this is not to remain a purely transitory phenomenon, but to take on the character of a permanent relationship, a "community" of disciples or followers, or a party organization, or any sort of political or hierocratic organization, it is necessary for the character of charismatic authority to become radically changed . . . it cannot remain stable, but becomes either traditionalized or rationalized, or a combination of both.
>
> The following are the principle motives underlying this transformation: (a) the ideal and also the material interest of the followers in the continuation and the continual reactivation of the community, (b) the still stronger ideal and also stronger material interests of the members of the administrative staff, the disciples, the party workers, or others in continuing their relationship . . . but they have an interest in continuing it in such a way that both from an ideal and a material point of view, their own position is put on a stable everyday basis. (Weber, 1968, Vol. 1, p. 246)

In the subsequent discussion of the routinization of charisma particularly after the succession crisis, Weber notes that a process of traditionalization or of legalization takes place and that one of the possible outcomes is a greater bureaucratization. For Weber, one of the decisive motives underlying all cases of the routinization of charisma is naturally the striving for security, the objective necessity of adapting the order and the staff organization to the normal everyday needs and conditions of carrying on administration, and the necessity that there should be some definite order introduced into the organization of the administrative staff itself.

There can be no doubt that the desire for security in the top elite after Stalin, the surrogate Stalins, and the experience of the purges, decisively influenced the top elite's decisions. The weakening of the police as a key political factor, perhaps its neutralization by the army, the emphasis on collective leadership and the rejection of the cult of personality, the distrust of an emerging powerful leader that led to the ouster of Khrushchev, the desire even on his part to use the procedures of the party statutes to resolve the leadership crisis, the growing concern for socialist legality, are all reflections of this desire for security in the top elite. Some of those changes were made easier by the formal rules and the conception of leadership institutionalized before Stalin, and in this respect it is doubtful that a post-Hitler *Fuhrerstaat* would have had as easy a transformation. The desire for security, however, also explains the reaffirmation of the role of the party, the reactivation of the party as a source of legitimacy of the leadership, even the slowing down of the de-Stalinization and of efforts to revise it, as well as the decisive reaction to the Czech reform. To be stable, post-totalitarianism can reject the totalitarian heritage only selectively and gradually, if it is not to lead to a revolutionary outbreak that could lead to a radical change of the system, endangering the continuity in power of the elite. The literature suggests, even when it provides only limited and indirect evidence, that the cleavages between conservatives and reformists cut across practically all organizations, groups, opinion milieux, or whatever units of analysis are used, largely along generational lines. There seems to be a difference between this and the crisis of succession or approaching succession in authoritarian regimes, in which in addition to such crosscutting and generational differences we find a greater tension between the elements constituting the limited pluralism of the regime on a more institutional basis, possibly with some of them breaking out of the system and contributing to its final crisis or overthrow (Linz, 1973a). Significantly no one expects in any of the communist countries a military intervention or coup that would establish a noncommunist regime.

Once the great break through constraining conditions had been accomplished, with destruction of traditional society by war communism, the secure establishment of Communist party rule without any need to share power with other leftist parties, collectivization of agriculture and forced industrialization, destruction of the sanitary cordon intended by the West, and a more complex society requiring greater expertise and consequently autonomy of individuals and groups had emerged, the leadership was probably right in assuming that a system could be run more efficiently and equally securely without the constant affirmation of moral political unity, emphasis on ideological orthodoxy, fear of "groupism," constant assertion of the power of the party, and the recurrent mobilization for radical changes. The fact that, perhaps due to Stalin's idiosyncrasies, the totalitarian effort had been accompanied by massive terror even against the elite, obviously legitimated a transition to what Tucker (1963) has called an "extinct movement regime" and others "administrative totalitarianism" (Kassof, 1969) or "rationalized totalitarianism" (Cocks, 1970). The transition to a post-totalitarian state implies less emphasis on the goal culture and greater concern for the functional requisites of the social system. This allows a process that had been described as liberalization: the emergence of group interest, or at least the expression of it by a few outstanding individuals (Skilling, 1971, p. 382); "the free expression and collision of opinions" while rejecting "groupism" (*gruppovshina*); the ideological recognition of "non-antagonistic contradictions"; and the effective and to some extent visible manifestation of group influences in decision making (Skilling, 1971, p. 401). A limited monocentrism, a less ideological politics, and a greater tolerance for depolitization show a tendency toward an authoritarian regime. Let us note that while most non-communist authoritarian rulers insistently warn against the return of political parties, rulers of the Soviet Union warn against "groupism" and factionalism—a recognition of tendencies within the party—showing the different starting points of change. These processes are accompanied by bureaucratization and professionalization, tendencies that run counter to the ideological tradition of participation and mobilization of the party activists and the citizens, a tradition that is potentially suspicious of the emerging social pluralism and legitimizes demands for greater participation. The initial post-totalitarian legitimacy of an emerging authoritarian regime is therefore likely to be questioned, not only by neo-Stalinists but by those wanting to return to some of the hopes in the Marxist-Leninist tradition for a more socially egalitarian, active, and participatory society. It is possible that some of the different paths followed after de-Stalinization and the tensions in this period are the result of these two, somewhat different, pressures. In fact, contrary to what many analysts believe, liberalization and "democratization" (in the sense of greater participation) are in tension. This is because, as other authoritarian regimes show, the pursuit of both tendencies would lead ultimately to a nonauthoritarian regime, endangering the position of the present ruling elite, but also because of an ideological heritage ambivalent on this point.

Richard Lowenthal has formulated very well the contradictory pressures leading to post-totalitarian authoritarianism when he writes:

> The Communist Party can no longer claim that its task is to use state power to transform the social structure in accordance with its utopian goals; it knows it must react to the pressures and demands of society. But wishing to keep its monopoly of power, it is not resigned to

conceive of government as a mere representative of the needs of society—for a truly representative regime would have to be a pluralistic regime, permitting independent organized groups to struggle for their opinions and interests and to reach decisions by coalitions and compromise. Rather, the postrevolutionary party regime sees itself as an indispensible, authoritative, arbiter of society's various interests, recognizing their existence but regulating their expression and limiting their representation while retaining for itself the ultimate right of decision. Unable to continue its revolutionary offensive against society and unwilling to be reduced to a mere expression of the constellation of social forces at a given moment, it is neither totalitarian nor democratic, but authoritarian: it is on the defensive against the forces of autonomous social development, a guardian clinging to a role after his ward has reached adulthood. (Lowenthal, 1970, pp. 114–15)

It might be argued that the emergence of post-totalitarian tendencies after stabilization of the revolutionary regime in China, specifically bureaucratization of the party, etc., led Mao, the old revolutionary still formally in power, to reverse the trend with the mobilizational response of the Great Cultural Revolution and the Red Guards, as the analysis of Schurmann (1968) suggests. Let us not forget that Khrushchev combined the detotalitarianization of the thaw with the revitalization of the party and new efforts to engage citizens in political participation, through activities like the citizens' courts and the activation of local volunteers, people's guards (*druzhiny*), and the Komsomol in functions of social control described by Leon Lipson (1967). To the extent that the mass of the population and the more active sectors of it share many of the values of a deprivatized, collectively oriented society, they might question the tendencies toward greater autonomy advocated by intermediate strata and support more consensually than terroristically imposed totalitarian tendencies. This would account for the quite different post-totalitarian character of the Soviet Union and the German Democratic Republic compared to those societies in which the totalitarian phase was much shorter and was largely imposed from outside and in which pluralistic elements of the pretakeover society and culture had survived.

In the literature we find a variety of attempts to conceptualize and describe post-totalitarian communist systems which reflect some of the dilemmas pointed out above.[64] Since the Soviet Union was in many ways, under Stalin, the most totalitarian, it is still not clear how far it will move in the authoritarian direction. In fact, it could be argued the Stalinist regime in its last stage had become a system characterized by considerable conservatism, inflexibility, inertia, and stagnation, which ran counter to the mobilizational aspects of a totalitarian movement regime. The kind of "late totalitarianism" characterized by a highly ritualized adherence to ideological formulae, a curbing of utopian expectations, extreme bureaucratic rigidity and few organizational innovations, a theoretical and actual downgrading of the party relative to the state and the police, and highly formalized popular participation with little real involvement could be conceived as a "totalitarian authoritarianism."

From that baseline the post-Stalinist development showed two somewhat different tendencies, one reflected in the scholarly discovery of interest and group politics and the other, well described by Azrael (1970a), "a populist model of rationalized totalitarianism" initiated by Khrushchev with his extensive use of the policy of "public participation." In this line we find the creation of so-called nonstaff party commissions by the district and city party committees, consisting of party volunteers who were not on the paid rosters of the party apparat assisting in the review of admission, discipline, and appeals. This contrasted with the pattern since 1934 in which such questions had been the privileged domain of party secretaries. Those instructors were also to observe party members who had been disciplined for "endlessly looking after their words" (Cocks, 1970, p. 172), an excellent example of why democratization and rationalization in the Soviet sense could not be equated with liberalization. Another example is control function assigned to "Komsomol Searchlight" detachments, of which in 1964 there were more than 260,000 groups and 500,000 posts of assistants (Cocks, 1970, p. 172). These activities under the Party State Control Committee (PSCC) implementing the policy described as *obshchestvennye nachala* (Cocks, 1970, pp. 165–66), or "public principles," with its dimension of "public participation" was naturally regarded with distrust by the *apparatchiki* and the economic managers. This trend toward "communist self-government" was reexamined and curtailed after the fall of Khrushchev by his successors, who turned toward a more bureaucratic formula for rationalization, deemphasizing the voluntarism and the populism with a turn to *nauchnaia organizatsiia truda* ("scientific organization of labor"). This policy, linked with another component of the Leninist tradition, his enthusiasm for scientific management, and practically with the needs of a socialist economy meant in practice an emphasis on retraining of party and government workers. The new spirit was reflected in a greater concern with information gathering and office organization, and technological aides aimed at administrative reform from above by experts. Cocks, whom we are following in this analysis of Soviet policies, concludes: "The alliance of economic managers and party bureaucrats which was forged out of the common interest and desire to maintain their own institutional structures against democratic intrusions and mass pressures, gives no guarantee of being long-lasting" (Cocks, 1970, p. 185). Zvi Gitelman also reflects this tension when he writes:

> Clearly the role of the party is a more delicate issue for systems opting for authentic participatory strategies since those opting for national performance strategies could retain the structure and the political position of the party while altering the content of its ideology, thus making it a party of "experts" for example. (Gitelman, 1970, p. 261)

This alternative course leads toward what Allen Kassof (1969) has called "the administered society, totalitarianism without terror." The aim was well expressed in 1969 by the editors of *Partiinaia Zhizn* as "systematic and fundamental control prevents mistakes and slips, holds people in constant state of creative stress and does not leave room for such manifestations as placidity, complacency, and conceit" (Cocks, 1970, pp. 186–87). Cocks notes that there is some tendency to fuse the two main trends we have just been discussing, to strike a balance between the populist and the bureaucratic formulas for rationalization. All this leads us to the question, How post-totalitarian (ignoring obviously the Stalinist idiosyncrasies and terror) is Soviet society?

Gordon Skilling's extensive writings and a number of monographic studies on policymaking and local politics have emphasized the role of group conflict. Much of the discussion hinges on what is meant by groups and to what extent the five types that he mentions—"leadership groups or factions, official or bureaucratic groups, intellectual groups, broad social groups, and opinion groups"—are comparable to the groups we discover in pretotalitarian or stable authoritarian regimes. He rightly notes that the first question is that of legitimacy or, rather, the presumed lack of legitimacy of political groups in Marxist-Leninist theory. There is obviously a thin line between the existence of such groups de facto and the limited legitimacy granted to them in pure authoritarian regimes. Certainly the talk about "nonantagonistic contradictions" opens the door to convergence. Skilling lists three additional major considerations: the question of group autonomy in the defense of its interest and opinions, the extent to which political groups have become organized or institutionalized, and the range of purposes and specific objectives of such groups. These dimensions lead him in a comparative analysis of communist systems to a classification of communist states in five types, to which in passing he adds the pre-totalitarian (pre-Stalinist) phase. Let us quote briefly his characterization of these types.

> In the quasi-totalitarianism state political groups are treated in theory as illegitimate, and in practice are severely limited in their capacity for independent action. In some cases, the leadership consciously sets out to destroy political groups, in others to infiltrate and emasculate them. If organized groups such as trade unions exist, they are manipulated and controlled by the leadership and do not articulate the interests of their constituency. In general the official groups, especially the party, are superior in power and influence to the intellectuals who are bereft of any real power. Even the official groups are relatively weak and are used as instruments by the leadership. (Skilling, 1970, pp. 222–23)

As he notes, this category coincides with totalitarianism except for the definitions that overstress the monopoly of power and make terror an essential characteristic. Stalin's Russia from 1929 to 1953, Hungary, Poland, Czechoslovakia after 1947–48, and Albania to the present might be in this category.

A second type may be called "consultative authoritarianism," to use the term suggested by Peter Ludz (1970) in reference to the German Democratic Republic, in which Skilling would include Rumania (Jowitt, 1971), Bulgaria (Oren, 1973), and in certain respects Hungary in the sixties, Poland (Wiatr, 1967; Lane and Kolankiewicz, 1973) after March 1968, and the Soviet Union after Khrushchev. In it:

> When group activity occurs spontaneously and expresses fundamental opposition, it is firmly repressed, and the dominant role of the top leadership is kept intact. Although the police remain an important force, the prominent position they held in the quasi-totalitarian state is occupied here by such bureaucratic groups as the party and state administrators. These grounds are valued for their expertise and thus acquire an opportunity to articulate their own and other groups' interests. There is also an increasing willingness to bring some of the professional groups, such as the economists and scientists, into the decision making process, although the party apparat continues to play the superior role, both in theory and in practice. Creative intellectuals . . . are subject to strict control but occasionally slip the leash and

assert their own viewpoint. Broader social groups continue to be impotent, and their interests are expressed, if at all, by more powerful official groups. (Skilling, 1970, p. 223)

Skilling notes how in response to particular crises and wishes of the leadership this type moves back and forth. Probably in terms of our general typology at a higher level of abstraction, this type is still closer to the totalitarian pole using our definition.

The third category of Skilling is "quasi-pluralistic authoritarianism," in which he includes Hungary and Poland during the thaw of 1953–56, the Soviet Union under Khrushchev, and Czechoslovakia and Poland in the mid-1960s. He characterized this type

as distinguished by a greater degree of group conflict, resulting usually from the initiative of the groups themselves. Although the party leadership remains the dominant factor in politics, there is greater interaction between the leaders and political groups and greater likelihood of some influence by the latter on the political process. Group conflict is often accompanied, and may be encouraged, by sharp factional conflicts among the leaders and serious divisions of opinion within the party as a whole. Although bureaucratic groups, especially the party hierarchy, remain powerful, they cannot entirely exclude the intellectual and opinion groups in general from participation. Both types of group show a greater determination to express interests and values in opposition to the party line, advancing alternative policies, criticizing official decisions and actions, and in some cases challenging frontally a whole series of official policies. Ironically, these active groups continue to be for the most part noninstitutionalized, whereas organized groups such as the trade unions remain impotent. (Skilling, 1970, p. 224)

It is in this context that we find for the first time a preregime institution mentioned as a significant group, the Catholic Church in Poland. His effort to locate a number of communist countries in the typology shows the instability of this type but also its frequency. It is perhaps the most dominant type of post-totalitarian communist regime.

A fourth type, characterized as "democratizing and pluralistic authoritarianism," includes Czechoslovakia between January and August 1968 and Yugoslavia after the break with the Soviet Union and most particularly after 1966. They are systems in which "with the endorsement of the leadership, political groups were to a substantial degree institutionalized and they played a significant role in policy making" (Skilling, 1970, p. 225). Czechoslovakia under Dubcek represents an interesting example "in which both centrally directed change designed and elaborated by the party leaders and powerful spontaneous forces from below with considerable freedom of expression, particularly for change oriented intellectual groups articulating a wide variety of group interests and opinions," a revitalization of dormant associations like trade unions and even distinctive opinion groups like the "club of the non-party committee" urged alternative policies on the leadership and even institutional change (Skilling, 1973a). However, the Soviet invasion cut short this development. Yugoslavia, in a more gradual way over the fifties and sixties, moved toward this type through the decentralization of public administration and the introduction of workers councils, institutionalizing expressions of local and regional interests and giving representation of economic interests in elected assemblies, on the basis of a kind of corporativism. Skilling suggests that this pluralistic development affected the cultural and intellectual sphere less in Yugoslavia than in Czechoslovakia and even in a short period in Hungary and Poland.

Yugoslavia, which would deserve more discussion in this context, would be in our basic typology an authoritarian regime, and the different degree of autonomy granted to various groups and their institutionalization fits well with our notion of limited pluralism (Neal, 1957; Hoffman and Neal, 1962; Zaninovich, 1968; Horvat, 1969; Barton, Denitch, and Kadushin, 1973). However, we should not ignore the opportunities for participation provided by self-management and workers' control (Roggemann, 1970; Pusić, 1973; Supek, 1973) and the potential for mobilization of the League of Communists. This participatory element is in conflict with bureaucratic and technocratic tendencies (Milenkovitch, 1971) and should—in principle—counteract the pressures of nationalism. A sign of the legitimacy gained by the new institutions is that criticism is often articulated in terms of discrepancies between ideal and reality of self-management. Yugoslavia also exemplifies that in the dynamics of authoritarian regimes there might be two alternative paths: one, liberalization, which might benefit particularly intellectual, cultural groups, opinion groups, making the pool from which the professional politicians are recruited more heterogeneous; and another path emphasizing more the ideology, retaining an important function for the party but allowing a greater democratization at the local and factory level. From this perspective a comparison of Yugoslavia with the Partido Revolucionario Institucional (PRI) regime in Mexico and even with Franco's Spain would be fruitful. It is our assumption that stable communist regimes created by a national revolution, fully independent of the USSR, are more likely to progress in the direction of partial democratization than of liberalization. Posttotalitarian, and in the case of Yugoslavia postadministrative-phase, independent communist regimes are likely to take this form. Or perhaps, if the break through the constraining conditions has not yet been achieved and the original ideologically committed leadership is still in power, the form will fit the Chinese model with its antibureaucratic mobilizational features under the cultural revolution.

It is this last model that is described by Skilling as "anarchic authoritarianism," in which few of the groups that clashed in the cultural revolution were institutionalized or "legitimate." Also they were permitted and even encouraged by Mao, using spontaneous and coercive methods that had little in common with the organized processes of group action in Czechoslovakia or Yugoslavia. It is this last type in Skilling's classification that seems less useful. His typology raises a basic question, which is not easy to answer: Under what conditions does "quasi-pluralistic authoritarianism" become "democratizing and pluralistic authoritarianism"?

John Michael Montias's (1970) "Types of Economic Systems," based on three coordinates—the degree of mobilization for the promotion of regime goals of participants in the system, particularly of peasants, workers, and employees by lower-level party cadres; the degree of reliance by central authorities on hierarchically transmitted commands for furthering regime goals; and the relative importance of markets for producer goods—makes little reference to other political and cultural changes in communist systems. However, in view of the central importance of the organization of the economy in the development of communist politics, the changing role of the party in the economy, the nature of incentives as they affect the citizen, the sources of discontent, etc., it would be most interesting to relate his types with other political changes. On the basis of the three mentioned coordinates, he distinguishes four main types of socialist economic systems: (1) mobilization, (2) centralized administered, and (3) decentralized administered, both of which are characterized by having hierarchically structured bureaucracies for affecting the party's economic policies, and (4) market socialist. The mobilization system, high on the mobilization coordinate and on that of command, is certainly in the economic sphere the most congruent with totalitarianism. This probably would be true for a mobilization system not relying heavily on hierarchically transmitted commands as it might have existed in China in the Great Leap Forward campaign. It seems reasonable that the post-totalitarian authoritarian systems will ruin the economy either as decentralized administered systems or in the form of market socialism.

In connection with the typology offered by Montias the question might be raised whether a totalitarianism aiming at a utopian transformation of society in spheres not directly related to the economy and social structure but to cultural and religious values, the mobilization for an imperialist policy, and changing the status structure rather than the class structure (as it was in the case of the Nazis) was totalitarian with an economic policy that would not fit in the mobilizational or centralized administrative system types. Perhaps this was the case because the German economy at that time was much further advanced. It seems, however, that given the close interconnection between the political and economic system in communist societies, changes in the economic system toward greater autonomy of various units will tend to have also political consequences. Montias in his analysis stresses that the transitions from one to another type of economic system are reversible and that there are cases of remobilization. He also seems to suggest that the dismantling of centralized systems and particularly the shift to market socialism is hard to achieve without "revolution from above" buttressed by suitable changes in ideology. In that context he notes that in Yugoslavia the ideological support for the economic reform was provided by inveighing against state capital monopoly and bureaucratization, which were made to be hallmarks of Soviet "degeneration," a process that did not take place in Czechoslovakia and Hungary, where the reforms were grafted to the old system. Without a change in political leadership it seems that the transformation to market socialism could not occur. Certainly the question of the relative weight of economic developments, social changes, and strictly defined political factors, in the process of transition from totalitarianism to a variety of post-totalitarian systems, deserves further analysis.

Certainly a number of social, economic, political, and historical variables would account for these different developments in post-totalitarian communist states, but as the case of Czechoslovakia shows, the international linkages with the Soviet Union are a far from negligible variable. We should not forget either, in any comparative analysis, the different ways in which the communists achieved power in different countries: the combination of national and social revolution in China, Yugoslavia, North Vietnam, Cuba, and Albania; and the largely externally imposed rule in Poland, Czechoslovakia, Rumania, Bulgaria, and East Germany. Nor can we neglect the characteristics of the Communist party before taking power: its size, its respectable showing in free elections in Czechoslovakia, and the ways in which it had developed in exile, illegality, and resistance in other countries like the Southern Balkans. In the case of East Germany the transition of a society from one totalitarian system to another obviously contributed to its stability, despite the discontent and the competition with the Federal Republic that before the Berlin Wall undermined its development. Nor can we ignore the demonstration effect of changes in one communist country on others, particularly the impact of the Yugoslav example and in a quite different direction of the Chinese.

In the short run we would argue that the stabilized Soviet sphere of influence, the Soviet intervention in Hungary and Czechoslovakia, and the détente with the United States should discourage those favoring a more open discussion of political institutional alternatives and questioning the dominant role of the party. On the other hand the complexity of tasks undertaken by the political system and the party should, in a less tense atmosphere and with greater economic resources, favor a more participatory authoritarian regime, in which at the local level, perhaps at the factory level, a certain decentralization would be combined with a freer participation of those loyal to the system. This would favor a "democratizing authoritarianism" at the lower levels and the "consultative authoritarianism" of Peter Ludz at the higher level rather than a further institutionalization of "quasi-pluralistic authoritarianism." It would favor economic rather than political reform even when these are obviously difficult to separate in communist states. Despite the convergence in many respects with other types of authoritarian regimes, particularly the "mobilizational one-party states" in the Third World and some of the "statist-organic authoritarian regimes" in the Western sphere of influence, we do not expect them to evolve in the same direction. In the West the pressures for liberalization are likely to be stronger than those for greater participation, while in the East those for liberalization are likely to be curtailed and those for participation, strengthened, at least at the lower levels, where they can be controlled. It depends very much on the values of the observer which of these two developments he or she would consider closer to the model of competitive democracy. But neither is likely to head ultimately to competitive democracy. The possibility of a reversal of post-totalitarian authoritarianisms in the communist world to "populist" or "bureaucratic" totalitarian tendencies cannot be excluded, but at present does not seem likely.

The question of post-totalitarianism particularly in the Soviet Union, is intimately linked with the theories of convergence of industrial or postindustrial society.[65] Alfred G. Meyer has summarized very well the intellectual and ideological context in which such theories have been formulated:

> Theories of convergence are as old as the Russian revolution itself, if we think of Waclaw Machajski's wry Saint-Simonian prognosis of the development of a stratified industrial society in which the educated and skilled would emerge as the new ruling class. Machajski was a disillusioned Marxist; and theories of convergence seem to suggest themselves easily to disillusioned Marxists, or at least to Marxists who have become disillusioned about the Soviet Union. Consider the theories of Trotsky, Achminov, Djilas, Mao, and the European and American New Left. In some fashion or other, they all describe the Soviet system as one in which a proletarian revolution gone wrong has resulted in the society reverting to some form of capitalism. Conversely, in the manner of James Burnham, another disillusioned Marxist, theories of the revolution betrayed correspond to assumptions about the end of capitalism and democracy in the West and foretell the emergence of a "managerial" society much like that projected by Saint-Simon, Machajski, and others. (Meyer, 1970, p. 319)

In addition to the disillusioned Marxists, writers disappointed with or suspicious of democracy, particularly among sociologists, starting with Tocqueville, have also noted the totalitarian tendencies of democracy. Another group is some economists who argue that the command economy has become dysfunctional and must be replaced by new and more rational planning methods. In their work, as in that of Isaac Deutscher, there is a strong element of technological economic determinism, which assumes a given technology causing a functionally corresponding social structure or system of social relations and similar systems of social relations developing similar political systems. The tendency from the days of the founding fathers of sociology to allow only limited autonomy to politics from the socioeconomic system and their areas of interest explain the favor that this perspective has found among them. The collection of readings edited by Paul Hollander (1969), *American and Soviet Society,* shows the fruitfulness and also the limitations of this perspective. Another source has been pacifist moralizing, wishful thinking, and sheer impatience with the cold war, based on the somewhat dubious assumption that similar systems are more compatible with each other than dissimilar ones. A newer theory of convergence proceeds from the assumption that industrial societies will converge in the form of bureaucratization rather than liberalization and democratization, which represented passing stages in the development of Western societies. Alfred G. Meyer (1970), without calling it convergence, contributes to that perspective when he asserts that the Soviet Union can be best understood as a giant bureaucracy, something like a modern corporation extended over the entire society, a "General Motors at large," even when he warns against pushing the analogy too far considering that in real life General Motors still exists within a larger society, culture, and political system.

The convergence theories, optimistic or apocalyptic, often on the basis of the opposite of ideological premises, have the merit of highlighting certain aspects of the study of societies and political systems that the type of analysis offered in this chapter tend to neglect but that cannot be fully dismissed.

5

THE PLACE OF THE WORLD'S STATES IN THE TYPOLOGY: AN ATTEMPT AND ITS DIFFICULTIES

It would have certainly been highly desirable to further operationalize our three main dimensions: the degree of monism versus limited pluralism, mobilization versus depoliticization of the population, and centrality of ideologies versus predominance of what we have called mentalities. The next step would have been to find systematic, valid, and reliable indicators of those three dimensions and to locate the countries of the world in the resulting attribute space. Finally, by selecting meaningful cutting points we would be able to define operationally the types and subtypes of nondemocratic regimes. The end product of such efforts would be a list of countries that at any particular point in time could be placed in each type.

Any reader of the now extensive literature on the conditions and measures of democracy, well summarized by John D. May (1973), will be fully aware of the difficulties in carrying out such an operation, even for the limited number of countries that generally are considered democratic or borderline cases. In spite of the availability of easily measurable indicators like the percentage of population eligible to vote, percentage voting, electoral support of majority and minority parties, share in seats of those parties, and constitutionally legitimate turnover of executives, as well as much richer information and other indicators like mass media control and the usual indices of economic development, no generally accepted classification or measure of the degree of democracy has resulted. The data that we would need to operationalize the dimensions of our typology are much more elusive, and in addition no one has yet made a deliberate effort to collect them systematically. To take just one obvious dimension, political mobilization of the citizens versus depoliticization, there is no easily available measure comparable to the percentage of citizen voting in competitive democracies.[66] Even leaving aside the differing meaning of the vote when there is no freedom to articulate and organize alternative opinion, it seems somewhat strange to find that in the Ivory Coast, Guinea, Gabon, the United Arab Republic, and Niger over 98 percent of the electorate actually votes, according to official reports (a similar report is made for seven communist countries), while among the polyarchies only the Netherlands reaches that high level of participation. It is, however, worth notice that among all the countries that we would not consider democracies according to our definition, those claiming an electoral participation rate above 90 percent happen to be totalitarian, post-totalitarian, or those we would have classified at the time as mobilizational postindependence regimes, generally with an officially established single party.[67] However, such an indicator would be useless for those countries that have not had national elections, like Cuba and China, obviously based on a high level of mobilization, and others like traditional Arab sheikhdoms, nor would such an indicator with its gross distortions and falsifications be of much value to classify countries between those extremes. Another possible indicator of mobilization, as we suggested in our discussion, would be the actual membership and participation in the activities of the officially established single party and its mass organizations for youth, women, etc. No one has systematically collected such data, and it is likely that the figures reported would in many cases be a wishful distortion of reality. Certainly the 1.1 million members claimed in the early sixties by Falange-Movimiento in Spain can in no meaningful way be compared with the 2.5 million members of the NSDAP in 1935, if we would consider even the most minimal indicators of involvement in the party. Actually in proportion to the population of each country, those figures would not be far apart. If this is the case with the most easily quantifiable indicator, the situation becomes even worse when we consider ones like the degree of limited pluralism or the monopoly of political power. Scholars unfamiliar with this type of system have fallen into the trap of considering the proportion of members of the government or high officeholders who are members of the party as an indicator, forgetting that they were legally considered members by the fact of holding such offices and their reaching those positions had nothing to do with previous involvement in the party but was based on quite different criteria, like military or bureaucratic careers, technical expertise, membership in influential religious associations, etc. Only a case-by-case sifting of the evidence for which the monographic research is often unavailable would allow us to make intelligent use of such operational criteria. We would obviously wish to have quantitative indicators of the importance of the official single parties in the political process of totalitarian and authoritarian regimes, and we would not deny that such indicators could be devised, like the ratio between government nonparty officials and paid officials of the party; the presence of men who made their careers in the party in other sectors of the political system like government, bureaucracies, the military, the academy, etc.; and the share of the party in the control of mass media. It would seem as if the degree of autonomy, development, interest articulation, and aggregation as defined by Gabriel Almond could serve to measure the degree of pluralism. But the efforts of Banks and Textor (1963; Banks and Gregg, 1965) to operationalize those concepts show the difficulty in using them outside of the democratic and a few other well-known countries. In fact, their coding of those dimensions is based not on any hard indicators but on the judgment of experts, using probably quite different frames of reference in classifying the country they know best.

In view of all these problems it seems unwarranted to attempt to place all the countries of the world within the types and subtypes we have developed here. But it seems appropriate, using our best judgment, to place a number of polities in the types we have theoretically and inductively developed. Certainly even more than in the case of the measurement of democracy found in the literature, scholars will disagree with our typology, but even accepting its usefulness they will question the placing of particular countries at a particular time in it, on account of a different reading of the available evidence or using different indicators than those implicitly used by us. Therefore our classification should be considered indicative and illustrative and be perfected by other scholars before it is used in sophisticated computer analysis in search for correlations with other nonpolitical variables. Our distinctions are qualitative rather than quantitative, and often quite far apart from those resulting from perhaps premature efforts of quantification of some relevant dimensions, like the scaling by Dahl and his associates of 114 countries in 31 types by the opportunities to participate in national elections and to oppose the government. This does not mean that the clusters of countries discovered by them using the admittedly debatable coding of Banks and Textor do not show significant coincidences with the groupings reached by us. When there could be such a profound disagreement as that between Banks and Textor and Dahl about the classification of a well-known country like France, we can imagine how precarious the data base for such refined classifications must be in the case of most countries that have reached independence recently and are characterized by unstable governments that have not been the object of monographic research from a comparative perspective. All this would account for the relatively low level of coincidence between the classifications in our typology and the scaling of those same countries by Dahl, Norling, and Williams (Dahl, 1971, Appendix A, pp. 231–45) disregarding changes in the nature of the political regime even over short periods of time. The difficulties encountered by Marvin E. Olsen, Dick Simpson, and Arthur K. Smith in measuring democratic performance, noted by John D. May (1973), should serve as warning against premature and specious quantification of any typological effort like ours. Elegant statistical operations built on weak foundations seem to us more misleading than a frankly qualitative judgment based on a mental and hopefully intelligent summation of a large amount of information.

6

CONCLUDING COMMENTS

After our panoramic overview of the variety of political systems that are not based on a regular free competition for power among organized groups emerging with more or less spontaneity from the society, that is, of all the regimes that cannot be called competitive democracies, it is difficult to discern some general trends about the prospects of different forms of government.[68] On the one hand, the successful stable democracies, with their political freedoms, the opportunities for political participation of the average citizen, particularly those with a calling for politics, and the predictability and relative peacefulness in handling political and social crises, continue to be a pole of attraction to people living under the variety of nondemocratic regimes. This accounts for the tendencies toward greater pluralism and more opportunities for participation to which the rulers in authoritarian regimes pay lip service or more or less sincerely and incompetently aim. On occasion we have noted how the processes of liberalization and democratization (in the sense of greater opportunities for active political participation) do not seem to have equally favorable prospects in different authoritarian and totalitarian systems. We can certainly expect the emergence of many transitional types of polities that, without losing their authoritarian character, might have a potential for becoming competitive democracies under favorable circumstances. In a small number of countries the fact that only recently they were ruled as competitive democracies creates pressures both from below and within the elite in that direction. However, we should not forget that the majority of countries we have been considering never have been under liberal democratic rule, never have had an opportunity to develop the traditions and values of a

Rechtstaat ("state of law") or the pluralism of institutions and corporate groups of the type that the West developed in centuries of feudalism, estate representation *(ständische-Verfassung)*, and autonomous corporate cities. Let us not forget that many of the regimes we have been considering have been established as successors of monarchical traditional despotisms or traditional political systems, where authority was limited by customs rather than by law and in which no other groups including religious organizations and authorities could challenge or limit political authority. A large number of polities, particularly in Africa, have emerged as a result of external colonial territorial divisions imposed upon smaller traditional political units, premodern tribal organizations, and communal structures. In those cases the modern and pseudomodern political systems have been imposed not upon a national community with civic consciousness but upon successors of an external authoritarian rule of the colonizer, and the task of building a civic and perhaps national consciousness may have to precede any attempt to organize a democratic state in which horizontal cleavages would crosscut and integrate vertical, territorial, and/or ethnic cleavages. In such societies we can expect a variety of authoritarian and perhaps occasionally totalitarian efforts to create stable regimes. In those societies in which authoritarian rule has succeeded with practically no discontinuity traditional premodern authoritarian forms or colonial rule, we can expect only limited popular pressures toward competitive democracy. Certainly, elites educated and/or oriented toward Western advanced societies are likely to be discontented with authoritarian rule and feel that modernization requires either competitive democracy or an imitation of the utopian totalitarian model. That discontent of sectors of the elite undoubtedly will contribute to the instability of authoritarian regimes, but it is doubtful that it will not lead to the successive reproduction of new and different authoritarian regimes. The transition from a desire by the elites for constitutional democratic forms after independence—first imitated and externally imposed or genuinely desired—to mobilizational or machine-type single parties and then to bureaucratic-military authoritarian rule in so many African states reflects those dilemmas. Authoritarian regimes of one or another type appeared to intellectuals, leaders, and even citizens of competitive democracies as basically illegitimate, and that value judgment in many ways contributes to delegitimize those regimes for important sectors in the elite of their societies but not necessarily for the masses. We therefore should be careful not to confuse the instability of authoritarian regimes with favorable prospects for competitive democracy. The alternative to a particular authoritarian regime might be change within the regime or from one type of authoritarian rule to another, if not permanent instability or chaos (of which the Congo after independence was an outstanding example, see Willame, 1972).

We should not forget either that even established competitive democracies in a period of social change and revived ideological passion might undergo crises that lead to authoritarian rule unless a last minute and deliberate effort of reequilibration succeeds (Linz and Stepan, 1978). The circumstances accompanying a breakdown of democracy, as cases in Latin America show, make the reestablishment very difficult. Competitive democracy seems to be the result of quite unique constellations of factors and circumstances leading to its inauguration and stability. Many developments in modern societies and in the not-so-modern, particularly in terms of economic well-being, should make stable democracies possible, but those same conditions do not assure a successful process of inauguration of such regimes. Certainly many societies satisfied the requirements for stable democracy we find in the literature, but did not become competitive regimes.

When Robert Dahl raised the question about the future of polyarchies he wrote, "As with a great many things, the safest bet about a country's regime a generation from now is that it will be somewhat different but not radically different from what it is today." We can make the same statement about today's nondemocratic regimes. We would, however, have to add that in contrast to the stabilized democracies, we would expect considerable change in the types of authoritarian regimes and within the regimes themselves. Paradoxically, great shifts in mass electorates in advanced societies, except in extreme crisis situations, are unlikely, and therefore evolutionary rather than basic change characterizes democratic politics. Since in authoritarian regimes change depends on few actors, less constrained by constituencies difficult to convince by persuasion rather than imposition, important changes can take place more unexpectedly and can change the system considerably. Perhaps the particular types of authoritarian regimes are less likely to be fully institutionalized, and therefore we can expect many changes within the genus authoritarian. Since the end of World War II and even earlier, the list of countries fitting into the basic subtypes of majoritarian and consociational democracies has changed little. Neither has that of nondemocratic political states over the same period. But the lists of countries fitting at different moments in time into the various subtypes has been far from stable. Irregular and violent changes have been frequent, as the overthrow of the postindependence single-party regimes in Africa by military coups establishing military-bureaucratic regimes shows. There are also evolutive tendencies within authoritarian regimes which seem to lead to a certain convergence toward some form of institutionalization of a limited pluralism based on a controlled and irresponsible representation of interests, limited and controlled forms of participation, and limited efforts of ideological justification of such institutional arrangements. That point of convergence in the development of authoritarian regimes seems to be relatively close to the model we have described as organic statism.[69] The regimes established as military dictatorships in the narrow sense of emergency interim rule by the army very quickly tend to become bureaucratic-military if not bureaucratic-technocratic-military. With the passing of time the variety of interests in society, particularly economic, professional, and sectorial, and to a certain degree labor and territorial, are included in one way or another into the limited and controlled pluralism. On the other hand, systems established by and through political parties gaining or aspiring to the monopoly of control or at least dominance over other pluralistic components with the effort of mass mobilization and declared ideological commitments seem to lose that dynamism and increasingly share their power with a variety of selected interest groups. Their totalitarian and arrested totalitarian tendencies are deflected toward various forms of conservative quasi-pluralistic or pluralistic authoritarian regimes, some of which seem to show a growing affinity to the model of organic statism. At some point the observer could think that the future was in the hands of mobilizational single parties that would hold at least dominant or predominant, if not exclusive, power. Contrary to that expectation we have seen the overthrow, transformation, or decay of single-party rule and organizations. Bureaucratic rule in cooperation with recognized organized interests seems to be the dominant model, sometimes supported by the military with its coercive capacity and organizational resources, other times legitimated by the continuing presence and influence at the top of a single party that provides some opportunity to organize a well-controlled mass participation and to recruit politically ambitious persons. It is important to be aware of the range and direction of dynamic tendencies within authoritarian regimes. It is this fact that makes it so difficult to place different countries in the types delineated above without reference to a particular moment in their development.

As to the future of totalitarianism, predictions are even more difficult. Certainly two of the historically most salient and well-known cases, the rule of Hitler and Stalin, seem to have weakened its attractiveness. But there can be no question that some of the underlying utopian ideological assumptions that made those distorted forms with their terror possible are still there. Ultimately, once the pluralistic conflict and accommodation model underlying democratic politics has been rejected in favor of a consensual society based on a deliberate active search for the common good according to a rational or irrational ideal conception under a leadership defined as competent and self-confident about achieving it, this model is not likely to lose its appeal. The totalitarian utopia is, for modern man, a pole of attraction not easily forgotten and is comparable in this respect to that of freedom for the individual to participate in democratic politics. Almost inevitably the elites in authoritarian regimes will feel the attraction of those two poles, even when the confining conditions of reality make it unlikely that most authoritarian regimes will evolve in one or another of those directions. Totalitarianism is ultimately as much if not more a result of a unique constellation of factors as is competitive democracy. Perhaps, fortunately, it is not easy to establish totalitarian systems. In spite of their many failures, and their lack of a distinctive legitimacy formula and ideology attractive to intellectuals, authoritarian regimes rather than totalitarian systems and democratic governments are the regimes most easily established and function under conditions neither too favorable nor unfavorable to the stability of government. Contrary to the hopes of free men and those of the *terribles simplificateurs* of which Burckhardt wrote, many if not most states will be ruled in the immediate future by authoritarian regimes, neither fully subordinating the individual to a great historical task of building a perfect society nor allowing him a free choice among a large set of alternatives or an opportunity to convince his fellow citizens to support him to implement those goals.

NOTES

This work was made possible by my stay at the Institute for Advanced Study, Princeton, supported by NSF Grant GS-31730X2. I would like to acknowledge the invaluable assistance of Rocío de Terán and the help of Claire Coombs.

Chapter 1: Introduction

1. An excellent comparative study of two societies under different political systems and the implications for the individual of living in the USSR and the U.S. is Hollander (1972). However, the impact of the generational and liberal-radical intellectual protest around 1970 colors some sections on the U.S. too much.

2. For Mussolini's and the Italian use of the term "totalitarian" see Jänicke (1971), pp. 20–36. This work is also the best review of the history of the uses of the term, its variants, and the polemics surrounding it, and includes an extensive bibliography. It should be noted that the use of the term for both fascist and communist regimes was not exclusive of liberals, Catholics, or conservatives, but that socialists like Hilferding already in 1939 did so. Hilferding also in 1936 abandoned a Marxist analysis of the totalitarian state (see Jänicke, 1971, pp. 74–75 and Hilferding, 1947b, p. 266).

3. On the concept of total war see Speier (1944).

4. For a discussion of the perception of the similarities of the Soviet and the fascist regimes by Trotsky and Italian Fascists see Gregor (1974b, pp. 183–88). For another example see the analysis by a Spanish left fascist, Ledesma Ramos (1968, pp. 288–91 passim). See also footnote 55.

5. For a review of the current typologies of political systems see Wiseman (1966, pp. 47–96). Almond and Coleman (1960) was a pioneer work in which Pye, Weiner, Coleman, Rustow, and Blanksten study politics in Asia, Africa, and Latin America. The typology by Shils is used in connection with the functional analysis by Almond. Almond and Powell (1966, chapters 9–11) present a typology according to the degree of structural differentiation and secularization, from

273

primitive political systems to modern democratic, authoritarian, and totalitarian. Another interesting contribution is Finer (1971, pp. 44–51 passim). Blondel (1972) organizes his comparative analysis of political systems, distinguishing traditional conservative, liberal democratic, communist, populist, and authoritarian conservative systems. Rustow (1967) distinguishes (1) traditional, (2) modernizing—personal charismatic, military, single-party authoritarian, (3) modern democratic, totalitarian, and (4) absence of government.

Organski (1965) has formulated another typology of regimes on the basis of their relation to stages of economic development, the function of politics in that process, and the type of elite alliances and class conflicts. Among them we might note the type he calls "syncratic" (from the Greek 'syn,' together, rule) in semideveloped countries based on a compromise between industrial and agrarian elites stimulated by a threat from below.

Apter (1965), on the basis of his extensive research experience in Africa, has developed a highly stimulating and influential typology of political systems based on two main dimensions: the type of authority and the values pursued. The first dimension distinguishes systems of hierarchical authority (centrally controlled systems) and of pyramidal authority (systems with constitutional representation); the second distinguishes consummatory (sacred) and instrumental (secular) values. The resulting types are, among the hierarchic authority systems: (1) mobilizational systems (like China) and (2) either modernizing autocracies or neomercantilist societies (of which Morocco and Kemalism in Turkey would be examples); among pyramidal authority systems: (3) theocratic or feudal systems and (4) reconciliation systems. Mobilization and reconciliation systems are compared in relation to coercion and information, which are in inverse relation. Unfortunately it would be too complex to present here how Apter relates these theoretically developed types to the analysis of concrete political systems and to problems of modernization.

6. The calculations used in this section on the ranking of countries by population, gross national product, GNP growth rates, and the population under different types of regimes in Europe are based on tables 5.1, 5.4, and 5.5 in Taylor and Hudson (1972).

7. Our delimitation and definition of democracy has been derived from the following major works: Sartori (1962a), Kelsen (1929), Schumpeter (1950), and Dahl (1971). On Dahl's contribution to the theory of democracy, or—as he now prefers to call it—polyarchy, see the critical review essay of Ware (1974). It refers to criticisms of what has been called "elitist theory of democracy." See for example Bachrach (1967). Since these critiques focus more on the "democratization" of polyarchies than on their distinction from nonpolyarchies, we shall not enter further into these important discussions. We have developed our ideas about democracy further in the context of a discussion of R. Michels's pessimistic and ultimately misleading analysis; see Linz (1966).

8. The most debated case is Mexico, where a presidential candidate only in 1952 obtained less than 75 percent of the vote and generally obtains close to or over 90 percent. Opposition leaders are fully aware that they are doomed to lose any election for the 200 governorships and 282 senatorial seats. The opposition party's only hope (a recent development) is to obtain, in exchange for a few positions as representatives or municipal presidents, recognition by the government

for its leaders in the form of contracts, loans, or services. Parties are financed in many cases by the government, and they support the government candidates or provisionally fight them in exchange for concessions for their supporters. "Thus they have participated in the political game and the ceremony of elections," as a Mexican social scientist puts it. See González Casanova (1970). Another critical analysis is Cosío Villegas (1972). An earlier analysis that emphasizes the oligarchic characteristics is Brandenburg (1964). The best monographic study of policymaking in Mexico as an authoritarian regime is Kaufman (1970). For an analysis of elections see Taylor (1960). However, there are other interpretations that emphasize the democratic potential, either within the party or as a long-term development; see Scott (1964, 1965), Needler (1971), Padgett (1966), and Ross (1966). The fact that elections do not serve as a channel to power and that the Partido Revolucionario Institucional (PRI) is a privileged party does not mean that there is not considerable freedom of expression and organization. For a study of the leading opposition party, its electoral support, and the handicaps it faces see Mabry (1973), pp. 170–82. On the continuing disagreement of scholars on the nature of the political system see Needleman and Needleman (1969).

Chapter 2: Totalitarian Systems

9. On intellectual and cultural life in the Soviet Union see Pipes (1961), Swayze (1962), Simmons (1971), and P. Johnson and Labedz (1965). For East Germany see Lange (1955). For communist China, MacFarquhar (1960) and Chen (1967). An interesting case study is Medvedev (1969) on Lysenko. For Nazi Germany, Brenner (1963), Mosse (1966), Wulf (1963a, 1963b, 1963c, 1964), and Strothmann (1963). For further particularly revealing bibliographic references to education, the world of knowledge, see Tannenbaum (1972). While not a theoretically significant contribution, the illustrations showing the heterogeneity and eclecticism in official Italian art contrast with the German equivalents and are another indicator of the doubtful totalitarian character of Italian Fascism. See Silva (1973). The contrast between totalitarian and authoritarian regime cultural policy should become apparent to the reader of the study of Spanish intellectual life under Franco by E. Díaz (1974).

10. On religion and the state in the Soviet Union see Curtis (1960). For more recent times see Bourdeaux (1968, 1969) and Hayward and Fletcher (1969). For communist China see Baier (1968), Bush (1970), MacInnis (1972), and H. Welch (1972). For Germany see Conway (1968), Zipfel (1965), Lewy (1965), Buchheim (1953). For a regional study rich in documentation see Baier (1968). The contrast with Italy can be found in Webster (1960).

11. Already in the SA, ranks were given without regard to wartime rank in the army; see Gordon (1972, pp. 84–85). This ideology breaking through the status structure of the society was reflected in the SA oath: "I promise that I will see in every member . . . without thought of class, occupation, wealth or poverty, only my brother and true comrade, with whom I feel myself bound in joy and sorrow." Later this meant that a high civil servant might have been quite intimidated by his janitor holding the position of party *Blockwart*.

12. We cannot enter into the complex problem of the relationship between political systems and foreign policy. Certainly, aggressive policies, intervention in the internal affairs of other countries, political and economic imperialism are no monopoly of any type of regime. There can be no question either that national-socialism and its ideological conceptions and the internal dynamic of the German regime led to aggressive expansion, war, and the creation of a hegemonic system of exploited and oppressed countries and dependent satellites. There are distinctive Nazi components in that policy, particularly its racist conception, that cannot be confused with those derived from German nationalism (regaining full sovereignty after Versailles, the Auschluss, incorporation of border ethnic minorities) and those of a Mitteleuropa economic dominance policy. See Bracher (1970, pp. 287–329, 400–8, and the bibliographic references on pp. 520–23); Jacobsen (1968), Hillgruber (1971), and Hildebrand (1973). Deakin (1966) and Wiskemann (1966) study the very revealing relationship between Hitler and Mussolini. Undoubtedly, Fascist Italy also pursued a policy of expansion in the Adriatic and Africa, but it could be argued that—leaving aside rhetorical claims—its goals were those of prefascist imperialism. All fascist movements are characterized by their exacerbated nationalism, anti-internationalism, antipacificism, exultation of military values, irredentism, and often pan-nationalism, contrasted with the ideological commitments of democratic parties of the left and center, even when some of those parties were not opposed to colonialism and national power and prestige politics.

The question of foreign policy of communist states presents the same problem of isolating national interests of the USSR—inherited from the Russian Empire—from those derived from the dynamics of the regime (particularly as the result of the civil war and foreign intervention, encirclement, isolation) and finally from those derived from international revolutionary solidarity and ideologically based perceptions of the international scene. The different points of view expressed by scholars can be found in Hoffmsan and Fleron (1971, part 3), in addition to Schulman (1969) and Ulam (1968). The literature on the Sino-Soviet dispute (Zagoria, 1969) brings out the complex interweaving of national interest and ideological conflicts. Obviously the literature on Eastern European communist countries (Seton-Watson, 1968; Ionescu, 1967; Brzezinski, 1960) reveals the inseparability of foreign and internal policy considerations with the Soviet hegemonic sphere. The relations of communist parties with the CPSU, particularly when the Soviet Union served as model socialist country, make it impossible to separate (specifically in the Stalin era) the politics of a worldwide revolutionary movement from those of the only country in which the party was in power. Polycentrism has obviously changed and complicated things. In spite of the affinities between fascist parties, influences and imitations, they never were linked by a common discipline comparable to the communists. Ideologically linked parties, ignoring any more direct dependency, are undoubtedly a factor in the foreign policy of movement regimes. The style and capacity for certain types of international political responses of regimes subject to free public criticism and overt dissent and of those not facing them must be different. However, it would be a mistake to deduct (for any type of regime) foreign policy at any point in time from ideological commitments, as the flexibility shown in the Hitler-Stalin pact or U.S–communist China relations prove; but it might be more valid to take them into account in long-range strategies of regimes. A related topic we have ignored (perhaps too much) is the link between foreign policy crises and the crises and breakdown of democratic regimes, particularly in the rise of fascism but also the turn to authoritarian solutions in the Third World, as well as the link between preparedness for war, more specifically total war, and totalitarian tendencies.

13. The problem of succession of leaders in nondemocratic constitutional regimes has been considered one of their weaknesses in contrast to hereditary monarchies and parliamentary or presidential democracies (Rustow, 1964). The succession of Lenin and the consequent struggle for power influenced that discussion, as well as the very personal leadership and life-long tenure of many single-party regime leaders. Already in 1933 Farinacci in a letter to Mussolini (Aquarone, 1965, pp. 173–75) raised the question of succession of a unique leader who would not allow the emergence of other leaders as a problem in this type of regime. In fact, the expectation was that in the absence of an heir apparent no smooth transition could be expected and that any effective legal method to remove leaders in life or after limited tenure could be institutionalized. Events did not allow us to see the succession of the founders of fascist regimes, and the longevity of other founders has left us with speculations about the future of their regimes. The rise of Khrushchev (Swearer, 1964; Rush, 1968) despite the conflicts involved proved that succession did not need to lead to a breakdown of the system or even another purge and reign of terror. For the problems surrounding the succession of Mao see Robinson (1974). However the relatively institutionalized and peaceful succession of Khrushchev and Ho Chi Minh, and that of Nasser and Salazar, among others, suggest that the institutions of such regimes might be better able to handle the problem than was thought. Even more noticeable is the tendency of newly established authoritarian regimes, like the Brazilian military, to forestall the emergence of personal leadership and to establish time limits for tenure of office. The not too distant passing away of a number of founders of authoritarian regimes should allow a comparative analysis of the problem.

14. A good measure of the importance of ideology is the growth of a distinctive language (for example in case of Germany see Berning, 1964, and Klemperer, 1966) and the frequency of its use.

15. Aquarone (1965). Quoted from the "Statuto del partito del 1938," Appendix 63, pp. 571–90; see page 577. The work of Aquarone is essential for the study of the ideology and organization of the Italian Fascist party and state and includes a wealth of documents and legal texts.

16. On the ruling and nonruling communist parties see the *Yearbook on International Communist Affairs* (Allen, 1969); on their strength see the annual reports of the U.S. Department of State. For the Soviet Union (Rigby, 1968); for China the figures are: 57 in 1921 to 300,000 in 1933, 40,000 in 1937, 1,211,128 in 1945, 4,438,080 in 1949, 7,859,473 in 1955, 17,000,000 in 1961. Ratios to population in other communist countries around 1961 range from 3.2 percent in Albania to 15.5 percent in North Korea, with most countries between 4 and 5 percent, and 4.2 percent in the USSR (Schurmann, 1968, pp. 129, 138). See also Brzezinski (1971, p. 86). For the Italian Fascist party see

Germino (1959), De Felice (1966a, pp. 6–11); for the NSDAP, see Schäfer (1957), Buchheim (1958), Orlow (1973, pp. 136–38), and the extremely useful and neglected *Parteistatistik,* published by the Reichsorganisationsleiter der NSDAP (1935); and Linz (1970a, pp. 202) for other fascist parties.

For those who would argue that intraparty democracy could be an alternative to political competition in the society at large, it is worth remembering that party membership ranges from 1.3 to over 1.5 percent of the population in Cuba (1969), 2.5 percent of the population in China, 4.2 percent in the USSR, to a high of 11.6 percent in Czechoslovakia (all in 1961) (Schurmann, 1968, p. 138). The figure of the PNF in Italy was 5.3 percent (1937) and the maximum for the NSDAP, 9.9 percent in 1943 (Linz, 1970a, p. 202).

17. See also Buchheim (1968a, pp. 391–96) on resignation from the SS, which confirms the in principle voluntary character of membership.

18. This point is well analyzed in Aquarone (1965, pp. 31–34, 262–63), with reference to the conflicts between prefects and party secretaries, and mayors and political secretaries, which generally (but not always) were decided in favor of the state authorities. In 1938 a confidant reported: "In the frequent changes of the guard the active, disinterested and revolutionary elements are substituted by elements that narcotize all activity of the party. . . the tendency to appoint secretary of the [local] Fasci, municipal employees that lack the necessary freedom to activate [potenziare] the party and control the activity of the administrative Enti [organizations]. The party loses, in those cases, its revolutionary activism, the possibility to reinvigorate and make the static element constituted by bureaucracy of the various Enti march in fascist step. In summary, there is lacking that healthy dualism between political and administrative power, indispensable factor in the revolutionary affirmation of fascism" (p. 263). The state-party relation was the object of constant debate among fascist theorists and constitutionalists (F. Neumann, 1963, pp. 75–77; for review of the literature see Conde, 1942, pp. 299–318; Manoilescò, 1938, pp. 97–108). The communists have constantly grappled with this difficult problem (see for example Schurmann, 1968, pp. 109–14). Mao's formulation: "The Party is the instrument that forges the resolution of the contradiction between state and society in socialism" is a response to this problem, as are the principle of vertical and dual rule (Schurmann, pp. 57, 88–89, 188–89) and the conflicts about decentralization. The Yugoslavs significantly criticized the early phase of the regime with the term "statism," and sophisticated Italian fascists like Bottai see in the statism that undermined corporativism and even the party the end of spontaneity and participation in the regime (Aquarone, pp. 216–21). It is no accident that the idea of a "withering away" of the party should have been discussed (Aquarone, p. 35) once the state would be fascisticized and the corporative system fully developed. Such ideas have also appeared with the emphasis on self-management in Yugoslavia and the development of a broadly based Marxist commitment. The Yugoslavs attempted to implement the principle of "separating the party from power," making state and party office incompatible, assigning to the party the role of leading ideological—"conscience of the revolution"—and political force of a society organized

along the lines of self-management of workers councils and communes (Zaninovich, 1968, pp. 141–46; Supek, 1973). The party was conceived as the unifying factor in a self-managed society bridging other cleavages and restraining bureaucratic, technocratic, as well as particularistic interests, even when in practice the older, bureaucratically entrenched party cadres resisted the "pluralization" of society. An interesting possible development is a role for the army-party members as a "vanguard" of the party, counteracting the nationalist tendencies in the society (Remington, 1974). It would be interesting to speculate if the duality state-party is not a functional analogue (equivalent would be too strong a statement) to the duality of state and church and the duality of authority in many traditional empires.

19. On the membership policy of the PNF see Aquarone, 1965, pp. 177–87. The purge of 1930–31 affected 120,000 members, but in 1932–33 the opening raised the membership from 1,007,231 to 1,413,407. (See also Germino, 1959.) On the NSDAP purge of SA members and the left wing particularly among the Politische Leiter, see Orlow, 1973, pp. 120–25 and Schäfer, 1957. See Orlow, pp. 204–7 on the disappointing 1937 membership drive, pp. 236–37 on membership composition and "planning," pp. 342 on difficulties in recruiting youth, p. 408 on membership figures for 1942.

For the USSR see the excellent monograph by Rigby (1968) who gives the official figures from 1917 to 1967 of full and candidate members, which show the impact of purges and membership drives, data on social and sex composition over time, regional variations, members in the armed forces, etc. The purge from May 1929 to May 1930 affected 170,000 members, about 11 percent of the membership, and in 1935, 16 percent.

20. The conception of democratic centralism formulated by Lenin in 1906 in these terms, "The principle of democratic centralism and autonomy of local institutions means specifically *freedom of criticism,* complete and everywhere, as long as this does not disrupt the unity of action *already decided upon*—and the intolerability of any criticism undermining or obstructing the *unity* of action decided on by the party," arouse the comments of Rosa Luxemburg and Trotsky, quoted by R. V. Daniels (1969, p. 12).

21. For excellent analyses of leader personality in totalitarian systems see Tucker (1965) and Vierhaus (1964). The general context of personal leadership in modern politics can be found in Hamon and Mabileau (1964), Willner (1968), and Schweitzer (1974). The peculiar hold of Hitler of the Nazi party before even taking power is studied by Nyomarkay (1967). See also Horn (1972). An obvious source not to be neglected are the biographies like the Bullock (1964) and the description of the world around the *Führer* by an insider like Speer (1971). The phenomenon of "court politics" that exists at the top in any political system but acquires special importance in authoritarian and totalitarian systems would deserve serious comparative analysis.

Some of the analyses of totalitarian systems, like the recent book by Schapiro (1972b), seem in our view to overemphasize the role of leadership. The blaming of Stalin has obviously excused many analysts from attempting to understand the conditions for "Stalinism." They should heed the advice in this criticism by Marx of Victor Hugo's *Napoleon the Little:* "He does not notice that he makes this individual great instead of little by ascribing to him a personal power of initiative such as would be without parallel in world history" (Karl Marx and Friedrich Engels, 1851, Vol. 1, p. 221).

22. For the change in *Mein Kampf* between the 1925 (second edition) and post-1930 editions, on the election of leaders in the party see Maser (1970, pp. 56–57).

23. The role of elections and the party in managing them in noncompetitive politics would deserve comparative analysis. Some interesting material can he found for the Soviet Union in Gilison (1970), Mote (1965), U.S. Department of State, Division of Research for Europe, Office of Intelligence Research (1948). For East Germany, Bundesministerium für Gesamtdeutsche Fragen (1963). For Poland, Pelczynski (1959). Yugoslav elections offer an interesting contrast; see Burks and Stanković (1967). The elections after Hitler's *Machtergreifung* have been analyzed by Bracher, Sauer, and Schulz (1960). There is unfortunately no comparable analysis of elections after Mussolini's March on Rome. Elections under authoritarian regimes (outside of Yugoslavia) could deserve more analysis in terms of their functions for the system, the responses of citizens, the patterns of participation, voiding of votes in relation to the social structure, as well as the techniques to discourage candidates of the "tolerated" opposition, electoral coercion, and falsification. The contrast between the election process in totalitarian and authoritarian pseudo- or "semi-" democratic regimes (that some would even claim to be democratic) can be seen in Penniman (1972) and the election factbooks for Latin American countries published by the Institute for Comparative Study of Political Systems. For a theoretical paper that could serve as a starting point see Rose and Mossawir (1967).

24. The problem of relationship between party, state, and society has always been discussed in the ideological literature of totalitarian regimes. For a good analysis in the German case, see Franz Neumann (1963, pp. 62–68, 71–80, an interesting comparison with Italy; and pp. 467–70).

25. For the USSR see Fainsod (1963). For China, Yang (1965) and Vogel (1971). For Cuba, Yglesias (1969). For Germany, Allen (1965), Peterson (1969), Heyen (1967), Meyerhoff (1963), and Görgen (1968). For a contrast with an authoritarian regime see Ugalde (1970), Fagen and Tuohy (1972), and Linz (1970b).

26. See below.

27. See below.

28. An approach that cannot be ignored is the emphasis on the historical and cultural continuity with prerevolutionary Russia (Berdyaev, 1948; Simmons, 1955; Pipes 1967; Vaker, 1962; and the excellent collection of essays edited by Black, 1967). Bell (1961) reviews this "Slavic" interpretation in his essay on "Ten Theories in Search of Soviet Reality," which also discusses (pp. 51–56) Leites's *A Study of Bolshevism* (1953), which sees Bolshevism as a conscious attempt to reverse traditional patterns of Russian character, in an interesting attempt of pyscho-history. On cultural continuity and Chinese communism see Solomon (1971) and Pye (1971).

29. The particular German historical and cultural-ideological background that made the rise of national socialism and its successful drive to power possible has been highly debated. A balanced view by a sociologist is Dahrendorf (1967). The ideological-cultural roots are studied by Stern (1965), Mosse (1964), Sontheimer (1968), Faye (1972), Struve (1973) and the earlier and less focussed studies by Butler (1941), Viereck (1961), and Vermeil (1955). Interesting but overstated is Lukács (1955). The essays by Buchheim (1953) and Plessner (1959) deserve mention. However, the general European climate of opinion cannot be ignored either, as the study by Hoepke (1968) on the German right and Italian Fascism shows. Anti-Semitism, which fueled the totalitarian drive of the Nazis and some other fascist movements, has been the subject of considerable research we cannot review here; see Massing (1949), Pulzer (1964), and the more psychological interpretations of Fromm (1941), Adorno *et al.* (1950), Bettelheim and Janowitz (1950), and more recent German sources quoted by Bracher (1970, pp. 506–7). A related problem is that of social Darwinism; see Conrad-Martius (1955) and Zmarzlik (1973).

30. For a review of the literature and bibliography see May (1973) and the already classic analyses by Lipset (1959), Neubaner (1967), Eckstein (1966), and Dahl (1971). A more general analysis of stability of regimes is Eckstein (1971).

31. For a detailed historical account see La Cierva (1969). For historical accounts in English see Jackson (1965) and Carr (1971). More directly relevant for a political scientist is the analysis by Malefakis (1970, Chapter 15, "Could the Disaster Have Been Avoided?" pp. 388–400). The chapter on Spain in Linz and Stepan (1978) will attempt to draw the theoretical implications.

32. We have already referred to the writings of S. M. Lipset, S. Rokkan, S. Neumann, W. Kornhauser, R. Lepsius among others. The specific conditions for the rise of fascism are discussed in Linz (1976). See also below for references to the literature on fascist movements and regimes.

33. The slow process of transition from negative integration, to use the expressions of Guenther Roth (1963), to participation of socialist parties is particularly illuminating in this respect. The monographs by Schorsky, Berlau, Gay, and G. A. Ritter on the German Social Democratic party and the theoretical analysis of Robert Michels are the most salient contributions.

34. In this section we have analyzed only the internal processes leading to the establishment or overthrow of one or another type of regime. Obviously, all types of regimes have been overthrown by external defeat (we have only to think of Nazi totalitarianism, Japanese bureaucratic-military, semitraditional authoritarianism after World War II) or established, maintained, or overthrown with foreign assistance playing more or less decisive role (communist regimes in Eastern Europe, the GDR, North Korea, authoritarian rule in Spain with fascist help, not to mention the impact of American aid or hostility on regime changes in Latin America). Certainly in economically dependent countries outside influences and the reactions to them, even short of direct intervention, are one more factor accounting for internal crises and through them for the success or failure of different regimes. However, the interests of outside economic forces might be equally well served—in different cases—by democratic and a

variety of authoritarian regimes, so that it is difficult to establish a direct link between *dependencia* and type of regime.

Another factor contributing to the emergence, consolidation, and permanence of authoritarian rule is a hostile international environment that makes the open debate of foreign policy alternatives of a democracy undesirable and justifies the outlawing of parties linked with a neighboring foreign power or the discrimination against irredentist minorities supported by it. This was a factor that contributed to the strengthening of antidemocratic tendencies in Finland in the thirties and the transformation of the three Baltic democracies into presidential dictatorships. Similar problems contributed to authoritarianism in Poland and a number of Balkan countries in the interwar period.

Chapter 3: Traditional Authority and Personal Rulership

35. Among the extensive literature see Winckler (1970), Krader (1968), Eisenstadt (1959), Mair (1962), Colsen and Midldleton (1957), Turner and Swartz (1966), Fortes and Evans-Pritchard (1940), Fallers (1965), Evans-Pritchard (1940 and 1948), Gluckman (1965a and 1965b).

36. The reader edited by Eisenstadt (1971) contains many contributions on premodern political systems and references to the literature. The same is true for Bendix (1968). The classic work in this field is Weber (1968), *Economy and Society*. Bendix (1960) is the best exposition in English of Weber's comparative historical-polititial sociology. The contemporary relevance of Weber's categories has been noted by Roth (1971, pp. 156–69). The major comparative study of classical empires is Eisenstadt (1962). For a typology of traditional systems see Apter (1965, pp. 85–122).

37. For essays showing the persistent significance of tradition for understanding contemporary politics see *Daedalus* (1973) on "Post-Traditional Societies." As examples of monographs showing the complex interaction between traditional and more modern political institutions we can mention Gellner and Micaud (1972) and Behrman (1970).

See for example the collection of papers edited by Swartz (1968) and the essays in *Political Systems and the Distribution of Power,* A.S.A. Monographs, No. 2.

38. The role of tradition in the political and social modernization of Japan has been the object of considerable research. As examples of different interpretations of modernization under the Meiji see Norman (1948), Craig (1961), and Jansen (1961). One of the few paired comparisons in social science is *Political Modernization in Japan and Turkey,* Ward and Rustow (1964). For the continuous role of the emperor and the court in modern times see Titus (1974).

39. There are a number of excellent studies on Moroccan politics: Ashford (1961, 1965a, 1967), Waterbury (1970), Zartman (1971), Moore (1970b), and Gellner and Micaud (1972). The latter focusses on the interaction between sectors of society—Arabs and Berbers—and its implications, including a discussion of the coup of 10 July 1971.

40. For a less extreme example see Anderson (1964). These regimes are classified as cases of "personal control" in the typology of Lanning (1974), based on the two dimensions: power relationships between authorities and groups (distinguishing group dominant, power balance, and authority dominance) and organizational basis (distinguishing functional, interest groups, and personal relations). The sixth of the resulting types is based on authority dominance and personal relations and includes Haiti, Nicaragua, and Paraguay and in the past Trujillo.

41. For life and politics in a rural community under Trujillo see Walker (1972, pp. 11–31).

42. Recent sociological and anthropological studies of local politics and even national politics in many societies have conceptualized them with the term *"clientela"*—from the Italian and Spanish—and described the patterns as "clientelism"; see for example Lemarchand (1972), Lemarchand and Legg (1972), Powell (1970), Heidenheimer (1970), Lande (1965), Leeds (1964), Leff (1968).

Chapter 4: Authoritarian Regimes

43. The descriptive literature on Latin Atnerican politics and particular countries in the area is extensive and we cannot refer to it in detail. A good exposition with country chapters by specialists (with bibliographies) is Needler (1970). See also Anderson (1967), with special emphsasis on the relation between politics and economic development. R. H. McDonald (1971) is informative on party systems and elections. See also our notes in this chapter on military in politics, corporativism, and Mexican politics. On the problems of instability see Kling (1956) and chapters in Linz and Stepan (1978).

There are a number of books on Middle East politics (Binder, 1964; Halpern, 1963; Karpat, 1968; Hurewitz, 1969; Abboushi, 1970; Rustow, 1971; Landau, 1972) that provide a wealth of descriptive information, bibliographic references, and analysis of ideological tendencies. These works and those on Egypt and the Maghreb (see note 60), particularly Morocco (see note 39), should provide the basis for a more comparative and theoretical analysis of the authoritarian regimes in Islamic societies and the variety of patterns of transition from traditional or colonial rule to more modern political systems in them. Our focus in this chapter precludes discussion of the link between cultural traditions, values, and even a culture-personality-psychological approach to the emergence of authoritarian rule in these societies in contrast to, let us say, the Hispanic or Southeast Asian societies, which would complement our analysis. For reviews of Southeast Asian politics see Kahin (1964) and Pye (1967).

44. The comparative study of communist systems and the variety of theoretical approaches has a long tradition; for recent bibliographic essays see Cohen and Shapiro (1974, pp. xix–xliv) and Shoup (1971). Kanet (1971), after others like Tucker (1969) and Fleron (1969), has argued that the study of communist systems should be incorporated more into a broader comparative framework. Without rejecting this point we would argue that a more systematic

theoretical comparative analysis of communist systems, not limited to the USSR and Eastern Europe or to paired comparisons of the USSR and China like those in the volume edited by Treadgold (1967) and implicitly in the better monographs on China, but including Cuba, North Vietnam, and North Korea, would be perhaps a prior step. The different phases in those regimes could provide us with even greater opportunities for "multivariate" comparative study, like the paper by Yeh (1967) on industrialization strategies in the USSR 1928–37 and China 1953–62. Area specialization, perhaps imposed by the linguistic skills required and the difficulties of access to data, has been an obstacle to such an effort. Cuba for example has attracted mostly the attention of American sympathizers and critics, French leftists, and a few Latin Americanists, but almost no students of other communist regimes. It has been the object of descriptive-historical studies (Huberman and Sweezy, 1969; Draper, 1965; Suárez, 1967; Dumont, 1970; Karol, 1970; Thomas, 1971; Halperin, 1972) and of collections of papers edited by MacGaffey and Barnett (1965), Mesa Lago (1971), and Horowitz (1972). Except for a study by Tang and Maloney (1962) on the Chinese impact and the greater similarity in patterns of participation with China than the Soviets (Fagen, 1969, p. 259), there has been little effort to study the regime in a comparative perspective, even among communist countries. The charismatic authority of Castro (Fagen, 1965; Lockwood, 1967), the relatively slow institutionalization of the party organization, the shifts in policy, the dependence on the USSR, the U.S. hostility, the growing militarization (Dumont, 1970; Domínguez, 1974), and the highly polemical responses to the revolution have probably contributed to this lack of comparative analyses.

It is impossible to present here an adequate bibliography on communist China. For a basic list of sources, Berton and Wu (1967), Schurmann (1968), Waller (1971, pp. 172–82). The excellent collections of papers edited by Treadgold (1967), Barnett (1969), Baum (1971), Lindbeck (1971), and Scalapino (1972), and the *Handbook* edited by Wu (1973) can serve as introduction to the best scholarship, in addition to monographs quoted in this essay, like those of Lewis (1963), Townsend (1972). Vogel (1971), and the classic works of Schram (1967. 1969) on Mao and his thought.

A useful review is Shaffer (1967), with chapters by Marxist and non-Marxist authors, including countries generally neglected (like Albania, Korea, Vietnam, Mongolia) in a comparative analysis, and bibliographic references. particularly to specialized periodicals.

45. On the long-lived Estado Novo of Salazar see Kay (1970), Lucena (1971), Schmitter (1973b, 1974), Wiarda (1974), as well as the primary sources they quote, including basic books on organization of the state published in Portugal.

46. To use the expression of Karl Marx in the *Eighteenth Brumaire of Louis Bonaparte* (1851–52, revised 1869; see 1955 edition, pp. 243–344, especially 333–34). Thalheimer (1930) (quoted from 1968 edition, pp. 19–38) is an interesting application of the ideas of Marx in the *Eighteenth Brumaire* to fascism, more sophisticated than most Marxist, particularly communist, interpretations. See also note 55 for Trotsky's use of "Bonapartism" in the analysis of Stalinism.

47. The difference between mobilizational authoritarianism and the military-bureaucratic variants is well reflected in this quote from a report by Guariglia, Italian ambassador and top Fascist leader, arguing for support for Spanish fascists in May 1933: "We may be at its side. We have to help them for the moment to overcome their purely Catholic, Monarchist and even reactionary prejudices. We must aid them to avoid taking up the ideology of Action Française, and to forget *primoderiverismo*. Military *pronunciamientos* like Sanjurjo's must be avoided. Propaganda among the agricultural and laboring masses is essential. In a word, they must leave behind the antiquated mentality of 1848 revolutionaries, and adopt the modern ideal of unanimous collaboration of all classes, united by the single superior principle of the authority of the State'" (Report of May 16, 1933, quoted by Coverdale, 1975).

48. On the Franco regime after the phase we might describe as "arrested totalitarianism" in addition to Linz (1964, 1970a, 1973a, 1973b) the work of von Beyme (1971), significantly entitled *From Fascist to Development Dictatorship: Power Elite and Opposition in Spain,* and Medhurst (1973) provide excellent overviews. In Spanish, Esteban *et al.* (1973) analyze the constitution from the point of view of possible changes in the system leading to changes of the system. Iglesias Selgas (1968, 1971) offers a useful "orthodox" description. Anderson (1970) analyzes the economic policymaking in the regime and Linz and De Miguel (1966b) study the business community, its formal and informal leadership and the disjunction between both in the corporative institutions, and the realities of organic statism and interest group politics in an authoritarian regime. On local politics and community power see Linz (1970a).

49. Andreski (1954, revised 1968), S. E. Finer (1962), and Janowitz (1964) offered the first systematic and comparative analyses, which should be read together with the collections of papers edited by Huntington (1962), Gutteridge (1965), Van Doorn (1968), Janowitz and Van Doorn (1971), Kelleher (1974), and the work of Feit (1973). An early bibliography is Lang (1965). For a typology of military regimes see Perlmutter (1969). The frequency of intervention in Latin America has led to area-wide analyses from the early writings of Lieuwen (1960, 1964), Germani and Silvert (1961). Johnson (1964) to those of Needler (1966), Horowitz (1967), Putnam (1967), Nun (1969), Ronfeldt (1972), Solaún (1973), Stepan (1973), Schmitter (1973a), and the bibliographic essays of McAlister (1966) and Lowenthal (1974). Among the country monographs we can mention North (1966) on Argentina, Chile, and Peru; Potash (1969), Evers (1972), O'Donnell (1973) on Argentina; Hector (1964) on Argentina and Bolivia; Puhle (1970) also on Bolivia; Stepan (1971, 1973) and Schneider (1971) on Brazil; Gilmore (1964), Needler (1964), Fitch (1973) on Ecuador and Einaudi (1969), Lowenthal (1974) and a 1975 collection of papers edited by him on Peru. Also on Peru and Brazil, Einaudi and Stepan (1971). The interventions and postcoup regimes in the Middle East have been studied by N. Fisher (1963), Hurewitz (1969), and Perlmutter (1970); in Egypt by Vatikiotis (1961) and Dekmejian (1971), in Iraq by Vernier (1963) and Dann (1969). For Indonesia see Feith (1962) and Pauker (1963), and for Korea, Kim (1971). The long history of the army in politics in Spain is covered by Payne (1967) and in the literature mentioned in the note on the origins of the civil war.

50. The literature on Italian corporativism is very extensive and little of it sociological. Among the many sources Sarti (1968, 1970, 1971) deserves special notice, in addition to Aquarone (1965) and Ungari (1963). Among studies published before the end of World War II see Schneider (1928 and 1936), Finer (1935), Schmidt (1938, 1939), Welk (1938). An interesting analysis of how the Italian experience was perceived by different sectors in Germany, from Conservatives to Nazis, see Hoepke (1968). For a contrast among the Catholic, Fascist, and Nationalist corporativist ideologies see Vallauri (1971).

51. The high member apathy and oligarchic control in a variety of voluntary associations, particularly trade unions and professional associations, has been noted by scholars inspired by the work of Michels (for references see Linz, 1966, pp. cv–cxiii).

52. Max Weber (1968), in *Economy and Society,* Vol. 1, pp. 297–99, in the section on "Representation by the Agents of Interest Groups" notes that "as a rule, this kind of representation is propagated with a view toward disenfranchising certain strata: a) either by distributing mandates among the occupations and thus *in fact* disenfranchising the numerically superior masses; or b) by *openly* and *formally* limiting suffrage to the nonpropertied and thus by disenfranchising those strata whose power rests on their economic position (the case of a state of Soviets)." Weber continues commenting on the absence of effective individual leadership in such bodies, the difficulty of reaching non-artificial majority decisions, etc. These patterns obviously reinforce the "non-representative," "non-elective" elements in the political system, that is, the authoritarian nonaccountable elements.

53. France under the Vichy government of Pétain also exemplifies the difference between an authoritarian regime with many characteristics of organic statism and a fascist mobilizational regime desired by some of those supporting it (Paxton, 1972).

54. On the three-cornered competition for power among the state—controlled by fascists, it is true, in alliance with the bureaucracy—the party organization and the *corporazioni,* as well as interests and ideological tendencies within them, ultimately decided in favor of the first, see Aquarone (1965, chapters 3 and 4, particularly pp. 151, 164–65, 188–89; and for those who argued that the *corporazioni* should substitute the party, pp. 220–21). On the conflicts between state and party, specifically the prefects and provincial party leaders, see pp. 262–63.

55. Significantly, Trotsky (1937, pp. 278–79), in attempting to describe and analyze Stalinism also uses the term "Bonapartism" in this text. We cannot resist quoting since it also reflects his view of the symmetry of Stalinism and Fascism "in spite of deep differences in social foundations."

> Bonapartism is one of the political weapons of the capitalist regime in its critical period. Stalinism is a variety of the same system, but upon the basis of a workers' state torn by the antagonism between an organized and armed soviet aristocracy and the unarmed toiling masses. . . .
>
> In the last analysis, Soviet Bonapartism owes its birth to the belatedness of the world revolution. But in the capitalist countries the

same cause gave rise to fascism. We thus arrive at the conclusion, un-expected at first glance, but in reality inevitable, that the crushing of Soviet democracy by an all-powerful bureaucracy and the extermina-tion of bourgeois democracy by fascism were produced by one and the same cause: the dilatoriness of the world proletariat in solving the problems set for it by history. Stalinism and fascism, in spite of a deep difference in social foundations, are symmetrical phenomena. In many of their features they show a deadly similarity. A victorious rev-olutionary movement in Europe would immediately shake not only fascism, but Soviet Bonapartism.

56. The literature on national socialism as an ideology, a movement and a party in power fills libraries. For a bibliography see Herre and Auerbach and supplement edited by Thile Vogelsang *Vierteljahrshefte für Zeitgeschichte* (since 1953). Basic in English is Bracher (1970), with bibliography, pp. 503–33. For annotated critical bibliography, Orlow (1969, 1973). See also Bracher and Jacobsen (1970). Useful reviews are Broszat (1966), Nolte (1963), the anthologies of documents with introductions by Hofer (1957), Remak (1969), and Noakes and Pridham (1974), and for the period 1933–35, Wheaton (1969). Still indispensable is the classic work by Franz Neumann (1963; origi-nally published 1944), *Behemoth*. An interesting overview of German politics, society, and culture under the Nazis is Grunberger (1971). For excellent bio-graphical sketches of the Nazi leadership, Fest (1970). To place Nazism in the context of German society and history see Dahrendorf (1965). An excellent documentary collection is Tyrell (1969). A most stimulating review of conflict-ing or complementary interpretations of Nazism is Sauer (1967).

57. In addition to the more sophisticated Marxist analyses of fascism we cannot ignore the partisan interpretations of Aquila, Zetkin, Togliatti, Dutt dis-cussed by Nolte (1967). De Felice (1969, 1970), and Gregor (1974b), the Trot-skyite Guerin (1939), and more recent writings of Lopukhov (1965), Galkin (1970), and Vajda (1972), reviewed by Gregor (1974c, pp. 129–70), as well as the responses of the Third International (Fetscher, 1962; Pirker, 1965).

58. The relation of fascism to modernization is a complex issue, object of a recent debate (Turner, 1972; Gregor, 1974c). See also Organski (1965) and the early essay by Borkenau (1933).

59. The politics of particular countries have been the object of mono-graphic study, although sometimes with little effort of comparison and theo-retical conceptualization; see for example on the Ivory Coast, in addition to Zolberg (1969), Potholm (1970, pp. 230–71) for a more critical view, and for a comparison of the PDCI with Tanzania's TANU, Zeller (1969); on Mali, Snyder (1965); on Sierra Leone, Cartwright (1970); on Madagascar, Spacen-sky (1970); on Guinea under the leadership of Sékou Touré, one of the few mobilizational single-party regimes left, see Ameillon (1964), Charles (1962), Voss (1971), and Zolberg (1966). On the authoritarian regime established in Congo (Zaire) by Mobutu after years of turmoil there is an interesting study (using the concept of patrimonialism) by Willame (1972).

60. The Maghreb and the Middle East countries after independence have experimented with military and single-party mobilizational regimes in addition

to the survival of semitraditional rulers (like Morocco, see note 39). For an overview see Clement Moore (1970b) and Hurewitz (1969), who distinguishes in the Middle East military republics, military-civilian coalitions, traditional monarchies, modernizing monarchies, and nonmilitary republics. The most stable civilian single-party regime born in the struggle for independence has been Tunisia under the personal leadership of Bour-guiba (Clement Moore 1965, 1970a; Camau, 1971; Hermassi, 1972), while Algeria, initially a mobilizational party regime, had from the beginning—due to the prolonged war with the French—a military component, which gained the upper hand when Boumedienne ousted Ben Bella (Quandt, 1969; Duprat, 1973). In Iraq (Vernier, 1963; Dann, 1969) and Syria (for bibliographic references see Hurewitz, 1969, p. 520), where the ideological Baathist party had considerable impact in alliance with the army, the military have attempted, like in Egypt, to create nationalist-socialist-populist mobilizational regimes, but ultimately personal rulership, the military and bureaucratic technocratic elements seem to have become dominant. The fate of the socialist Baath party has not been too different from minor fascist parties in authoritarian regimes. Ethnic and religious heterogeneity contributed to the instability of these regimes.

The politics of Egypt since the military coup against the monarchy, under Naguib, Nasser, and Sadat, has been the object of considerable analysis and debate. Among the main studies, Vatikiotis (1961), Lacouture and Lacouture (1958), Lacouture (1969), Wheelock (1960), Abdel-Malek (1968, first published 1962), Binder (1965), Moore (1970, 1973, 1974), Dekmejian (1971), Kosheri Mahfouz (1972), and Harik (1973) deserve mention. It is a perfect example of the changes "within" a regime approaching changes "of" the regime, from strictly military rule to the complex, shifting, and indecisive attempts to create a mobilizational single party, from a military mentality to efforts to develop an ideology, from popular passivity to efforts to create channels of participation. It shows the range of possibilities of change but also the difficulties of change within the framework of an authoritarian regime established by the army.

61. The case of Nkrumah, who moved from charismatic leadership to personal rulership with the forms of a single-party mobilizational authoritarian regime (that some perceived as totalitarian in ambitions), is an example of how even the period of rule of one person cannot be pigeonholed into a typology but how different conceptualizations can serve the analysis; Wallerstein (1961), Apter (1963), Bretton (1966), Fitch and Oppenheimer (1966).

62. For references to different patterns of colonialism see Potholm (1970), pp. 70–77.

63. A decisive factor in the potential for mobilization, control, and participation of new regimes—and with it for totalitarianism—is the strength of the party conquering power before takeover. Let us not forget that the Italian Fascists in March 1921 already had 80,476 members, in December claimed 218,453, and by May 1922, 322,310 (the March on Rome would be at the end of October) (De Felice, 1966, pp. 10–11), even though those members were mostly north of Rome. The NSDAP in 1930 had 129,563 and on January 30, 1933, on the eve of the Machtergreifung, 719,446 (Schäfer, 1957, p. 17); the Hitler Youth at the end of 1931 had already organized 5.1 percent of those

eligible (Orlow, 1969, p. 237). That kind of support can obviously be gained only in an open and relatively modern society, or one undergoing total disintegration, when war and revolution combine, like in Russia, Yugoslavia, China, and Vietnam.

64. In the context of the application to communist systems in Eastern Europe, including the Soviet Union, of the interest-group politics approach, the early and still very fruitful alternatives of "technical-rational traditionalist and ideological revolutionary'" models of development offered by Barrington Moore (1954) have unfortunately been somewhat neglected.

65. For two reviews of the literature on convergence see Meyer (1970) and Weinberg (1969). Also, Halm (1969), Linnemann, Pronk, and Tinbergen (1965), Tinbergen (1961), Mills (1958), Sorokin (1964), Wolfe (1968), Black (1970), Aron (1967), and Brzezinski and Huntington (1964, pp. 9–14, 419–36), for a critical discussion of convergence. While far from accepting the convergence theory, the authors point to similarities, functional equivalents, and differences between the U.S. and the USSR in many spheres in a suggestive comparative study.

Chapter 5: The Place of the World's States in the Typology: An Attempt and Its Difficulties

66. A basic source for comparative study of noncompetitive or semi- or pseudocompetitive elections under authoritarian regimes are the *Election Factbooks* for Latin American countries, published by the Institute for the Comparative Study of Political Systems, and the volumes edited by Sternberger and Vogel (1969–).

67. The empirical and systematic study of the organization, function, and composition of political parties (as reflected in the contribution to [the original] *Handbook)* has tended to center on parties in a democratic competitive context (including antisystem parties) and the parties in power in communist noncompetitive regimes and Nazi Germany but has relatively neglected parties in authoritarian pseudo-multiparty, officially single party, and often de facto nonparty regimes. The International Comparative Political Parties Project covering 50 countries at Northwestern University directed by Kenneth Janda (with its careful coding of data and exhaustive bibliographic guides) is filling that gap (including countries like Guinea, Ecuador, Dominican Republic, Congo-Brazzaville, Greece, Iran, and among the communist countries Bulgaria, Hungary, and North Korea of those in our purview).

Chapter 6: Concluding Comments

68. One objection that can legitimately be made to our analysis is that we have focussed on sovereign states, ignoring the clear and not so clear cases of foreign dependence. Certainly we did not include in our purview colonial rule

in all its varieties, from intervention in fiscal affairs of state, protectorate of traditional rulers, to indirect and direct administration by foreigners. Nor have we paid due attention to rule established by a foreign power by the threat of use of force—like the rest-Czech state under the Nazi *Reichsprotektorat*—or the creation of a regime headed by nationals of the country with the military and political assistance of another country, which even after withdrawing its forces exercises influence or veto of its policies and reserves itself the right to intervene by force to sustain the regime.

The satellite regimes that during WWII became identified with the name of Quisling accurately describe that relationship. Such rule of limited or practically no legitimacy is by definition nondemocratic in origin. Continuity, specific successes, and a growing autonomy might transform it into stable regimes not based only on coercion. The delimitation of international spheres of influence and the ideological affinities and personal links between national parties identified with an international movement, particularly in communist states, have contributed to the stabilization of such regimes. Internal political, social, and economic developments, even when not directly decided by the hegemonic power—as they were obviously by Hitler and Stalin—are deeply affected by changes in policy in the dominant power in the bloc or hegemonic area.

In addition there are more subtle types of linkages that affect the internal political development of many states, especially outside the major powers (Rosenau, 1969).

Intervention in internal crises and regime changes is not new, nor is the support for rebels and secessionist independence movements. Since the French Revolution, Napoleon, and the Holy Alliance, outside support on grounds of ideological affinity—not always easy to separate from power politics—has been normal. International parties made their appearance with the revolutionary movements—anarchism and socialism. Later, the ideological affinities created more or less tight relations between parties, from the Comintern and Cominform to the Christian Equipes Internationales and nowadays between nationalist terrorists. At each historical moment one or another successful regime kindles the admiration and desire of imitation by people in many countries, and without such an external reference internal political developments can not be understood. International and internation organizations have attempted to influence the development of regimes by mediation, nonrecognition, exclusion, political economic boycott, peace-keeping forces, etc., with varying degrees of success. Other nations, international movements, or organizations under their influence are therefore factors in the establishment of totalitarian, authoritarian, and on rare occasions democratic regimes, which we cannot ignore (even when we cannot discuss them here).

69. De facto, however, the process often leads to a more personal rule of the leader or the executive, who appoints, intervenes, or controls all institutions, preventing independent leadership and real institutional autonomy, but is without resources (given the deliberation of the single party) for mobilization of support and dynamic social change. These processes have been well described by Aquarone (1965).

BIBLIOGRAPHY

Abboushi, W. F. (1970). *Political Systems of the Middle East in the 20th Century*. New York: Dodd, Mead.

Abdel-Malek, Anouar (1968). *Egypt: Military Society. The Army Regime, the Left, and Social Change under Nasser*. New York: Random House (Vintage).

Abendroth, Wolfgang (1969). *Faschismus und Kapitalismus: Theorien über die sozialen Ursprünge und die Funktion des Faschismus*. Frankfurt: Europäische Verlagsanstalt.

Abraha, Gedamu (1967). "Wax and gold." *Ethiopian Observer* (Addis Ababa) 11:226–43.

Adam, Heribert (1971). *Modernizing Racial Domination: The Dynamics of South African Politics*. Berkeley: University of California Press.

Adorno, Theodor W., Else Frenkel-Brunswick, Daniel J. Levinson, and R. Nevitt Sanford (1964). *The Authoritarian Personality*, 2 vols. New York: Wiley.

Allen, Richard V., ed. (1968, 1969). *Yearbook on International Communist Affairs*. Stanford: Hoover Institution Press.

Allen, Williams Sheridan (1965). *The Nazi Seizure of Power: The Experience of a Single German Town 1930–1935*. Chicago: Quadrangle Books.

——— (1975). "The Appeal of Fascism and the Problem of National Disintegration." In Henry A. Turner, Jr. *Reappraisals of Fascism*. New York: New Viepoints/Franklin Watts.

Almond, Gabriel, and James S. Coleman, eds. (1960). *The Politics of the Developing Areas*. Princeton: Princeton University Press.

Almond, Gabriel, and G. Bingham Powell (1966). *Comparative Politics: A Developmental Approach*. Boston: Little, Brown.

Ameillon, B. (1964). *La Guinée: Bilan d'une Independence*. Paris: Maspero.

Anderson, Charles W. (1967). *Politics and Economic Change in Latin America: The Governing of Restless Nations*. New York: Van Nostrand Reinhold.

——— (1970a). "Nicaragua: The Somoza Dynasty." In Martin Needler (ed.), *Political Systems of Latin America*. New York: Van Nostrand Reinhold.

—— (1970b). *The Political Economy of Modern Spain.* Madison: University of Wisconsin Press.

Andreski, Stanislav (1968). *Military Organization and Society.* Berkeley: University of California Press.

The Anti-Stalin Campaign and International Communism (1956). New York: Columbia University Press.

Apter, David E. (1963). *Ghana in Transition.* New York: Atheneum.

—— (1965). *The Politics of Modernization.* Chicago: University of Chicago Press.

Aquarone, Alberto (1965). *L'organizzazione dello Stato totalitario.* Torino: Einaudi. Quoted by permission.

Arendt, Hannah (1963). *Eichmann in Jerusalem: A Report on the Banality of Evil.* New York: Viking Press.

—— (1966). *The Origins of Totalitarianism.* New York: Harcourt, Brace & World.

Armstrong, John A. (1967). *The Soviet Bureaucratic Elite: A Case Study of the Ukrainian Apparatus.* New York: Praeger.

Aron, Raymond (1967). *The Industrial Society: Three Essays on Ideology and Development.* New York: Praeger.

—— (1968). *Democracy and Totalitarianism.* London: Weidenfeld and Nicolson.

Ashford, Douglas E. (1961). *Political Change in Morocco.* Princeton: Princeton University Press.

—— (1965a). *The Elusiveness of Power: The African Single Party State.* Ithaca, N.Y.: Center for International Studies, Cornell University.

—— (1965b). *Morocco-Tunisia: Politics and Planning.* New York: Syracuse University Press.

—— (1967). *National Development and Local Reform: Political Participation in Morocco, Tunisia and Pakistan.* Princeton: Princeton University Press.

Azpiazu, Joaquín (1951). *El Estado Corporativo.* Madrid: Fomento Social.

Azrael, Jeremy R. (1966). *Managerial Power and Soviet Politics.* Cambridge, Mass.: Harvard University Press.

—— (1970a). "Varieties of de-Stalinization." In Chalmers Johnson (ed.), *Change in Communist Systems.* Stanford: Stanford University Press.

—— (1970b). "The internal dynamics of the CPSU, 1917–1967." In S. Huntington and C. Moore (eds.), *Authoritarian Politics in Modern Society.* New York: Basic Books.

Bachrach, Peter (1967). *The Theory of Democratic Elitism: A Critique.* Boston: Little, Brown.

Baier, Helmut (1968). *Die Deutschen Christian Bayerns im Rahmen des bayerischen Kirchenfampfes.* Nürenberg: Verein für bayerische Kirchengeschichte.

Banks, Arthur S., and Robert B. Textor (1963). *A Cross-Polity Survey.* Cambridge, Mass.: M.I.T. Press.

Banks, Arthur S., and Phillip M. Gregg (1965). "Grouping political systems: Q-factor analysis of *A Cross-Polity Survey.*" *American Behavioral Scientist* 9:3–6.

Barber, Benjamin (1969). "Conceptual foundations of totalitarianism." In Carl J. Friedrich, M. Curtis, and B. Barber (eds.), *Totalitarianism in Perspective: Three Views*. New York: Praeger.

Barghoorn, Frederick G. (1971). "The security police." In H. Gordon Skilling and F. Griffiths (eds.), *Interest Groups in Soviet Politics*. Princeton: Princeton University Press.

——— (1972). *Politics in the USSR*. Boston: Little, Brown.

——— (1973). "Factional, sectoral, and subversive opposition in Soviet politics." In Rohert A. Dahl (ed.), *Regimes and Oppositions*. New Haven: Yale University Press.

Barnett, A. Doak, ed. (1969). *Chinese Communist Politics in Action*. Seattle: University of Washington Press.

Bärnthaler, Irmgard (1971). *Die Vaterländische Front: Geschichte und Organisation*. Vienna: Europa Verlag.

Barton, Allen H., Bogdan Denitch, and Charles Kadushin, eds. (1973). *Opinion-Making Elites in Yugoslavia*. New York: Praeger.

Bauer, Raymond A., Alex Inkeles, and Clyde Kluckholn (1956). *How the Soviet System Works*. Cambridge, Mass.: Harvard University Press.

Bauer, Otto, Herbert Marcuse, Arthur Rosenberg et al. (1968). *Faschismus und Kapitalismus*. Frankfurt: Europäische Verlag.

Baum, Richard, ed. (1971). *China in Ferment: Perspectives on the Cultural Revolution*. Englewood Cliffs, N.J.: Prentice-Hall.

Baylis, Thomas A. (1974). *The Technical Intelligentsia and the East German Elite: Legitimacy and Social Change in Mature Communism*. Berkeley: University of California Press.

Beck, Carl (1970). "Career characteristics of Eastern European leadership." In R. Barry Farrell (ed.), *Political Leadership in Eastern Europe and the Soviet Union*. Chicago: Aldine.

Beck, F., and W. Godin [pseuds.] (1951). *Russian Purge and the Extraction of Confession*. New York: Viking.

Behrman, Lucy G. (1970). *Muslim Brotherhoods and Politics in Senegal*. Cambridge, Mass.: Harvard University Press.

Bell, Daniel (1961). "Ten theories in search of Soviet reality." In Alex Inkeles and Kent Geiger (eds.), *Soviet Society: A Book of Readings*. Boston: Houghton Mifflin.

Bendix, Reinhard (1960). *Max Weber: An Intellectual Portrait*. Garden City, N.Y.: Doubleday.

———, ed. (1968). *State and Society: A Reader in Comparative Political Sociology*. Boston: Little, Brown.

Berdyaev, Nicholas (1948). *The Origin of Russian Communism*. London: Geoffrey Bles.

Berghahn, Volker R. (1969). NSDAP und 'Geistige Führung' der Wehrmacht 1939–1943." *Vierteljahrshefte für Zeitgeschichte* 7:17–71.

Berman, Harold J. (1963). *Justice in the USSR*. New York: Random House (Vintage).

——— (1972). *Soviet Criminal Law and Procedure: The RSFSR Codes*. Cambridge, Mass.: Harvard University Press.

Berman, Harold J., and James W. Spindler (1972) *Soviet Criminal Law and Procedure: The RSFSR Codes*. Cambridge, Mass.: Harvard University Press.

Berning, Cornelia (1964). *Vom "Abstamnmungsnachweis" zum "Zuchtwart":*
Vokabular des Nationalsozialismus. Berlin: de Gruyter.
Berton, Peter, and Eugene Wu (1967). *Contemporary China: A Research*
Guide. Stanford: Hoover Institution on War, Revolution and Peace, Stan-
ford University.
Bettelheim, Bruno, and Morris Janowitz (1950). *Dynamics of Prejudice*. New
York: Harper.
Beyme, Klaus von (1971). *Vom Faschismus zur Entwicklungsdiktatur: Mach-*
telite und Opposition in Spanien. Munich: R. Piper.
Bienen, Henry, ed. (1968). *The Military Intervenes: Case Studies in Political*
Development. New York: Russell Sage Foundation.
——— (1970). *Tanzania*. Princeton: Princeton University Press.
——— (1974). "Military and society in East Africa: thinking again about
praetorianism." *Comparative Politics* 6:489–517.
Binder, Leonard (1962). *Iran: Political Development in a Changing Society*.
Berkeley: University of California Press.
——— (1964). *The Ideological Revolution in the Middle East*. New York:
Wiley.
——— (1965). "Egypt: the integrative revolution." In L. W. Pye and S. Verba
(eds.), *Political Culture and Political Development*. Princeton: Princeton
University Press.
Black, Cyril, ed. (1967). *The Transformation of Russian Society: Aspects of*
Social Change since 1861. Cambridge, Mass.: Harvard University Press.
———, (1970). "Marx and modernization." *Slavic Review* 29:182–86.
Black, Cyril E., and Thomas P. Thornton, eds. (1964). *Communism and Revo-*
lution: The Strategic Uses of Political Violence. Princeton: Princeton Uni-
versity Press.
Blackmer, Donald L. M. (1968). *Unity in Diversity: Italian Communism and*
the Communist World. Cambridge, Mass.: M.I.T. Press.
Blackmer, Donald L. M., and Sidney Tarrow, eds. (1975). *Communism in Italy*
and France. Princeton: Princeton University Press.
Bloch, Charles (1970). *Die SA und die Krise des NS-Regimes 1934*. Frankfurt
am Main: Suhrkamp Verlag.
Blondel, Jean (1972). *Comparing Political Systems*. New York: Praeger.
Boberach, Heinz, ed. (1965). *Meldungen aus dem Reich: Auswahl aus den*
geheimen Lageberichten des Sicherheitsdienstes der SS 1939–1944.
Neuwied: Luchterhand.
Borkenau, Franz (1933). "Zur Soziologie des Faschismus." In Ernst Nolte
(ed.), *Theorien über den Faschismus*. Cologne: Kiepenheuer & Witsch.
Bourdeaux, Michael (1968). *Religious Ferment in Russia: Protestant Opposi-*
tion to Soviet Religious Policy. New York: St. Martin's Press.
——— (1969). *Patriarch and Prophets: Persecution of the Russian Orthodox*
Church Today. London: Macmillan.
Bourricaud, François (1967). *Pouvoir et société dans le Pérou cotemporain*.
Paris: Colin.
Bowen, Ralph H. (1947). *German Theories of the Corporate State*. New York:
Russell & Russell.

Bracher, Karl Dietrich (1957). *Die Auflösung der Weimarer Republik: Eine Studie zum Problem des Machverfalls in der Demokratie.* Stuttgart: Ring.

——— (1970). *The German Dictatorship.* New York: Praeger.

Bracher, Karl Dietrich, amid Hans-Adolf Jacobsen, eds. (1970). *Bibliographic zur Politik in Theorie und Praxis.* Düsseldorf: Droste Verlag.

Bracher, Karl Dietrich, Wolfgang Sauer, and Gerhard Schulz (1960). *Die nationalsozialistische Machtergreifung: Studien zur Errichtung des totalitären Herrschaftssystems in Deutschland 1933/34.* Cologne: Westdeutscher Verlag.

Bradenburg, Frank R. (1964). *The Making of Modern Mexico.* Englewood Cliffs: Prentice-Hall.

Brandenburg, Hans-Christian (1968). *HJ-Die Geschichte der HJ.* Cologne: Wissenschaft u. Politik.

Brenner, Hildegard (1963). *Die Kunstpolitik des Nationalsozialismus.* Reinbek bei Hamburg: Rowohlt.

Bretton, Henry L. (1966). *The Rise and Fall of Kwame Nkrumah: A Study of Personal Rule in Africa.* New York: Praeger.

——— (1971). *Patron-Client Relations: Middle Africa and the Powers.* New York: General Learning Press.

——— (1973). *Power and Politics in Africa.* Chicago: Aldine.

Broszat, Martin (1966). *German National Socialism, 1919–1945.* Santa Barbara: Clio Press.

Brown, J. F. (1966). *The New Eastern Europe: The Khrushchev Era and After.* New York: Praeger.

Brzezinski, Zbigniew (1956). *The Permanent Purge.* Cambridge, Mass.: Harvard University Press.

——— (1960). *The Soviet Bloc.* Cambridge, Mass.: Harvard University Press. Enlarged and revised paperback edition, 1971.

——— (1962). *Ideology and Power in Soviet Politics.* New York: Praeger.

——— (1971). *The Soviet Bloc: Unity and Conflict.* Cambridge, Mass.: Harvard University Press.

Brzezinski, Zbigniew, and Samuel P. Huntington (1964). *Political Power: USA/USSR.* New York: Viking Press.

Buchheim, Hans (1953). *Glaubenskrise im Dritten Reich: Drei Kapitel Nationalsozialistischer Religionspolitik.* Stuttgart: Deutsche Verlags-Anstalt.

——— (1958). "Mitgliedschaft bei der NSDAP." In Paul Kluke (ed.), *Gutachten des Instituts für Zeitgeschichte.* Munich: Institut für Zeitgeschichte.

——— (1968a). *Totalitarian Rule: Its Nature and Characteristics.* Middletown, Conn.: Wesleyan University Press.

——— (1968b). "Command and compliance." In Helmut Krausnik, Hans Buchheim, Martin Broszat, and Hans-Adolf Jacobsen (eds.), *Anatomy of the SS State.* New York: Walker.

Bullock, Alan (1964). *Hitler: A Study in Tyranny.* New York: Harper & Row.

Bundesministerium für Gesamtdeutsche Fragen (1963). *Die Wahlen in der Sowjetzone: Dokumente und Materialien.* Bonn: Deutscher Bundes-Verlag.

Burke, Melvin, and James Malloy (1972). "Del Populismo Nacional al Corpo-rativismo Nacional: El caso de Bolivia 1952–1970." *Aportes* 26:66–97.

Burks, R. V. (1961). *Time Dynamics of Communism in Eastern Europe.* Prince-ton: Princeton University Press.

Burks, R. V., and S. A. Stanković (1967). "Jugoslawien auf dem Weg zu halb-freien Wahlen?" *Osteuropa* 17:131–46.

Burrowes, Robert (1969). "Totalitarianism: the revised standard version." *World Politics* 21:272–94.

Bush, Richard C., Jr. (1970). *Religion in Communist China.* Nashville: Abing-don Press.

Busshoff, Heinrich (1968). *Das Dollfuss-Regime in Österreich in geistes-geschichtlicher Perspektive unter besonderer Berücksichtigung der "Schöneren Zukinft" und "Reichspost."* Berlin: Duncker & Humblot.

Butler, Rohan (1941). *The Roots of National Socialism 1783–1933.* London: Faber and Faber.

Camau, Michel (1971). *La notion de démocratie dans la pensée des dirigeants maghrébins.* Paris: CNRS.

Cardoso, Fernando Henrique (1973). "'As contradiçoes do Desenvolvimento-associado." Paper presented at the International Meeting on Sociology of Development: Dependency and Power Structure, Berlin, 1973.

Carr, Raymond, ed. (1971). *The Republic and the Civil War in Spain.* London: Macmillan.

Carsten, Francis L. (1967). *The Rise of Fascism.* Berkeley: University of Cal-ifornia Press.

Carter, Gwendolen M., ed. (1962). *African One-Party States.* Ithaca: Cornell University Press.

Cartwright, John R. (1970). *Politics in Sierra Leone 1947–67.* Toronto: Uni-versity of Toronto Press.

Chapman, Brian (1970). *Police State.* London: Pall Mall.

Charles, Bernard (1962). "'Un parti politique africain: le Parti Démocratique de Guinée." *Revue Française de Science Politique* 12:312–59.

Chen, S. H. (1967). "Artificial 'flowers' during a natural 'thaw.'" In Donald W. Treadgold (ed.), *Soviet and Chinese Communism: Similarities and Differ-ences.* Seattle: University of Washington Press.

Chen, Theodore H. E., ed. (1967). *The Chinese Communist Regime: Docu-ments and Commentary.* New York: Praeger.

Clausewitz, Karl von (1911). *On War,* 3 vols. (Originally published 1832). London: Kegan Paul, Trench, Trübner & Co.

Cliffe, Lionel, ed. (1967). *One-Party Democracy.* Nairobi: East African Pub-lishing House.

Clogg, Richard, and George Yannopoulos, eds. (1972). *Greece under Military Rule.* New York: Basic Books.

Cocks, Paul (1970). "The rationalization of party control." In Chalmers John-son (ed.), *Change in Communist Systems.* Stanford: Stanford University Press.

Cohen, Lenard (1973). "The social background and recruitment of Yugoslav political elites, 1918–1948." In Allen H. Barton, Bogdan Denitch, and

Charles Kadushin (eds.), *Opinion-Making Elites in Yugoslavia.* New York: Praeger.

Cohen, Ronald, and John Middleton, eds. (1957). *Comparative Political Systems: Studies in the Politics of Pre-industrial Societies.* New York: Natural History Press.

Cohn, Norman (1966). *Warrant for Genocide.* New York: Harper & Row.

Coleman, James S., and Carl G. Rosberg, Jr., eds. (1964). *Political Parties and National Integration in Tropical Africa.* Berkeley: University of California Press.

Conde, Francisco Javier (1942). *Introducción al Derecho Político actual.* Madrid: Escorial.

Conquest, Robert (1960). *The Soviet Deportation of Nationalities.* New York: St. Martin's Press.

——— (1968). *The Great Terror: Stalin's Purge of the Thirties.* New York: Macmillan.

Conrad-Martius, Hedwig (1955). *Utopien der Menschenzüchtung: der Sozialdarwinismus und seine Fölge.* Munich: Kösel-Verlag.

Conway, John S. (1968). *The Nazi Persecution of the Churches, 1933–1945.* New York: Basic Books.

Conze, Werner, and Hans Raupach, eds. (1967). *Die Staats- und Wirtschaftskriese des Deutschen Reiches 1929/33.* Stuttgart: E. Klett.

Cornell, Richard (1970). *The Soviet Political System: A Book of Readings.* Englewood Cliffs, N.J.: Prentice-Hall.

Cosío Villegas, Daniel (1972). *El sistema político mexicano: las posibilidades de cambio.* Mexico City: Editorial Joaquin Mortiz.

Cotler, Julio (1972). "Bases del Corporativismo en el Perú." *Sociedad y Política* 1:3–11.

Coverdale, John F. (1975). *Italian Intervention in the Spanish Civil War.* Princeton: Princeton University Press.

Craig, A. M. (1961). *Cho-Shu in the Meiji Restoration.* Cambridge, Mass.: Harvard University Press.

Crassweller, Robert D. (1966). *Trujillo: The Life and Times of a Caribbean Dictator.* New York: Macmillan.

Croan, Melvin (1970). "'Is Mexico the future of East Europe: institutional adaptability and political change in comparative perspective." In S. Huntington and C. Moore (eds.), *Authoritarian Politics in Modern Society.* New York: Basic Books.

Curtis, John S. (1960). "Church and state." In Cyril E. Black (ed.), *The Transformation of Russian Society.* Cambridge, Mass.: Harvard University Press.

Curtis, Michael (1969). "Retreat from totalitarianism." In Carl J. Friedrich, M. Curtis, and Benjamin Barber (eds.), *Totalitarianism in Perspective: Three Views.* New York: Praeger.

Daalder, Hans (1974). "The consociational democracy theme: a review article." *World Politics* 26:604–21.

Daedalus (Winter, 1973). "Post-traditional societies." Essays by several authors.

Dahl, Robert A. (1971). *Polyarchy: Participation and Opposition.* New Haven: Yale University Press.

Dahrendorf, Ralf (1967). *Society and Democracy in Germany.* Garden City, N.Y.: Doubleday.

Dallin, Alexander, and George W. Breslauer (1970). *Political Terror in Communist Systems.* Stanford: Stanford University Press.

Dallin, David J., and Boris I. Nicolaevsky (1947). *Forced Labor in Soviet Russia.* New Haven: Yale University Press.

Daniels, Robert Vincent (1969). *The Conscience of the Revolution: Communist Opposition in Soviet Russia.* New York: Simon & Schuster.

Dann, Uriel (1969). *Iraq under Quassem: A Political History 1958–1963.* New York: Praeger.

Deakin, F. W. (1966). *The Brutal Friendship: Mussolini, Hitler and the Fall of Italian Fascism.* Garden City, N. Y.: Doubleday.

De Felice, Renzo (1965). *Mussolini il rivoluzionario: 1883–1920.* Torino: Einaudi.

—— (1966a). *Mussolini il fascista. I: La conquista del potere. 1921–1925.* Torino: Einaudi.

——, ed. (1966b). *Il Fascismo e I Partiti politici Italiani: Testimonianze del 1921–1923.* Rocca San Casciano: Cappelli.

—— (1968). *Mussolini il fascista. II: L'organizzazione dello Stato fascista. 1925–1929.* Torino: Einaudi.

—— (1969). *Le Interpretazioni del Fascismo.* Bari: Laterza.

—— (1970). *Il Fascismo: Le Interpretazioni dei contemporanei e degli storici.* Bari: Laterza.

Dekmejian, R. Hrair (1971). *Egypt under Nasir: A Study in Political Dynamics.* Albany: State University of New York Press.

Delzell, Charles F., ed. (1970). *Mediterranean Fascism 1919–1945.* New York: Harper & Row.

Diamant, Alfred (1960). *Austrian Catholics and the First Republic: Democracy, Capitalism, and the Social Order, 1918–1934.* Princeton: Princeton University Press.

Díaz, Elías (1974). *Pensamiento español 1939–73.* Madrid: Edicusa.

Dicks, Henry V. (1972). *Licensed Mass Murder: A Socio-Psychological Study of Some SS Killers.* New York: Basic Books.

Diederich, Bernard, and Al Burt (1969). *Papa Doc: The Truth about Haiti Today.* New York: McGraw-Hill.

Domínguez, Jorge I. (1974). "The civic soldier in Cuba." In Catherine McArdle (ed.), *Political-Military Systems: Comparative Perspectives.* Beverly Hills: Sage.

Döring, Hans Joachim (1964). *Die Zigeuner im Nationalsozialistischen Staat.* Hamburg: Kriminalistik Verlag.

Drachkovitch, Milorad M., ed. (1965). *Marxism in the Modern World.* Stanford: Stanford University Press.

Draper, Theodore (1965). *Castroism: Theory and Practice.* New York: Praeger.

Dumont, René (1970). *Cuba est-il socialiste?* Paris: Editions du Seuil.

Duprat, Gérard (1973). *Révolution et autogestion rurale in Algérie.* Paris: A. Colin.

Durkheim, Emile (1902). *De la division du travail social: Etude sur l'organisation des sociétés supérieures.* 2nd ed., with a new preface: "Quelques remarques sur les groupements professionels." Paris: Alcan.

Duverger, Maurice (1963). *Political Parties.* New York: Wiley.

Eckstein, Harry (1966). *Division and Cohesion in Democracy: A Study of Norway.* Princeton: Princeton University Press.

────── (1971). *The Evaluation of Political Performance: Problems and Dimensions.* Beverly Hills: Sage.

Eichholtz, Dietrich (1969). *Geschichte der deutschen Kriegwirtschaft: 1939–1945.* (East) Berlin: Akademie Verlag.

Einaudi, Luigi R. (1969). *The Peruvian Military: A Summary Political Analysis.* Rand Memorandum RM-6048-RC. Santa Monica: The Rand Corporation.

Einaudi, Luigi, and Alfred Stepan (1971). *Latin American Institutional Development: Changing Military Perspectives in Peru and Brazil.* Santa Monica: The Rand Corporation.

Eisenstadt, S. N. (1958). "The study of Oriental despotisms as systems of total power." *The Journal of Asian Studies* 17:435–46.

────── (1959). "Primitive political systems: a preliminary comparative analysis." *American Anthropologist* 61:205–20.

────── (1962). *The Political Systems of Empires.* New York: Free Press of Glencoe.

────── (1967). *Israeli Society.* New York: Basic Books.

──────, ed. (1971). *Political Sociology: A Reader.* New York: Basic Books.

Elbow, Matthew H. (1953). *French Corporative Theory, 1789–1948.* New York: Columbia University Press.

Eschenburg, Theodor, et al. (1966). *The Path to Dictatorship 1918–1933: Ten Essays by German Scholars.* Garden City, N.Y.: Doubleday (Anchor).

Esteban, Jorge de, et al. (1973). *Desarrollo político y Constitución española.* Esplugues de Llobregat, Barcelona: Ariel.

Evans-Pritchard, E. E. (1940). *The Political System of the Annuak of the Anglo Egyptian Sudan.* London: London School of Economics.

────── (1948). *The Divine Kingship of the Shilluk of the Nilotic Sudan.* Cambridge: Cambridge University Press.

Evers, Tilman Tönnies (1972). *Militärregierung in Argentinien.* Frankfurt am Main: A. Metzner Verlag.

Fagen, Richard R. (1965). "Charismatic authority and the leadership of Fidel Castro." *Western Political Quarterly* 18:275–84.

────── (1969). *The Transformation of Political Culture in Cuba.* Stanford: Stanford University Press.

Fagen, Richard R., Richard A. Brody, and Thomas J. O'Leary (1968). *Cubans in Exile: Disaffection and the Revolution.* Stanford: Stanford University Press.

Fagen, Richard R., and William S. Tuohy (1972). *Politics and Privilege in a Mexican City.* Stanford: Stanford University Press.

Fainsod, Merle (1963). *Smolensk under Soviet Rule.* New York: Random House (Vintage).

Fallers, Lloyd A. (1965). *Bantu Bureaucracy: A Century of Political Evolution among the Basoga of Uganda.* Chicago: University of Chicago Press.

Farrell, R. Barry (1970a). "Top political leadership in Eastern Europe." In R. Barry Farrell (ed.), *Political Leadership in Eastern Europe and the Soviet Union.* Chicago: Aldine.

————, ed. (1970b). *Political Leadership in Eastern Europe and the Soviet Union.* Chicago: Aldine.

Faye, Jean Pierre (1972). *Langages totalitaires.* Paris: Hermann.

Fein, Leonard J. (1967). *Politics in Israel.* Boston: Little, Brown.

Feit, Edward (1973). *The Armed Bureaucrats: Military-Administrative Regimes and Political Development.* Boston: Houghton Mifflin.

Feith, Herbert (1962). *The Decline of Constitutional Democracy in Indonesia.* Ithaca: Cornell University Press.

Fernández-Carvajal, Rodrigo (1969). *La Constitución Española.* Madrid: Editora Nacional.

Fest, Joachim C. (1970). *The Face of the Third Reich: Portraits of the Nazi Leadership.* New York: Pantheon Books.

Fetscher, Iring (1962). "Faschismus und Nationalsozialismus: Zur Kritik des sowjet-marxistischen Faschismusbegriffs." *Politische Vierteljahresschrift* 3:42–63.

Finer, Herman (1935). *Mussolini's Italy.* New York: Holt.

Finer, S. E. (1962). *The Man on Horseback: The Role of the Military in Politics.* New York: Praeger.

———— (1971). *Comparative Government.* New York: Basic Books.

Fischer, George (1968). *The Soviet System and Modern Society.* New York: Atherton Press.

Fischer, Sydney Nettleton, ed. (1963). *The Military in the Middle East.* Columbus: Ohio State University Press.

Fishman, Joshua A. (1968). "Some contrast between linguistically homogeneous and linguistically heterogeneous polities." In Joshua A. Fishman, Charles A. Fergurson, and Jyatirindra das Gupta (eds.), *Language Problems of Developing Nations.* New York: Wiley.

Fitch, John S., III (1973). "Toward a model of the coup d'état as a political process in Latin America: Ecuador 1948–1966." Ph.D. dissertation in political science, Yale University.

Fitch, Bob, and Mary Oppenheimer (1966). "Ghana: end of an illusion." *Monthly Review.* 18:1–130.

Fleischman, V. (1971). *Aspekte der Sozialen und Politischen Entwicklung Haitis.* Stuttgart: Klett.

Fleron, Frederic, ed. (1969). *Communist Studies and the Social Sciences: Essays on Methodology and Empirical Theory.* Chicago: Rand McNally.

————, (1970). "Representation of career types in Soviet political leadership." In R. Barry Farrell (ed.), *Political leadership in Eastern Europe and the Soviet Union,* Chicago: Aldine.

Foltz, William J. (1965). *From French West Africa to the Mali Federation.* New Haven: Yale University Press.

Fortes, M., and E. E. Evans-Pritchard, eds. (1940). *African Political Systems.* London: Oxford University Press.

Fraenkel, Ernst (1941). *The Dual State: A Contribution to the Theory of Dictatorship.* New York: Oxford University Press.

Fraga Iribarne, Manuel (1959). *El reglamento de las Cortes Españolas.* Madrid: S.I.P.S.

Friedland, William H., and Carl G. Rosberg, Jr., eds. (1964). *African Social-ism*. Stanford: Stanford University Press.

Friedrich, Carl J., ed. (1954). *Totalitarianism: Proceedings of a Conference held at the American Academy of Arts and Sciences, March 1953*. Cambridge, Mass.: Harvard University Press.

————, (1969). "The evolving theory and practice of totalitarian regimes." In C. Friedrich, Michael Curtis, and Benjamin R. Barber (eds.), *Totalitarianism in Perspective: Three Views*. New York: Praeger.

Friedrich, Carl J., and Zbigniew K. Brzezinski (1965). *Totalitarian Dictatorship and Autocracy*. New York: Praeger.

Fromns, Erich (1941). *Escape from Freedom*. New York: Rinehart.

Galíndez, Jesús de (1973). *The Era of Trujillo Dominican Dictator*. Tuscon: University of Arizona Press,

Galkin, Alexander (1970). "Capitalist society and fascism." *Social Sciences* (Published by the USSR Academy of Sciences) 1:128–38.

Gamm, Hans-Jochen (1962). *Der braune Kult. Das Dritte Reich und seine Ersatzreligion: Ein Beitrag zur politischen Bildung*. Hamburg: Rütten & Loening.

Geertz, Clifford (1968). *Islam Observed: Religious Development in Morocco and Indonesia*. New Haven: Yale University Press.

Geiger, Theodor (1932). *Die soziale Schichtung des deutschen Volkes*. Stuttgart: F. Enke.

Gellner, Ernest, and Charles Micaud, eds. (1972). *Arabs and Berbers: From Tribe to Nation in North Africa*. Lexington: D. C. Heath.

Germani, Gino (1965). *Política y sociedad en una época de transición*. Buenos Aires: Paidos.

———— (1973). "El surgimiento del peronismo: el rol de los obreros y de los migrantes internos." *Desarrollo Económico* 13:435–88.

Germani, Gino, and Kalman Silvert (1961). "Politics, social structure and military intervention in Latin America." *Archives Européennes de Sociologie* 2:62–81.

Germino, Dante L. (1959). *The Italian Fascist Party in Power*. Minneapolis: University of Minnesota Press.

Gibson, Richard (1972). *African Liberation Movements: Contemporary Struggles against White Minority Rule*. London: Oxford University Press.

Gilison, Jerome M. (1970). "Elections, dissent, and political legitimacy." In Richard Cornell (ed.), *The Soviet Political System: A Book of Readings*. Englewood Cliffs, N.J.: Prentice-Hall.

Gilmore, Robert (1964). *Caudillism and Militarism in Venezuela 1810–1910*. Athens, Ohio: Ohio University Press.

Gimbel, John H. (1968). *The American Occupation of Germany: Politics and the Military, 1945–1949*. Stanford: Stanford University Press.

Gitelman, Zvi Y. (1970). "Power and authority in Eastern Europe.'" In Chalmers Jolsnson (ed.), *Change in Communist Systems*. Stanford: Stanford University Press.

Gittings, John (1967). *The Role of the Chinese Army*. London: Oxford University Press.

Gliksman, Jerzy G. (1954). "Social prophylaxis as a form of Soviet terror.'" In Carl J. Friedrich (ed.), *Totalitarianism*. Cambridge, Mass.: Harvard University Press.

Gluckman, Max (1965a). *Politics, Law and Religion in Tribal Society*. Chicago: Aldine.

————— (1965b). *The Ideas of Barotse Jurisprudence*. New Haven: Yale University Press.

González Casanova, Pablo (1970). *Democracy in Mexico*. New York: Oxford University Press.

Gordon, Harold J., Jr. (1972). *Hitler and the Beer Hall Putsch*. Princeton: Princeton University Press.

Görgen, Hans-Peter (1968). "Düsseldorf und der Nationalsozialismus." Dissertation, Cologne University.

Greene, Nathanael, ed. (1968). *Fascism: An Anthology*. New York: Crowell.

Gregor, A. James (1968). *Contemporary Radical Ideologies*. New York: Random House.

————— (1969). *The Ideology of Fascism: The Rationale of Totalitarianism*. New York: Free Press.

————— (1974a). *The Fascist Persuasion in Radical Politics*. Princeton: Princeton University Press.

————— (1974b). *Interpretations of Fascism*. Morristown, N.J.: General Learning Press.

————— (1974c). "Fascism and modernizations: some addenda." *World Politics* 26:370–84.

Gripp, Richard C. (1973). *The Political System of Communism*. New York: Dodd, Mead.

Groth, Alexander J. (1964). "The 'isms' in totalitarianism." *The American Political Science Review* 58:888–901.

Grunberger, Richard (1971). *The 12-Year Reich: A Social History of Nazi Germany 1933–1945*. New York: Holt, Rinehart and Winston.

Gueyt, Rémi (1969). *La mutation tchècoslovaque*. Paris: Editions Ouvrières.

Gulijew, W. E. (1972). *Demokratie und Imperialismus*. East Berlin: Staats-Verlag der Deutschen Demokratschen Republik.

Gutteridge, William F. (1965). *Military Institutions and Power in the New States*. New York: Praeger.

Hale, Oron J. (1964). *The Captive Press in the Third Reich*. Princeton: Princeton University Press.

Halm, George N. (1969). "Will market economies and planned economies converge?" In Erich Streissler (ed.). *Roads to Freedom: Essays in Honor of Friedrich A. von Hayek*. London: Routledge & Kegan Paul.

Halperin, Maurice (1972). *The Rise and Decline of Fidel Castro: An Essay in Contemporary History*. Berkeley: University of California Press.

Halpern, Manfred (1963). *The Politics of Social Change in the Middle East and North Africa*. Princeton: Princeton University Press.

Hamilton, Alastair (1971). *The Appeal of Fascism*. New York: Avon.

————— (1973). *The Appeal of Fascism: A Study of Intellectuals and Fascism 1919–1945*. New York: Avon.

Hammond, Thomas T. (1955). "Yugoslav elections: democracy in small doses." *Political Science Quarterly* 70:57–74.

Hamon, Léo, and Albert Mabileau (1964). *La personnalisation du pouvoir.* Paris: Presses Universitaires de France.

Harasymiw, Bohdan (1972). "Nomeklatura: the soviet communist party's leadership recruitment system." *Canadian Journal of Political Science* 2:493–512.

Harik, Iliya (1973). "The single party as a subordinate movement: the case of Egypt." *World Politics* 26:80–105.

Hartz, Louis (1964). *The Founding of New Societies: Studies in the History of the United States, Latin America, South Africa, Canada and Australia.* New York: Harcourt, Brace and World.

Hayes, Paul M. (1973). *Fascism.* New York: Free Press.

Hayward, Max, and William C. Fletcher eds. (1969). *Religion and the Soviet State.* New York: Praeger.

Hector, Cary (1964). *Der Staatsstreich als Mittel der politischen Entwicklung in Südamerika: Dargestellt am Beispiel Argentiniens und Boliviens von 1930 bis 1955.* Berlin: Colloquium Verlag.

Heidenheimer, Arnold J., ed. (1970). *Political Corruption: Readings in Comparative Analysis.* New York: Holt, Rinehart and Winston.

Hennig, Eike (1973). *Thesen zur deutschen Sozial und Wirtschaftsgeschichte 1933 bis 1938.* Frankfurt/a.M.: Suhrkamp.

Hermassi, Elbaki (1972). *Leadership and National Development in North Africa: A Comparative Study.* Berkeley: University of California Press.

Hermet, Guy (1973). "Les fonctions politiques des organisations religieuses dans les régimes à pluralisme limité." *Revue Française de Science Politique* 23:439–72.

Herre, Vorher F., and H. Auerbach (1955). *Bibliographie zur Zeitgeschichte und zum Zweiten Weltkrieg für die Jahre 1945–1950.* Munich: Instituts für Zeitgeschichte.

Hess, Robert L. (1970). *Ethiopia: The Modernization of Autocracy.* Ithaca: Cornell University Press.

Hess, Robert L., and Gerhard Loewenberg (1964). "The Ethiopian no-party state: a note on the functions of political parties in developing states." *American Political Science Review* 58:947–50.

Heyen, Franz Josef (1967). *Nationalsozialismus im Alltag.* Boppard am Rhein: Harald Beldt Verlag.

Hildebrand, Klaus (1973). *The Foreign Policy of the Third Reich.* London: B. T. Batsford.

Hilferding, Rudolf (1947a). "The modern totalitarian state." *Modern Review* 1:597–605. (First published under the pseudonym Richard Kern, "Die Weltwirtschaft in Kriegsgefahr," *Neuer Vorwärts* 289: January 1939.)

——— (1947b). "State capitalism or totalitarian state economy. (Written in 1940.) *Modern Review* 1:266–71.

Hillgruber, Andreas (1971). *Kontinuität und Diskontinuität in der deutschen Aussenpolitik von Bismarck bis Hitler.* Düsseldorf: Droste Verlag.

Hitler, Adolf (1924–26). *Mein Kampf.* Page references are to the 1943 English edition, translated by Ralph Manheim. Boston: Houghton Mifflin.

Hodgkin, Thomas (1961). *African Political Parties: An Introductory Guide.* Harmondsworth, Middlesex: Penguin Books.

Hoepke, Klaus-Peter (1968). *Die deutsche Rechte und der italienische Faschismus.* Düsseldorf: Droste Verlag.

Hofer, Walther, ed. (1957). *Der Nationalsozialismus: Dokumente 1933–1945.* Frankfurt am Main: Fischer Bücherei.

Hoffmann, Erik P., and Frederic J. Fleron, Jr., eds. (1971). *The Conduct of Soviet Foreign Policy.* Chicago: Aldine-Atherton.

Hoffman, George W., and Fred W. Neal (1962). *Yugoslavia and the New Communism.* New York: Twentieth Century Fund.

Höhne, Heinz (1969). *The Order of the Death's Head: The Story of Hitler's SS.* London: Seeker & Warburg.

Hollander, Gayle D. (1972). *Soviet Political Indoctrination.* New York: Praeger.

Hollander, Paul (1969). *American and Soviet Society.* Englewood Cliffs, N.J.: Prentice-Hall.

———— (1973). *Soviet and American Society: A Comparison.* New York: Oxford University Press.

Hopkins, Raymond F. (1971). *Political Roles in a New State: Tanzania's First Decade.* New Haven: Yale University Press.

Horn, Wolfgang (1972). *Führerideologie und Parteiorganisation in der NSDAP (1919–1933).* Düsseldorf: Droste.

Horowitz, Irving Louis (1967). "The military elites." In S. M. Lipset and A. Solari (eds.), *Elites in Latin America.* New York: Oxford University Press.

————, ed. (1972). *Cuban Communism.* New Brunswick, N.J.: Transaction Books.

Horvat, Branko (1969). *An Essay on Yugoslav Society.* White Plains, N.Y.: International Arts and Sciences Press.

Hough, Jerry F. (1969). *The Soviet Prefects: The Local Party Organs in Industrial Decision-making.* Cambridge, Mass.: Harvard University Press.

———— (1971). "The party apparatchiki." In H. Gordon Skilling and Franklyn Griffiths (eds.), *Interest Groups in Soviet Politics.* Princeton: Princeton University Press.

———— (1974). "The Soviet system: petrification or pluralism?" In Lenard J. Cohen and Jane P. Shapiro (eds.), *Communist Systems in Comparative Perspective.* Garden City, N.Y.: Doubleday (Anchor).

Huberman, Leo, and Paul M. Sweezy (1969). *Cuba: Anatomy of a Revolution.* New York: Monthly Review Press.

Huntington, Samuel P. (1956). "Civilian control of the military: a theoretical statement." In H. Eulau, S. Eldersveld, and M. Janowitz (eds.), *Political Behaviour: A Reader in Theory and Research.* New York: Free Press.

————, ed. (1962). *Changing Patterns of Military Politics.* New York: Free Press.

———— (1964). *The Soldier and the State: The Theory and Politics of Civil-Military Relations.* New York: Random House (Vintage).

———— (1968). *Political Order in Changing Societies.* New Haven: Yale University Press.

———— (1970). "Social and institutional dynamics of one-party systems." In S. P. Huntington and C. H. Moore (eds.), *Authoritarian Politics in Modern Society.* New York: Basic Books.

Huntington, Samuel P., and Clement H. Moore (1970). "Conclusion: authoritarianism, democracy, and one-party politics." In S. P. Huntington and C. H. Moore (eds.), *Authoritarian Politics in Modern Society.* New York: Basic Books.

Hurewitz, J. C. (1969). *Middle East Politics: The Military Dimension.* New York: Praeger.

Iglesias Selgas, Carlos (1968). *La via española a la democracia.* Madrid: Ediciones del Movimiento.

────── (1971). *Comentarios a la Ley Sindical.* Madrid: Cabal.

Inkeles, Alex (1954). "The totalitarian mystique: some impressions of the dynamics of totalitarian society." In Carl J. Friedrich (ed.), *Totalitarianism.* Cambridge, Mass.: Harvard University Press.

Inkeles, Alex, and Raymond A. Bauer (1959). *The Soviet Citizen: Daily Life in a Totalitarian Society.* Cambridge, Mass.: Harvard University Press.

Inkeles, Alex, and Kent Geiger, eds. (1961). *Soviet Society: A Book of Readings.* Boston: Houghton Mifflin.

Institut für Zeitgeschichte (1958). *Gutachten des Instituts für Zeitgeschichte.* Münich: Institut für Zeitgeschichte.

Institute for the Comparative Study of Political Systems, A Division of Operations and Policy Research Inc. (from 1962 onwards). *Election Factbook* . . . (for different countries and dates). Washington, D.C.

International Journal of Politics (1973). Vol. 2, no, 4. "Critiques of fascism theory from the West German New Left." Several essays.

Ionescu, Ghita (1967). *The Politics of the European Communist States.* New York: Praeger.

Jäckel, Eberhard (1972). *Hitler's Weltanschauung. A Blueprint for Power.* Middletown: Wesleyan University Press.

Jackson, Gabriel (1965). *The Spanish Republic and the Civil War 1931–1939.* Princeton: Princeton University Press.

Jacobsen, Hans-Adolf (1968). *Nationalsozialistische Aussenpolitik 1933–1938.* Frankfurt a.M.: A. Metzner.

Jacobson, Jason, ed. (1972). *Soviet Communism and the Socialist Vision.* New Brunswick, N.J.: New Politics Publishing Company.

Jäger, Herbert (1967). *Verbrechen unter Totalitärer Herrschaft. Studien zur nationalsozialistischen Gewaltkriminalität.* Olten: Walter-Verlag.

James, Robert Rhodes, ed. (1969). *The Czechoslovak Crisis, 1968.* London: Weidenfeld and Nicolson.

Janda, Kenneth, ed. (1972). "International Comparative Political Parties Project: ICPP variables and coding manual." Multilith. Evanston: Northwestern University.

Jänicke, Martin (1971). *Totalitäre Herrschaft. Anatomie eines politischen Begriffes.* Berlin: Duncker & Humblot.

Janos, Andrew C. (1970a). "The one-party state and social mobilization: East Europe between the wars." In S. Huntington and C. Moore (eds.), *Authoritarian Politics in Modern Society.* New York: Basic Books.

────── (1970b). "Group politics in communist society: a second look at the pluralistic model." In S. Huntington and C. Moore (eds.), *Authoritarian Politics in Modern Society.* New York: Basic Books.

Janowitz, Morris (1964). *The Military in the Political Development of New Nations: An Essay in Comparative Analysis.* Chicago: University of Chicago Press.

—— (1971). *On Military Intervention.* Rotterdam: Rotterdam University Press.

Janowitz, Morris, and Jacques Van Doorn, eds. (1971). *On Military Ideology.* Rotterdam: Rotterdam University Press.

Jansen, M. B. (1961). *Sakamoto, Ryoma and the Meiji Restoration.* Princeton: Princeton University Press.

Jasper, Gotthard, ed. (1968). *Von Weimar zu Hitler, 1930–1933.* Cologne: Kiepenheuer & Witsch.

Joffe, Ellis (1965). *Party and Army-Professionalism and Political Control in the Chinese Officer Corps, 1949–1964.* Cambridge, Mass.: Harvard University East Asian Research Center.

—— (1971). "The Chinese army under Lin Piao: prelude to political intervention.'" In J. M. H. Lindbeck (ed.), *China: Management of a Revolutionary Society.* Seattle: University of Washington Press.

Johe, Werner, ed. (1967). *Die gleichgeschaltete Justiz.* Frankfurt: Europäische Verlaganstalt.

Johnson, Chalmers, ed. (1970). *Change in Communist Systems.* Stanford: Stanford University Press.

Johnson, John J. (1964). *The Military and Society in Latin America.* Stanford: Stanford University Press.

Johnson, Priscilla, and Leopold Labedz, eds. (1965). *Khrushchev and the Arts: The Politics of Soviet Culture, 1962–1964.* Cambridge, Mass.: M.I.T. Press.

Jowitt, Kenneth (1971). *Revolutionary Breakthroughs and National Development: The Case of Romania, 1944–1965.* Berkeley: University of California Press.

Jünger, Ernst (1934). *Die totale Mobilmachung.* (First ed. 1930). Berlin: Junker und Dunnhaupt.

Kahin, Georg McTurrsan (1964). *Governments and Politics in Southeast Asia.* Ithaca: Cornell University Press.

Kaltefleiter, Werner (1968). *Wirtschaft und Politik in Deutschland: Konjunktur als Bestimmungsfaktor des Parteiensystems.* Cologne: Westdeutscher Verlag.

Kanet, Roger E., ed. (1971). *The Behavioral Revolution and Communist Studies.* New York: Free Press.

Karol, K. S. (1970). *Guerrillas in Power: The Course of the Cuban Revolution.* New York: Hill & Wang.

Karpat, Kemal H. (1959). *Turkey's Politics: The Transition to a Multiparty System.* Princeton: Princeton University Press.

——, ed. (1968). *Political and Social Thought in the Contemporary Middle East.* New York: Praeger.

Kase, Francis, J. (1968). *People's Democracy: A Contribution to the Study of the Communist Theory of State and Revolution.* Leyden: A. W. Sijthoff.

Kassof, Allen (1965). *The Soviet Youth Program.* Cambridge, Mass.: Harvard University Press.

——, ed. (1968). *Prospects for Soviet Society.* New York: Praeger.

—— (1969). "The administered society: totalitarianism without terror." In Frederick J. Fleron, Jr. (ed.), *Communist Studies and the Social Sciences.* Chicago: Rand McNally.

Kaufman, Susan Beth (1970). "Decision-making in an authoritarian regime: the politics of profit-sharing in Mexico." Ph.D. dissertation, Columbia University.

Kautsky, John H., and Roger W. Benjamin (1968). "Communism and economic development." In John H. Kautsky (ed.), *Communism and the Politics of Development.* New York: Wiley.

Kay, Hugh (1970). *Salazar and Modern Portugal.* New York: Hawthorn Books.

Kedward, H. R. (1969). *Fascism in Western Europe 1900–45.* Glasgow: Blackie.

Kele, Max H. (1972). *Nazis and Workers: National Socialist Appeals to German Labor, 1919–1933.* Chapel Hill: University of North Carolina Press.

Kelleher, Catherine McArdle, ed. (1974). *Political-Military Systems: Comparative Perspectives.* Beverly Hills: Sage.

Kelsen, Hans (1929). *Vom Wesen und Wert der Demokratie.* Tübingen: J. C. B. Mohr.

——— (1948). *The Political Theory of Bolshevism: A Critical Analysis.* University of California Publications in Political Science, Vol. 2. Berkeley: University of California Press.

Kern, Robert, and Ronald Dolkart eds. (1973). *The Caciques: Oligarchical Politics and the System of Caciquismo in the Luso-Hispanic World.* Albuquerque: University of New Mexico Press.

Kilson, Martin (1963). "Authoritarian and single-party tendencies in African politics."' *World Politics* 15:262–94.

Kim, Se-Jin (1971). *The Politics of Military Revolution in Korea.* Chapel Hill: University of North Carolina Press.

Kirchheimer, Otto (1969). *Politics, Law, and Social Change.* New York: Columbia University Press.

Kirkpatrick, Jeane (1971). *Leader and Vanguard in Mass Society: A Study of Peronist Argentina.* Cambridge, Mass.: M.I.T. Press.

Klemperer, Victor (1966). *Die unbewältigte Sprach: Aus dem Notizbuch eines Philologen LTI.* Darmstadt: Melzer.

Kling, Merle (1956). "Towards a theory of power and political instability in Latin America." *Western Political Quarterly* 9:21–35.

Klönne, Arno (1957). *Hitlerjugend. Die Jugend und ihre Organisation im Dritten Reich.* Hannover: Norddeutsche Verlagsanstalt.

Kluke, Paul (1973). "National Socialist Europe ideology." In Hajo Holborn (ed.), *Republic to Reich: The Making of the Nazi Revolution.* New York: Random House (Vintage).

Koehl, Robert (1972). "Feudal aspects of National Socialism." In Henry A. Turner (ed.), *Nazism and the Third Reich.* New York: Quadrangle Books.

Kogon, Eugen (1950). *The Theory and Practice of Hell.* London: Secker and Warburg.

Kolkowicz, Roman (1967). *The Soviet Military and Communist Party.* Princeton: Princeton University Press.

——— (1971). "The military." In H. Gordon Skilling and Franklyn Griffiths (eds.), *Interest Groups in Soviet Politics.* Princeton: Princeton University Press.

Kool, Frits, and Erwin Oberländer, eds. (1967). *Arbeiterdemokratie oder Parteidiktatur.* Olten: Walter Verlag.

Korbell, J. (1959). *Communist Subversion of Czechoslovakia, 1938–1948: The Failure of Coexistence.* Princeton: Princeton University Press.

Korbonski, Andrzej (1974). "Comparing liberalization processes in Eastern Europe: a preliminary analysis." In Lenard J. Cohen and Jane P. Shapiro (eds.), *Communist Systems in Comparative Perspective.* Garden City, N.Y.: Doubleday (Anchor).

Kornhauser, W. (1959). *The Politics of Mass Society.* Glencoe, Ill.: Free Press.

Kosheri Mahfouz, El (1972). *Socialisme et pouvoir en Egypte.* Paris: Librairie générale de droit et de jurisprudence.

Krader, Lawrence (1968). *The Origins of the State.* Englewood Cliffs, N.J.: Prentice-Hall.

Krausnick, Helmut, Hans Buchheim, Martin Broszat, and Hans-Adolf Jacobsen (1968). *Anatomy of the SS State.* New York: Walker.

Kriegel, Annie (1972). *Les grands procès dans les systèmes communistes.* Paris: Gallimard.

Kühnl, Reinhard (1966). *Die nationalsozialistische Linke 1925–1930.* Meisenheim am Glan: Anton Hain.

Labedz, Leopold, ed. (1962). *Revisionism: Essays on the History of Marxist Ideas.* New York: Praeger.

La Cierva, Ricardo de (1969). *Historia de la Guerra Civil española,* Vol. l. Madrid: San Martín.

Lacouture, Jean (1969). *4 hommes et leurs peuples: Surpourvoir et sousdeveloppment.* Paris: Editions du Seuil.

Lacouture, Jean, and Simoune Lacouture (1958). *Egypt in Transition.* New York: Criterion.

Lamounier, Bolivar (1974). "Ideologia ens regimes autoritários: uma crítica a Juan J. Linz." *Estudos Cebrap* (São Paulo) 7:69–92.

Landau, Jacob M., ed. (1972). *Man, State, and Society in the Contemporary Middle East.* New York: Praeger.

Lande, Carl H. (1965). *Leaders, Factions, and Parties: The Structure of Philippine Politics.* New Haven: Southeast Asia Studies, Yale University.

Lane, David, and George Kolankiewicz, eds. (1973). *Social Groups in Polish Society.* New York: Columbia University Press.

Lang, Kurt (1965). "Military sociology: a trend report and bibliography." *Current Sociology* 13:1–55.

Lange, M. G. (1955). *Wissescaft im Totalitären Staat: Die Wissenschaft der Sowjetischen Besatzngszone auf dem Weg zum 'Stalinismus.'* Stuttgart: Ring Verlag.

Lanning, Eldon (1974). "A typology of Latin Americans political systems." *Comparative Politics* 6:367–94.

Laqueur, Walter, and Leopold Labedz, eds. (1962). *Polycentrism: The New Factor in International Communism.* New York: Praeger.

Laqueur, Walter, and George L. Mosse, eds. (1966). *International Fascism, 1920–1945.* New York: Harper & Row.

Lasswell, Harold D., and Daniel Lerner, eds. (1966). *World Revolutionary Elites: Studies in Coercive Ideological Movements.* Cambridge, Mass.: M.I.T. Press.

Ledeen, Michael Arthur (1972). *Universal Fascism: The Theory and Practice of the Fascist International, 1928–1936.* New York: Fertig.

Ledesma Ramos, Ramiro (1968). *¿Fascismo en España? Discurso a las juventudes de España.* Reprinted. (Originally published 1935). Esplugues de Llobregat, Barcelona: Ariel.

Lee, J. M. (1969). *African Armies and Civil Order.* New York: Praeger.

Leeds, Anthony (1964). "Brazilian careers and social structure." *American Anthropologist* 66:1321–47.

Lefever, Ernest W. (1970). *Spear and Scepter: Army, Police, and Politics in Tropical Africa.* Washington. D.C.: The Brookings Institutition.

Leff, Nathaniel H. (1968). *Economic Policy-Making and Development in Brazil 1947–1964.* New York: Wiley.

Leites, Nathan C. (1953). *A Study of Bolshevism.* Glencoe, Ill.: Free Press.

Leites, Nathan, and Elsa Bernaut (1954). *Ritual of Liquidation: The Case of the Moscow Trials.* Glencoe, Ill.: Free Press.

Lemarchand, René (1972). "Political clientelism and ethnicity in tropical Africa: competing solidarities in nation-building." *The American Political Science Review* 66:68–90.

Lemarchand, René, and Keith Legg (1972). "Political clientelism and development: a preliminary analysis." *Comparative Politics* 4:149–78.

Lenin, V. I., *One Step Forward, Two Steps Back,* as quoted in Daniels, Robert Vincent (1969). *The Conscience of the Revolution: Communist Opposition in Soviet Russia.* New York: Clarion Book.

Lepsius, Rainer (1968). "The collapse of an intermediary power structure: Germany 1933–1934." *International Journal of Comparative Sociology* 9:289–301.

——— (1971). "Machtübernahme und Machtübergabe zur Strategie des Regimewechsels." In Hans Albert *et al.* (eds.), *Sozialtheorie und sozial Praxis.* Meisenheim am Glan: Verlag Anton Hain.

Lerner, Daniel, Ithiel de Sola Pool, and George K. Schueller (1966). "The Nazi elite." In H. Lasswell and D. Lerner (eds.), *World Revolutionary Elites: Studies in Coercive Ideological Movements.* Cambridge, Mass.: M.I.T. Press.

Levine, Donald N. (1965). *Wax and Gold: Tradition and Innovation in Ethiopian Culture.* Chicago: University of Chicago Press.

Levytsky, Borys, ed. (1974). *The Stalinist Terror in the Thirties: Documentation from the Soviet Press.* Stanford: Hoover Institution Press.

Lewis, John Wilson (1963). *Leadership in Communist China.* Ithaca, N.Y.: Cornell University Press.

Lewy, Guenter (1965). *The Catholic Church and Nazi Germany.* New York: McGraw-Hill.

Lieuwen, Edwin (1960). *Arms and Politics in Latin America.* New York: Praeger.

——— (1964). *Generals vs. Presidents: Neo-Militarism in Latin America.* New York: Praeger.

Lifton, Robert Jay (1968). *Revolutionary Immortality: Mao Tse-tung and the Chinese Cultural Revolution.* New York: Vintage Books.

Lijphart, Arend (1968a). "Typologies of democratic systems." *Comparative Political Studies* 1:3–44.

——— (1968b). *The Politics of Accommodation: Pluralism and Democracy in the Netherlands.* Berkeley: University of California Press.

——— (1969). "Consociational democracy." *World Politics* 21:207–25.

——— (1975). "Review article: the Northern Ireland problem: cases, theories, and solutions." *British Journal of Political Science* 5:83–106.

Lindbeck, J. M. H. (1967). "Transformation in the Chinese Communist Party." In Donald W. Treadgold (ed.). *Soviet and Chinese Communism: Similarities and Differences.* Seattle: University of Washington Press.

———, ed. (1971). *China: Management of a Revolutionary Society.* Seattle: University of Washington Press.

Linnemann, H., J. P. Pronk, and Jan Tinbergen (1965). *Convergence of Economic Systems in East and West.* Rotterdam: Netherlands Economic Institute.

Linz, Juan J., (1964). "An authoritarian regime: the case of Spain." In Erik Allard and Yrjo Littunen (eds.), *Cleavages, Ideologies and Party Systems.* Helsinki: Westermarck Society. Reprinted in Erik Allard and Stein Rokkan, eds. (1970), *Mass Politics: Studies in Political Sociology.* New York: Free Press. Page references are to the 1970 edition.

——— (1966). "Michels e il suo contributo alla sociologia politica." Introduction to Roberto Michels, *La sociologia del partito politico nella democrazia moderna.* Bologna: Il Mulino.

——— (1970a). "From Falange to Movimiento-Organización: the Spanish single party and the Franco regime 1936–1968." In S. Huntington and C. Moore (eds.), *Authoritarian Politics in Modern Societies: The Dynamics of Established One Party Systems.* New York: Basic Books.

——— (1970b). *Elites locales y cambio social en la Andalucía rural.* Vol. 2 of *Estudio Socioeconómico de Andalucía.* Madrid: Instituto de Desarrollo Económico.

——— (1973a). "Opposition in and under an authoritarian regime: the case of Spain." In Robert A. Dahl (ed.), *Regimes and Oppositions.* New Haven: Yale University Press.

——— (1973b). "The Future of an authoritarian situation or the institutionalization of an authoritarian regime: the case of Brazil," In Alfred Stepan (ed.), *Authoritarian Brazil: Origins, Policies, and Future.* New Haven: Yale University Press.

——— (1973c). "Continuidad y discontinuidad en la élite política española: de la restauración al régimen actual." In *Libro Homenaje al Prof. Carlos Ollero.* Madrid: Gráficas Carlavilla.

——— (1976). "Some notes towards a comparative study of fascism in sociological-historical perspective." In Walter Laqueur (ed.), *A Guide to Fascism.*

Linz, Juan J., and Amando De Miguel (1966a). "Within-nation differences and comparisons: the eight Spains." In Richard L. Merritt and Stein Rokkan (eds.), *Comparing Nations.* New Haven: Yale University Press.

——— (1966b). *Los empresarios ante el poder público: El liderazgo y los grupos de intereses en el empresariado español.* Madrid: Instituto de Estudios Políticos.

Linz, Juan J., and Alfred Stepan, eds. (1976). *Breakdown and Crises of Democracies.*

Lipset, Seymour Martin (1959). "Some social requisites of democracy: economic development and political legitimacy." *American Political Science Review* 53:69–105.

—— (1960). "'Fascism'—left, right, and center." In S. M. Lipset, *Political Man: The Social Bases of Politics.* Garden City, N.Y.: Doubleday.

—— (1973). "Commentary: social stratification research and Soviet scholarship." In Murray Yanowitch and Wesley A. Fisher (eds.), *Social Stratification and Mobility in the USSR.* White Plains, N.Y.: International Arts and Sciences Press.

Lipset, Seymour M., and Richard B. Dobson (1973). "Social stratification and sociology in the Soviet Union." *Survey* 3:114–85.

Lipset, S. M., and S. Rokkan (1967). "Cleavage structures, party systems, and voter alignment: an introduction." In Lipset and Rokkan (eds.), *Party Systems and Voter Alignments: Cross-National Perspectives.* New York: Free Press.

Lipson, Leon (1967). "Law: the functions of extra-judicial mechanisms." In Donald W. Treadgold (ed.), *Soviet and Chinese Communism: Similarities and Differences.* Seattle: University of Washington Press.

—— (1968). "Law and society." In Allen Kassof (ed.), *Prospects for Soviet Society.* New York: Praeger.

Lockwood, Lee (1967). *Castro's Cuba: Cuba's Fidel.* New York: Macmillan.

Lopukhov, Boris R. (1965). "Il problema del fascismo italiano negli scritti di autori sovietici." *Studi storici* 6:239–57.

Lowenthal, Abraham F. (1974). "Armies and politics in Latin America." *World Politics* 27:107–30.

——, ed. (1975). *The Peruvian Experiment: Continuity and Change Under Military Rule.* Princeton: Princeton University Press.

Lowenthal, Richard (1970). "Development vs. utopia in communist policy." In Chalmers Johnson (ed.), *Change in Communist Systems.* Stanford: Stanford University Press.

Lucena, Manuel (1971). *L'Evolution du Systeme Portugais à travers les Lois (1933–1971),* 2 vols. Paris: Institut des Sciences Sociales du Travail. Quoted by permission.

Ludendorff, Erich (1935). *Der Totale Krieg.* Munich: Ludendorff Verlag.

Ludz, Peter Christian (1964). "Entwurf Einer soziologischen Theorie Totalitär Verfasster Gesellschaft." In P. C. Ludz (ed.), *Soziologie der DDR.* Cologne-Opladen: Westdeutscher Verlag.

—— (1970). *The German Democratic Republic from the Sixties to the Seventies: A Socio-Political Analysis.* Cambridge, Mass.: Center for International Affairs, Harvard University.

—— (1972). The *Changing Party Elite in East Germany.* Cambridge. Mass.: M.I.T. Press.

Lukács, Georg (1955). *Die Zerstörung der Vernunft.* Berlin: Aufbau-Verlag.

Mabry, Donald J. (1973). *Mexico's Acción Nacional: A Catholic Alternative to Revolution.* Syracuse: Syracuse University Press.

Macartney, C. A. (1962). *October 15: A History of Modern Hungary, 1929–1944,* 2 vols. Edinburgh: Edinburgh University Press.

MacFarquhar, Roderick (1960). *The Hundred Flowers Campaign and the Chinese Intellectuals.* New York: Praeger.

MacGaffey, Wyatt, and Clifford R. Barnett (1965). *Twentieth-Century Cuba: The Background of the Castro Revolution.* Garden City, N.Y.: Doubleday (Anchor).

MacInnis, Donald E. (1972). *Religious Policy and Practice in Communist China.* New York: Macmillan.

Mair, Lucy (1962). *Primitive Government.* Harmondsworth: Penguin Books.

Malefakis, Edward E. (1970). *Agrarian Reform and Peasant Revolution in Spain: Origins of the Civil War.* New Haven: Yale University Press.

Malloy, James M. (1974). "Authoritarianism, corporatism and mobilization in Peru." *The Review of Politics* 36:52–84.

Manoïlesco, Mihail (1936). *Le Siècle du Corporatisme.* (Original ed. 1934.) Paris: Félix Alcan.

———(1938). *El partido único,* Zaragoza: Heraldo de Aragón.

Mansilla, H. C. F. (1971). *Faschismus und eindimensionale Gesellschaft.* Neuwied: Luchterhand.

Marcuse, Herbert (1964). *One-Dimensional Man.* Boston: Beacon Press.

———(1969). "Repressive tolerance." In Robert Paul Wolff, Barrington Moore, Jr., and H. Marcuse (eds.), *A Critique of Pure Tolerance.* Boston: Beacon Press.

Markovitz, Irving Leonard, ed. (1970). *African Politics and Society: Basic Issues and Problems of Government and Development.* New York: Free Press.

Maruyama, Masao (1963). *Thought and Behaviour in Modern Japanese Politics.* London: Oxford University Press.

Marx, Karl (1851–52; revised 1869). *The Eighteenth Brumaire of Louis Bonaparte.* Reprinted in Karl Marx and Frederick Engels, *Selected Works in Two Volumes.* Moscow: Foreign Language Publishing House, 1955.

Maser, Werner (1970). *Hitler's Mein Kampf: An Analysis.* London: Faber and Faber.

Mason, T. W. (1968). "The primacy of politics—politics and economics in National Socialist Germany." In S. J. Woolf (ed.), *The Nature of Fascism.* London: Weidenfeld & Nicolson.

Massing, Paul W. (1949). *Rehearsal for Destruction: A Study of Political Anti-Semitism in Imperial Germany.* New York: Fertig.

Matossian, Mary (1958). "Ideologies of delayed industrialization: some tensions and ambiguities." *Economic Development and Cultural Change* 6:217–28.

Matthias, Erich, and Rudolf Morsey, eds. (1960). *Das Ende der Parteien 1933.* Düsseldorf: Kommission für Geschichte des Parlamentarismus und der politische Parteien.

Mau, Hermann (1953). "Die 'Zweite Revolution' der 30. Juni 1934." *Vierteljahrshefte für Zeitgeschichte* 1:119–37.

May, John D. (1973). *Of the Conditions and Measures of Democracy.* Morristown, N.J.: General Learning Press.

McAlister, Lyle N. (1966). "'Recent research and writings on the role of the military in Latin America." *Latin American Research Review* 2:5–36.

McDonald, Ronald H. (1971). *Party Systems and Elections in Latin America.* Chicago: Markham.

McRae, Kenneth D., ed. (1974). *Consociational Democracy: Political Accommodation in Segmented Societies.* Toronto: McClelland and Stewart.

Medhurst, Kenneth N. (1973). *Government in Spain: The Executive at Work.* Oxford: Pergamon Press.

Medvedev, Zhoros A. (1969). *Rise and Fall of T. D. Lysenko.* New York: Columbia University Press.

Merkl, Peter H. (1975). *Political Violence under the Swastika: 581 Early Nazis.* Princeton: Princeton University Press.

Mesa-Lago, Carmelo, ed. (1971). *Revolutionary Change in Cuba.* Pittsburgh: University of Pittsburgh Press.

Messerschmidt, Manfred (1969). *Die Wehrmacht im NS-Staat.* Hamburg: v. Decker.

Meyer, Alfred G. (1957). *Leninism.* Cambridge, Mass.: Harvard University Press.

—— (1964). "USSR, incorporated." In Donald W. Treadgold (ed.), *The Development of the USSR: An Exchange of Views.* Seattle: University of Washington Press.

—— (1965). *The Soviet Political System: An Interpretation.* New York: Random House.

—— (1967). "Authority in communist political systems." In Louis J. Edinger (ed.), *Political Leadership in Industrialized Societies.* New York: Wiley.

—— (1970). "Theories of convergence." In Chalmers Johnson (ed.), *Change in Communist Systems.* Stanford: Stanford University Press.

Meyerhoff, Hermann (1963). *Herne 1933–1945—Die Zeit des Nationalsozialismus: Ein kommunalhistorischer Rückblick.* Herne: Stadt(verwaltung).

Michels, Robert (1928). "Some reflections on the sociological character of political parties." *The American Political Science Review* 21:753–72.

—— (1962). *Political Parties: A Sociological Study of the Oligarchical Tendencies of Modern Democracy.* (Originally published 1911). New York: Collier Books.

Mickiewicz, Ellen Propper (1967). *Soviet Political Schools: The Communist Party Adult Instruction System.* New Haven: Yale University Press.

Milenkovitch, Deborah (1971). *Plaint and Market in Yugoslav Economic Thought.* New Haven: Yale University Press.

Mills, C. Wright (1958). *The Causes of World War Three.* New York: Simon & Schuster.

Milne, R. S. (1967). *Government and Politics in Malaysia.* Boston: Houghton Mifflin.

Milward, Alan S. (1966). *Die Deutsche Kriegswirtschaft, 1939–1945.* Stuttgart: Deutsche Verlags-Anstalt.

Montias, John Michael (1970). "Types of communist economic systems." In Chalmers Johnson (ed.), *Change in Communist Systems.* Stanford: Stanford University Press.

Montgomery, John D., and Albert O. Hirschman, eds. (1968). *Public Policy* 17. Articles on military government and reconstruction by C. J. Friedrich, L. Krieger, and P. H. Merkl.

Moore, Barrington, Jr., (1951). *Soviet Politics: The Dilemma of Power. The Role of Ideas in Social Change.* Cambridge, Mass.: Harvard University Press.

———— (1954). *Terror and Progress USSR: Some Sources of Change and Stability in the Soviet Dictatorship.* Cambridge, Mass.: Harvard University Press.

———— (1965). *Political Power and Social Theory.* New York: Harper (Torchbooks).

———— (1966). *Social Origins of Dictatorship and Democracy: Lord and Peasant in the Making of the Modern World.* Boston: Beacon Press.

Moore, Clement H. (1965). *Tunisia since Independence.* Berkeley: University of California Press.

———— (1970a). *Politics in North Africa, Algeria, Morocco, and Tunisia.* Boston: Little Brown.

———— (1970b). "The single party as source of legitimacy." In S. Huntington and C. Moore (eds.), *Authoritarian Politics in Modern Society.* New York: Basic Books.

———— (1973). "Raisons de la faillite du parti unique dans les pays arabes." *Revue de l'Occident Musulman et de la Méditerranée* 15–16:242–52.

———— (1974). "Authoritarian politics in unincorporated society: the case of Nasser's Egypt." *Comparative Politics* 6:198–218.

Morris, Ivan, ed. (1968). *Japan 1931–1945: Militarism, Fascism, Japanism?* Lexington, Mass.: D. C. Heath.

Morrison, Donald George, *et al.* (1972). *Black Africa: A Comparative Handbook.* New York: Free Press.

Morton, Henry W., and Rudolf L. Tökés, eds. (1974). *Soviet Politics and Society in the 1970's.* New York: Free Press.

Mosse, George L. (1964). *The Crisis of German Ideology: Intellectual Origins of the Third Reich.* New York: Grosset & Dunlap.

———— (1966). *Nazi Culture: Intellectual, Cultural and Social Life in the Third Reich.* New York: Grosset & Dunlap.

Mote, Max E. (1965). *Soviet Local and Republic Elections: A Description of the 1963 Elections in Leningrad Based on Official Documents, Press Accounts, and Private Interviews.* Stanford: The Hoover Institution on War, Revolution and Peace, Stanford University.

Moy, Roland F. (1971). *A Computer Simulation of Democratic Political Development: Tests of the Lipset and Moore Models.* Sage Professional Papers in Comparative Politics, No. 01–019:2. Beverly Hills: Sage.

Nagy-Talavera, Nicholas M. (1970). *The Green Shirts and the Others: A History of Fascism in Hungary and Rumania.* Stanford: Hoover Institution Press.

Neal, Fred W. (1957). *Titoism in Action.* Berkeley: University of California Press.

Needleman, Carolyn, and Martin Needleman (1969). "Who rules Mexico? A critique of some current views of the Mexican political process." *Journal of Politics* 81:1011–84.

Needler, Martin (1964). *Anatomy of a Coup d'état: Ecuador 1963.* Washington, D.C.: Institute for the Comparative Study of Political Systems.

———— (1966). "Political development and military intervention in Latin America." *American Political Science Review* 60:616–26.

——— (1967). *Latin American Politics in Perspective.* Princeton: D. Van Nostrand.
———, ed. (1970). *Political Systems of Latin America.* New York: Van Nostrand Reinhold.
——— (1971). *Politics and Society in Mexico.* Albuquerque: University of New Mexico.
Neubauer, Deane E. (1967). "Some conditions of democracy." *American Political Science Review* 61:1002–09.
Neumann, Sigmund (1942). *Permanent Revolution: Totalitarianism in the Age of International Civil War.* New York: Harper.
Neumann, Franz (1957). *The Democratic and the Authoritarian State.* Glencoe, Ill.: Free Press.
——— (1963). *Behemoth: The Structure and Practice of National Socialism 1933–1944.* (First ed. 1944). New York: Octagon.
Newton, Ronald C. (1974). "Natural corporatism and the passing of populism in Spanish America." *The Review of Politics* 86:84–51.
Noakes, Jeremy, and Geoffrey Pridham, eds. (1974). *Documents on Nazism 1919–1945.* London: Jonathan Cape.
Nolte, Ernst (1963). *Der Nationalsozialismus.* Munich: R. Piper & Co.
——— (1966). *Die faschistischen Bewegungen.* Munich: Deutscher Taschenbuch Verlag.
——— (1968a). *Die Krise des liberalen Systems und die faschistischen Bewegungen.* Munich: Piper.
——— (1968b). *Der Faschismus von Mussolini zu Hitler: Texte, Bilder und Dokumente.* Munich: Verlag Kurt Desch.
———, ed. (1967). *Theorien über den Faschismus.* Cologne: Kiepenheuer.
——— (1969). *Three Faces of Fascism: Action Française, Italian Fascism, and National Socialism.* New York: Mentor Book.
Nordlinger, Eric A. (1970). "Soldiers in mufti: the impact of military rule upon economic and social change in the non-Western states." *The American Political Science Review* 64:1131–48.
——— (1972). *Conflict Regulation in Divided Societies.* Cambridge, Mass.: Center for International Affairs, Harvard University.
Norman, H. (1948). *Japan's Emergence as a Modern State.* New York: Institute of Pacific Relations.
North, Liisa (1966). *Civil-Military Relations in Argentina, Chile, and Peru.* Berkeley: Institute of International Studies.
Nove, Alec (1964). *Economic Rationality and Soviet Politics; Or Was Stalin Really Necessary?* New York: Praeger.
NSDAP, Reichsorganisationsleiter (1935?). *Partei-Statistik,* Stand: 1935, 4 vols. Munich: Internal publication.
Nun, José (1968). "A Latin American phenomenon: the middle-class military coup." In James Petras and Maurice Zeitlin (eds.), *Latin America: Reform or Revolution?* New York: Fawcett.
——— (1969). *Latin America: The Hegemonic Crisis and the Military Coup.* Berkeley: Institute of International Studies, University of California.
Nyomarkay, Joseph (1967). *Charismna and Factionalism in the Nazi Party.* Minneapolis: University of Minnesota Press.

O'Connor, Dennis M. (1963). "Soviet People's Guards: an experiment with civic police." *New York University Law Review* 39:580–87.

O'Donnell, Guillermo (1973). *Modernization and Bureaucratic-Authoritarianism: Studies in South American Politics.* Berkeley: Institute of International Studies, University of California.

Oren, Nissan (1973). *Revolution Administered: Agrarianism and Communism in Bulgaria.* Baltimore: Johns Hopkins University Press.

Organski, A. F. K. (1965). *The Stages of Political Development.* New York: Knopf.

Orlow, Dietrich (1965). "Die Adolf-Hitler-Schulen." *Vierteljahrshefte für Zeitgeschichte* 23:272–84.

——— (1969). *The History of the Nazi Party: 1919–1933.* Pittsburgh: University of Pittsburgh Press.

——— (1973). *The History of the Nazi Party: 1933–1945.* Pittsburgh: University of Pittsburgh Press.

Padgett, Vincent (1966). *The Mexican Political System.* Boston: Houghton Mifflin.

Palmer, David Scott (1973). *"Revolution from Above": Military Government and Popular Participation in Peru, 1968–1972.* Cornell University Dissertations Series, No. 47. Ithaca: Cornell University.

Pauker, Guy J. (1963). *The Indonesian Doctrine of Territorial Warfare and Territorial Management.* Santa Monica: The Rand Corporation.

Paxton, Robert O. (1972). *Vichy France: Old Guard and New Order, 1940–44.* New York: Knopf.

Payne, Stanley G. (1967). *Politics and the Military in Modern Spain.* Stanford: Stanford University Press.

Pelczynski, Zbigniew (1959). "Poland 1957." In David E. Butler (ed.), *Elections Abroad.* London: Macmillan.

Penniman, Howard R. (1972). *Elections in South Vietnam.* Washington, D.C.: American Enterprise Institute for Public Policy Research.

Perham, Margery (1947). *The Government of Ethiopia.* London: Faber and Faber.

Perlmutter, Amos (1969). "The praetorian state and the praetorian army: toward a taxonomy of civil-military relations in developing polities." *Comparative Politics* 2:382–404.

——— (1970). "The Arab military elite." *World Politics* 22:269–300.

Peterson, Edward N. (1969). *The Limits of Hitler's Power.* Princeton: Princeton University Press.

Pike, Frederick B., and Thomas Stritch, eds. (1974). *The New Corporatism: Social-Political Structures in the Iberian World.* Notre Dame: University of Notre Dame Press.

Pipes, Richard , ed. (1961). *The Russian Intelligentsia.* New York: Columbia University Press.

——— (1967). "Communism and Russian history." In Donald W. Treadgold (ed.), *Soviet and Chinese Communism: Similarities and Differences.* Seattle: University of Washington Press.

Pipping, Knut, Rudolf Abshagen, and Anne-Eva Brauneck (1954). *Gespräche mit der Deutschen Jugend: Ein Beitrag zum Authoritätsproblem.* Helsingfors: Akademische Buchhandlung.

Pirker, Theo, ed. (1965). *Komintern und Faschismus, 1920–1940: Dokumente zur Geschichte und Theorie des Faschismus.* Stuttgart: Deutsche Verlag-Anstalt.

Plessner, Helmuth (1959). *Die verspätete Nation: Über die politische Verführbarkeit bürgerlichen Geistes.* Stuttgart: W. Kohlhammer.

Ploss, Sidney I. (1965). *Conflict and Decision-Making in Soviet Russia: A Case Study of Agricultural Policy, 1953–1963.* Princeton: Princeton University Press.

Political Systems and the Distribution of Power. A.S.A. Monographs, No. 2. London: Tavistock.

Pollack, Jonathan D. (1974). "The study of Chinese military politics: toward a framework for analysis." In Catherine McArdle Kelleher (ed.), *Political-Military Systems: Comparative Perspectives.* Beverly Hills: Sage.

Potash, Robert A. (1969). *The Army and Politics in Argentina, 1928–1945: Yrigoyen to Perón.* Stanford: Stanford University Press.

Potholm, Christian P. (1970). *Four African Political Systems.* Englewood Cliffs, N.J.: Prentice-Hall.

Potholm, Christian P., and Richard Dale, eds. (1972). *Southern Africa in Perspective: Essays in Regional Politics.* New York: Free Press.

Powell, John Duncan (1970). "Peasant society and clientelist politics." *American Political Science Review* 64:411–25.

Puhle, Hans-Jürgen (1970). *Tradition und Reformpolitik in Bolivien.* Hannover: Verlag für Literatur und Zeingeschehen.

Pulzer, P. G. J. (1964). *The Rise of Political Anti-Semitism in Germany and Austria.* New York: Wiley.

Pusić, Eugen, ed. (1973). *Participation and Self-Management.* Zagreb: Institute for Social Research.

Putnam, Robert (1967). "Toward explaining military intervention in Latin American politics." *World Politics* 20:83–110.

Pye, Lucian W. (1967). *Southeast Asia's Political Systems.* Englewood Cliffs, N.J.: Prentice-Hall.

——— (1971). "Mass participation in Communist China: its limitations and the continuity of culture." In John M. H. Lindbeck (ed.), *China: Management of a Revolutionary Society.* Seattle: University of Washington Press.

Quandt, William B. (1969). *Revolution and Political Leadership: Algeria 1954–1968.* Cambridge, Mass.: M.I.T. Press.

Rämisch, Raimund (1957). "Der Berufsstäudische Gedanke als Episode in der nationalsozialistischen Politik." *Zeitschrift für Politik* 4:268–72.

Reitlinger, Gerald (1968). *The Final Solution: The Attempt to Exterminate the Jews of Europe, 1939–1945.* South Brunswick, N.J.: T. Yoseloff.

Remak, Joachim, ed. (1969). *The Nazi Years: A Documentary History.* Englewood Cliffs, N.J.: Prentice-Hall.

Remington, Robin A. (1969). *Winter in Prague: Documents on Czechoslovak Communism in Crisis.* Cambridge, Mass.: M.I.T. Press.

———, ed. (1974). "Armed forces and society in Yugoslavia." In Catherine McArdle Kelleher (ed.), *Political-Military Systems: Comparative Perspectives.* Beverly Hills: Sage.

Rigby, T. H. (1968). *Communist Party Membership in the U.S.S.R. 1917–1967.* Princeton: Princeton University Press.

———— (1969). "Traditional market and organizational societies and the USSR." In Frederic J. Fleron, Jr. (ed.), *Communist Studies and the Social Sciences.* Chicago: Rand McNally.

Riggs, Fred W. (1967). *Thailand: The Modernization of a Bureaucratic Polity.* Honolulu: East-West Center Press.

Roberts, Henry L. (1951). *Rumania: Political Problems of an Agrarian State.* New Haven: Yale University Press.

Robinson, Thomas W. (1974). "Political succession in China." *World Politics* 27:1–38.

Roggemann, H. (1970). *Das Modell der Arbeiterselbstverwallung inn Jugoslanwien.* Frankfurt am Main: Europäische Verlagsanstalt.

Rogger, Hans, and Eugen Weber, eds. (1966). *The European Right: A Historical Profile.* Berkeley: University of California Press.

Rokkan, Stein (1966). "Norway: numerical democracy and corporate pluralism." In Robert Dahl (ed.), *Political Oppositions in Western Democracies.* New Haven: Yale University Press.

Ronfeldt, David (1972). Patterns of civil-military rule." In Luigi Einaudi (ed.), *Latin America in the 1970's.* Santa Monica: The Rand Corporation.

Rose, Leo E., and Margaret W. Fisher (1970). *The Politics of Nepal: Persistence and Change in an Asian Monarchy.* Ithaca: Cornell University Press.

Rose, Richard (1971). *Governing without Consensus: An Irish Perspective.* Boston: Beacon Press.

Rose, Richard, and Harve Mossawir (1967). "Voting and elections: a functional analysis." *Political Studies* 15:173–201.

Rosenau, James N., ed. (1969). *Linkage Politics: Essays on the Convergence of National and International Systems.* New York: Free Press.

Ross, Stanley R., ed. (1966). *Is the Mexican Revolution Dead?* New York: Knopf.

Rossiter, Clinton L. (1948). *Constitutional Dictatorship: Crisis Government in the Modern Democracies.* Princeton: Princeton University Press.

Rotberg, Robert I., with Christopher K. Clague (1971). *Haiti: The Politics of Squalor.* Boston: Houghton Mifflin.

Roth, Guenther (1963). *The Social Democrats in Imperial Germany.* Totowa, N.J.: Bedminster.

———— (1971). "Personal rulership, patrimonialism, and empire-building." In Reinhard Bendix and Guenther Roth (eds.), *Scholarship and Partisanship: Essays on Max Weber.* Berkeley: University of California Press.

Rush, Myron (1968). *Political Succession in the USSR.* New York: Columbia University Press.

Rustow, Dankwart A. (1964). "Succession in the twentieth century." *Journal of International Affairs* 18:104–13.

———— (1967). *A World of Nations: Problems of Political Modernization.* Washington, D.C.: The Brookings Institution.

———— (1971). *Middle Eastern Political Systems.* Englewood Cliffs, N.J.: Prentice-Hall.

Sabine, George H. (1934). "The state." In Edwin R. A. Seligman and Alvin Johnson (eds.), *Encyclopedia of the Social Sciences.* New York: Macmillan.

Salvemini, Gaetano (1961). *Scritti sul fascismo.* Milano: Feltrinelli.
Sarti, Roland (1968). "Fascism and the industrial leadership in Italy before the March on Rome." *Industrial and Labor Relations Review* 21:400–17.
—— (1970). "Fascist modernization in Italy: traditional or revolutionary?" *American Historical Review* 75:1029–45.
—— (1971). *Fascism and the Industrial Leadership in Italy 1919–1940.* Berkeley: University of California Press.
Sartori, Giovanni (1962a). *Democratic Theory.* Detroit: Wayne State University Press.
—— (1962b). "Dittatura." *Enciclopedia del Diritto,* Vol. 11. Milano: A. Giuffrè.
—— (1968). "Political development and political engineering." In John D. Montgomery and Albert O. Hirschman (eds.), *Public Policy,* Vol. 17. Cambridge, Mass.: Harvard University Press.
—— (1970a). "Concept information in comparative politics." *The American Political Science Review* 64:1033–53.
—— (1970b). "The typology of party systems—proposals for improvement." In Erik Allardt and Stein Rokkan (eds.), *Mass Politics: Studies in Political Sociology.* New York: Free Press.
—— (1974). "Rivistando il 'pluralismo polarizzato.'" In Fabio L. Cavazza and Stephen R. Graubard (eds.), *Il Caso Italiano: Italia anni '70.* Milano: Garzanti.
Sauer, Wolfgang (1967). "National Socialism: totalitarianism or fascism?" *American Historical Review* 73:404–24.
Scalapino, Robert A. (1953). *Democracy and the Party Movement in Prewar Japan: The Failure of the First Attempt.* Berkeley: University of California Press.
——, ed. (1972). *Elites in the People's Republic of China.* Seattle: University of Washington Press.
Schäfer. Wolfgang (1957): *NSDAP Entwicklung und Struktur der Staatspartei des Dritten Reiches.* Hannover: Norddeutsche Verlagsanstalt O. Goedel.
Schapiro, Leonard (1965). *The Origin of the Communist Autocracy: Political Opposition in the Soviet State, First Phase, 1917–1922.* New York: Praeger.
—— (1972a). *Totalitarianism.* New York: Praeger.
——, ed. (1972b). *Political Opposition in One-Party States.* London: Macmillan.
Schein, Edgard H., with Inge Schneier and Curtis H. Baker (1961). *Coercive Persuasion: A Socio-psychological Analysis of the "Brainwashing" of American Civilian Prisoners by the Chinese Communists.* New York: Norton.
Schmidt, Carl T. (1938). *The Plough and the Sword.* New York: Columbia University Press.
—— (1939). *The Corporate State in Action: Italy under Fascism.* New York: Oxford University Press.
Schmitt, Carl (1928). *Die Diktatur: Von den Anfängen des modern Souveränitätsgedankens bis zum proletarischen Klassenkampf.* Munich: Duncker & Humblot.

———— (1940). "Die Wendung zum totalen Staat." *Positionen und Begriffe im Kampf mit Weimar—Genf—Versailles 1923–1939.* Hamburg: Hanseatische Verlagsanstalt.

Schmitter, Philippe C. (1971). *Interest Conflict and Political Change in Brazil.* Stanford: Stanford University Press.

———— (1973a). *Military Rule in Latin America: Functions, Consequences and Perspectives.* Beverly Hills: Sage.

———— (1973b). "Corporatist interest representation and public policy-making in Portugal." Paper presented at the Conference on Modern Portugal, October 10–14, 1973, University of New Hampshire, Durham, N.H.

———— (1974). "Still the century of corporatism?" *Review of Politics* 36:85–131. Quoted by permission.

Schneider, Herbert W. (1928). *Making the Fascist State.* New York: Oxford University Press.

———— (1936). *The Fascist Government of Italy.* New York: Van Nostrand.

Schneider, Ronald M. (1971). *The Political System of Brazil: Emergence of a "Modernizing" Authoritarian Regime, 1964–1970.* New York: Columbia University Press.

Schoenbaum, David (1967). *Hitler's Social Revolution: Class and Status in Nazi Germany 1933–1939.* Garden City, N.Y.: Doubleday (Anchor).

Scholtz, Harold (1967). "Die 'NS-Ordensburgen.'" V*ierteljahrshrefte für Zeitgeschichte* 15:269–98.

Schöpflin, George, ed. (1970). *The Soviet Union and Eastern Europe: A Handbook.* New York: Praeger.

Schorn, Hubert (1959). *Der Richter im Dritten Reich: Geschichte und Dokumente.* Frankfurt: Klostermann.

Schram, Stuart R. (1967). *Mao Tse-tung.* Harmondsworth: Penguin.

———— (1969). *The Political Thought of Mao Tse-tung.* New York: Praeger.

Schueller, George K. (1966). "The politburo." In Harold D. Lasswell and Daniel Lerner (eds.), *World Revolutionary Elites: Studies in Coercive Ideological Movements.* Cambridge, Mass.: M.I.T. Press.

Schumann, Hans-Gerd (1958). *Nationalsozialismus und Gewerkschaftsbewegung.* Hannover: Norddeutsche Verlagsanstalt O. Goedel.

Schumpeter, Joseph A. (1950). *Capitalism, Socialism, and Democracy.* New York: Harper & Row.

Schurmann, Franz (1968). *Ideology and Organization in Communist China.* Berkeley: University of California Press.

Schweitzer, Arthur (1965). *Big Business in the Third Reich.* Bloomington: Indiana University Press.

———— (1974). "Theory of Political Charisma." *Comparative Studies in Society and History* 16:150–81.

Scott, Robert E. (1964). *Mexican Government in Transition.* Urbana: University of Illinois Press.

———— (1965). "Mexico: the established revolution." In Lucian W. Pye and Sydney Verga (eds.), *Political Culture and Political Development.* Princeton: Princeton University Press.

Seidel, Bruno, and Siegfried Jenkner, eds. (1968). *Wege der Totalitarismus-Forschung.* Darmstadt: Wissenschaftliche Buchgesellschaft.

Seton-Watson, Hugh (1967). *Eastern Europe between the Wars 1918–1941.* New York: Harper & Row.

────── (1968). *The East European Revolution.* New York: Praeger.

Shaffer, Harry G., ed. (1967). *The Communist World: Marxist and Non-Marxist Views.* New York: Appleton-Century-Crofts.

Shils, Edward (1960). *Political Development in the New States.* The Hague: Mouton.

Shoup, Paul (1971). "Comparing communist nations: prospects for an empirical approach." In Roger E. Kanet (ed.), *The Behavioral Revolution and Communist Studies.* New York: Free Press.

Shulman, Marshall D. (1969). *Stalin's Foreign Policy Reappraised.* New York: Atheneum.

Silva, Umberto (1973). *Ideologia e Arte del Fascismo.* Milano: Gabriele Mazzotta.

Simmons, Ernest J. (1955). *Continuity and Change in Russian and Soviet Thought.* Cambridge, Mass.: Harvard University Press.

────── , ed. (1971). "The writers." In H. Gordon Skilling and Franklyn Griffiths (eds.), *Interest Groups in Soviet Politics.* Princeton: Princeton University Press.

Skilling, H. Gordon (1966). *The Government of Communist East Europe.* New York: Crowell.

────── (1970). "Leadership and group conflict in Czechoslovakia." In R. Barry Farrell (ed.), *Political Leadership in Eastern Europe and the Soviet Union.* Chicago: Aldine.

────── (1971). "Group conflict in Soviet politics: some conclusions." In H. G. Skilling and F. Griffiths (eds.), *Interest Groups in Soviet Politics.* Princeton: Princeton University Press.

────── (1973a). "Opposition in Communist East Europe." In Robert A. Dahl (ed.), *Regimes and Oppositions.* New Haven: Yale University Press.

────── (1973b). "Czechoslovakia's interrupted revolution." In Robert A. Dahl (ed.), *Regimes and Oppositions.* New Haven: Yale University Press.

Skilling, H. Gordon, and Franklyn Griffiths, eds. (1971). *Interest Groups in Soviet Politics.* Princeton: Princeton University Press.

Snyder, Frank Gregory (1965). *One-party Government in Mali: Transition Toward Control.* New Haven: Yale University Press.

Solaún, Mauricio (1969). "El fracaso de la democracia en Cuba: un régimen 'patrimonial' autoritario (1952)." *Aportes* 13:57–80.

Solaún, Mauricio, and Michael A. Quinn (1973). *Sinners and Heretics: The Politics of Military Intervention in Latin America.* Urbana: University of Illinois Press.

Solomon, Richard H. (1971). *Mao's Revolution and the Chinese Political Culture.* Berkeley: University of California Press.

Solzhenitsyn, Aleksandr I. (1973). *The Gulag Archipelago 1918–1956: An Experiment in Literary Investigation.* Paperback ed. New York: Harper & Row.

Sontheimer, Kurt (1968). *Antidemokratisches Denken in der Weimarer Republik.* Munich: Nymphenburger Verlagshandlung.

Sorokin, Pitirim (1964). *The Basic Trends of our Times.* New Haven: College and University Press.

Spacensky, Alain (1970). *Madagascar: 50 ans de vie politique (de Ralaimongo à Tsiranana).* Paris: Nouvelles Editions Latines.

Speer, Albert (1971). *Inside the Third Reich.* New York: Avon Books.

Speier, Hans (1944). "Ludendorff: the German concept of total war." In Edward Mead Earle (ed.), *Makers of Modern Strategy.* Princeton: Princeton University Press.

Spiro, Herbert J. (1968). "Totalitarianism." *International Encyclopedia of the Social Sciences,* Vol. 16. New York: Crowell, Collier and Macmillan.

Staff, Ilse, ed. (1964). *Justiz im Dritten Reich: eine Dokumentation.* Frankfurt am Main: Fischer-Bücherei.

Stalin, Joseph (1924). *The Foundations of Leninism.* Reprinted in Bruce Franklin, ed. (1972). *The Essential Stalin: Major Theoretical Writings, 1905–1952.* Garden City, N.Y.: Doubleday, Anchor.

Stepan, Alfred (1971). *The Military in Politics: Changing Patterns in Brazil.* Princeton: Princeton University Press.

———— (1973). "The new professionalism of internal welfare and military role expansion." In A. Stepan (ed.), *Authoritarian Brazil: Origins, Policies, and Future.* New Haven: Yale University Press.

Stern, Fritz (1965). *The Politics of Cultural Despair.* Garden City, N.Y.: Doubleday.

Sternberger, Dolf, and Bernhard Vogel, eds. (1969–). *Die Wahl der Parlamente und anderer Staatsorgane.* Vol. I for Europe, others in progress; with extensive bibliographic references. Berlin: De Gruyter.

Stewart, Philip (1968). *Political Power in the Soviet Union: A Study of Decision-Making in Stalingrad.* Indianapolis: Bobbs-Merrill.

Strothmann, Dietrich (1963). *Nationalsozialistische Literaturpolitik.* Bonn: H. Bouvier u. Co.

Struve. W. C. (1973). *Elites against Democracy: Leadership Ideals in Bourgeois Political Thought in Germany, 1890–1933.* Princeton: Princeton University Press.

Suárez, Andrés (1967). *Cuba: Castroism and Communism, 1959–1966.* Cambridge, Mass.: M.I.T. Press.

Supek, Rudi (1973). "The Statist and self-managing models of socialism." In Allen H. Barton, Bogdan Denitch, and Charles Kadushin (eds.), *Opinion-Making Elites in Yugoslavia.* New York: Praeger.

Swartz, Marc J. (1968). *Local-Level Politics: Social and Cultural Perspectives.* Chicago: Aldine.

Swayze, Harold (1962). *Political Control of Literature in the USSR, 1946–1959.* Cambridge, Mass.: Harvard University Press.

Swearer, Howard R., with Myron Rush (1964). *The Politics of Succession in the U.S.S.R.: Materials on Khrushchev's Rise to Leadership.* Boston: Little, Brown.

Talmon, J. L. (1961). *The Origins of Totalitarian Democracy.* New York: Praeger.
Tang, Peter S. H., and Joan Maloney (1962). *The Chinese Communist Impact on Cuba.* Chestnut Hill, Mass.: Research Institute on the Sino-Soviet Bloc.
Tannenbaum, Edward R. (1972). *The Fascist Experience: Italian Society and Culture, 1922–1945.* New York: Basic Books.
Taylor, Charles Lewis, and Michael C. Hudson (1972). *World Handbook of Political and Social Indicators.* 2d ed. New Haven: Yale University Press.
Taylor, George E. (1967). "Communism and Chinese history." In Donald W. Treadgold (ed.), *Soviet and Chinese Communism: Similarities and Differences.* Seattle: University of Washington Press.
Taylor, Philip B., Jr. (1960). "The Mexican elections of 1958: affirmation of authoritarianism?" *Western Political Quarterly* 13:722–44.
Thalheimer, August (1930). "Über den faschismus." *Gegen den Strom: Organ der KPD (Opposition).* Reprinted in O. Bauer, H. Marcuse, and A. Rosenberg (1967), *Faschismus und Kapitalismus.* Edited by Wolfgang Abendroth. Frankfurt: Europäische Verlagsantalt.
Thomas, Hugh (1971). *Cuba: The Pursuit of Freedom.* New York: Harper & Row.
Thompson, Leonard M. (1966). *The Republic of South Africa.* Boston: Little, Brown.
Tigrid, Pavel (1969). *La chute irrésistible d'Alexander Dubcek.* Paris: Calmann-Lévy.
Timashef, Nicholas S. (1960). "The inner life of the Russian Orthodox Church." In Cyril E. Black (ed.), *The Transformation of Russian Society.* Cambridge, Mass.: Harvard University Press.
Tinbergen, Jan (1961). "Do communist and free economies show a converging pattern?" *Soviet Studies* 1:133–41.
Titus, David Anson (1974). *Palace and Politics in Prewar Japan.* New York: Columbia University Press.
Toharia, José Juan (1974). "The Spanish judiciary: a sociological study. Justice in a civil law country undergoing social change under an authoritarian regime." Ph.D. dissertation in sociology, Yale University.
Tökés, Rudolf L. (1974). "Dissent: the politics for change in the USSR." In Henry W. Morton and Rudolf L. Tökés (eds.), *Soviet Politics and Society in the 1970's.* New York: Free Press.
Tomasevich, Jozo (1955). *Peasants, Politics, and Economic Change in Yugoslavia.* Stanford: Stanford University Press.
Townsend, James R. (1972). *Political Participation in Communist China.* Berkeley: University of California Press.
——— (1974). *Politics in China.* Boston: Little, Brown.
Travaglini, Thomas (1963). *Der 20 Juli. Technik und Wirkung seiner propagandistischen Behandlung nach den amtlichen SD-Berichten.* Berlin: Freie Universität. (Inaug. Diss.)
Treadgold, Donald W., ed. (1967). *Soviet and Chinese Communism: Similarities and Differences.* Seattle: University of Washington Press.

Trindade, Helgio (1974). *Integralismo: O Fascismo Brasileiro na Decada de 30.* São Paulo: Difusao Europeia do Livro.

Triska, Jan F., ed. (1969). *Communist Party-States: Comparative and International Studies.* Indianapolis: Bobbs-Merrill.

Trotsky, Leon (1937). *The Revolution Betrayed.* New York: Doubleday.

Tucker, Robert C. (1961). "Towards a comparative politics of movement-regimes." *American Political Science Review* 55:281–89.

――― (1963). *The Soviet Political Mind.* New York: Praeger.

――― (1965). "The dictator and totalitarianism." *World Politics* 17:555–84.

――― (1969). "On the comparative study of communism." In F. J. Fleron, Jr. (ed.), *Communist Studies and the Social Sciences.* Chicago: Rand McNally.

Turner, Henry A. (1972). "Fascism and modernization." *World Politics* 24:547–64.

Turner, Victor, and Marc Swartz, eds. (1966). *Political Anthropology.* Chicago: Aldine.

Tyrell, Albrecht, ed. (1969). *Führer Befiehl . . . Selbstzeungnisse aus der "Kampfzeit" der NSDAP Dokumentation und Analyse.* Düsseldorf: Droste.

Ueberhorst, Horst (1968). *Elite für die Diktatur.* Düsseldorf: Droste.

Ugalde, Antonio (1970). *Power and Conflict in a Mexican Community: A Study of Political Integration.* Albuquerque: University of New Mexico Press.

Uhlig, Heinrich (1956). *Die Warenhäuser im Dritten Reich.* Cologne: Westdeutscher Verlag.

Ulam, Adam B. (1968). *Expansion and Coexistence: The History of Soviet Foreign Policy from 1917–67.* New York: Praeger.

Ungari, Paulo (1963). *Alfredo Rocco e l'Ideologia giuridica del Fascism.* Brescia: Morcelliana.

U.S. Department of State, Bureau of Intelligence and Research (1971). *World Strength of the Communist Party Organizations.* Washington, D.C.: Government Printing Office.

U.S. Department of State, Division of Research for Europe, Office of Intelligence Research (1948). *Direct Popular Elections in the Soviet Union.* OIR Report No. 4711. Washington, D.C.: Government Printing Office.

Vaker, Nicholas (1962). *The Taproot of Soviet Society.* New York: Harper & Row.

Vallauri, Carlo (1971). *Le radici del corporativismo.* Roma: Bulzoni.

Van den Berghe, Pierre L. (1967). *South Africa: A Study in Conflict.* Berkeley: University of California Press.

Van Doorn, Jacques, ed. (1968). *Armed Forces and Society.* The Hague: Mouton.

Vatikiotis, P. J. (1961). *The Egyptian Army in Politics: Pattern for New Nations?* Bloomington: Indiana University Press.

Vermeil, Edmond (1955). "The origin, nature and development of German nationalist ideology in the 19th and 20th centuries." In Maurice Baumont, John H. E. Fried, and Edmond Vermeil (eds.), *The Third Reich.* International

Council for Philosophy and Humanistic Studies, with the assistance of UNESCO. New York: Praeger.

Vernier, Bernard (1963). *L'Irak d'aujourd'hui.* Paris. A. Colin.

Viereck, Peter (1961). *Metapolitics: The Roots of the Nazi Mind.* New York: Capricorn.

Vierhaus, Rudolf (1964). "Faschistisches Führerturm: Ein Beitrag zur Phänomenologie des europäischen Faschismus." *Historische Zeitschrift* 198:614–39.

Voegelin, Erich (1936). *Der Autoritäre Staat.* Vienna: Julius Springer.

Vogel, Ezra (1967). "Voluntarism and social control." In Donald W. Treadgold (ed.), *Soviet and Chinese Communism.* Seattle: University of Washington Press.

——— (1971). *Canton under Communism: Programs and Politics in a Provincial Capital, 1949–1968.* New York: Harper & Row.

Vogelsang, Thilo (1962). *Reichswehr, Staat und NSDAP: Beiträge zur deutschen Geschichte 1930–1932.* Stuttgart: Deutsche Verlags-Anstalt.

Voss, Joachim (1971). *Der progressistische Entwicklungsstaat: Das Beispiel der Republik Guinea.* Hannover: Verlag für Literatur und Zeitgeschehen.

Wagner, Albrecht (1968). *Die Umgestaltung der Gerichtsverfassung und des Verfahrens- und Richterrechts im nationalsozialistischen Staat.* Stuttgart: Deutsche Verlags-Anstalt.

Walker, Malcolm T. (1972). *Politics and the Power Structure: A Rural Community in the Dominican Republic.* New York: Teachers College Press.

Wallerstein, Immanuel (1961). *Africa: The Politics of Independence. An Interpretation of Modern African History.* New York: Random House (Vintage).

——— (1966). "The decline of the party in single-party African states." In Joseph LaPalombara and Myron Weiner (eds.), *Political Parties and Political Development.* Princeton: Princeton University Press.

Ward, Robert E., and Dankwart A. Rustow, eds. (1964). *Political Modernization in Japan and Turkey.* Princeton: Princeton University Press.

Ware, Alan (1974). "Polyarchy." *European Journal of Political Research* 2: 179–99.

Waterbury, John (1970). *The Commander of the Faithful: The Moroccan Political Elite. A Study in Segmented Politics.* New York: Columbia University Press.

Weber, Eugen (1964). *Varieties of Fascism.* Princeton: Nostrand.

Weber, Hermann (1969). *Die Wandlung des deutschen Kommunismus: Die Stalinisierung der KPD in der Weimarer Republik.* Frankfurt am Main: Europäische Verlagsanstalt.

Weber, Max (1968). *Economy and Society.* Edited and translated by Guenther Roth and Claus Wittich, 3 vols. New York: Bedminster Press.

Webster, Richard A. (1960). *The Cross and the Fasces: Christian Democracy and Fascism in Italy.* Stanford: Stanford University Press.

Weeks, Albert L. (1970). *The Other Side of Coexistence: An Analysis of Russian Foreign Policy.* New York: Pitman.

Weiker, Walter F. (1963). *The Turkish Revolution: 1960–1961.* Washington, D.C.: The Brookings Institution.

—— (1973). *Political Tutelage and Democracy in Turkey: The Free Party and Its Aftermath.* Leiden: E. J. Brill.

Weinberg, Gerhard L., ed. (1964). "Adolf Hitler und der NS-Führungsoffizier (NSFO)." *Vierteljahrshefte für Zeitgeschichte* 12:443–56.

Weinberg, Ian (1969). "The problem of convergence of industrial societies: a critical look at the state of a theory." *Comparative Studies in Society and History* 11:1–15.

Weiner, Stephen M. (1970). "Socialism legality on trial." In Abraham Brumberg (ed.), *In Quest of Justice.* New York: Praeger.

Weinkauff, Hermann (1968). *Die deutsche Justiz und der Nationalsozialismus.* Stuttgart: Deutsche Verlags-Anstalt.

Welch, Claude E., Jr., ed. (1970). *Soldier and State in Africa: A Comparative Analysis of Military Intervention and Political Change.* Evanston: Northwestern University Press.

Welch, Holmes (1972). *Buddhism under Mao.* Cambridge, Mass.: Harvard University Press.

Welk, William G. (1938). *Fascist Economic Policy: An Analysis of Italy's Economic Experiment.* Cambridge, Mass.: Harvard University Press.

Werner, Andreas (1964). *SA und NSDAP. SA: "Wehrverband," "Parteitruppe" oder "Revolutionsarmee"?* Erlanden: A. Werner.

Wheaton, Eliot Barculo (1969). *Prelude to Calamity. With a Background Survey of the Weimar Era.* Garden City, N.Y.: Doubleday.

Wheelock, Keith (1960). *Nasser's New Egypt.* New York: Praeger.

Wiarda, Howard J. (1968). *Dictatorship and Development: The Methods of Control in Trujillo's Dominican Republic.* Gainesville: University of Florida Press.

—— (1973a). "Toward a framework for the study of political change in the Iberic-Latin tradition: the corporative model." *World Politics* 25:206–35.

—— (1973b). "The Portuguese corporative system: basic structures and current functions." *Iberian Studies* 2:73–80.

—— (1974). "Corporatism and development in the Iberic-Latin word: persistent strains and new variations." *The Review of Politics* 36:3–33.

Wiatr, Jerzy J. (1962). "Elections and voting behavior in Poland." In A. Ranney (ed.), *Essays on the Behavioral Study of Politics.* Urbana: University of Illinois Press.

——, ed. (1967). *Studies in Polish Political System.* Warsaw: Polish Academy of Sciences.

Wiatr, Jerzy J., and Adam Przeworski (1966). "Control without Opposition." *Government and Opposition* 1:227–39.

Wiles, P. J. D., and Stefan Markowski (1971). "Income distribution under communism and capitalism." *Soviet Studies* 22:344.

Willame, Jean-Claude (1972). *Patrimonialism and Political Change in the Congo.* Stanford: Stanford University Press.

Willner, Ann Ruth (1968). *Charismatic Political Leadership: A Theory.* Center of International Studies Research Monograph 32. Princeton: Princeton University.

Wilson, David A. (1962). *Politics in Thailand.* Ithaca: Cornell University Press.

Winckler, Edwin A. (1970). "Political anthropology." In Bernard J. Siegel (ed.), *Biennial Review of Anthropology, 1969.* Stanford: Stanford University Press.

Windsor, Philip, and Adam Roberts (1969). *Czechoslovakia, 1968: Reform, Repression and Resistance.* London: Chatto and Windus.

Winkler, Heinrich August (1972). *Mittelstand, Demokratie und National-sozialismus, Die Politische Entwicklung von Handwerk und Kleinhandel in der Weimarer Republik.* Cologne: Kiepenheuer und Witsch.

Wiseman, H. V. (1966). *Political Systems: Some Sociological Approaches.* London: Routledge & Kegan Paul.

Wittfogel, Karl A. (1957). *Oriental Despotism: A Comparative Study of Total Power.* New Haven: Yale University Press.

Wolf, Eric R., and Edward C. Hansen (1967). "Caudillo politics: a structural analysis." *Comparative Studies in Society and History* 9:168–79.

Wolfe, Bertram D. (1968). "Russia and the USA: a challenge to the convergence theory." *The Humanist* 28:3–8.

Woolf, S. J., ed. (1968). *The Nature of Fascism.* London: Weidenfeld and Nicolson.

———, ed. (1969). *European Fascism.* New York: Random House (Vintage).

Wu, Yuan-li, ed. (1973). *China: A Handbook.* New York: Praeger.

Wulf, Joseph (1963a). *Literatur und Dichtung im Dritten Reich: Ein Dokumentation.* Güterlosh: Sigbert Mohn.

——— (1963b). *Die Bildenden Künste im Dritten Reich: Ein Dokumentation.* Gütersloh: Sigbert Mohn.

——— (1963c). *Musik im Dritten Reich: Ein Dokumentation.* Gütersloh: Sigbert Mohn.

——— (1964). *Theater und Film im Dritten Reich: Ein Dokumentation.* Gütersloh: Sigbert Mohn.

Yang, C. K. (1965). *Chinese Communist Society: The Family and the Village.* Cambridge, Mass.: M.I.T. Press.

Yeh, K. C. (1967). "Soviet and Chinese industrialization strategies." In D. Treadgold (ed.), *Soviet and Chinese Communism: Similarities and Differences.* Seattle: University of Washington Press.

Yglesias, José (1969). *In the Fist of the Revolution: Life in a Cuban Country Town.* New York: Random House (Vintage).

Young, William B. (n.d.) "Military regimes shape Africa's future. The military: key force." Unpublished paper.

Zagoria, Donald S. (1969). *The Sino-Soviet Conflict 1956–1961.* New York: Atheneum.

Zaninovich, M. George (1968). *The Development of Socialist Yugoslavia.* Baltimore: Johns Hopkins University Press.

Zapf, Wolfgang (1965). *Wandlungen der deutschen Elite: Ein Zirkulations-modell Deutscher Führungsgruppen 1919–1961.* Munich: Piper.

Zartman, I. William, ed. (1971). *Man, State and Society in the Contemporary Maghreb.* New York: Praeger.

Zeller, Claus (1969). *Elfenbeinküste: Ein Entwicklungsland auf dem Wege zur Nation.* Freiburg: Rombach.

Zeman, Zbynek A. (1968). *Prague Spring: A Report on Czechoslovakia 1968.* Harmondsworth: Penguin.

Ziegler, Heinz O. (1932). *Autoritärer oder Totaler Staat.* Tübingen: J. C. B. Mohr (Paul Siebeck).

Zipfel, Friedrich (1965). *Kirchenkampf in Deutschland.* Berlin: de Gruyter.

Zmarzlik, Hans-Günter (1973). "Social Darwinism in Germany, seen as a historical problem." In Hajo Holborn (ed.), *Republic to Reich: The Making of the Nazi Revolution.* New York: Random House (Vintage).

Zolberg, Aristide R. (1966). *Creating Political Order: The Party-States of West Africa.* Chicago: Rand McNally.

——— (1969). *One-Party Government in the Ivory Coast.* Princeton: Princeton University Press.

Zonis, Marvin (1971). *The Political Elite of Iran.* Princeton: Princeton University Press.

INDEX

Abendroth, Wolfgang, 226
Abraha, Gedamu, 145
Absolutism, 51
Adam, Heribert, 234
Afghanistan: Taliban regime in, 36, 37
Africa, 143; authoritarian regimes in,
 174, 227; mobilizational regimes in,
 193; single-party regimes in, 178,
 229, 230
Albania, 258
Algeria, 237; authoritarian regimes in,
 146, 148; colonialism and, 149, 151;
 deculturation of, 149, 151
Allen, Sheridan, 18, 217
Alltagsgeschichte, 27
Almond, Gabriel, 55, 171, 265
Angola, 237
Anti-anticommunism, 29
Anticommunism, 29
Antifascism, 29
Anti-Semitism, 15, 17, 27, 120, 190,
 221, 222
Apartheid, 233–237
Apter, David, 227
Aquarone, Alberto, 79, 83, 92, 103,
 166, 167, 211, 214
Arabian peninsula, 145
Arditi, 18
Arendt, Hannah, 4, 7, 18, 33, 66, 72,
 95, 100, 105, 107, 111, 130
Argentina: authoritarian regimes in,
 193, 194, 195; democracy in, 60;

military regimes in, 26, 200, 201;
 nationalism in, 192; stability in, 195
Armstrong, John, 245
Aron, Raymond, 22, 24
Asia, Southeast, 143
Australia, 234
Austria, 216; authoritarian regimes in,
 192, 215; clerical-fascists in, 77;
 democracy in, 62; nondemocratic
 regimes in, 12
Authoritarian regimes, 159–261. *See
 also* Nondemocratic regimes;
 anarchic, 174, 257; Bonapartist
 model, 190, 218; Chinese, 66;
 conservative, 171; consultative, 174,
 259; cultural explanations for,
 17–18; defective, 240–245; defining,
 159–171; democratizing, 34, 174,
 259; electoral, 34; ethnocratic, 34,
 233–240; exclusionary, 178;
 expressive functions of, 171, 172*tab;*
 future of, 35–38; ideology in, 163,
 164, 173; inauthenticity of claims,
 173; instrumental functions of, 171,
 172*tab;* judicial system in, 109;
 Latin American, 36, 194, 215;
 limited pluralism of, 36, 168, 175;
 mentality of, 162, 163, 164, 165,
 179; military, 62, 172; modernizing,
 171, 173; monopolistic control in,
 65, 72; multiparty, 34; national
 culture and, 17–18; nationalism as

329

Van den Berghe, Pierre, 234
Venezuela: authoritarian regimes in, 36, 154
Vierhaus, Rudolf, 87, 98
Vietnam, 258; civil war in, 99; social revolution in, 193
Violence. *See also* Terror; communism and, 16; habit of, 111; legitimization of, 111; organizations of, 98; privatization of, 25, 37, 186; in revolutionary thought, 111; spiral of, 111; terrorism and, 35; use of, 37
Voegelin, Erich, 52, 215
Vogel, Ezra, 109
Vogelsang,, 205
Volksgemeinschaft, 94, 117, 120, 214
Vorsehung, 23

Wagner, Albrecht, 109
Wallerstein, Immanuel, 227, 228
Weber, E., 219
Weber, Max, 80, 116, 144, 151, 152, 209, 212, 248
Weiker, Walter, 60
Weimar Republic, 14, 137
Weinberg, Ian, 125

Weiner, Stephen, 101
Weinkauff, Hermann, 107
Welch, C.E., 227
Werner, Andreas, 98
Wiarda, Howard, 153, 215
Wiatr, Jerzy, 254
Williams, Mary Frase, 55
Wilson, David, 145
Windsor, Philip, 245
Winkler, Heinrich, 221
Wittfogel, Karl, 141–142
Woolf, S.J., 220

Young, William, 56, 227
Yugoslavia, 116, 216, 245, 255, 256, 257; authoritarian regimes in, 194

Zaninovich, M. George, 256
Zapf, Wolfgang, 106, 118
Zartman, I. William, 147
Zeitgeist, 9
Zeman, Zbynek, 245
Ziegler, Heinz, 52
Zionism, 120, 221, 238
Zolberg, Aristide, 229, 230, 231

ABOUT THE BOOK

In this classic work, noted political sociologist Juan Linz provides an unparalleled study of the nature of nondemocratic regimes.

Linz's seminal analysis develops the fundamental distinction between totalitarian and authoritarian systems. It also presents a pathbreaking discussion of the personalistic, lawless, nonideological type of authoritarian rule that he calls (following Weber) the "sultanistic regime."

The core of the book (including a 40-page bibliography) was published in 1975 as a chapter in the *Handbook of Political Science,* long out of print. The author has chosen not to change the original text for this new edition, but instead has added an extensive introduction reflecting on some of the contributions to the literature and the changes that have taken place in world politics and in the nature of regimes since the 1970s.

Juan J. Linz is Sterling Professor of Political and Social Science at Yale University. His work on authoritarianism, the breakdown of democratic regimes, and transitions to democracy has had a wide-ranging impact not only on scholarship, but also in the world of politics.